THE
CREATION-EVOLUTION
CONTROVERSY

THE
CREATION - EVOLUTION
CONTROVERSY

(Implications, Methodology and Survey of Evidence)

TOWARD A RATIONAL SOLUTION

by

R.L. WYSONG, D.V.M.

INQUIRY PRESS

1880 North Eastman   Midland, Michigan 48640

First Printing 1976
Second Printing 1976
Third Printing 1978
Fourth Printing 1980
Fifth Printing 1981
Sixth Printing 1984
Seventh Printing 1987
Eighth Printing 1991

Published by
INQUIRY PRESS

1880 North Eastman   Midland, Michigan 48640

FIRST EDITION

LIBRARY OF CONGRESS CATALOG CARD NUMBER 75-31486
ISBN 0-918112-01-X: Hardbound
ISBN 0-918112-02-8: Kivar

TO *those who rise above the prevalent*
   inclination and comfort of holding to
   untested popular beliefs
 to *those who welcome change when it is the*
   product of open unbiased investigation
 to *those who work to actuate the belief*
   that the human condition is better
   served by the search for truth than
   conformity

ℭontents

List of Figures

Acknowledgements

The author wishes to express special appreciation to the following individuals who have helped the most with various aspects of the preparation of the manuscript: Typing--Jeannie Amboy, Penny Salisbury, Kim Olney, Sylvia VanCamp, Bonnie Friend, Kathy Cheadle; Proof reading and index preparation--Steve Robertson, Borys Ryzyj, Jeff Salisbury, Charles Amboy, Art Rasher, Hal Flemings, Peter Karch, Bill Crickmore, Edward Sedlack, Margaret Frissel, Julie Hartman; Art--Larry Cole(cover), Walter Horton(four of the cartoons), Betty Jo Wysong(numerous drawings, diagrams and letterings); Photography--Rod Cranson(conversion of slides and various other photographic preparations). Many have graciously allowed the use of photographs, these individuals are cited in the legends.

FOREWORD

    The creation-evolution controversy has been raging for near-
ly a century. Recently there has been increased interest as a
result of legislative proposals in several States concerning the
teaching of creation, as well as evolution, in the public school
systems. The importance of this subject, however, does not change
with time or circumstance. To those who seek intellectual content-
ment the issue is timeless. Likewise, origins--which the evolution-
creation controversy is all about--has universal appeal. Origins
is sexless, not circumscribed by political boundaries, raceless,
and of interest to all ages. Even tender young children with
practically their first words importune parents with "Where did
I come from?"
    The resolution of this controversy is vital to the formulation
of a life-philosophy and, consequently, affects life itself. But,
interestingly, there is probably no subject of greater interest or
impact that wallows in so much public ignorance. True, dogmatic
assertions are made by proponents of each side, but the topic of
origins is rarely treated rationally. Teachers are increasingly
becoming afraid even to mention the topic, for fear of retaliation
by parents taking opposing views. On the other hand, most parents
are incapable of competently dealing with the question of origins
and simply assume one side or the other, guessing that someone,
somewhere, has the necessary supporting proofs all worked out. Thus,
in the end, the controversy is not resolved, but dismissed, ignored,
forgotten, avoided--it is dissolved.
    There are, although one has to do no little hunting to find
them, many fine writings that treat both sides of the subject cur-
rently in print. Thus, some of what I discuss here will be a review and restating, hopefully from a fresh viewpoint, for those
versed in evolution-creation argumentation. I humbly recognize the
work done by so many others and express my indebtedness to those
who have expended so much effort and time.

My objective is to present some new information and approach the controversy in a way that I believe will allow one to see the questions, issues, implications and evidence in a rational perspective. Resolving this issue is intimately tied with honest, unprejudiced thinking, for which hopefully this book will be an aid.

In making this attempt, however, I realize I will not appear to come off entirely clean. Surely my biases will filter through here and there. For this I apologize in advance. Optimistically, my failures will not cause alienation, prejudgments or a reactionary sharpening of reader biases.

The presentation will assume the reader has a working knowledge of common creation-evolution arguments, especially the widely disseminated evolutionary proofs. To give balance, I will concentrate on evidence and reasonings--many that are creationistic in slant--which are not popularly known.

Our goal is to resolve the controversy. Therefore, the opening chapters basically deal with why we should and how we can accomplish this goal. The importance of the subject is emphasized by showing the effect each of the two alternatives can have upon society and the individual. Then the propriety of laymen attempting to resolve the controversy and the method by which it can rationally be accomplished is pursued. With this preliminary and essential groundwork laid, the positions are defined and the data examined. Finally, you are invited to reach a conclusion within the methodological context prescribed.

I must confess that in addressing this topic I have found myself wandering into several diverse disciplines, many for which I can claim no special expertise. However, the more qualified readers of certain sections will find the material heavily documented and specifically referenced for their more exacting questions and research. For others, however, the treatment here may prove to be somewhat of a strain on their academic knowhow. However, I must make clear at the outset, due to the specific nature and quantity of the scientific data accumulated over the past generation, the subject of origins cannot be adequately treated in a cursory "lay" fashion. If it were, the serious attention of most modern educated inquirers would be dulled. So the book is designed for the serious student of origins, the searcher, the prober looking for an indepth treatment, the investigator wanting to understand and make the material his own and not just be dogmatically told; the book is not meant for a simple light reading. Therefore, trying not to compromise technical credibility, I have attempted simplicity with a view toward making comprehension accessible to the modern-day average highschool educated person.

The book is structured so the logic and argumentation flows sequentially. Even though each chapter is somewhat self-contained, a front to back reading is encouraged if one desires to reach an informed conclusion consistent with the definitional and methodological frameworks outlined in the early chapters.

THE
1 { CONTROVERSY'S
IMPORTANCE

Who among thinking people has not asked: "From where did man come?" "From where did the plants and animals come?" "What is the source of the stars, the earth and the universe?"

To some, the answer to these questions is that they are unanswerable. Perhaps their own reasoning or that of another convinced them that questions about origins can't be resolved and, furthermore, that such questions are only academic and unimportant. It may be that they have convinced themselves such issues belong to the scientist, philosopher and theologian--not the layman.

Many who have dismissed these questions feel they can go on living their lives with no resultant discomfort. "Why expend energy on meaningless questions when man is faced with so many more profound questions that need resolution?" they ask.

Others, convinced that such questions are of vital importance, have met them head on and resolved to find their truthful answers. These individuals have perhaps spent countless hours reading, thinking and conversing on the subject of origins. Through much deliberation they may have formulated answers they feel are correct, or frustrated, arrived at answers they recognize are probably not consistent with truth but with which they are at least comfortable.

Origins and World-View

Is the controversy worthy of our time and energy? Is it important? Wouldn't getting involved in such a problem be pure intellectual calisthenics, fitting only for a late-night, opinionated, philosophical jam session in a dormitory?

Oparin, the Russian biochemist and pioneer researcher on

the origin of life, claims:

> "The deeper the human mind penetrates into the myster-
> ies of life, the greater is the potential for healthy,
> fruitful, and happy human life. The understanding of
> the essence of life and of the mode of organization of
> living matter is thus full of obvious and overpowering
> fascination for human beings. This understanding, how-
> ever, is impossible without a knowledge of the origin of
> life."[1]

Elsewhere he wrote, reflecting the earlier views of Heraclitus
of Ephesus, and Aristotle:

> "One can only understand the essence of things when one
> knows their origin and development."[2]

The resolution of the origin of life is crucial to one's understanding of life, its meaning, purpose, and "essence" (Oparin).
If we do not believe this, the chances are that we have simply
been deceived and lulled into thinking origins is not a significant
issue.

Truthful answers to the questions of origin especially gain
importance because our world-view, our philosophy of life, is related to their answers. The framework from which we approach life's
varied problems is, in a large part, supplied to us by our view of
origins.

Unlike the indifference the material universe has for the
conclusions drawn from and laws imposed upon it by man, our understanding of man's origin and essence profoundly affects the subject matter, man himself. Eisenberg, a psychiatrist, wrote:

> ". . . the motions of the planets are sublimely indif-
> ferent to our earth bound astronomy. But the behavior
> of men is not independent of the theories of human be-
> havior men adopt."[3]

Both creation and evolution are theories of human behavior and
therefore affect human behavior.

Additionally, one's position on origins acts like a plumb
line guiding the erection of his life-philosophy. Life-philosophy
in turn affects human behavior. In this regard, Drane wrote:

> "Every ethic is founded in a philosophy of man, and
> every philosophy of man points toward ethical behavior."[4]

Specifically pointing to these behavioral, ethical and philosophical effects produced, for example, by the evolutionary position on origins, John Dewey wrote of Charles Darwin's book:

> ". . . the *ORIGIN OF SPECIES* introduced a mode of think-

1. *MOLECULAR EVOLUTION: PREBIOLOGICAL AND BIOLOGICAL, EDS.*
D.L. ROHLFING AND A. I. OPARIN (NEW YORK: PLENUM, 1972), P.1
2. *A.I. OPARIN: LIFE, ITS NATURE ORIGIN AND DEVELOPMENT (N.Y.:*
ACADEMIC, 1964), P. 37.
3. *L. EISENBERG: "ON THE HUMANIZING OF HUMAN NATURE," IN IMPACT*
OF SCIENCE ON SOCIETY, 23 (1973):213.
4. *J. DRANE: "A PHILOSOPHY OF MAN AND HIGHER EDUCATION," IN MAIN*
CURRENTS IN MODERN THOUGHT, 29 (1972):98.

ing that in the end was bound to transform the logic of knowledge, and hence the treatment of morals, politics, and religion."[5]

And, Raven said in review of the impact of Darwin's ideas on origins: "In Darwin's case the consequences were still more revolutionary; for his doctrine dealt not with the laws governing inanimate objects, not with physics and chemistry, but with living creatures, with man's position in the scheme of things, and with religion."[6]

To illustrate the relationship between origins and life-philosophy, a student asks a learned group gathered for discussion: "Why does man seem to be continually at war?"

"That's the nature of man," someone answers.

"Why?" the student retorts.

Another in the group follows up, "War is simply a part of social evolution. Why, we even see the violent struggle for survival among the animals. War is the means by which the earth's population is kept in check and the weak societies are culled to make room for the more fit. So, you see, war actually serves for the betterment of the human race in the long run."

Feeling a cold chill, the student replies, "Isn't that inhuman? Isn't it wrong to kill others? I certainly don't want to be one of those sacrificed for the 'betterment of the human race!'"

"Who is to say what is right or wrong? Our primary responsibility is to ourselves and what we feel is right for the occasion," pops back another in the group.

The group: "Yeah, we want to do our own thing! Animals struggle for survival and do what they want, why shouldn't we?"

"What does what the animals do have to do with us?" says the student.

"Animals are our relatives, everybody knows that. They're here as a result of blind purposeless forces and so are we. Who is to dictate what is right or wrong for us? Chance? Natural laws? Nonsense! **Phooey** on religious morality!" says the group leader.

What happened during the course of the conversation? Did not the group find justification for their war philosophy in the assumption that life arose by blind, unintelligent forces? If the student proceeded to query them on the evidences that life arose by evolution, and their arguments were found wanting, he could then dismiss their whole explanation for why man wars as purely a foundationless guess. On the other hand, if they were able to show him the factual basis for their evolutionary beliefs, he must then consider with all seriousness the explanation for wars they advanced.

---

5. JOHN DEWEY: "THE INFLUENCE OF DARWINISM ON PHILOSOPHY," IN *GREAT ESSAYS IN SCIENCE*, ED. M. GARDNER (N.Y.: POCKET BOOKS, 1957), P. 16.

6. C. RAVEN: "DARWIN AND HIS UNIVERSE," IN *A SHORT HISTORY OF SCIENCE* (N.Y.: DOUBLEDAY, 1951)P. 103.

Our student now turns his attention to another group: "Why does man seem to be continually at war?"

"Because man is basically evil," someone replies.

"Why?" the student says.

"Because God cursed him after he ate the apple," another replies confidently.

"How do you know there is a God?" the student says.

"Because it says so in the Bible," he answers.

"What if I don't believe in the Bible?" the student asks timidly.

"I don't even want to talk to you, you demonized, hippy atheist!" he snorts.

"Please, without the Bible, how do you know there is a God?" the student pleads.

"Look at the creation, the beauty all around you!" another takes over.

"But how do you know God created it?" the student presses.

If this group can proceed to show the student a solid basis for their beliefs, the student will have to consider very seriously their answer to his question about wars. If they cannot, he can dismiss their answer as mythology.

POSITION ON ORIGINS

WORLD-VIEW

APPROACH TO LIFE

We should note three important points from the above illustration: (1) An understanding of a very serious problem facing man, war, is linked to convictions which are in turn linked to one's position on origins. (2) One's attitude toward war is only as correct as the truthfulness of his position on origins. (3) Most importantly, the solutions to life's problems, war being one of them, will likely be, a priori, dependent upon the correct resolution of origins.

This third statement is made because the solution to any problem is dependent, a priori, upon a proper approach to and understanding of the problem itself. The problems man faces today (social, political, racial, ecological) are a direct result of human behavior. Human behavior is a manifestation or dynamic outworking of world-view; e.g., if one's world-view, his life-philosophy, justifies pollution, he will pollute, if it justifies racism he will be a racist, etc. In turn, world-view is directly linked to one's position on origins. Problems, behavior, world-view and origins are intimately related. Therefore, resolution of problems depends upon a change to proper behavior which demands a change to right world-view which demands a correct view on origins. Similarly, in medicine, cures for infectious disease depend upon correct treatment which depends upon proper diagnosis which in turn relies upon a correct understanding of pathogenic microbiology (science of disease producing organisms). Blood letting, manure packs, and secret brews only aggravate an infectious disease. Why? Improper treatment reflects an incorrect understanding of infectious causes. Likewise, solutions to man's great social problems depend upon a correct understanding of origins. Attempts at cures within the framework of an incorrect understanding of origins will likely be ineffective or perhaps even aggravating.

CORRECT ON ORIGINS

CORRECT WORLD-VIEW

SOLUTIONS

Why are people starving? Why is there so much strife, lawlessness and violence in the world? Why does man seem to be inept in governing himself? When all people basically want peace, prosperity and security, why is it so manifestly absent in our modern "brain-age?" Why the evil, hypocrisy, immorality and selfishness not only among the masses, but also in politics and religion? Why does this world system seem to be facing annihilation from so many quarters with apparently no way out? A person's position not only on war, but on these matters can likewise be linked through questioning to one's view on origins.

No one denies the importance of these issues and similar problems of life. Therefore, if our attitude toward these most plaguing problems of man is linked to our position on origins, who will deny the subject's importance?

A person can basically take one of two positions on origins. One is there is a creator, the other is there is not; or, evolution explains origins or it does not. Creation versus evolution, theism versus materialism or naturalism, and design versus chance, are all ways of expressing the two alternatives. (I will demon-

strate the fallacy of so-called theistic evolution, which is held
by some as a third alternative, in a later chapter.)
    Let's now examine specifically how the two positions on ori-
gins have manifested themselves throughout history.

The Evolutionary Position's Effect

Orgel has stated:
> "The replacement of 'will' by 'chance' as the mediator
> of biological change has transformed our view of man's
> relation to the rest of the universe."[7]

If life came into existence through purely natural, materialistic,
chance processes, then, as a consequence, we must conclude life
is without moral direction and intelligent purpose. This absence
of direction would in effect mean man could direct his own life,
or be guided by a situation ethic. Answers to life's many questions would come from materialistic philosophy. Materialistic
philosophy relieves one of moral responsibility to anyone, including the supernatural. Atoms have no morals, thus, if they
are our progenitors, man is amoral. (I am not saying that an evolutionist is necessarily "immoral," rather, I am saying that
philosophically, logically, the term morality loses meaning in
the context of true atheistic materialism.)

George Gaylord Simpson wrote that man:
> ". . . stands alone in the universe, a unique product
> of a long, unconscious, impersonal, material process
> with unique understanding and potentialities. These
> he owes to no one but himself and it is to himself
> that he is responsible. He is not the creature of un-
> controllable and undeterminable forces, but he is his
> own master. He can and must decide and manage his own
> destiny."[8]

Morality and ethics are purely relative to an evolutionist
who follows through with the logical implications of his philosophy. Motulsky said, regarding religious absolutes:
> "An ethical system that bases its premises on absolute
> pronouncements will not usually be acceptable to those
> who view human nature by evolutionary criteria."[9]

Thompson, in his introduction to Charles Darwin's *ORIGIN OF SPE-
CIES*, said similarly of the rise of evolutionary thought with
the publication of Darwin's book:
> "For the majority of its readers, therefore, the *ORIGIN*
> effectively dissipated the evidence of providential

---

7. L. E. ORGEL: *THE ORIGINS OF LIFE: MOLECULES AND NATURAL SELECTION* (N.Y.: JOHN WILEY, 1973), P. 183.
8. G. G. SIMPSON: "THE WORLD INTO WHICH DARWIN LED US," IN *SCIENCE*, 131(1960):966.
9. A. G. MOTULSKY: "BRAVE NEW WORLD," IN *SCIENCE*, 185(1974):654.

control."

The philosopher, Bahnsen, explains the popularity of evolution this way:

> "The real issue is whether man must think God's thought after him in order to understand the world correctly or whether man's mind is the ultimate assigner of meaning to brute and orderless facts . . . Evolutionary thought is popular because it is a worldview which facilitates man's attempt to rid himself of all knowledge of the transcendent Creator and promises to secure man's autonomy (especially his ability to interpret the 'facts' oblivious to God)."[10]

Evolutionists wonder if man has simply concocted a creator because of an inability to explain naturally occurring events, out of the need for some sort of security, some sort of foundation upon which to build, out of a need for a scapegoat for presently unexplainable phenomena. Or, is man truly a graceless parasite of deity, as the British barrister Dewar has said? Is man to be ultimately the master of the Universe, the controller and mastermind of its workings and his own destiny, or is he simply a created thing, a puny creature held captive within the realm of physical and moral laws by a creator personage?

But these questions, to most evolutionists, are rhetorical. Man is indeed believed to be his "own master, liberated from the myth of providential control."

Many have drawn conclusions from evolution and made applications to various facets of life, (i.e., they have followed through from origins to world-view to behavior). Social evolution provided in part the basis for Fascism and its oppressive racist actions. Evolution pervaded Mussolini's thinking to the point that he justified war, as did Nietzsche, on the basis that it provided the means for evolutionary progress.[11]

One need not read far in Hitler's *MEIN KAMPF* to find that evolution likewise influenced him and his views on the master race, genocide, human breeding experiments, etc.[12] Arthur Keith, an evolutionary anthropologist, said of Hitler:

> "The German Fuhrer . . . has consciously sought to make the practice of Germany conform to the theory of evolution."[13]

The class struggles and anti-religious policies of Communism owe their existence to evolutionary political and social philos-

---

10. *G.L.BAHNSEN: "ON WORSHIPPING THE CREATURE RATHER THAN THE CREATOR," IN JOURNAL OF CHRISTIAN RECONSTRUCTION, 1(1974):84.*
11. *R. CLARK: DARWIN: BEFORE AND AFTER (LONDON: PATERNOSTER, 1948), P. 115; OSCAR LEVY: THE COMPLETE WORKS OF NIETZSCHE(1930), P.75.*
12. *R. CLARK, (REF.11) PP. 115-117.*
13. *ARTHUR KEITH: EVOLUTION AND ETHICS (NEW YORK: G.P.PUTNAM'S, 1949), P. 230.*

ophy.[14] It is well known that Marx, the father of communism
wanted to dedicate his second book, *DAS KAPITAL* to Darwin.[15]
The ruthless and unethical competition found in capitalistic nations, as well as imperialistic warmongering, likewise find justification in evolutionary philosophy.

One of the primary goals of the space effort is to try to
find extraterrestrial life and perhaps gain insight into the origin of life on earth. By the end of the 1960's, over 20 billion
dollars were spent by the U.S. alone for the purpose of exploring
the moon. A massive economic effort such as this and its relation
to the question of the origin of life certainly show the degree to
which man will go to try to resolve the question.

Modern psychology, and especially the "sex drive psychology"
of Freud, also find a basis in evolutionary thinking.[16] Education, history, sociology, and all scientific and academic disciplines, including religion, have been heavily influenced by evolution.[17] Children's books, television, newspapers, and magazines are also replete with the doctrines of evolution. And
racism, both modern and ancient, is a sequel to evolutionary philosophy.[18]

Even our language has incorporated words and phrases that
assume the truth of evolution. For example, proto means primitive
or first. Thus we have pro-tons in the nuclei of atoms--assumed
to have come first; proto-plasm in cells--assumed to have come
first; proto-zoans as single celled microscopic organisms--assumed
most simple and coming first; proto-humans--assumed primate precursor to humans; and proto-history--assumed evolutionary prere-
corded history. Single cells are considered "simple" and man is
termed "complex." Unruly children are spoken of as "just passing
through a stage" and spanking the "sweet lil darlins" is considered "primitive" and "brutish."

Julian Huxley contends that evolution is an explanation of
the whole of reality:

"The whole of evolution was soon extended into other

14. *J. D. BERNAL: MARR AND SCIENCE (N.Y.: INTERNATIONAL, 1952),
P. 17.*
15. *R. HOFSTADLER: SOCIAL DARWINISM IN AMERICAN THOUGHT
(N.Y.: GEORGE BRAZILLER, 1959), P. 115.*
16. *R. J. FAIRBANKS: "SIGMUND FREUD," IN TWENTIETH CENTURY ENCY-
CLOPEDIA OF RELIGIOUS KNOWLEDGE, ED. L.A.LOETSCHER (GRAND RAPIDS:
BAKER, 1955),P. 446; E. FROMM: BEYOND THE CHAINS OF ILLUSION--MY
ENCOUNTER WITH MARR AND FREUD (N.Y.: SIMON AND SCHUSTER,1962)P.33.*
17. *E. G. BEWKES AND OTHERS: EXPERIENCE REASON AND FAITH
(N.Y.: HARPER AND BROS., 1940), P. 549.*
18. *A.M.ROSE: "THE SLOW PAINFUL DEATH OF THE RACE MYTH," IN SO-
CIETY TODAY AND TOMORROW, EDS. E. HUNT AND J. KARLIN (N.Y.:
MACMILLAN, 1961), P. 194.; J.S.HALLER, JR.: OUTCASTS FROM EVOLU-
TION: SCIENTIFIC ATTITUDES OF RACIAL INFERIORITY (URBANA: U. OF
ILLINOIS, 1971).*

than biological fields. Inorganic subjects such as the life-histories of stars and the formation of chemical elements on the one hand, and on the other hand subjects like linguistics, social anthropology, and comparative law and religion, began to be studied from an evolutionary angle, until today we are enabled to see evolution as a universal, all-pervading process.

"Furthermore, with the adoption of the evolutionary approach in non-biological fields, from cosmology to human affairs, we are beginning to realize that biological evolution is only one aspect of evolution in general.

"Evolution in the extended sense can be defined as a directional and essentially irreversible process occurring in time, which in its course gives rise to an increase of variety and an increasingly high level of organization in its products. Our present knowledge indeed forces us to the view that the whole of reality is evolution--a single process of self transformation."[19]

If evolution has permeated practically the entire fabric of society and provides a basis for many of man's actions, can we say that the issue of origins is unimportant? Furthermore, the need to be sure we are right on the question of origins becomes manifestly crucial, does it not?

The Creation Position's Effect

If, on the other hand, life owes its existence to a creator, a supernatural force, then life is the result of his will and purposes. Understanding these purposes would be the only way to understand life's varied questions and problems.

To illustrate this, consider that when we buy an automobile we also have access to an owner's manual. That manual is an expression of the automobile's creator concerning the purposes and functions of the machine. If one has questions regarding the operation of the machine or its mechanical failures, he seeks the answers as given in the manual. If we don't familiarize ourselves with the correct purpose of the automobile, we can't expect to understand its operation or its failures.

Likewise, if we exist due to an intelligent being's purpose, then an understanding of how to operate properly is absolutely dependent upon knowledge of that purpose. Failures, problems, and malfunctions in the created world will only be understood in light of those purposes. To keep our lives in touch with reality and

19. J. HUXLEY: "EVOLUTION AND GENETICS," IN <u>WHAT IS SCIENCE</u>, ED. J.R.NEWMAN (N.Y.: SIMON AND SCHUSTER, 1955),PP.272-278.

truth, and to avoid problems, we would be in constant pursuit of correct knowledge of the creator and strive to live our lives consistent with his will. In short, as opposed to evolution, creationism demands submission to "absolute pronouncements" (Motulsky) and means "providential control" (Thompson). Our lives could only take on real meaning within the context of his purposes, not our own. Obviously then, creationsim is going to have far-reaching impact just as does evolutionism. (Fig. 1)

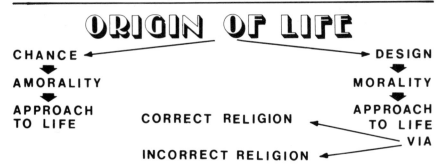

Fig. 1-Possible Routes
There are two possible explanations for the origin of life. If we owe our existence to chance, then our approach to life could be amoral, i.e., it could take any direction and be justified. On the other hand, if we were created, we are responsible to that creator. We must then seek his will--the correct religion.

Without regard for whether particular actions are correct relative to the true will of a creator, let's examine the far-reaching effects creationism has had. Belief in a supernatural creator, or "religion" as it is commonly termed, is or has been part of every human society. Religion has held sway from the African witchdoctor menacing his tribe under an iron hand, to modern political church-State marriages. Religion, up to the present century, ruled practically absolute on all aspects of human activity. Not only was a moral code dictated, but imprimatur was required for scientific inquiry and even philosophical thought.

For example, from the early seventeenth century the church proscribed the teaching that the earth revolved around the sun. Luther castigated Copernicus; and the Catholic Church, through the Inquisition, forced Galileo to recant.

The political influence of religion has been profound. The American Constitution was formulated by men of intense religious persuasion. Hitler assumed a messianic, millenial role and signed concordats with religion condoning his actions.[20] The Inquisition, the Thirty Years War, and the Crusades were "religious."

20. *R. HOCHHUTH: THE DEPUTY (N.Y.: GROVE PRESS, 1964).*

Both World Wars were sanctioned by religions on each side. The French newspaper, *LA DERNIERE HEURE*, in its January 7, 1967 issue, quoted a French clergyman's words to his country's soldiers during World War I:

> "My brothers, comrades of the French army and of their glorious allies, the Almighty God is on our side . . . God is near to our brave soldiers in battle, he gives them strength and fortifies them against the enemy . . . God will give us the victory."

Then it quoted a clergyman of the same denomination from Cologne Germany:

> "God is with us in this fight for righteousness . . . We command you in the name of God, to fight to the last drop of your blood for the honor and glory of the country. . . God knows we are on the side of righteousness and he will give us the victory."

No one can deny the financial influence of religion. No one can deny the impact of religion upon family structure and child rearing. Millions upon millions have experienced the total personal commitment religion can require. And, sadly, religion has and does, to some extent, foster racial ideas and nationalism.

Now, as I have stated, these various religious influences speak nothing to the "rightness" or "wrongness" of particular courses of action in terms of the "true will" of a creator (as opposed to the free license of evolutionism, creationism implies the subsequent step of seeking the true will of the creator), but they do show the remarkable and far-reaching impact religion can have on human activity. Should origins then be treated lightly? Since one's position on origins provides the basic philosophical premise upon which human actions can or cannot be justified, should we not be careful here just as we should cautiously check the stability of the soil upon which we build a home?

Extraterrestrial Life VS a Creator

The degree to which one's life can revolve like spokes around the hub of origins is fantastic. The parallel influences both creation and evolution have on their respective devotees is striking. These parallels are especially made apparent in the attempts by both evolutionists and creationists to communicate with the "products" of their philosophies.

If evolution is true and is an all-pervading universal process, as Huxley suggested above, then it is eminently reasonable for the Universe to be abundant in intelligent civilizations(10^{16} or more are estimated). Some of these would more than likely be far more advanced than ours(an estimated five hundred trillion).[21]

21. W. T. KEETON: *BIOLOGICAL SCIENCE* (N.Y.:NORTON, 1972),p.699.

Consequently, as stated above, the space effort is very much geared toward finding this extraterrestrial life. Facetiously, it is said, there are so many satellites and other devices being pumped into space that if it is kept up the flying saucers won't be able to get through; and the time is now being lamented when space exploration taxed only the imagination.

A division of NASA is space bioscience, or, as it is also called, exobiology. Exobiology is a study of extraterrestrial life. The evolutionary assumption of extraterrestrial life has thus produced a "science" for which there is no known subject matter. Life beyond the earth is not known to exist nor are even planetary systems outside our own. But there is every hope and confident expectation that the subject matter of exobiology will soon be discovered.

During the filming of the 10.5 million dollar film entitled: *2001--A SPACE ODYSSEY*, Lloyd's of London was approached for insurance. The producers of the film, concerned about whether their plot might be botched if extraterrestrial life were found before showing the film, wanted insurance against such an eventuality.

Lloyd's refused.

Thus we can see the certainty with which people believe in the fulfillment of the evolutionary implication of extraterrestrial life. In this case, a movie maker was willing to spend large sums for insurance against finding extraterrestrial life, and an insurance company was afraid to take the money and write a policy against finding it.

A natural consequence of belief in extraterrestrial life is an attempt toward communication. Evolutionists have followed through with this by spending massive amounts of money and almost countless hours in research devoted to devising codes and equipment to send and receive messages. A noted example is the plaque aboard the Pioneer 10 spacecraft launched in 1972.[22] (Fig. 2). Other efforts involve the use of giant radio telescopes like Cornell's at Puerto Rico.

Many evolutionists believe their position offers mankind much hope. On the back cover of the book, *EVOLUTION IN ACTION*, by Julian Huxley, these comments are made:

"Without some knowledge of evolution one cannot hope to arrive at a true picture of human destiny . . . He has brought renewed hope and faith that the frontiers are not all closed; that a new world does lie ahead."[23]

More specifically, contact with extraterrestrial life is expected to bring us essentials for betterment, perhaps even salvation. Pointing first to the importance of origins, Sagan wrote: ". . . it would be a great mistake to ignore where we

22. *C. SAGAN: THE COSMIC CONNECTION(N.Y.:DELL,1973); C. SAGAN, ED.: COMMUNICATION WITH EXTRATERRESTRIAL INTELLIGENCE(MASS.:M.I.T.,1973).*
23. *J. HUXLEY: EVOLUTION IN ACTION(N.Y.:NEW AMERICAN LIBRARY,1953).*

have come from in our attempt to determine where we are going . . . It has been suggested that the contents of the initial message received will contain instructions for avoiding our own self-destruction, a possibly common fate of societies shortly after they reach the technical phase."24

So if evolution is true we should expect extraterrestrial life. If there is extraterrestrial life we should expect communication with it and from it. In turn, the messages received might be expected to offer mankind some sort of renewed hope.

Perhaps you can see the superstructure of effort, thought and even hope that can be built upon evolution.

On the other hand, the creationist also contends that he can with equal logic expect communication from an intelligent creator. He likewise expects the message to contain hope and perhaps a formula for salvation: a revelation to man informing him of his role in the purposes and will of the creator. The parallel implications of the two positions are remarkable in this regard.

To say the least, communication with either a superintelligent extraterrestrial creature or a supernatural creator would be highly exciting. However, we have no contact at present with extraterrestrial life. But there are claims that we have had visitations in the past. On the other hand, there is no direct dial to a creator, voices booming from the heavens or Creator TV Channel we can turn to. But there are claims that certain "holy" books are communiques from the creator to man.

The astronomer, Carl Sagan, in a recent writing, considered the possibility that we have had visitations from UFO's and extraterrestrial beings. He states:

"There is surely no way in which we could exclude such a contingency. How could we prove it?. . . The arguments are of two sorts, legend and artifact. . . There is only one category of legend that would be convincing: When information is contained in the legend that could not possibly have been generated by the civilization that created the legend--if, for example, a number transmitted from thousands of years ago as holy turns out to be the nuclear fine structure constant. This would be worthy of considerable attention.

"Also convincing would be certain classes of artifact. . . An example would be an illuminated manuscript, rescued from an Irish monastery, that contains the electronic circuit diagram for a superheterodyne radio receiver."

He concludes:

"To the best of my knowledge, there are no such legends and no such artifacts."25

---

24. *C. SAGAN:THE COSMIC CONNECTION(N.Y.:DELL, 1973), PP.6,219.*
25. *IBID., PP. 204,205.*

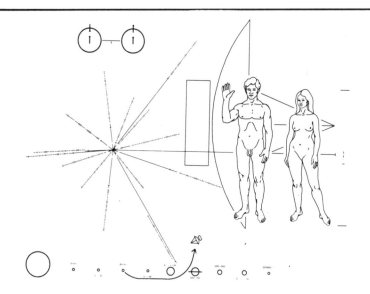

Fig. 2 - A Cosmic Message

The above message was placed aboard the Pioneer 10 spacecraft launched March 3, 1972. The etching was made on a long-wearing gold-anodized aluminum plate attached to the antenna support struts. The spacecraft left the solar system in December of that year and was the first vessel to do so. It will reach the nearest star in 80,000 years. The message is in a scientific code--likened to a bottled message cast into the cosmic ocean by earth sailors--believed to be decipherable by any advanced extraterrestrial civilization. The various symbols communicate locale, epoch and nature of the spacecraft builders. For example, the bottom symbols represent the initial trajectory launched by earth--third planet from the sun--and passage by Jupiter. Understanding this message requires deductions from proton and electron spins, binary math and pulsars. The desire to communicate is natural for intelligent beings. (Courtesy of Carl Sagan)

Although Sagan believes there is extraterrestrial life, he believes there is no evidence that we have had visitations, *a la, CHARIOTS OF THE GODS.*

In a similar fashion creationists check the authenticity of the holy books. They feel three criteria could be used to check validity:

1. The picture presented of the real world, the cosmology, must be accurate for surely the creator must know the structure

and dynamics of the universe he has made.
2. The writing must be reasonable and consistent, mirroring a
   creator's super-mind. The writings must reflect this high
   degree of intelligence since even reasonable humans can write
   consistent literature.
3. To mark the writing as extraordinary, as explicable only by
   invoking the supernatural, it must have features that distin-
   guish it from the literature of mere humans. It must, so to
   speak, describe the "nuclear fine structure constant" and
   "superheterodyne radio receivers" long before their discovery.
   In this way creationists feel they could make sure that "in-
spired" writings were not merely the product of someone writing
under the inspiration of a flower, tree, rock or maiden, since,
of course, anyone can claim to have produced "holy" writings.
   Then we have the problem of interpretation of extraterrestrial messages and holy writings. Carl Sagan found himself in
the position of having to defend his plaque. (Fig. 2) Some have
suggested extraterrestrial beings would interpret the man in the
drawing as giving a Nazi greeting, the crosshatched lines as a
metropolitan railroad, the space vehicle as a garden trowel, the
five extended fingers as antennae, and the capability of the one
figure to throw arrows from the shoulder, and the whole of the
message as a delaration of war! Sagan didn't scrap the message,
but rather defended its contents by appealing to reason, context,
and honesty.
   Holy writings, if they are indeed supernatural in origin,
could also be misinterpreted. A defender of them would also have
to appeal to reason, honesty and context.
   Many devote their entire lives to the philosophical hope of
contact with extraterrestrial life. Millions of others have dedicated themselves to the pronouncements and directives in holy
writings. Hopefully you can see that both courses depend upon resolving the creation-evolution controversy in a rational manner
and then, at each step thereafter, remaining true to that method,
i.e., rationally resolve the controversy, rationally resolve the
possibility of communication, rationally resolve if artifacts or
writings are valid, rationally resolve the interpretation of the
writings or artifacts.
   Again, let me emphasize the parallels between the two positions:
1. Evolution implies extraterrestrial intelligence;
   Creation implies supernatural, higher intelligence.
2. Evolution implies the expectation of communication with extraterrestrial life;
   Creation implies the expectation of communication with supernatural life.
3. Evolution implies a hope, salvation from this communique;
   Creation does likewise.
4. Evolution would demand a critical evaluation of messages as
   to authenticity;
   Creation would also.

5. Evolution would demand a reasonable, honest and contextual analysis of the contents of the message;
Creation would as well.

There are three things I would like to emphasize. One is that the evolution-creation controversy does not end with its resolution. It is not enough to simply conclude that one or the other is right. This would only be the beginning. The sequel to our decision would lead us to such things logically and naturally as the hope for communication with extraterrestrial life or to religious apologetics and exegesis. The second point of importance is that the correct resolution of the controversy depends upon a rational methodology, and the correctness of the steps subsequent to that demands rational methodology. My third point is that the controversy has far-reaching impact and importance, and we do ourselves no favor by glossing over it perfunctorily.

The scope of this book is to take step one--to rationally resolve the controversy and point to implications. Hopefully, the reader will follow through with a rational treatment of these implications.

The Need for a Rational Approach

Many at least intuitively realize the importance of their position on origins. Why can we say this? Because usually we can measure the degree with which any issue affects us personally--its importance--by the thermometer of emotions. It seems the more critical an issue is, the more emotional our attitude toward it.

Thus, when people refuse to talk about origins and treat it as a hush hush topic, something personal and private, impugn the motives of those who do talk about it, or give vent to emotion when it is discussed, we are being given indirect testimony to the subject's importance.

Why not face up to the issue and level our best tools against it? Those tools are not emotions but are our reasoning faculties. This would not mean just to think privately and formulate our own biased ideas. It would not mean we should dismiss one side or the other simply because of prejudice, pressure or a superficial knowledge. It does not mean that we should exclude the idea that the truth of the matter in a very real and satisfying sense could be found. What it does mean is to proceed as Calvin suggests:

"The true student will seek evidence to establish fact rather than confirm his own concept of truth, for truth exists whether it is discovered or not."[26]

26. M. CALVIN: _CHEMICAL EVOLUTION_(N.Y.:OXFORD U., 1969), P.252.

2. CAN LAYMEN QUESTION ?

Dogmatic and authoritative pronouncements fulminate from both religious and evolutionary camps. The layman is intimidated. He asks, "Who am I to question recognized authority?" The man on the street, fearing some sort of ostracism or humiliation if he would dare raise his voice as a skeptic, simply allows himself to be swept along by the edicts--the course of least resistance.

In this chapter we will consider the propriety of laymen entering the controversy and deciding for themselves in a reasonable way the truth on origins. This will require sifting through some of the more popular argumentation foisted on the public and encouragement individually to dissect and openly challenge dogma. Nothing said here is intended to point at specific individuals, organizations, or groups. We will necessarily generalize and speak of two categories, religion and evolution, but not all that we say will apply to all evolutionists or all religionists. And, since there are many in religion who accept evolution and many evolutionists who accept religion, this categorization is artificial and is not meant to set up a rigid dichotomy. The intent of this exposé is simply to reveal attitudes we must watch out for in our pursuit of truth on origins.

Are Credentials Necessary ?

Are we audacious feeling that we, as laymen, can resolve the controversy? There are those who would say so. Some feel this controversy is open game only for theologians with "proper" credentials. We simply don't have the proper schooling, they may say. So the argument is that the laity must have tacit faith and trust the pronouncements of those religiously qualified. But why so? The "original theologians" were lay people. If they could for-

mulate creationistic concepts we need no special credentials to
challenge or validate them. Issues that affect us personally
should be resolved personally.

Others may be timid in approaching the subject of origins,
feeling only recognized scientific authorities could be competent
to reach a decision on such a "scientific question." Since evolution is imputed to be a scientific conclusion, are laymen in a
position to scrutinize scientific generalizations, propositions,
interpretations of data? Most certainly. The evolutionary proposition, by and large, was generated by laymen! The Greeks, who
were among the first to concoct evolutionary notions, were philosophers; Darwin was a novice in biology prior to his *Beagle*
tour; Charles Lyell, who advocated the concept of geological uniformity so necessary to evolutionary thinking, was a lawyer, not
a geologist or paleontologist; others were theologians (what?!),
mathematicians, and what have you. Those who developed evolutionary thought had no special credentials, we need none to evaluate
it and decide upon its legitimacy.

Similarly, in courts of law jurors decide upon verdicts.
These individuals usually have no special competency in penology,
retributive justice, judication or forensic medicine, yet the
scales are held in their hands. The decisions do not rest with
the "qualified," yet biased, pleading counselors. If the jurors
are fair-minded, honest, discerning, and open, and if they follow
the methodological guidelines laid down by the judge, prudent decisions will be made.

Further justification for the jury members in the court of
origins being laymen lies with the realization, as we mentioned
in the previous chapter, that origins has far-reaching impact upon human activity. Origins is not merely an academic matter; it
is not an esoteric abstruse philosophical problem fit only to be
ricocheted back and forth between the minds of mental giants in
university or theological conclaves. Origins affects you and I
through its effect upon education, politics, sociology, psychology
and individual, man-on-the-street philosophy and ethics. This
makes the subject of origins open game for Joe Public.

In this regard, Marshall and Sandra Hall wrote:

> "Who is to say, after all, that ordinary citizens don't
> have the right to question any group of experts if that
> group's actions affect the entire spectrum of everybody's
> life, young, old, working or at leisure? If an engineer
> designs a bridge and it falls down during the five
> o'clock rush and kills eighty-two nonengineers, who will
> say the victims' survivors can make no effective com-
> plaint because they are not engineers? If atomic
> scientists make some little slip and wipe out Oregon,
> are citizens from neighboring states to allow new atomic
> sites to be built near them because they feel unquali-
> fied as nonscientists in making such a decision?"[1]

1. M & S. HALL:*THE TRUTH:GOD OR EVOLUTION*(NEW JERSEY:CRAIG,1974)P.99.

Argument from Expert Testimony

Expert testimonials are a common crutch for the limp in one's ability to muster a rational argument. Creationists often cite theologians or scientists as experts "proving" their position. Evolutionists proffer the scientific community almost en masse as expert testimonial "proving" their case. But does expert testimony prove anything if we rely on it alone? We'll examine the evolutionary use of expert testimony, although our conclusions will apply equally well to the creationist who relies solely upon expert testimony.

Evolutionists agree to the historicity, actuality, reality and fact of evolution. There is, however, no consensus on the exact mechanism by which the process took place. Thus we will find evolutionary expert vying with evolutionary expert on all facets of the proposed evolutionary scheme. Apropos are the words of Hilaire Belloc:

"But scientists who ought to know,
Assure us that it must be so . . .
Oh! Let us never, never doubt
What nobody is sure about."

If a layman were to choose to disagree with both sides of a given point, would he then be naive, credulous, moronic, an uninformed imbecile? Certainly not, for he could cite experts that reject either side, thus, the layman would have expert backing.

We might illustrate this point by turning to one of the many points of contention among origin of life researchers. The Nobel Prize winner, Harold Urey, argues that life originally formed in a methane-ammonia atmosphere. On the other hand, Abelson, a geologist, contends that the historical evidence from the rocks militates against a methane-ammonia atmosphere and, in lieu of this, proposes an atmosphere of a different compostion, one resulting from planetary outgassing.

Both of these men are considered experts. Yet they disagree on a very fundamental point. We could disagree with Urey and have the expert backing of Abelson, or we could disagree with Abelson and have the expert backing of Urey. Or, we could disagree with both of them and argue that neither a methane-ammonia atmosphere(Abelson's backing) nor a planetary outgassing atmosphere(Urey's backing) existed to precipitate the spontaneous formation of life.

I am not saying that the above example would prove creationism, or refute evolution. Arguing solely from expert testimony proves nothing. The creationist can effectively argue from expert testimony to disprove evolution just as the evolutionist can so argue to disprove creation. The arguments from expert testimonials produce stalemates not solutions.

1. IF EXPERT A DISAGREES WITH EXPERT B
   ON A GIVEN POINT;

2. AND EXPERT B DISAGREES WITH EXPERT A
   ON THE SAME POINT;

3. THEN LAYMEN CAN DISAGREE WITH A AND
   HAVE THE BACKING OF B, AND ALSO
   DISAGREE WITH B AND HAVE THE EXPERT
   BACKING OF A;

4. THUS LAYMEN CAN DISAGREE WITH BOTH OF
   THE EXPERTS ON THE SAME POINT IN
   QUESTION AND HAVE EXPERT BACKING IN
   SO DOING.

Does this discussion mean we cannot use any testimonials from experts? No. We simply mean that an expert's interpretation of the facts, his conclusions, taken alone and detached from reason, should not be sufficiently convincing. It is, of course, proper to cite experts to establish facts and acquaint us with evidences and, if necessary, counter an opposing expert testimony.

Argument from Popularity

Truth is never determined on the basis of a popularity poll. Citing this scholar or that one as holding beliefs similar to ours is tenuous support. The argument from popularity(*argumentum ad populum*) is logically invalid.

We often hear statements to the effect that the entire scientific community believes in the fact of evolution. Or, in the past era, theologians could argue the same about creationism. Pronouncements from popularity convey impact on the layman and have the effect of dead-ending inquiry. Few wish to be unique, odd, renegades or intellectual dropouts. So, in self-defense, laymen side with whatever is vogue.

Tactics based upon group pressure--popularity--are also the basis for many of the commericals we encounter daily: Since everyone is doing it, eating it, wearing it, seeing it, using it, buying it and believing it, shouldn't you!? Children especially feel the pressure from the slogan, "everbody's doing it," as evidenced by the fads in dress, drugs, language and morals.

Surely the gimmickry in advertising is obvious, and the naive need for acceptance by the crowd is expected of children, but should mature thinkers succumb? Certainly not, for under the guise of popularity and authoritarian pressure is cheap advertising and tactics fit only to convince impressionable youth.

Popularity in Reverse

Up until the present century, creationism held the upper hand in terms of popularity. But now evolution is secured by the vote of the masses--at least the educated masses. So the argument that the entire scientific community believes is now commonly heard.

But this is not true, and even if it were, of what value is the argument? The vote of the scientific community has never mandated truth. These elections, if you will, are strewn with the wreckages of shattered "truths" like the flat earth, phlogistan and ether.

Although it is true that most in academia believe evolution, there are not an insignificant number who hold the opposite position, or have at least rejected evolution. In England there is the Evolution Protest Movement, and the United States has the Bible-Science Association, Institute for Creation Research and Creation Research Society. These organizations deny evolution and are made up of members numbering in the several thousands. Many have advanced graduate degrees and some hold significant positions in the academic and scientific community. So we could say that there is definitely a growing popularity in reverse. But we could also say, "so what!" Exactly, popularity means nothing regardless of the side it is on.

Propaganda

Religionists have been noted for their submission to propaganda and blind faith. Dogmatic statements of doctrine are thundered from the pulpits and the laity is to acquiesce. The faithful are even asked not to entertain contrary views in literature or discussion. If one questions accepted doctrine, if he finds it weak under close scrutiny, he throws his "spirituality" and "faith" into question. Answers like "have faith my son" or "it's a divine mystery" are foisted as adequate rebuttal to any challenge. Thus, reason and the rational approach is abandoned. Propaganda is substituted.

It is interesting how religionists will argue against the use of reason through the use of reason. This is like arguing that shovels are a contemptible tool, condemning them by putting all of the world's shovels in a large hole and covering them over with dirt shoveled in by a shovel.

Everyone will press reason into service when, by so doing, they can bolster their own cherished beliefs. But when reason contradicts preconceived ideas, reason is forsaken and even turned upon. If reason is of no value, or only limited worth, then all men would be led to universal skepticism. No system of thought, religious or secular, could stand.

It is true that reason can be abused and even lead to error. Does this mean that reason should be universally abandoned? No, this would be like throwing the baby out with the bath water. The use of reason should not be feared, rather, its lack of use should be. The worst perpetuated errors have been those demanding implicit faith and submission to propaganda.

If one dares to challenge traditional religious teachings, counterarguments and castigations will often follow this general line: (1) One must assume the doctrine as true before examining the facts; (2) Contrary facts are deemed not properly understood, shelved as mysteries and thought of as tests of faith; (3) That which is most popular must be true; (4) Appropriate credentials (obtained by being selectively trained--propogandized--in a sanctioned religious school) are prerequisites to discussion, criticism, or free thought on religious matters; (5) The search for supporting evidences must be made by neglecting the material which might crimp the proof.

So much for religious propaganda. What about evolutionism? The same type of propaganda syndrome is found there also. Note these comments by Julian Huxley, an outspoken evolutionist:

> "The first point to make about Darwin's theory is that it is no longer a theory but a fact. No serious scientist would deny the fact that evolution has occurred just as he would not deny the fact that the earth goes around the sun.

> "Darwinism removed the whole idea of God as the creator of organisms from the sphere of rational discussion. Darwin pointed out that no supernatural designer was needed; since natural selection could account for any known form of life, there is no room for a supernatural agency in its evolution."[2]

The television, newspapers, magazines and childrens books are replete with either blatant or subtle comments similar to these. A university president stated in a New Orleans newspaper:

> "It takes an overwhelming prejudice to refuse to accept the facts, and anyone who is exposed to the evidence supporting evolution must recognize it as an historical fact."[3]

Consider these comments in a scientific book written especially for young people:

> "When the theory of evolution was first thought of as an explanation of the family resemblances of plants and animals, it was only a reasonable guess. But by the

2. J. HUXLEY:"AT RANDOM: A TELEVISION PREVIEW," IN EVOLUTION AFTER DARWIN, ED. S. TAX(CHICAGO: UNIVERSITY OF CHICAGO, 1960), P. 41.
3. THE NEW ORLEANS TIMES--PICAYUNE(MAY 7,1964).

time it was developed in its present form by the English
biologist, Darwin, in 1859, it was no longer just a
guess. It was a scientific law proved by many lines of
evidence."[4]

Theodosius Dobzhansky, the famous geneticist, said:

"Evolution as a historical fact was proved beyond reasonable doubt not later than in the closing decades of
the 19th century. No one who takes the trouble to become familiar with the pertinent evidence has at present
a valid reason to disbelieve that the living world,
including man, is a product of evolutionary development."[5]

Savage, in his book, *EVOLUTION*, wrote:

"No serious biologist today doubts the fact of evolution
. . . the fact of evolution is amply clear . . . We do
not need a listing of evidences to demonstrate the fact
of evolution any more than we need to demonstrate the
existence of mountain ranges."[6]

And Richard Goldschmidt, of the University of California,
asserted:

"Evolution of the animal and plant world is considered
by all those entitled to judgement to be a fact for
which no further proof is needed."[7]

Recently, a local college sent letters of invitation to several scientists asking them to participate in a creation-evolution
seminar. Some of the scientists were evolutionists and some were
creationists. Noteworthy were a couple of the replies.

The first is from a scientist, author, and vehement proponent
of evolution. He answered:

"Thank you for your kind invitation to participate in
your seminar. The so-called Special Creation is not
a topic fit for scientific analysis, since no evidence
can either prove or disprove it, and discussing it as
if it were such a topic can only be misleading. I
must decline your invitation."

The second letter is not quite so subtle in deprecating a
consideration of both sides of the issue:

"I am indeed aware of increased publicity for 'creationism,' as also for astrology and witchcraft. I believe
that the flat earth is not now so much discussed, but
doubtless that will come too.

---

4. IRVING ADLER: *HOW LIFE BEGAN*(N.Y.: NEW AMERICAN LIBRARY, 1957),P.18.
5. T. DOBZHANSKY IN *EVOLUTION OF MAN*, ED. L. B. YOUNG(NEW JERSEY:
OXFORD U., 1970), P. 58.
6. J. SAVAGE: *EVOLUTION*(N.Y.:HOLT, RINEHART,WINSTON, 1965), PREFACE.
7. R. GOLDSCHMIDT IN *AMERICAN SCIENTIST*, 40(1952):84.

"In spite of my evident distaste for anti-intellect-
ualism and regression to the Middle Ages . . . I am
quite unable to accept your invitation . . ."
These words are from a world renowned paleontologist. Did
you catch the fact that if you were to even consider creation as
an option, you would automatically become anti-intellectual,
regressed, unscientific, and would be displaying a mentality given
to serious consideration of astrology, witchcraft and a flat
earth? What can the layman do but recoil in fear?

The prevalence of this and like propaganda is to be expected
though because propoganda, like manure, is of no value unless it
is spread.

To be sure, in the minds of many, those who consider the
creation alternative are a reproachful lot. In the minds of others
those who consider evolution are likewise reproachful. But an
intolerant attitude is merely a symptom of the age-old "follow
the crowd" syndrome. To many, nonconformity in itself is sufficient reason to heap reproach on another.

Rickover wrote of those who dare not conform to fashionable
thought:

"The 'controversial' tag makes him a 'flawed' personality, not group-adjusted, one-sided, ill-informed,
frustrated and motivated by ill will. Epithets may
therefore be thrown at him with impunity; he may be
misquoted and misrepresented, and what he says may be
contemptuously dismissed as requiring no refutation
whatever."[8]

Our desire for truth, regardless of our personal credentials,
should not allow us to be intimidated by the possibility that open
inquiry may lead us to a position ostracizing us from the norm--
religious or scientific.

Why not, as Darwin suggested in the conclusion to his book,
THE ORIGIN OF SPECIES, ". . .view both sides of the question with
impartiality . . ." This means we must cull propaganda and savor
an open rational investigation.

Necessity of Criticism

Both creationists and evolutionists believe they have the
truth. A quality of truth is its ability to hold up under criticism. But some in religion feel it improper to even raise questions, much less criticize, what is traditional. Some evolutionists also insulate their views from critical probings.

To win men to the truth, their minds must be won. Minds are
not won by dogmatism. Dogmaticism produces, at best, menial

8. H. G. RICKOVER: "DECLINE OF THE INDIVIDUAL," IN SATURDAY
EVENING POST, 236(MARCH 30, 1963): 11.

robots. Minds are won by openness.

When the scientific community originally accepted Darwin's ideas, they did so to be emancipated from religion's intellectually stifling effects. Mora pleaded with origin-of-lifers(scientists involved in origin of life experimentation) not to put up a mental block against teleology, by implication, religion, and asks:

> ". . .are we not avoiding this consideration of purpose because of bad memories teleology evokes?"[9]

Elsewhere he wrote:

> "Furthermore, in physics we avoid teleology of any kind, again apparently because of good historical reasons."[10]

Price says even more pointedly:

> "As new knowledge develops, it has increasingly provided natural explanations for facts and phenomena formerly ascribed to the supernatural. Perhaps new understanding of chemical evolution and biological function can develop a philosophy of man more unified, less divisive, less of a major breeding ground for man's inhumanity to man than the many religious dogmas now so much used to inflame feelings of hatred, suspicion and prejudice in human society."[11]

The authors, Marshall and Sandra Hall, wrote:

> "Organized religions' record of intolerance and superstition drives many people to accept evolutionary answers . . . let us add a third thing for you to remember. There is nothing wrong with using straw men in debates. Evolutionists have been doing it for years. 'Look at the churches,' they will say. 'See how corrupt and rich and ungodly they are. Who could believe they have the correct assumption.' That's one straw man they use . . .Up to then, those who had turned away from organized religion had done so primarily as a reaction against the corruption, intolerance, and often cruelty of the Roman Catholic Church; defects often equalled in the 16th through 19th centuries by the Protestants. Thus out of reaction against the rigidity of the Church, and fortified by science in their doubts relating to church dogma, many were ripe indeed for the 'book that shook the world.' Few, prior to Darwin, had gone so far as to reject God; it was organized religion that had been under attack. . . .With the advent of

9. P. MORA: "URGE AND MOLECULAR BIOLOGY," IN NATURE, 199(1963): 218.

10. P. MORA: "THE FOLLY OF PROBABILITY," IN THE ORIGINS OF PRE-BIOLOGICAL SYSTEMS AND THEIR MOLECULAR MATRICES, ED. S. FOX(N.Y.: ACADEMIC, 1965), P. 49.

11. C. PRICE IN MOLECULAR EVOLUTION:PREBIOLOGICAL AND BIOLOGICAL, EDS. D. ROHLFING & A. OPARIN(N.Y.:PLENUM, 1972), P. 462.

Darwin's theory, and its acceptance by evergrowing
numbers of people, religion looked steadily more foolish and science more reasonable. Not only did science
appear more reasonable, but it appeared also to be
more dedicated to truth."[12]

On the other hand, many evolutionists are now simply repeating the mentality of religions that originally drove them to their
position. Thompson, in the introduction to THE ORIGIN OF SPECIES,
by Charles Darwin, said:

"As we know, there is a great divergence of opinion
among biologists, not only about the cause of evolution
but even about the actual process. This divergence exists because the evidence is unsatisfactory and does
not permit any certain conclusion. It is therefore
right and proper to draw the attention of the non-
scientific public to the disagreements about evolution.
But some recent remarks of evolutionists show that
they think this unreasonable. This situation, where
men rally to the defense of a doctrine they are unable
to define scientifically, much less demonstrate with
scientific rigor, attempting to maintain its credit
with the public by the suppression of criticism and
the elimination of difficulties, is abnormal and unde-
sirable in science."[13]

Also note these pointed comments by a creationist organization in reaction to the affront by the evolutionary community:

"If evolution has a strong case, it should welcome examination. But when evolutionists assume their theory
proved, that it is no longer debatable, that only the
ignorant will attack it; when they meet opposition
with a haughty air of superiority, smear the Bible, and
belittle the intellect of Bible believers--does not all
that make evolution's case suspect? Are such tactics
necessary to cover over a weak case, or no case? Mature and proved science does not have to erect a psy-
chological front to ward off inquiry, does not have to
smear opposition to protect its discoveries. Then why
does evolution?"[14]

A recent biology textbook has even taken the novel position
of criticizing the evolutionist's attitude:

"Finally, we cannot imagine that the cause of truth is
served by keeping unpopular or minority ideas under
wraps. Today's students are much less inclined than

12.   M.&S.HALL: THE TRUTH: GOD OR EVOLUTION (NEW JERSEY: CRAIG,
1974), PP. 5,98,122.
13.   W.R.THOMPSON: "INTRODUCTION," IN THE ORIGIN OF SPECIES, BY
CHARLES DARWIN (N.Y.: E.P.DUTTON, 1956).
14. EVOLUTION VERSUS THE NEW WORLD (N.Y.: WATCHTOWER BIBLE & TRACT
SOCIETY, 1950), P.4.

those of former generations to unquestionably accept the pronouncements of 'authority.' Specious arguments can only be exposed by examining them. Nothing is so unscientific as the inquisition mentality that served, as it thought, the truth, by seeking to suppress or conceal dissent rather than by grappling with it."[15]

Has evolution triumphed over dogmatic religious attitudes? Or is, as some boast, evolution synonymous with science? Science hinges on investigation. Without investigation and criticism, discovery stops. If evolutionism suppresses critics, then its status as a science is questionable. On the other hand, if religion suppresses critics, then it cannot be the vicar of truth it claims to be.

Truth welcomes deliberate criticism, perusal, inspection, scrutiny, and review. If evolution is true, or creation is true, they should bare themselves to this action.

Although we will not be using the "scientific method" in resolving the controversy (for reasons made apparent in the next chapter), we should follow in attitude the open, rational approach advocated by that method.

Speaking of Francis Bacon and the rise of the inductive scientific method, the author of *BACON AND THE EXPERIMENTAL METHOD* states:

"What was wanted was a method by which we could slowly and cautiously rise from observed facts to wider and deeper generalizations, testing every such generalization at each step by deliberately looking out for possible exceptions to it, and rejecting or modifying it if we actually found such exceptions."[16]

Sir Karl Popper, a leader in the development of the scientific method, would argue that scientific advancement toward truth hinges upon the falsification of theories. (*THE LOGIC OF SCIENTIFIC DISCOVERY*-1959) This, he would argue, is evidenced by history leaving an immense trail, not of proven truths, but of falsified and discarded theories.

Should creation or evolution be exempt from attempts to falsify them? Can one only investigate or criticize after he has accepted the fact of either one or the other? One has a basis for his faith, be it in evolution or creation, or he does not. A faith built upon a solid rational foundation invites criticism and welcomes refinement; faith built upon a bubble jealously protects itself from the ravages of attack for fear it may burst.

If truth is our goal, why not open our views to close scrutiny? If we have the truth, our views will stand, if we don't, let them fall.

---

15. P. DAVIS AND E. SOLOMON: *THE WORLD OF BIOLOGY*(N.Y.:MCGRAW-HILL, 1974), P. 414.
16. C. D. BROAD: "BACON AND THE EXPERIMENTAL METHOD," IN *A SHORT HISTORY OF SCIENCE--A SYMPOSIUM*(N.Y.:DOUBLEDAY, 1951), P.32.

28

Suppression of Heretics

Unfortunately, the intimidation of the layman has often been extended beyond propagandizing and gentle authoritarian nudgings. In some cases it has become outright persecution and suppression.

In the past, especially, religions viciously and mercilessly attacked dissenting individuals. A noteworthy example is the Inquisition. Cruelty, torture, sadism and ostracism have all been done in the spirit of "truth preservation."

Religion has lost much of her power. Today evolutionists have it. And suprisingly they are known to use the same inquisitorial tactics against heretics. It is deemed apostate by some evolutionary minds to even mention creationism as a possible alternative. If creation is considered one might make suspect his ability to walk and chew bubble gum at the same time.

Abundant are the sad stories of students who have pursued advanced degrees, only to be denied them because they rejected evolutionism. It is also next to impossible to publish material that is pro-creationism or anti-evolutionism through the well known trade publishing houses, even though these same houses copiously publish evolutionary material. Those siding for creation usually must publish their research through their own channels or through sectarian religious houses.

Mora, an origin of life researcher, confirms this intolerant attitude in academia:

> "In one respect, in the consideration of purposes, we seem to have a complete mental block. One who brings teleology into science might expose himself to a little ridicule, if not to a gentle inquisitorial castigation by editors of scientific journals or to the expression of exasperation by fellow scientists."[17]

Velikovsky, who theorized a catastrophic evolutionary history for this planet, met considerable opposition in trying to publish his work. Traditional evolutionary science holds to the position of historical uniformity (all things continue today as they have in the past). The uniformity proposition is believed key to evolutionary mechanisms.

Scientists in this country evidently felt Velikovsky's ideas on historical catastrophism would have cataclysmic effects on their coddled philosophies. These scientists brought such pressure to bear on the MacMillan publishers, threatening to boycott their textbooks, that MacMillan gave way and turned Velikovsky's works over to a publisher not producing scientific

17. P. T. MORA: "URGE AND MOLECULAR BIOLOGY," IN NATURE, 199 (1963):218.

textbooks.[18]

Has freedom of the press become the freedom to be sure that all of the propaganda is on one side, and a free land a place where you can say what you think if the majority thinks the same thing?

Society today is very concerned about human rights and equality. There is the black movement, the chicano movement, gay liberation, woman's liberation, student liberation, and child liberation. The need for freedom to express individuality seems to be keenly before the public. Why cannot such freedom be extended to laymen who wish to rationally consider the topic of origins? Does the fact that a religious world once suppressed freedom of thought and scientific inquiry justify the scientific community's like action today?

Those who cling to their doctrines in a cynical way, have no true foundation for what they believe, and avoid discussion, criticism, or thought on the matter, both the religionist and evolutionist who display these attitudes, are in dangerous positions. For without inquiry, criticism and thought, one has no real assurance that his convictions are valid. Our lives could be revolving around a philosophical lie. Truth is our goal. We have only to gain from searching it out and reconciling ourselves to it.

So, can a layman question? Yes! He has every right. The layman should be able to see that expert testimonials, *argumentum ad populum*, propaganda and suppression are flimsy, specious substitutes for rational arguments.

Let's decide upon a method by which we can resolve the controversy, set up definitions, then examine the evidences. If we are to be intimidated, let's let the evidences do it.

---

18. *FORT WAYNE NEWS SENTINEL(JULY 11, 1950), EDITORIAL PAGE; THE VELIKOVSKY AFFAIR*, ED. A. DEGRAZIA(N.Y.: UNIVERSITY BOOKS, 1966), PP. 20-74; S. TALBOTT: "A SHORT BIOGRAPHY," IN *PENSÉE*, 2(1972):5.

3 ᴄᴍETHODOLOGY

If any aspect of the subject of origins could be singled out for its importance, it would be methodology. Just as one is dependent upon a map to reach a desired destination, so must one follow the guidelines of proper methodology to find truth.

It is by giving only superficial attention to this facet of our subject that so many have become frustrated in their search for answers. The method by which we can rationally resolve the question of origins will provide the funnel through which we can channel our thoughts and research. It will tell us when our thinking is wrong, when our thinking is right, and how to make corrections, adjustments, modifications and progress. Individuals with various backgrounds, skills, biases, motives and desires will find common footing in a logical, well defined methodology. If our goal is to achieve real, truthful answers, it is preeminently important that we carefully construct the methodological framework for achieving that end, agree to it, use it and stick to it.

Two Positions

Why does a consideration of the topic of origins have to be a pitting of creationism against evolution? Aren't there other possibilities? No, in a broad sense there are not. All explanations of origins are reducible to these two. Consequently, Huxley, an evolutionist, states:

> "There are only three possible alternatives as regards the origin of living substance on this earth. Either it was naturally created; or it was brought to the earth from some other place in the universe in the interior of a meteorite; or it was produced naturally out of less complicated substances."

Huxley then proceeds to eliminate the second possibility by stating:

> ". . . it only removes the problem one step further back: we still have to face the question of how this supposed extraterrestrial life originated."[1]

In other words, the two possibilities remain creation and evolution.

L. T. More corroborates Huxley's comments:

> "The more one studies paleontology, the more certain one becomes that evolution is based on faith alone; exactly the same sort of faith which is necessary to have when one encounters the great mysteries of religion. . . The only alternative is the doctrine of special creation, which may be true, but is irrational."[2]

Watson has averred the same:

> "Evolution itself is accepted by zoologists, not because it has been observed to occur. . . or can be proved by logical coherent evidence, but because the only alternative, special creation, is clearly incredible."[3]

Note also these comments by Arthur Keith:

> "Evolution is unproved and unprovable. We believe it only because the only alternative is special creation, and that is unthinkable."[4]

Zucherman wrote concerning the origin of the mind:

> "Either evolutionary change or miraculous divine intervention lies at the back of human intelligence."[5]

The authors, Davis and Solomon, in their new biology text penned:

> "Such explanations tend to fall into one or the other of two broad categories: special creation or evolution. Various admixtures and modifications of these two concepts exist, but it seems impossible to imagine an explanation of origins that lies completely outside the two ideas."[6]

Newman asserted:

> "There is no rival hypothesis except the outworn and completely refuted one of special creation, now retained only by the ignorant, the dogmatic,

---

1.   *J.HUXLEY:EVOLUTION IN ACTION (N.Y.: NEW AMERICAN LIBRARY 1963),
PP. 20,21.*
2.   *WHY I BELIEVE IN CREATION (GREAT BRITAIN: EVOLUTION PROTEST
MOVEMENT PAMPHLET, 1968).*
3.   *D. WATSON: "ADAPTATION," IN NATURE, 123(1929):233.*
4.   *WHY I BELIEVE IN CREATION (GREAT BRITAIN: EVOLUTION PROTEST
MOVEMENT PAMPHLET, 1968).*
5.   *S. ZUCHERMAN: FUNCTIONAL ACTIVITIES OF MAN, MONKEYS AND APES
(1933),P. 155.*
6.   *P. DAVIS AND E. SOLOMON: THE WORLD OF BIOLOGY (N.Y.: MCGRAW
HILL, 1974), P. 395.*

and the prejudiced."[7]

George Wald concurs that

". . . there are only the two possibilities: either
life arose by spontaneous generation. . . or it arose
by supernatural creation. . . There is no third position."[8]

And elsewhere he has stated:

"Evolution advances, not by a priori design, but by the
selection of what works best out of whatever choices
offer. We are the products of editing, rather than of
authorship."[9]

Finally, we will quote the words of E. A. Schaffer in the
"Presidential Address to the British Association for the Advancement of Science," (1912):

". . . setting aside as devoid of scientific foundation
the idea of immediate supernatural intervention in the
first production of life, we are not only justified in
believing, but compelled to believe, that living matter
must have owed its origin to causes similar in character
to those which have been instrumental in producing all
other forms of matter in the universe, in other words,
to a process of gradual evolution."[10]

Evolutionary authorities, in the main, agree that there are
only the two basic possibilities. Creationists feel the same.
Therefore, we will proceed upon the premise there are only two.

Two Possible Positions:

1— Supernatural Creation

2—Naturalistic Evolution

Creationism is generally understood to mean belief in a supernatural being creating in a very literal historical sense.
Evolutionism, in its strictly materialistic, atheistic sense, is

7. H.NEWMAN:_OUTLINES OF GENERAL ZOOLOGY_(N.Y.:MACMILLAN,1924),P.407.
8. G. WALD: "THEORIES OF THE ORIGIN OF LIFE," IN _FRONTIERS OF
MODERN BIOLOGY_ (BOSTON: HOUGHTON MUFFLIN,1962),P. 187; G. WALD:
"THE ORIGIN OF LIFE," IN _THE PHYSICS AND CHEMISTRY OF LIFE_ (N.Y.:
SIMON & SCHUSTER, 1955),P.5.
9. G. WALD: "THE ORIGIN OF OPTICAL ACTIVITY," IN _ANNALS OF THE
NEW YORK ACADEMY OF SCIENCE_, 66(1957):367.
10. J. KEOSIAN:_THE ORIGIN OF LIFE_(N.Y.:REINHOLD,1968),P.12.

naturalism, i.e., all things owe their existence to natural causes and chance.

Other proposed possibilities, as Huxley brought out, such as life arising on earth from extra-terrestrial beings dropping protoplasm from UFO's or from "seeds" contained within meteorites, (cosmozoic or panspermia theories) simply postpone the problem to another planet or source--they relocate unanswered questions. (Fig. 3)

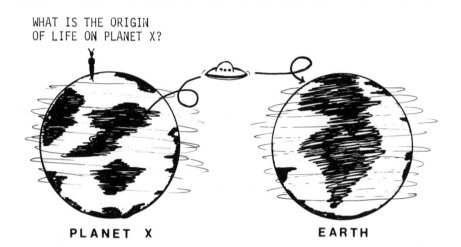

WHAT IS THE ORIGIN
OF LIFE ON PLANET X?

PLANET X   **EARTH**

Fig. **3** - Panspermia

Arguing that life could have come to earth from outer space does not create a third position on origins. This contention would simply remove the question of origins to another planet. There we would meet the same question, and again face the only two possible explanations for origins: life was created, or life was spontaneously generated. (Aside from this, it is generally accepted that life as we know it could not have survived the lethal radiations of outer space during its interplanetary sojourn. If life was brought to earth not by seeds within meteorites but by intelligent visitations, we face the difficulty in explaining the vast distances that would have been traveled and the unlikelihood of the compatibility with our environment.)

It would not lend to a rational discussion about the origin of life to speculate the possibility of extraterrestrial seeding, natural laws and forces yet undiscovered,or a third position for which there is no evidence. In our quest for a resolution to the controversy, we will limit ourselves to the real world about us, the natural laws we can observe in action, the actual record of past events and real experience.

We don't need authorities to tell us there are only two possible explanations for life. It is logical and obvious. It is a fact there are real things about us: rocks, flowers, clouds, animals, man, etc. There are also forces that cannot be seen yet their observed effects prove their reality, e.g., gravity, magnetism, wind. These real things owe their existence to a real cause. That cause can ultimately be only one of two possibilities: natural forces and chance, or supernatural intelligent design.

The Unknown Third Position

Some disagree that there are only the two positions. However, when asked to describe a third alternative they are at a loss. "But," they say, "just because we can't envision one at this time doesn't mean the potential is not there." So it is felt the assertion that there are only two alternatives is a narrowed view and precludes the possibility of further investigation and discovery.

To be sure, knowledge exists only as potential prior to its discovery. For example, the sphericity of the earth, nuclear physics, the automobile, electricity, airplanes, etc., at one time were not even conceivable. That obviously did not mean they were impossible. Therefore, it is reasoned, how can we rule out a third possibility?

We can't--philosophically at least. But in a practical and realistic sense we can for two main reasons:
1. Our goal is to resolve the controversy. To speculate a third position we can't define much less even imagine and then try to deal with this phantom intelligently would be impossible. Similarly, no fact or truth or law could stand if alternatives that could not be imagined (the logically fallacious argument from ignorance) were waged as refutation. Additionally, science would cease: everyone would fear acting on truths that were not truths because of imaginable alternatives.
2. Evolutionists believe in their position and argue it is established, or proven if you will, because of the evidence in support of it; creationists feel the same about their case. Neither reject their beliefs because of a possible third position. So, in a practical sense, why should we allow this abstract argument to prevent us from resolving the controversy and forming a belief in one or the other just as both creationists and evolutionists do? Why make a double standard? So, we will proceed under the very practical and legitimate assumption that there are only the two alternatives. When and if another alternative is defined, we'll consider it. But for now let's deal with what we know, with the real world as we presently perceive it.

Reality and Faith

The average man is about sixty-five pounds of muscle and three pounds of brain. This explains a lot of things, outstanding among which is the bizarre opinion of some that all of reality is an illusion.

Our investigation demands that we begin with faith there is a real world about us, and faith we can know it. Many led by the philosophies of the acclaimed intellectually elite have found it fashionable to doubt reality.

So often we find those who mock faith in reality as they exhale, laud science as they inhale. Actually, these two beliefs-- belief in science and disbelief in reality--are contradictory. Scientists must have faith in the predictability of real laws, the trustworthiness of real instrumentation, and the ability to decipher real truth through a real understanding of the principles of real mathematics, real probability and real logic. Without the exercise of faith in reality, nothing scientific nor material could ever be accomplished.

The very fact we are actually able to question reality testifies to its existence. Consequently, the well known 17th century philosopher, René Descartes, stated what has become an aphorism: "I think, therefore I am."

The absurdity of doubting reality, or existence, is further illustrated in the following conversation:

An emerging intellectual asks a friend: "Prove to me you exist!"

His astute friend replies, "Who are you talking to?"

"You!" he replies.

"Are you sure?" his friend says, "Because if I'm not here, and this is all just some kind of dream or illusion, then you're not there. Therefore, the question is not being asked, since you're not there to ask it. Furthermore, if I'm not here, how can I answer it?"

If during the course of a conversation you find someone seriously doubting the existence of reality, ask him to hand you his billfold. Open it before his puzzled eyes and proceed to remove all of the money you can find. Then pad your scrawny billfold with it. Nonplussed, your victim will usually fidget and ask: "What do you think you're doing?" Nonchalantly tell him you took his money thinking he wouldn't mind since, of course, neither the billfold, the money nor the whole event was actually real. Then watch his abstract philosophy fade in the dust and racket raised by insistent demands for the money's return to his real person and real billfold!

Plain old everyday living testifies to the existence of reality. Doubting it does not save us in a traffic jam, does not cancel the poisonous effects of a bad can of tuna, does not earn us wages, does not negate the real fact that we must eat and eliminate to survive, and does not void the plethora of very real problems facing the human race.

When one performs a simple act like sitting in a chair, he does so based upon the assumption that the chair will support him. That assumption is based upon faith in reality. Such faith was probably founded upon past experience with this or other similar chairs. If he is skeptical about the chair's ability to support him he may test it by pushing on it with his hand, kicking its legs, examining its components or he might even have his wife try it first. In any case, his decision to sit is based upon faith in what is real, the predictability of past experience, the chemical cohesiveness of glue, the strength of wood or steel, or in his wife's willingness to try it first.

Having faith in reality is certainly not a credulous concession to make. Everyone is subject to reality, and all people have faith. Even the person who doubts reality has faith that it does not exist, based in turn upon faith in his thinking faculties--which, of course, don't exist (?) In our investigation, as in all truly scientific work, we must have faith in reality.

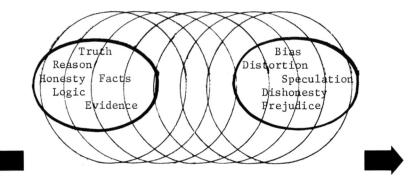

CIRCLES CONTAINING PEOPLE
WHO HAVE FAITH WITH
FOUNDATION

CIRCLES CONTAINING PEOPLE
WHO HAVE BLIND CREDULOUS
FAITH

Fig. 4 - Types of Faith

All people have faith. Faith can be founded in truth or be blind and credulous. The circles contain people with types of faith based upon the components within the ovals. Of course, one's faith is always based upon some of the components in each oval. However, truthseekers will constantly strive to be in the circles to the left, and those individuals content with naive faith will gravitate to the circles on the right.

"Having faith," however, is not something the intellectual likes to admit. "Faith" carries with it the connotation of emotionalism and fanaticism, not reason and logic. This is because of its misapplication by religionists though, and not as if having faith is necessarily the same as credulity.

All people have faith, even if it is faith that there is no such thing as faith. Faith can be built upon fiction or reality. If one ceases to have faith with foundation, faith based upon facts, he must in turn take up faith in the credulous--blind faith. In other words, since all people have faith, the question is: do we wish to have faith in line with truth, or faith in line with fancy? A faith with foundation follows belief and conviction which in turn is based upon facts and reality. This faith, then, is simply a continuation of reason. On the other hand, blind credulous faith has its basis in bias, distortion, error and fantasy. This blind faith would be a cessation of reason. (Fig. 4)

It is reasonable to believe in reality, to trust it and have faith in it. Faith in reality will allow us to use truth, facts, concrete evidences, laws and data in our investigation. If we prove one explanation of origins true at the expense of the other, we will believe that proven explanation to be truth, we will trust it, we will have faith in it. We will then be able to use the correct explanation of origins to understand other facets of life. Continued belief in the explanation of origins not consistent with reality would be blind credulity.

Origin Questions Have Answers

Most of us recognize there are answers in a very real, truthful and absolute sense to all questions.

A feeling of incompetence to find the answers is no justification for reasoning that absolute answers do not exist.

A primitive bushman may feel totally unable to understand the workings of an internal combustion engine. Does that mean the mechanism can't be understood, or that answers don't exist? Certainly not. We know that given the proper schooling and tools the bushman would soon understand the truthful answers to his questions.

Likewise, there must be truthful, absolute answers to questions about the origin of life and the physical world. Something (natural or supernatural) caused matter to form, something caused life to form. Gleaning answers will simply require the proper schooling and tools.

The philosopher, Descartes, argued reality owes its existence to a cause. Concerning that cause, he asks:

> "How could this cause communicate reality to
> the effect, unless it possessed it in

itself?"11
    Just as the physical and biological worlds are real, so must be their cause. Our objective here is to gain the competency, the education, the openness to find the real cause for the existence of life. If we approach the subject in an informed, unbiased manner, recognizing the limitations of our finite mind, our search should not be frustrated.

Superficial Impressions

    The competency to answer the question of origins may not come easy. The issues can be complex and the arguments detailed. Ferreting out truth will demand exertion on our part and willingness to look beyond the surface.

    Deceptively, geometric figures can be drawn to look different than they really are. Through the proper use of shading, curved lines and three dimensional perspective, we can easily be deceived. To discern the truth we often need to look beyond the shading and perhaps even make exacting appropriate measurements. (Fig. 5)

    The need to look beyond the surface, beyond personal ignorance or prejudice, was once illustrated to me in a short story.

    A young man from the east, a city slicker, was once walking down the street in a small western town. Upon reaching the horse stables he heard a clang from the hammer of the town's blacksmith. Curious, he peered into the darkened barn. Looking through the dust he could see the robust, muscular figure of the blacksmith apparently doing something to what looked like a young horse. Tantalized by naive curiosity the young man stepped into the barn for a closer look. As he timidly shuffled his way over the raw dirt and straw covered floor, he noted that the blacksmith had the front leg of the horse flexed backward and resting upon an apron covered knee. Why, he was nailing the final horseshoe on the hoof of the young colt. Amazed!   The young man then ran from the barn out into the street. Looking and sounding every bit like an eager young hound taking his first bite of a waddling porcupine, he exclaimed: "I just saw a horse get done bein' built!"

    Perhaps this was a logical conclusion forced from a sheltered life that imparted no knowledge of how horses come into the world. But the conclusion was naive, and most importantly, it was wrong! To discern the truth, the young man needed to talk to someone knowledgeable about the birds and the bees--and horses--and perhaps inquire about the blacksmith's engineering abilities. He needed to look beyond the surface.

    Without in depth examination we may be misled to our detri-

---

11. RENE DESCARTES: _DISCOURSE ON METHOD AND MEDITATIONS_ (N.Y.: BOBBS MERILL, 1960), P. 97.

ment. We know that many substances, including sugar and poisons, can exist in the form of white granules. Should we confidently eat all white granules because they look like sugar?

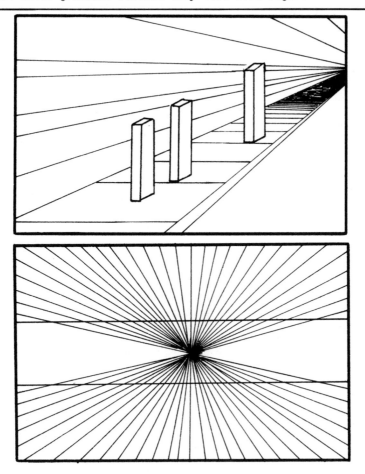

Fig.-5 Looking Beyond the Surface

Superficial impressions can often be misleading. Does the highest block in the top drawing appear larger than the other two blocks? Do the two lines in the bottom drawing appear bowed? Close examination may be needed to give the correct answer to these questions. Would it not also be wise to closely scrutinize schemes on the origin of life to be sure we determine truth?

Is it not true that the erroneous thinking of the scholars of past centuries was due to insufficient investigation--making judgements based upon surface impressions, e.g., the earth being flat? Superficialities often do not expose truth.

Many arguments used in creation-evolution debating appear reasonable at first glance but crumble under the weight of close scrutiny. If we are interested in not being misled--and we should be sensitive to this danger in an important matter like origins--why not measure arguments, taste them carefully. Both sides should be willing to open themselves for close dissection. So an important part of our method will involve wielding the scalpel of criticism, filleting arguments and casting aside superficially cute veneers and relishing the raw truth remaining.

Scientific Method

It is commonly taught that materialistic evolution is synonymous with science, empiricism and emotional neutrality; whereas creation is imputed to be religious doctrine based upon blind faith. Typifying this view, the zoologist, Theodosius Dobzhansky, stated in regard to the evolutionary proposition:

> "Most people, however, greeted the scientific proof of this view as a great liberation from spiritual bondage, and saw in it the promise of a better future."[12]

However, the evolutionist, G. G. Simpson, argues:

> "It is inherent in any definition of science that statements that cannot be checked by observation, are not really saying anything--or at least they are not science."[13]

And, the Oxford dictionary defines science:

> "A branch of study which is concerned either with a connected body of demonstrated truths or with observed facts systematically classified and more or less colligated and brought under general laws, and which includes trustworthy methods for the discovery of new truth within its own domain." (emphasis mine)

This definition could be stated yet another way: science is knowledge gained and verified through trained observation. Scientific work revolves around experimental repeatability, predictability and control.

One applies the scientific method by first of all observing and recording certain natural phenomena. He then formulates a generalization (scientific hypothesis) based upon his observations.

---

12. DUNN AND DOBZHANSKY: HEREDITY, RACE AND SOCIETY (N.Y.: THE NEW AMERICAN LIBRARY, 1952), P. 63.
13. G. G. SIMPSON: "THE NONPREVALENCE OF HUMANOIDS," IN SCIENCE 143 (1964):770.

In turn, this generalization allows him to make predictions. He then tests his hypothesis by conducting experiments to determine if the predicted result will obtain. If his predictions prove true, then he will consider his hypothesis verified. Through continual confirmation of the predictions the hypothesis will become a theory, and the theory, with time and test, will graduate to the status of a law. (Fig. 6)

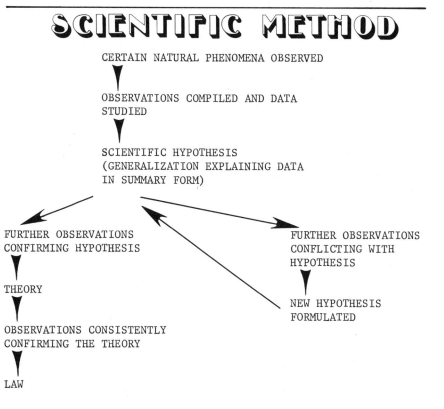

Fig.-**6** The Scientific Method

For example, one could observe that all bodies in the earth's sphere fall toward the earth. The observer seeks to explain this phenomenon by invoking a force, which he calls gravity. He states his hypothesis: Terrestrial Gravitation--all bodies in the earth's sphere will be acted upon by gravity and drawn toward the earth. He then tests his hypothesis by dropping objects from buildings, watching apples fall, rain dropping, etc. He finds his predicted results always true. His hypothesis then becomes a theory, and as he and other scientists through the years find the theory consistently true, the theory graduates to the status of a law. (Fig.7)

1 OBSERVATION

2 PROBLEM
HOW COME? WHY DOES
IT HAPPEN?

3 HYPOTHESIS
GUESS WHY SUCH AND
SUCH HAPPENS

4 EXPERIMENT
ASSUME HYPOTHESIS TRUE
AND TEST IT

5 THEORY
WHEN HYPOTHESIS IS
SUPPORTED BY A LOT OF
EXPERIMENTS

6 LAW
AFTER THEORY HAS WITH
TIME AND TEST PROVEN
TRUE

Fig.- **7** Establishing a Scientific Law

The question is, considering these definitions of the scientific method, is the materialistic proposition that life arose by chance a scientific hypothesis, or theory, or law, as Professor Dobzhansky implied above?

Evolution Is Philosophy

If the materialist's proposition is a scientific hypothesis, then it must be based upon observed phenomena--according to definition. Are scientists observing the spontaneous generation of life today in test tubes,swamps or mud puddles? Or, are organisms observed evolving into new and different organisms? No, they are not! If that be the case, and evolution is still considered a scientific hypothesis, then a trained scientist must have observed and recorded the original formation of life. Likewise,scientists must have observed evolution through the hundreds of millions of years it is said to have taken place.

Was a scientist present observing life popping into existence in the primeval oceans? Did he wonder about the cause? Did he record the temperature, analyze the components of the solutions, perform various chemical and physical tests, and then formulate a scientific hypothesis describing the cause of the formation of life? Did he,as well as future scientists,conduct experiments utilizing the exact conditions extant at the time of the original formation of life to determine if their predicted results would occur?

Of course such a primeval scientist is purely fictitious. Everyone realizes there was no scientist around when life arose to record observations and formulate a scientific hypothesis. Also, there are no experiments utilizing known early earth conditions to test the hypothesis that life arose by chance. (We will examine these experiments in detail in a later chapter.)

Candidly admitting the inexact nature of research on the origin of life, Pirie laments:

> "We now have little expectation of being able to conclude a discussion with the statement 'this is how life did arise'; the best we can hope for is 'this is one of the ways life could have arisen'. . . . We do not know what we are trying to generate or from what."[14]

The materialistic explanation for the origin of life is not an inductive scientific hypothesis based upon observations. Realizing this, Mora states:

> ". . . how life originated, I am afraid that, since Pasteur, this question is not within the sci-

---

14. *N. W. PIRIE: "SOME ASSUMPTIONS UNDERLYING DISCUSSION ON THE ORIGINS OF LIFE," IN ANNALS OF THE NEW YORK ACADEMY OF SCIENCE,66 (1957):369,376.*

entific domain."[15]

Along the same vein, Oparin, the Russian chemist, concedes: "Proof in the sense in which one thinks of it in chemistry and physics is not attainable in the problem of primordial biogenesis."[16]

Mathews stated in the most unlikely place, namely the introduction to *THE ORIGIN OF SPECIES*, by Charles Darwin: "In accepting evolution as fact, how many biologists pause to reflect that science is built upon theories that have been proved by experiment to be correct, or remember that the theory of animal evolution has never been thus proved."[17]

Prefacing his statements on the proposed mechanisms by which life was to have spontaneously evolved, Lipmann admits: "I am afraid what I have to say will be just as much natural philosophy as necessarily most discussions on the origin of life need be at present."[18]

These men are among the few evolutionary scientists who realize evolution is not a formulation of the true scientific method. They realize evolution means the initial formation of unknown organisms from unknown chemicals produced in an atmosphere or ocean of unknown composition under unknown conditions, which organisms have then climbed an unknown evolutionary ladder by an unknown process leaving unknown evidence.

The evolutionist's proposition is in reality only an extension, a deduction, from naturalistic philosophy as Lipmann said above. Evolutionary ideas began with ancient Greek philosophers like Epicurus, Anaximander, Thales, and Empedocles (2nd to 7th centuries B.C.) not scientists.

C. S. Lewis said it is a philosophy far predating Darwin's *ORIGIN OF SPECIES*.[19] Also, the University of Cambridge Professor, Pantin, wrote in the same vein: "Even the idea that men are descended from animals is common enough among savage races--a tribe may think they are descended from a boar or a beaver."[20]

15. *P. T. MORA: "URGE AND MOLECULAR BIOLOGY," IN NATURE,199 (1963):212.*

16. *A. I. OPARIN: LIFE: ITS NATURE, ORIGIN AND DEVELOPMENT (EDINBURGH: OLIVER AND BOYD, 1961), P. 33.*

17. *L. H. MATHEWS: "INTRODUCTION," IN THE ORIGIN OF SPECIES BY CHARLES DARWIN (LONDON:J.M.DENT AND SONS, 1971).*

18. *F. LIPMANN: "PROJECTING BACKWARD FROM THE PRESENT STAGE OF EVOLUTION OF BIOSYNTHESIS," IN THE ORIGINS OF PREBIOLOGICAL SYSTEMS AND THEIR MOLECULAR MATRICES, ED. S. W. FOX (N.Y.: ACADEMIC PRESS, 1965), P. 259.*

19. *C. S. LEWIS: CHRISTIAN REFLECTIONS (GRAND RAPIDS: EERDMANS, 1967), P. 83.*

20. *C. PANTIN: "THE ORIGIN OF SPECIES," IN A SHORT HISTORY OF SCIENCE (N.Y.: DOUBLEDAY, 1951), P. 94.*

The biologists, Davis and Solomon, wrote:
> "Less well known to us today are the evolutionary spec-
> ulations of ancient Greek philosophers which coexisted
> with their ideas of supernatural creationism."21

And finally, the evolutionist Simpson wrote:
> ". . . there is practically nothing in Darwin's theories
> that had not been expressed by others long before him."22

Thus, evolution is pre-scientism, it is philosophy. Naturalism explains that all things exist as a result of natural order
and chance. Therefore, assuming this philosophy correct, life a-
rose by natural processes and chance. Scientific knowledge may
then be used in an attempt to validate the philosophy, but that
philosophy cannot be validated by the scientific method, since, as
we have stated, the scientific method hinges upon observation and
no one observed the events at the time of the origin of life or
through the millenia evolution has supposedly spanned. Therefore,
could the evolutionary description of the formation of life be science? No! Philosophy? Yes!

∽ ∾

Is Evolution Scientifically Derived?

1. Scientific hypotheses are based upon observed phenomena.

2. Evolution explains the origin of life.

3. Life has not been observed spontaneously arising.

4. Therefore, evolution is not a scientifically derived hypothesis.

✖

Is Evolution Philosophy?

1. Naturalistic philosophy explains the existence of all things
   in terms of natural phenomena and chance occurrences.

2. Therefore, life must exist as a result of natural processes
   and chance occurrences--evolution.

∽ ∾

---

21. *P. DAVIS AND E. SOLOMON: THE WORLD OF BIOLOGY (N.Y.: MCGRAW-
HILL, 1974), P. 395.*
22. *G. G. SIMPSON: LIFE OF THE PAST (NEW HAVEN: YALE U., 1953),
P. 143; FURTHER DOCUMENTATION IN: W. LINDSEY: PRINCIPLES OF ORGAN-
IC EVOLUTION (ST. LOUIS: MOSBY, 1952),PP.18-25; W. GUTHRIE:A HIS-
TORY OF GREEK PHILOSOPHY(CAMBRIDGE:UNIVERSITY PRESS,1962),PP.142-144.*

Further proof that the evolutionary notion is an extension of naturalistic philosophy comes from carefully noting the manner in which scientists engaged in research on the origin of life attack the problem. Their research characteristically begins with the assumption that creation is false. This is not necessarily because the data militates against it, but because creation and evolution could not be true at the same time. It follows, since there are only two possible explanations for origins, and creation is false, naturalism must be true.

The reader might review the quotes made above where scientists admit creation as the alternative position to evolution, but dismiss it with simple strokes of the pen. Some further quotations will also bear out the a priori dismissal of creation. Keosian, in his book summarizing the current status of scientific inquiries into the origin of life, concludes:

> "There is general agreement on only one broad point--that organic compounds, abiotically synthesized, preceeded the origin of life. . . But there is no general agreement on the constitution of the primitive atmosphere nor on the mechanism of synthesis of organic compounds."[23]

In other words there is no agreement on how it happened (science), just agreement on the fact it did occur naturally (philosophy).

Mora accuses his scientific colleagues of redefining the scientific method such that one would proceed in this manner:
1. Avoid teleology
2. Verify by observation
3. Simplify[24]

Bernal, responding to his colleague, Mora, said:

> "The present laws of physics, I would agree with him, are insufficient to describe the origin of life. To him this opens the way to teleology, even, by implication, to creation by an intelligent agent. . . If he thinks he has shown conclusively that life cannot have originated by chance, only two rational alternatives remain. The first is that it did not arise at all, and that all we are studying is an illusion. . .The other alternative is that life is a reality but that we are not yet clever enough to unravel the nature of its origin. . ."[25]

Thus, rather than even concede creation as an alternative, Bernal argues that if life did not get here by naturalistic means, then life is an illusion! He also admits, by implication, that spontaneous generation has not been observed in the laboratory or elsewhere. But rather than confess any problem with his naturalistic position, he claims that any difficulty is only because

---

23. J.KEOSIAN:THE ORIGIN OF LIFE(N.Y.:REINHOLD, 1968),PP.13,54.
24. P. T. MORA,(REF.15) P.218.
25. THE ORIGINS OF PREBIOLOGICAL SYSTEMS AND THEIR MOLECULAR MATRICES, ED. S.W.FOX (N.Y.: ACADEMIC,1965),PP. 53-55.

"we are not clever enough yet." Addressing himself further to the objections made by Mora, Bernal says:

> "He said that the cardinal rule in science is that a statement must be provable--but that does not mean that it has to be proved now."[26]

Surely, if creation is false, then evolution remains as the only explanation for the origin of life, and must be true. Then, and only then, would it be right to pass over problems in the evolution of life and even express faith in future discoveries that will clear up annoying problems in current theory. But creation has not been proven false. The a priori dismissal of the creation position betrays the evolutionary position as biased naturalistic philosophy, not inductive science.

Some evolutionary advocates argue against the idea that evolutionary thinking predated Darwin and his contemporaries, and that it has foundation roots in philosophy rather than science. They argue that naturalistic thinking has proved the key to understanding nature, and that it has shown repeatedly the error in ascribing mysticism to things not understood. Naturalists reason that since many of life's mysteries have been resolved through an understanding of material phenomena, then likewise can the origin of life be so explained. In other words, since we now understand the details about processes such as reproduction, disease, growth, metabolism, physiology, anatomy, and many other things that were previously hidden under the cloak of "divine mystery," need we look beyond the material for answers about the origin of life? Since the driving force for many of life's phenomena has been shown to be in accord with natural law, and not in the hands of fire-breathing, lightning-throwing gods, should we not learn from history?

Thus, it is argued, evolutionary thinking was formulated inductively--a conclusion forced by the lessons of history, and by the observations of nature. The evolution idea has come after the facts, so they say. But this is not true, for there is no direct observational evidence of life arising spontaneously (with the exception of certain "incorrect observations" like flies arising from decaying matter, and mice from dirty rags heaped in a corner), or evolving, in the amoeba to man sense, through millions of years. Evolutionary thinking begins with a deduction from naturalistic philosophy, not empiricism, and in reality originated historically long before Darwin boarded the ship *Beagle*. More simply stated, the naturalist reasons: since life is here, it must have arisen through natural means--evolution.

Creation Is an Antithesis

The only logical alternative to naturalistic origins

---

26. *IBID.*

(evolution) is supernaturalistic origins (creation). So we could say that creationism, like evolutionism, is a philosophy. The creationist could deduce, as do evolutionists, that since life is here, life was created. But where would this leave us? The creationist would simply be claiming the correctness of his position because of simple bias, and the evolutionist would simply be claiming the correctness of his position because of bias. Neither position holds water to those yearning for rational truth. Since both positions are not subject to the experimental scientific method, how do we resolve the controversy?

We begin by admitting both positions to be models, guesses, or propositions equally viable. I will omit the use of the terms hypothesis or theory with regard to either, for this nomenclature would argue that the scientific method was used in their formulation. Let's agree that both are simply propositions or models at this point.

The Method

Beginning with these two possible propositions, by what means then can we decide upon the cause of the origin of life? Thus far we have simply established that the true scientific method cannot be used in resolving the controversy. This does not mean we cannot prove one position or the other true logically, by weighing evidences, as is done in a court of law. Lawyers present facts, data and evidence to dislodge or support cases; the jury, through a consideration of the facts and guided by proper methodology from the judge, makes a judgement. Similarly, we can examine the facts related to the evolution-creation controversy and make a judgement. (Fig. 8) The method simply involves determining which position is consistent with the evidence, the facts, the real world around us.

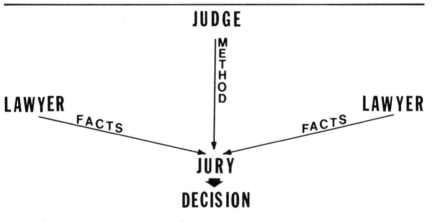

Fig. 8 - The Jury Method

It will be proper in our investigation to cite fallacies in one position or the other and offer these as corroborative proof for the validity of the opposite position. In other words, apart from direct supporting evidence, errors in the positions will be noted. Since there are only two possible positions, disproving one substantiates the other. If we prove creation wrong, i.e., inconsistent with the facts, we prove evolution true, and vice versa.

IF EXPLANATIONS **A** AND **B** ARE THE ONLY TWO POSSIBLE EXPLANATIONS FOR A PARTICULAR EVENT:

THE DISPROOF OF **A** PROVES **B**
or
THE DISPROOF OF **B** PROVES **A**

The medieval times are noted for impeding knowledge and truth. In those days new ideas were only accepted if they fit vogue orthodoxy. Some would even debate how many teeth a horse should have according to philosophical dogma without looking in the horse's mouth to see for themselves. Progress was stultified. The lesson to be learned from that portion of history is that open-mindedness is crucial to advancement, and the search for or the assertion of absolute knowledge with no test in reality is folly. Therefore, we will examine all of the pertinent real data and not just that fitting our preconceived ideas of truth. Lovers of truth will not fear giving an equal ear to all of the facts, for we know if our position is correct it will withstand rigorous investigation and cross examination.

It would not be fair to distort and twist facts that are inconsistent with the proposition we wish to be true. Likewise it would be improper to jockey our proposition as the contrary facts roll in. Our propositions must be defined specifically enough so that not every imaginable evidence, hypothetical or real, could be used as proof. In other words, each of the propositions must be falsifiable. There must be, at least in the imagination, evidences that could disprove one or the other. If a proposition cannot be falsified, if we cannot even conceive of possible facts that could prove it wrong, then the chances are our proposition is not really saying anything or is so ambiguous as to be virtually meaningless.

We must get clearly in mind what each of the propositions is and is not saying. Then concede that creation is possibly true, possibly false; or evolution is possibly true, possibly false. Since proponents of each side say their position is most consistent with the real world, the evidence, then it is to the evidence, unadulterated, that we will look to render a decision. (Fig. 9)

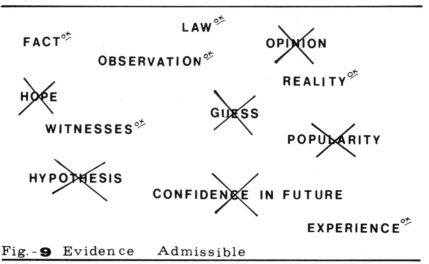

Fig.-9 Evidence Admissible

The Gnoof–Xert Controversy

We might draw a parallel between the method we are to use in determining the means by which life arose, to the method one would use in determining the kind of animal that has left tracks in the mud. First, we must agree that the tracks are there, they are real. Second, we must have faith in reality, facts, scientific truth, and logic. Third, and you'll have to bear with this hypothetical situation, we know the track was made by either a gnoof or a xert. We know this because all other animals are restrained from this particular area by impassable barriers of laser beams and antimatter. (Dr. Seuss has had his influence.) No one saw which animal made the track, so one can either speculate as to origin or examine the evidences. If the evidence is consistent with all we know of gnoof prints, then we would conclude a gnoof made the track. If the evidence supports the argument that the track was made by a xert, then we will believe that. The lack of evidence expected, or refuting evidence, for one side of the controversy would in effect be supporting evidence for the other side, since there are only two possibilities. Fair enough?

To debate this issue Professor Xerxes will take the xertist position, and Professor Goof, the gnoofist side. Both have asserted they have overwhelming evidence to support their contentions. They are both knowledgeable, zealous, sincere, and have agreed to the conditions stated above.

Dr. Xerxes opens: "This track has fifteen toes and it is axiomatically true that only xerts have fifteen toes. Gnoofs always have eleven."

Professor Goof replies haughtily: "That may be true for the cases we have examined and the tracks we have experimentally reproduced so far, but who is to say what modern science has in store for the future. Why..."

"I'm sorry Dr. Goof, speculation and accolades for science are not admissable for evidence. You have already agreed to the conditions. Only the facts Dr. Goof, please!" commands the moderator.

"Well, perhaps this particular gnoof overlapped his feet when he ran such that four extra toes were impressed in the track giving the appearance of fifteen toes," replies Dr. Goof defensively.

"Yes, that may be true, Dr. Goof, but all tracks show front and back feet having fifteen toes as they lead to and from this track," counters Dr. Xerxes.

Moderator: "The fact that this print has fifteen toes fits well with the xertist position, but apparently can't be reconciled with gnoofism."

The moderator then proceeds to list this fact under xertism as supporting evidence.

Dr. Xerxes: "It is also universally true that when a gnoof runs, his tail always drags behind. There is no impression of such in this bed of tracks."

"I know that is a scientific law," replies Dr. Goof, "But there are always exceptions, and besides scientists have been wrong in the past. Also..."

"Hold it," the moderator breaks in.

"May I reply to that?" asks Dr. Xerxes.

"Fine, but I'm warning you again about speculation, Dr. Goof!"

Dr. Xerxes continues: "The law of gnoof tail dragging knows no exceptions. Although it is true that scientists have been wrong in the past, reality and concrete established laws remain fixed and indeed applicable to our debate Dr. Goof. You are confusing scientific speculations with concrete established laws. Besides, if you could use 'possible exceptions' to laws, exceptions for which you have no evidence, or faith in future discoveries as evidence, nothing could be proven by our debate. After all I could as well argue from possible exceptions and future discoveries that the tracks were made from miniature atomic bombs dropped from UFO's containing little obnoxious moldy creatures made of cheese that have whizzed here from a dimension of time and space that we know nothing about yet!"

"Okay, I see your point," concedes Dr. Goof. "But nearly everyone I have talked to about these tracks, and that includes trackologists and other authorities, agree with me that these are gnoof prints."

XERTISM FACTS:

GNOOFISM FACTS:

1. 15 TOES
2. NO TAIL IMPRESSION
3. MUD-SAND INTERCALATIONS
4. NAIL IMPRINTS
5. STRIDE LENGTH
6. RUNNING PLANTAR ROTATION
7. ARCH LENGTH
8. NO KNEE IMPRINTS
9. RESIDUAL DERMAL BIOASSAYS
10. LAW OF FRICTION THERMOPHYSICS
11. FOOT-SLIP PRINCIPLES
12. GOOK-YIK ANALYSES

Fig. **10** - The Gnoof-Xert Controversy

"This isn't a popularity contest, Dr. Goof. Where is the substantiating data?" queries the moderator.

"Well, according to mud-ooze calibrations, the depth of these prints could only be produced by an animal within the thirty to fifty pound range. We know this is consistent with gnoof size, but certainly not with any xert."

"Again you are proposing speculation to support your position," Dr. Xerxes replies confidently. "The assumptions used in mud-ooze calibrations and computations are only valid up to five pounds. Any determination beyond that is strictly based upon assumptions that are unproven and, therefore, cannot be used here."

So on and on it goes. Dr. Xerxes thrusts established facts into the discussion, and Dr. Goof, only high sounding speculation. During the course of the debate the moderator lists the data under the hypothesis with which it is consistent. At the end of the discussion all data proves to be consistent with the proposition that the xert made the prints. (Fig. 10) The conclusion is that the prints must be those of a xert. No one saw the xert make the prints, yet the truth of the matter was determined. Dr. Goof, being a lover of truth, concedes.

This, by analogy, is essentially the method that can be used in determining what is responsible for the physical and biological world (tracks) around us. True, no one was there to observe and record the original formation of life, yet the truth can be ascertained by examining established facts to see which of the two propositions they support. Honesty will force us to accept that which is consistent with reality and reject that which is not. (Fig. 11)

CREATION FACTS:

EVOLUTION FACTS:

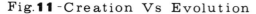

Fig.**11**-Creation Vs Evolution

The method for resolving the creation-evolution controversy will be the same as that used in the gnoof-xert controversy. Thus we can use a similar chart. Positive evidence will be listed under the appropriate proposition. Since there are only two positions, deficiencies in either can be listed under the opposite position as supporting evidence like we did in the gnoof-xert chart. Our listing, therefore, will contain both positive and negative pleas.

It is said: There are two kinds of people, those who agree with you, and the bigots; a logical person is anyone who can prove that you are right; there is no one so narrow as the fellow who disagrees with you; there is no sound more pleasing to the ears than that of someone admitting you are correct.

All of us are egocentric to one degree or another and have our minds filled with preconceived notions and prejudices which we tend to jealously defend and protect. I the writer plead guilty to this, and you the reader must also. Recognizing this frailty of human nature, but not letting it preclude the possibility that any of us can open our minds, let's proceed with our discussion of the controversy of origins in the belief that truth will prevail if we honestly seek it and stick to the pursuit long enough. Let's first clearly define the two positions, then proceed into the evidence.

4 ꟼDEFINITIONS

If we were to ask the average man on the street what evolution was, he would probably say: "Evolution means man came from an ape." If we asked him what is meant by creation, he would probably say: "Well, creation means everything was created in six days." Even highly educated teachers, and often origin of life researchers, can be heard parroting similar statements.

Both of these responses have inklings of accuracy. But any misunderstanding of definitions can efficiently serve to confuse, muddle and cloud one's view of the controversy. Misunderstandings have resulted in misrepresentations. Misrepresentations, in turn, produce bitter and heated exchanges.

Many have made up their minds on the controversy without having ever really understood what either model says. Thus, biases are established and become deep-seated. Minds close without there ever being an understanding of the most essential and elementary prerequisite to resolving any issue--definitions. How could justice be done to either side if definitions were inaccurate?

In this chapter we will try to define each position as precisely as possible. The definitions we establish will provide the baselines against which we can measure the evidence. Otherwise, if we don't know what we're trying to prove, how will we know when we're correct?

Evolution

Evolution, here, is taken in its most general form and its most materialistic sense. It is the philosophy having its roots in the pre-Christian naturalistic notions of the Grecian philosophers. An example is Anaximander who argued we had our beginnings as a fish which later moved to land and slowly transformed into increasingly complex animals eventually culminating in man.

Darwin, Spencer, and others since, have simply modified the

details, proposed mechanisms, and popularized evolution. The evolutionary proposition holds that the universe as well as the living fauna and flora upon the earth have arisen spontaneously.
There is much debate as to the exact mechanism by which the universe, matter, and life arose, but the materialist subscribes to
the basic tenant that unintelligent processes (as opposed to intelligent, i.e., a creator) are the fundamental causes. Life is
suggested to have originally sprung from nonliving matter through
a series of increasingly complex chemical gradations. Then the
simple life forms, through natural processes, changed to more and
more complex forms pinnacling in man. The hypothesis also teach-
es that man, as well as other living forms, are slowly, inevitably, continuing to evolve.

It is of extreme importance to emphasize that evolution is
not just a description of the variation in life forms we see about
us, but rather, and most importantly, a description of transmutation. Just as the Middle Age's transmutation was understood to
mean the conversion of base metals into gold and silver by alche-
my, evolutionary transmutation is understood to mean (in overview)
the change of distinct kinds of living organisms, through immense
time and accumulation of small variations, into other kinds.

Kerkut, of the University of Southhampton, calls the amoeba
to man thesis the general theory of evolution, and he calls simple
biological variation, or microevolution, the special theory of evolution.[1] It is this "general theory" that we will concern ourselves with, for it is the one at odds with the creation model.
(Fig. 12)

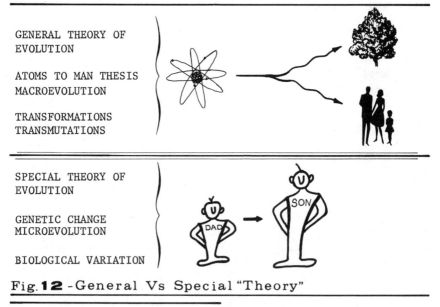

GENERAL THEORY OF
EVOLUTION

ATOMS TO MAN THESIS
MACROEVOLUTION

TRANSFORMATIONS
TRANSMUTATIONS

SPECIAL THEORY OF
EVOLUTION

GENETIC CHANGE
MICROEVOLUTION

BIOLOGICAL VARIATION

Fig. 12 -General Vs Special "Theory"

1. G. KERKUT: IMPLICATIONS OF EVOLUTION (N.Y.: PERGAMON, 1960).

Evolution ultimately hinges upon the concept of gross change --macroevolution, megaevolution--not microchanges and simple genetic variations. Even though most evolutionists contend that macrochanges occurred by slow variations, not by leaps (fish into frog), the sum total of microchanges, these small variations, are believed to have resulted in the change of one kind of organism into another, i.e., gross changes.

Some, of course, will be at odds with any definition of evolution we might suggest. However, all should be able to agree that, in essence, evolution suggests that all life forms owe their existence to natural processes and chance, not to supernatural synthesis. This is the proposition the evidence will be weighed against in subsequent chapters.

Creation

The alternative to evolution is creation. The two positions make exactly opposite arguments: "mindless" natural origins versus intelligent supernatural origins; unlimited variation and transmutation versus fixity and reversion to type.

EVOLUTION CREED:

IN THE BEGINNING, THERE WAS BIOPOIESIS; AND THE KINDS OF LIFE THUS FORMED WILL TRANSFORM INTO NEW AND DIFFERENT KINDS

CREATION CREED:

IN THE BEGINNING, THERE WAS CREATION; AND THE KINDS OF LIFE THUS FORMED WILL REPRODUCE ONLY ACCORDING TO THEIR KINDS

Fixity Vs Evolution

The polarity between the two positions on the origin of life is usually unambiguous. One argues a slow spontaneous naturalistic transformation of atoms into life, the other a sudden synthesis. However, there is much confusion about what the two models say regarding the degree of change possible once life is present.

Evolutionists, of course, contend unlimited variation is possible. It follows from this that evolutionary classification could be based upon somewhat arbitrary grounds since it is reasoned all life is "blood" related. For example, protozoa are classified on the basis of motility; sponges on the basis of external structure; worms on the basis of segmentation or whether they are parasitic or free-living; and subspecies have been formed on the basis of geographical distribution. (Some modern taxonomists say "species" is the only legitimate classification and it

58

should be based upon natural reproducibility.)

The evolutionary view of classification (Kingdom, Phylum, Class, Order, Genus, Species) is not toward showing definite immutable demarcations, but rather biased toward demonstrating phylogeny (evolutionary life histories) and simply providing a nomenclature for the convenience of biological study and research. Thus the criteria used for determining "species" are not especially critical to the evolutionist. Actually, the more confusion in classification--the less organisms are distinctly demarcated--the more it will appear as though organisms blend one into the other, i.e., the more evolution will appear true.

Now there is a very definite philosophical difference between this view and that of the creationist. The creationist's case hangs on classification and nomenclature. The creationist believes basic kinds were created in the not too distant past. These kinds were not blood related to other kinds but were interfertile with members of the same kind. Thus the creationist would argue, in opposition to evolution, (1) all life is not "blood" related and, (2) there are natural immutable reproductive demarkations in the biological world.

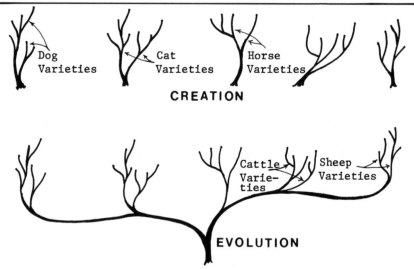

Fig. 13 - A Tree or a Forest

According to the evolutionary proposition, all life is related. All living things should be traceable to a common origin (monophyletic origin). On the other hand, the creation model allows for family trees but would stipulate that the geneological trunks would terminate in the original created organisms (polyphyletic origins), and not merge with other trunks. So the question is not whether there can be branching, but whether the trunks join.

The informed creationist would not argue that kinds have remained static since creation but rather would maintain they have produced variants which, although perhaps not exact duplicates of the original kind, are still interfertile. The evolutionist would insist all life belongs to one big family tree, (monophyletic origins) whereas the creationist pleads a forest (polyphyletic origins). (Fig. 13)

It is important to understand that the "species" classification was not built entirely upon the criteria used to delineate creation kinds, i.e., interfertility. (It must be noted, however, the father of modern taxonomy, Linnaeus, was a creationist. However, he had the wrong impression creation kinds could be separated on morphology alone. He, in large part, is directly responsible for the confusion between "kind" and "species.") Thus, it would not be fair to use the modern "species" classification to disprove the fixity of creation kinds. For example, there are many interfertile organisms classified as different species. The zebra x horse are interfertile but different species, as are also the lion x tiger, the cow x yak, rye x wheat, radish x cabbage, etc., for dozens of other examples. Thus the fact different "species" interbreed does not disprove the creationist's contention that different "kinds" don't interbreed. Many species have been classified on purely morphological criteria (looks). For example, the Galapagos finches studied by Darwin were classified on the basis of beak size and shape; the dog, wolf, fox and jackal were likewise separated as species on the basis of morphology.

Probably the most exacting and comprehensive treatment of "kind" I have come across is found in the book: *EVOLUTION, CREATION AND SCIENCE* (1947), by the biologist F. L. Marsh. To avoid confusion with "species", he calls the creation "kind", "baramin." He defines baramin (kind) in this way. Members of a baramin would be interfertile in the sense that at least a zygote is formed by the union of their sex cells, whether or not fertile or viable offspring are produced. Thus, the rat x mouse, goat x sheep, cow x bison, horse x ass, etc. crosses, although not always producing fertile offspring or even live offspring, are of the same baramin because there occurs true fertilization of the sex cells. The fertility problems in the mule (which is usually, but not always, sterile), Marsh explains, for example, are due to derangements in reproductive physiology brought about by mutations and perhaps other factors operating through time on the original horse-mule kind genetic apparatus.

In some cases, organisms once interfertile have become reproductively isolated (races develop which only rarely if ever interbreed) although they remain morphologically identical (they look alike) to the parent population. Some examples are the pekingese and Saint Bernard which look alike in every detail except for proportions and size, but don't breed because of obvious mechanical difficulties; one interfertile race of fruit flies develops two varieties which are no longer interfertile

(Drosophila pseudoobscura x *Drosophila persimilis* and *D. equinoxialis* x *D. willistoni)*; some varieties of gulls, mice and squirrels are reported to have lost interfertility after being separated geographically. In these cases Marsh expands his definition somewhat to include morphology. He contends, if two organisms breed, even though it is infrequent, they are of the same kind; if they don't breed but are clearly of the same morphological type, they are of the same kind by the logic of the axiom which states two things equal to the same thing are equal to each other.

I can see some difficulties with the precise details of this definition but it can nevertheless serve us well here as a working hypothesis. The creationist is essentially saying basic kinds of life (demarcated by interfertility or clear morphologic sameness) cannot become new and different kinds, or transmutate as evolutionists say. Dogs stay dogs, cats stay cats, peas remain peas, mosquitoes remain mosquitoes (drat!), even though these kinds can vary a tremendous amount within the circumscription of the kind, e.g., note the vast differences between the chihuahua and Great Dane of the interfertile dog kind. The "fixity" creation speaks to, and the "transformations" evolution speaks to, are best understood when compared and contrasted with each other. If there is no confusion as to what the term "species" means, the two positions can usually be quite easily contrasted, at least enough to enable us to see which is more consistent with the facts.

In summary, the creationist avers:
1. All organisms which are or were interfertile are genetically (or geneologically) unrelated to any other interfertile groups.
2. All organisms belonging to an interfertile group ("kind") can be traced back in time to the same original created ancestor.
3. All of nature is chopped up by discontinuities, genetically and morphologically.

On the other hand, the evolutionist contends:
1. All organisms are related and dovetail genetically to the first spontaneously generated cell.
2. All of nature is continuous genetically and morphologically. (Fig. 14)

Significance of Change

Even though it is thought to be, the creation proposition is not at odds with the commonly observed fact of genetic variation. Recall the trees in the creationist's forest have many branches representing varieties of the kind. (See Fig. 13) Nor is the creationist at odds with natural selection, survival of the fittest (same thing as natural selection), or mutations.

creation-fixity

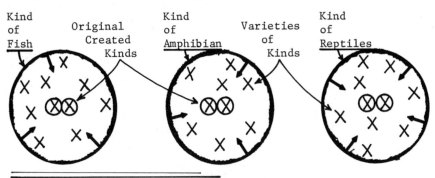

Kind of Fish

Original Created Kinds

Kind of Amphibian

Varieties of Kinds

Kind of Reptiles

evolution - transformation

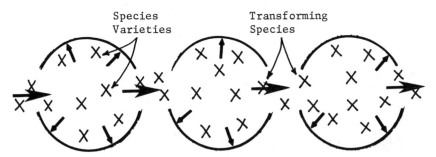

Species Varieties

Transforming Species

Fig.**14** - Fixity Vs Transformation
*The creation proposition describes the formation of basic units
(kinds) of life. Although these can vary, adapt, mutate and
change, they will only do so within prescribed bounds(circles),
the set limits of their kinds. Evolution describes life as having
inherent ability, through the aid of time, mutations and selection,
to transmutate from one form into another. Thus, according to evolution, life forms are not enclosed by genetic barriers restrict-
ing the amount of change possible.*

(Fig. 15) Creationism does not deny the possibility that these
processes could be operative on "kinds," perhaps even allowing
them to vary and adapt to different environments. But as the
creation model is generalized in its cataloging of various
plants and animals, it is specific in demanding that kinds would
remain true to their reproductive and morphologic kind--no
transmutations.

These points are crucial to an understanding of the evolution-creation controversy. Many cite the simple change, birth,
growth, death and variation we see about us as negating creation

62

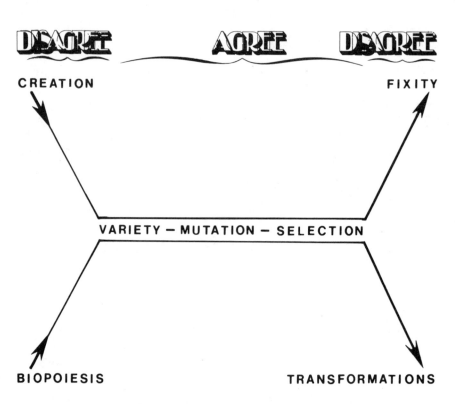

Fig. **15** - Agreement and Disagreement
Both creation and evolution agree that change, variety, mutation, selection and geographical distribution occur. They disagree on the means by which life arose, and also on the degree to which living forms can change.

and substantiating evolution.   Actually, these observations do not speak directly for or against either proposition.

Some simply reason:
1. Evolution is change, variety and growth.
2. Change, variety and growth are observed.
3. Therefore, evolution is observed.

Dunn and Dobzhansky have reasoned this way in their writings. They argue that the change and variety we see about us is simply "nature." Then they equate "nature" with evolution and state: "Even now occasional misguided persons try to fight the view that man is a part of nature."[2]

In their minds, a person who would doubt evolution would

2. *DUNN AND DOBZHANSKY: HEREDITY, RACE AND SOCIETY (N.Y.: NEW AMERICAN LIBRARY, 1952), P. 63.*

doubt nature! However, I repeat, the creationist does not deny
that man is a part of nature and that it is the nature of things
to change and vary. The creationist is simply putting a ceiling
on the amount of change possible; the evolutionist says the sky
is the limit. To prove evolution, therefore, the evolutionist
must show that organisms can vary beyond the confines of the
basic kinds, i.e., produce continuously, reproductively isolated
and morphologically unique forms--the amoeba to man idea. The
creationist must show fixity.

Theistic Evolution

Many hold to evolution while at the same time espousing belief in a creator. The result is a sort of hybrid, a baptized
evolution called theistic evolution.

Basically, theistic evolution contends that abiogenesis
(the spontaneous formation of life from chemicals) and evolution
(amoeba to man through eons) have occurred, but a creator was
instrumental in forming the initial matter and laws, and more or
less guided the whole process. The creator is used here as a
vindicator of evolutionary difficulties. With time, as evolutionists explained more and more by naturalism, the creator was
crowded further and further back in time and given less and less
responsibility. For many, theistic evolution is only believed
transitorily. The position is often only a filler, an easily
passed bridge from theism to atheism.

Theistic evolution has been advocated in the past by both materialists and theologians. Today it is vogue. It is downright
hard to find anyone who does not believe in evolution in one
form or another, and it is also difficult to find anyone who
does not believe in a creator in one form or another. This hybrid belief has given reprieve to those not wishing to make a
total commitment to either side. But is this position correct?
If so, how could it be proven true? On the other hand, if
false, how could it be falsified?

Some dismiss theistic evolution believing the position is a
self-contradiction: Since evolution is naturalism and theism is
supernaturalism, the two taken together as "theistic evolution"
would mean "supernatural naturalism." Others reject theistic
evolution because they believe evolution is entirely self-
explanatory, self-propagating through totally natural mechanisms.

But the acid test for theistic evolution is as follows:
Since theistic evolution rests upon the premise that evolution
is true, the proof or disproof of this premise provides the
means for checking the validity of theistic evolution. On the
one hand, if evolution is true, then theistic evolution might be
true--not necessarily, but might. If evolution is shown to be
true, the chore would still remain to establish whether natural
processes alone could cause evolution, or whether some sort of

divine guidance is essential. On the other hand, if evolution is false (if there is no evidence that it has occurred and if evidence militates against it), theistic evolution could not be true. To associate a creator with a falsity could throw him into suspicion.

So, although we are dichotomizing and challenging creation with strict atheistic evolutionism, the outcome (whether evolution is true or not) will also resolve the question regarding theistic evolution. If evolution (theistic or naturalistic) is true, then the data must demonstrate it; if creation is true, the data must support it. Which is true? Let's specifically define the two proposed mechanisms for the origin of life then proceed through the evidence.

Focusing on Origins

Evidence relevant to the controversy can basically be divided into two categories. The first category contains data pertinent to the original formation of life. The second category (amoeba to man) contains information pertinent to whether life will transmutate, as opposed to remaining fixed and reproducing only according to kinds.

In the not too distant past, if one wanted to attempt resolution of the controversy, he would have had to confine his investigation to the biological level, the amoeba to man category. Research would be limited to fossils, species variability, geographical distribution, genetics, hybridization, etc. Little was known about life at the chemical level. So informed discussion of the origin of life was not possible. This is not the case today. Details of biochemistry and molecular biology have virtually come in a flood, opening a vast, important fertile field of evidence relevant to the controversy.

Actually the step from chemicals to life is most significant. Investigation at this level surfaces essentially every piece of relevant evidence and allows us to peer into the innards of life and talk intelligently about mechanisms. Simpson, an evolutionist, concurs:

> "Above the molecular level, the simplest fully living unit is almost incredibly complex. It has become commonplace to speak of evolution from amoeba to man, as if the amoeba were the simple beginning of the process. On the contrary, if, as must almost necessarily be true, life arose as a simple molecular system, the progression from this state to that of the amoeba is at least as great as from amoeba to man. All the essential problems of a living organism are already solved in the one-celled protozoan, and these are only elaborated in

man or the other multicellular animals."3

The complexity of a cell is so great that Simpson feels if we can prove the chance formation of the cell and its molecular precursors, the problems related to subsequent evolution up the ladder, so to speak, are likewise solved. This would also mean if the chance formation of life is untenable, then probably so would be the evolution leading to man.

Since the origin of life takes on such importance, I will give it priority. We will focus on the origin of life giving special attention to chemical details, mechanisms and related principles and laws. This is not to say we will not venture into other interesting areas such as geology, dating methods, fossils, mutations, genetics, etc. Rather, these topics will be treated as they splinter from our more concerted investigation of mechanisms and origins. For example, when we consider the formation of DNA the discussion will veer from the question about the original formation of DNA to questions about whether DNA could or did evolve, or whether it has remained fixed. We then discuss data that speaks to this: fossils, genetics, mutations, natural selection, etc. When we discuss the effect of time on origins, we will also then diverge to the question of whether we do or do not have vast time to work with. This will require an examination of dating methods and geological timetable. Thus, we will not treat each discipline of evidence separately, but rather relate them to the theme of origins and to, in turn, our greater theme of resolving the evolution-creation controversy. In the end, however, we will have touched upon practically every discipline relevant to the controversy.

The Two Mechanisms

The problem of the formation of life is a chemical one. The creationist describes a creator as the cause and, therefore, the chemist. The evolutionist attributes the cause of life to innate chemical abilities, time and chance. The evolutionist must show tenable (historically valid) chemical processes and mechanisms that could spontaneously produce life from elemental matter; the creationist must show the insufficiency of naturalism and the sufficiency of creation to explain origins. By examining the evidence in this regard, we can determine whether Simpson's assertion is truth or fiction:

> "There is no reason to postulate a miracle (creator), nor is it necessary to suppose the origin of the processes of reproduction and mutation (life) was anything but naturalistic."4 (parenthetical words added)

---

3. *G. G. SIMPSON: THE MEANING OF EVOLUTION (NEW HAVEN: YALE UNIVERSITY, 1967), P. 17.*

4. *IBID, P. 16.*

The evolutionary proposition states that the first cell slowly formed over millions of years from an organic brew in the primitive oceans. Inorganic elements (atoms) of Carbon (C), Hydrogen (H), Oxygen (O), Nitrogen (N), Sulfur (S), Phosphorus (P) and others, are said to have combined under suitable conditions to form simple organic molecules (carbon-containing materials characteristically found in life). These chemical building blocks (biomonomers) in turn are said to have combined to form more and more complex chains of chemicals (macromolecules), some of which were to have had the capacity for self-reproduction.

The primordial soup thickened as more and more molecules were generated. It is postulated that the large macromolecules then became housed within globular-like spheres known as microspheres and coacervates (prebiological systems). This would result in providing stable environmental conditions for the fragile chemical precursors of life, comparable to the way in which the membrane surrounding a cell protects the delicate life-chemicals within. Then simple forms such as viral particles were to have developed. In turn, these are considered to have experienced progressive transformations culminating in the cell, the first living entity.

There is much debate as to the exact sequence and mechanism by which the first evolutionary steps were taken. But in general it is held that the progression was from simple to complex, and that random assortment was solely responsible for evolution.(Fig.16

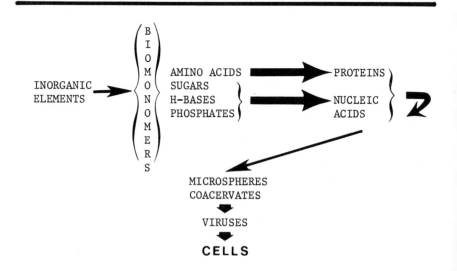

Fig.**16** - Chemical Evolution
The evolutionist explains the origin of life by proposing a series of increasingly complex chemical gradations. The driving forces behind the progression are believed to be chance, time and innate chemical properties.

On the other hand, the creationist describes a supernatural designer creating the various life forms, suddenly and decisively, through the use of intelligence and energy. (Fig. 17)

Fig. **17**- Creation of Life

The creationist accounts for life by implicating a creator. The creator is understood to have intelligently applied energy to create inorganic elements which were in turn miraculously fashioned into the basic kinds of life. Complex biochemicals would postdate life in this scheme, not predate it as with biopoiesis.

Which of the two schematics will withstand the rigors of close scrutiny?

Final Admonitions

Before proceeding into the evidence, it is of utmost importance that we, the jurors, see the importance of and be in agreement on methodology and definitions. No end statement can mean anything without the method. We must agree the methodological framework of Chapter 2 allows equal opportunity for each proposition to be correct in their end statements--provided each faction agrees their position must coincide with evidence from the real world.

The precise details of the definitions I have given can be disputed. However, the two factions must be saying something different otherwise there would be no controversy. It is the differences I have tried to emphasize. Hopefully we will at least be able to see the general contrasts.

There is no intent here to establish straw men. Certainly a real danger exists in purposely setting up a methodology and definitions which (1) fit our own set of data; and (2) are discordant with our opponent's data. Preliminaries can be appropriately fabricated to bias toward any outcome. On the other hand, one can easily claim definitions and methodology are biased after he finds himself in the losing position.

Therefore, it is essential the creationist and evolutionist see eye to eye now, before the evidence is examined. In other words, let's make sure the dice are not loaded before we begin to lose our shirt, not assume they are loaded just because we are losing. Without prerequisite agreement on methodology and definitions, debating the data would be superfluous.

Do we agree on these preliminaries? Yes? Then we're prepared to examine the evidence and adjudicate on the controversy.

5 { ORIGIN OF PROTEINS

A fundamental component of living tissue is protein. About
15% of living tissue and approximately ½ of the dry matter of
the body are composed of it. Proteins are long chains of smaller molecules called amino acids. There are about twenty different common amino acids, and the specific arrangement of these
in sequences dictates the function of the respective proteins.

Proteins are very diversified. Some of the body's proteins
are: the collagen of bone, cartilage and other connective tissues, which provide strength and support; the keratin in the
skin which has a protective function; the actin and myosin of
muscle which provide contractile ability and movement; the various hormones such as insulin and adrenalin which serve to control metabolism and various other vital functions; and the antibodies which protect against infection. The importance of tissue and cellular proteins is such that life in the absence of
protein is impossible.

What is the origin of proteins? What is the origin of
their building blocks (biomonomers), the amino acids? Could the
amino acids and proteins characteristic of life arise through
natural mechanisms, or would their formation depend upon supernatural synthesis? Let's answer this by first looking at the
amino acids.

Enantiomers

All of the twenty amino acids except one, glycine, can
exist in two different forms.[1] Thus the amino acid alanine can

---

1. *A FEW EXCEPTIONS TO THIS SHOULD BE NOTED. THE AMINO ACIDS*

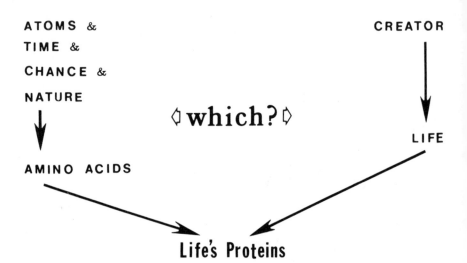

exist as L-alanine, or D-alanine; the amino acid threonine, as
L-threonine, or D-threonine; the amino acid phenylalanine, as
L-phenylalanine, or D-phenylalanine; and so forth. (Fig. 18)
All of these different forms of amino acids are known as enan-
tiomers (enantiomorphs, stereoisomers).

The two enantiomers of alanine are alike in that they contain the same atoms, but not alike in that the arrangement of
the constituent atoms three-dimensionally is different. They
are spoken of as mirror images of each other, or as being right-
and left-handed forms of the same molecule. They differ in that
they are not superimposable. (Fig. 19)

The significance of this is that although enantiomers can
link up in proteins as L to L, D to D, or D to L, all proteins
derived from living organisms, with insignificant exceptions,
are composed of only the L forms of the various twenty amino
acids.[2] In other words, if we examined a strand of protein
from muscle, the sequence of amino acids would perhaps be something like this:
(L-valine)-(L-alanine)-(L-threonine)-(L-alanine)-(L-valine)-
etc.; but never:

THREONINE, HYDROXYLYSINE, CYSTINE, ISOLEUCINE AND TWO HYDROXY-
PROLINES CAN EXIST IN FOUR DIFFERENT FORMS KNOWN AS DIASTEREO-
ISOMERS. FOR EXAMPLE, THE FOUR FORMS OF THREONINE WOULD BE L-
THREONINE, D-THREONINE, L-ALLO THREONINE AND D-ALLO THREONINE.
2. A. WHITE, P. HANDLER AND E. L. SMITH: PRINCIPLES OF BIO-
CHEMISTRY (N.Y.: MCGRAW-HILL, 1964), PP. 11, 99, 100.

1. Glycine	————
2. D-Alanine	L-Alanine
3. D-Valine	L-Valine
4. D-Leucine	L-Leucine
5. D-Isoleucine	L-Isoleucine
6. D-Serine	L-Serine
7. D-Threonine	L-Threonine
8. D-Cysteine	L-Cysteine
9. D-Cystine	L-Cystine
10. D-Methionine	L-Methionine
11. D-Glutamic Acid	L-Glutamic Acid
12. D-Aspartic Acid	L-Aspartic Acid
13. D-Lysine	L-Lysine
14. D-Arginine	L-Arginine
15. D-Histidine	L-Histidine
16. D-Phenylalanine	L-Phenylalanine
17. D-Tyrosine	L-Tyrosine
18. D-Tryptophan	L-Tryptophan
19. D-Proline	L-Proline
20. D-Hydroxyproline	L-Hydroxyproline

Fig.18-Amino Acids
There are approximately 20 different amino acids. Each amino acid, except glycine, can exist in both D and L stereoisomer forms.

(D-valine)-(L-alanine)-(D-threonine)-(D-alanine)-(L-valine)-etc.

When amino acids are synthesized in the laboratory for commercial use, or when they are formed under conditions supposedly duplicating early earth conditions, there is always a 50% mixture of D and L- amino acids formed (racemic D-L mixtures).[3]

Wald has conceded this point and stated that outside of life all syntheses yield racemic mixtures.[4] The researchers, Amie and Henri Amariglio, agree and assert: "Racemization is a thermodynamically favored transformation."[5]

Only through the use of intelligently controlled sophisticated measures, can D-forms be separated from L-forms to form

---

3. *IBID, PP. 11, 100.*
4. *G. WALD: "THE ORIGIN OF OPTICAL ACTIVITY," IN ANNALS OF THE NEW YORK ACADEMY OF SCIENCE, 66(1957):352.*
5. *AMIE AND HENRI AMARIGLIO: "UNSUCCESSFUL ATTEMPTS OF A-SYMMETRIC SYNTHESIS UNDER THE INFLUENCE OF OPTICALLY ACTIVE QUARTZ. SOME COMMENTS ABOUT THE POSSIBLE ORIGIN OF THE DIS-SYMMETRY OF LIFE," IN CHEMICAL EVOLUTION AND THE ORIGIN OF LIFE, EDS. R. BUVER AND C. PONNAMPERUMA (N.Y.: AMERICAN ELSELVIER, 1971), P. 63.*

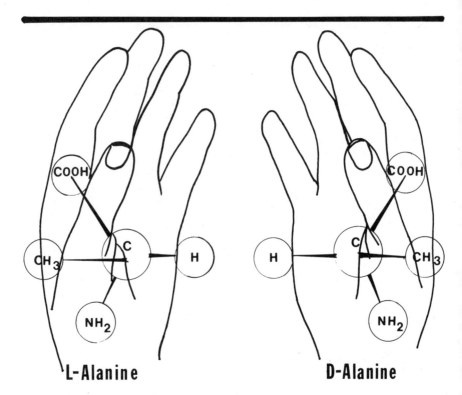

Fig.**19** - Enantiomers

Most amino acids can exist as D and L enantiomers. The enantiomers of the same amino acid are alike in containing the same atoms, but are different three-dimensionally. They are mirror images of one another but not superimposable. So, just as the right and left hand cannot be matched when superimposed, or a right-handed glove cannot fit a left hand, neither can the D and L forms of alanine be matched when superimposed.

pure (optically active) solutions of one enantiomer or the other.
Looking at the evolutionary position, if amino acids formed in the primitive oceans spontaneously, then the resultant brew would consist of 50% L, and 50% D-forms; and if these would in turn link up (polymerize) to form proteins, the proteins would be expected to consist of approximately equal amounts of D and L-forms. Also, since these proteins were the "ancient ancestors" of todays proteins, as found in living systems, one would expect the proteins of life today to be 50% D and 50% L-mixtures of amino acids. But, on the contrary, they are all L!

The fact that amino acids form in biopoiesis (origin of life) experiments is really no support that these experimental models portray or prove the spontaneous formation of life. For, to repeat, all living protein (with the exception of a miniscule few forms of life) contains 100% L-amino acids, whereas all spontaneous processes and laboratory syntheses yield a mixture of amino acids. Blum wrote:

> "Amino acids synthesized in the laboratory are a mixture of the right- and left-handed forms, and thermodynamically the two forms are indistinguishable."[6]

This problem for "origin-of-lifers" is the subject of intense research. Investigators argue there were conditions at the time of the origin of life that would have biased the formation of L-amino acids. Some have described the selective radiolysis of D amino acids by C^{14} beta rays leaving only L-forms;[7] others suggest light reflected from water, the moon, or crystal surfaces may have resulted in the selective formation of L amino acids;[8] and some have even suggested L-amino acids crystallized and settled out of solution and were later transported by the wind to another locale where they could become redispersed as a solution containing only L-amino acids.[9]

The question, though, is not whether scientists can devise experiments that will cause the selective formation of L-amino acids, but rather, whether such an event would be feasible as a spontaneous process. Even so, in spite of efforts of several thousand brainy kilocalories of thought and experiment, no 100% yields of pure optically active solutions of amino acids have been formed.[10]

---

6. H. BLUM: *TIME'S ARROW AND EVOLUTION* (NEW JERSEY: PRINCETON U., 1968), P. 159.

7. W. J. BERSTEIN, R. M. LEMMON AND M. CALVIN: "AN INVESTIGATION OF THE POSSIBLE DIFFERENTIAL RADIOLYSIS OF AMINO ACID OPTICAL ISOMERS BY ^{14}C BETAS," IN *MOLECULAR EVOLUTION: PRE-BIOLOGICAL AND BIOLOGICAL*, EDS. D. L. ROHLFING AND A. I. OPARIN (N.Y.: PLENUM, 1972), P. 151.

8. J. KEOSIAN: *THE ORIGIN OF LIFE* (N.Y.: REINHOLD, 1968), P. 93.

9. A. I. OPARIN: *LIFE: ITS NATURE ORIGIN AND DEVELOPMENT*, (EDINBURGH: OLIVER AND BOYD, 1961), P. 280.

10. K. HARADA: *NATURE*, 200(1963):200; S. AKABORI: "ASYMMETRIC HYDROGENATION OF CARBONYL COMPOUNDS," IN *THE ORIGINS OF PRE-BIOLOGICAL SYSTEMS AND THEIR MOLECULAR MATRICES*, ED. S. W. FOX (N.Y.: ACADEMIC, 1965), PP. 127-135; D. ROHLFING AND C. E. FOUCHE, JR.: "STEREO-ENRICHED POLY ALPHA AMINO ACIDS: SYNTHESIS UNDER POSTULATED PREBIOTIC CONDITIONS," IN *MOLECULAR EVOLUTION: PREBIOLOGICAL AND BIOLOGICAL*, (REF. 7) PP. 219-231.

Orgel contends, concerning the experimental conditions used to try to form pure L-amino acids:

"It is doubtful that any of the biases so far suggested was significant."[11]

Amie and Henri Amariglio state that all of the theories on the formation of optical activity have failed.[12] Oparin concludes that all proposals for explaining the optical activity of life (all L-amino acids) are feeble:

". . . we really cannot make any conclusive statement at this state of knowledge as to how such uniqueness evolved in nature."[13]

Sagan considered the various abiological mechanisms for the formation of optically active molecules (all L, or all D) and concluded:

"But none of these mechanisms can explain the origin of optical activity in biochemistry, because in the large each stereoisomer (enantiomer) of a pair should be produced in equal amounts. The amount of left-handed polarized light striking the surface of the Earth is balanced by right-handed polarized light; the amount of left-asymmetric quartz equals the amount of right-asymmetric quartz; and the extent of spontaneous synthesis of levo-rotary compounds should be exactly balanced by the rate of synthesis of dextrorotary compounds. It seems highly probable that the organic molecules synthesized on the primitive Earth at the time of the origin of life were not on the average optically active."[14]

Wald believes the various inorganic devices yielding optical activity are not relevant and, instead, poses natural selection as the key. He feels the reason life is composed of L-amino acids is because they "won in the fight."[15] In answer to Wald, we must point out first of all that it is fallacious to cite natural selection as a driving force for systems that do not have the ability to reproduce![16] (I will consider this in more detail later.) Also, there is no evidence that L-amino acids would be more viable to the extent of completely excluding the D enantiomers.

But evolutionists believe that since life is here, life evolved. Therefore, since the biases proposed to explain the

11. L. E. ORGEL: *THE ORIGINS OF LIFE: MOLECULES AND NATURAL SELECTION* (N.Y.: JOHN WILEY AND SONS, 1973), P. 167.
12. AMIE AND HENRI AMARIGLIO, (REF. 5) P. 63.
13. A. I. OPARIN, (REF. 9) PP. 215, 217, 280.
14. I. S. SHKLOVSKII AND C. SAGAN: *INTELLIGENT LIFE IN THE UNIVERSE* (N.Y.: DELL, 1966), PP. 244, 245.
15. G. WALD, (REF. 4) PP. 352-358, 360, 365.
16. T. DOBZHANSKY IN *THE ORIGINS OF PREBIOLOGICAL SYSTEMS AND THEIR MOLECULAR MATRICES*, (REF.10) PP. 309, 310.

spontaneous formation of all L-amino acids are untenable, the only alternative is to resort to the notion that L forms of amino acids are "better" (they must be, of course, since all life is made up of L-forms--or so it is reasoned). But the "L-preference" has not been demonstrated in the laboratory, even allowing the results from experiments that use conditions that could not have been relevant at any time in earth's history.

Even if by some quirk only the L-amino acids were formed in the beginning stage, this pure mixture of amino acids would soon degenerate, for 50% of the L-forms would revert to the D-forms spontaneously through the process known as racemization. (Especially would such racemization occur if the amino acids are subjected to hot or alkaline conditions, both conditions would probably have been present in the early earth.)[17] The enantiomers racemize toward an equilibrium rather than remaining as optically pure D or optically pure L:

$$\text{D-A. ACID} \overset{\text{racemization}}{\longleftrightarrow} \text{A. ACID-L}$$

Thus, even if we started with 100% L-amino acids, we would soon have a mixture of D and L-forms (racemic mixture), and be faced with the same original problem of forming all L-amino acid proteins from a D-L mixture.

(This automatic racemization is the basis for a new method being devised to date organic material. The rate at which L-amino acids revert to D-amino acids is determined and then applied to organic remains that have been undergoing this automatic change since death. In other words, the more D-amino acid in a bone, the older the bone; the less D-amino acid, the more recent the bone.)[18]

It seems that regardless of the concerted attempts to solve this problem for evolutionists, there remains no answer. Recently, at a seminar, Harold Urey, the noted scientist who won a Nobel prize for his experiments on the origin of life, was asked how life could be based on all L-amino acids yet spontaneous processes always yield racemates. Dr. Urey, a somewhat outspoken confirmed atheist and evolutionist, answered:

>"Well, I have worried about that a great deal and it is a very important question . . . and I don't know

17. *A. I. OPARIN, (REF. 9) P. 215; R. T. MORRISON AND R. N. BOYD: ORGANIC CHEMISTRY (BOSTON: ALLYN AND BACON, 1963), P. 868.*
18. *J. BADA AND OTHERS: "CONCORDANCE OF COLLAGEN-BASED RADIO-CARBON AND ASPARTIC-ACID RACEMIZATION," IN PROC. NATIONAL ACADEMY OF SCIENCE, 71(1974):914.*

the answer to it"[19]

This is not to say he does not believe an answer will be forthcoming. But it does point out the very real present inability to explain the natural origin of biological amino acids.

What conclusions can we draw from this examination? Namely, our present knowledge is insufficient to explain the natural origin of biologically viable amino acids, about the most simple building blocks of life. The evolutionist would express faith further research will surface an answer. The creationist would say this is true, the future may produce an explanation, but evolution is believed because of what is presently known, not because of what is hoped to be known at some indefinite time in the future. So, at present, our knowledge does not lend to a naturalistic interpretation of the origin of amino acids. On the other hand, the creationistic interpretation (1) is consistent with research showing pure amino acids can be formed only through intelligent manipulations, and (2) is, as agreed previously, the only logical alternative. The creationist has current evidence on his side and faith further research will not explain the naturalistic origin of L-amino acids.

But, one might still argue the formation of an all L-amino acid protein from a mixture of enantiomers is still possible from a probabilistic standpoint. Let's examine this thesis. We will see that the "possible" is quite impossible.

Possible Vs Impossible

The tendency today is to speak in terms of just how "probable" or "improbable" events are, and not whether they are possible or not. Anything is spoken of as being possible, even if the odds against it are huge.

But is this really coming to grips with reality? Is everything possible, practically speaking? The probability of events like a chair turning to dust just before you sit in it, throwing a ball to the moon, stomping your foot hard on the earth and throwing it out of orbit, dictionaries being formed from explosions in printers shops, extracting sunbeams from cucumbers, skinning a flint, weaving ropes of sand, squaring a circle, making a silk purse from a sow's ear, or milking a hegoat are so remote as to be considered for all practical purposes impossible.

To illustrate this point further and to get a feel for the calculations involved in probabilities, let's review some math and consider the probability of throwing heads with a penny one hundred times in succession. As Blum of Harvard has said:

> "Discussions of the mode of origin of life always involve, sooner or later, questions of chance. . ."[20]

---

19. *CREATION-EVOLUTION SEMINAR, LANSING COMMUNITY COLLEGE, 1974.*
20. *H. BLUM, (REF.6) P. 152.*

(If the details of mathematics bore (or snow) you, you might wish to skim this section. However, understanding this material will greatly aid your understanding of the argument that "all things are possible" and subsequent calculations relevant to origins.)

Powers of Ten

In this and subsequent discussions on probabilities we will be expressing numbers as 10 raised to a power. Expressing numbers in this notation is a convenience when dealing with large figures. The number 10 would be expressed as 10^1, 100 as 10^2, 1,000 as 10^3 and 1,000,000 as 10^6. The hazard in this notation, however, is that one can easily lose the feel for what the numbers are in reality.

As the exponents (superscripts) of 10 increase, the number represented increases with tremendous rapidity. To illustrate this, consider that although when 10^9 is increased to 10^{10}, and the exponent only increases by one, the real number, 10^9, is increased by 9,000,000,000:

$$10,000,000,000 = 10^{10}$$
$$- \ 1,000,000,000 = 10^9$$
$$\overline{ \ 9,000,000,000}$$

If we were to subtract 10^{20} (one followed by 20 zeros) from 10^{30}, the answer, for all practical purposes, expressed in this form of notation, is 10^{30}! Although 10^{20} is huge, 10^{30} is so much larger that it is barely dented by the subtraction.

To further elucidate the convenience, and seeming deception, of expressing numbers as exponents of ten, note: ten billion years $=(10^{10}$ years$)=(10^{18}$ seconds$)=(10^{24}$ millionths of seconds$)$! The earth weighs only (?) 10^{26} ounces! There are only (?) 10^{28} inches across the universe, and only (?) 10^{80} elementary particles (electrons, protons, neutrons) contained therein! Keeping these ideas in mind let's begin flipping coins.

Coin Probabilities

The chance of flipping a head at any one time is: number of favorable events possible (one head), to the total number of possibilities (two--one head plus one tail), or 1/2. Chance has no memory or consciousness, so each time we flip the penny the odds will still be 1/2 that we will get heads. The probability of getting heads twice in succession is: 1/2 X 1/2 =$1/2^2$ =1/4; three times in succession is: 1/2 X 1/2 X 1/2 =$1/2^3$ =1/8; and

the probability of getting heads one hundred times in succession
is 1/2 X 1/2 X 1/2 X 1/2 . . . one hundred times = $1/2^{100}$.

$1/2^{100}$ is approximately $1/10^{30}$; i.e., one chance in one
followed by thirty zeros we will get heads one hundred times in
succession.[21] Practically speaking, we are saying it will take
100,000,000,000,000,000,000,000,000,000,000 (10^{32}) tosses (10^{30}
sets of 100 tosses = 10^{30} X 10^2 = 10^{32}), on the average, to have
one chance of throwing heads one hundred times in succession.

We say this for the same reason that "on the average", it
would take two flips of a coin to obtain the 1/2 chance of getting heads once, eight flips "on the average" to get the 1/4
chance of getting heads twice in a row (four series of two
flips), 16 flips "on the average" to get the 1/8 chance of getting heads three times in a row. Thus, "on the average", to get
the $1/2^{100}$ ($1/10^{30}$) chance of throwing heads one hundred times
in a row, we just flip the coin 2^{100} X 100 (10^{32}) times. Also,
just as we may flip a coin 8 times and not realize the 1/4
chance of getting two heads in succession and, consequently,
have to flip several series of 8 to realize the chance, so likewise, several series of 10^{32} flips might be necessary to ever
get heads 100 times in succession.

If it would take about 10^{32} flips to get heads one hundred
times in succession, and if we were to flip the coin once every
second, how long would it take us to flip the penny this number
of times? We know that there are 10^7 seconds in one year, so we
should be flipping the coin 10^7 times every year.

If we divide 10^7 into 10^{32} we find it will take 10,000,000,-
000,000,000,000,000,000 (10^{25}) years to have one chance, on the
average, of throwing heads one hundred times in succession.
(Fig. 20)

It is interesting to note the longest age for the universe,
based upon the very liberal assumptions of evolutionists, is
only 10^{10} (ten billion) years. We are thus faced with the em-
barrassing situation of not having enough time, even if we began
flipping at the supposed beginning of the universe some 10,000,-
000,000 years ago, to even have one chance, not surety, of
throwing heads one hundred times in succession. This is not

---

21. *CHANGING NUMBERS OTHER THAN 10 RAISED TO A POWER, TO 10
RAISED TO A POWER, IS A CONVENIENCE FOR MAKING CALCULATIONS.
THE CONVERSION IS ACCOMPLISHED IN THE FOLLOWING MANNER:*
A. *DERIVING THE FORMULA:* $\cdots A^n = 10^y$

$$n \times logA = y \times log10$$

$$y = \frac{nlogA}{log10}$$

B. *CONVERTING* 2^{100}: $\cdots\cdots\cdots 2^{100} = 10^y$

$$100 \times log2 = y \times log10$$

$$y = \frac{100 \times .3}{1}$$

$$y = 30 \ APPROXIMATELY$$

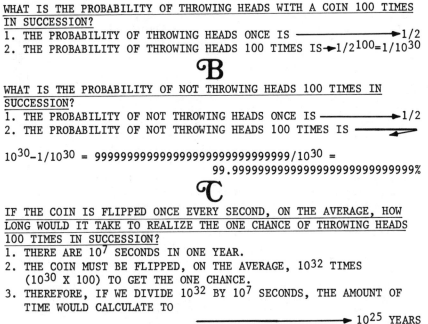

𝒜

WHom IS THE PROBABILITY OF THROWING HEADS WITH A COIN 100 TIMES IN SUCCESSION?
1. THE PROBABILITY OF THROWING HEADS ONCE IS ────────► $1/2$
2. THE PROBABILITY OF THROWING HEADS 100 TIMES IS ►$1/2^{100} = 1/10^{30}$

ℬ

WHAT IS THE PROBABILITY OF NOT THROWING HEADS 100 TIMES IN SUCCESSION?
1. THE PROBABILITY OF NOT THROWING HEADS ONCE IS ────────► $1/2$
2. THE PROBABILITY OF NOT THROWING HEADS 100 TIMES IS ────────►

$10^{30} - 1/10^{30} = 999999999999999999999999999999/10^{30} =$
$99.9999999999999999999999999999\%$

𝒞

IF THE COIN IS FLIPPED ONCE EVERY SECOND, ON THE AVERAGE, HOW LONG WOULD IT TAKE TO REALIZE THE ONE CHANCE OF THROWING HEADS 100 TIMES IN SUCCESSION?
1. THERE ARE 10^7 SECONDS IN ONE YEAR.
2. THE COIN MUST BE FLIPPED, ON THE AVERAGE, 10^{32} TIMES (10^{30} X 100) TO GET THE ONE CHANCE.
3. THEREFORE, IF WE DIVIDE 10^{32} BY 10^7 SECONDS, THE AMOUNT OF TIME WOULD CALCULATE TO ────────────► 10^{25} YEARS

* *

Fig. **20** - Coin Probabilities

even mentioning the problem of wearing your thumb down to the knuckle, or better yet, to the shoulder. And there would probably not be enough pennies ever produced to withstand the wear and tear of being flipped 10^{32} times.

Reasoning on Probabilities

So when we speak of events being practically impossible, we are saying events whose probabilities are infinitely slight just plain won't happen. Emil Borel, in his book on probabilities, stated that the "law of probability" is: "events whose probabilities are extremely small never occur."[22]

22. E. BOREL: *ELEMENTS OF THE THEORY OF PROBABILITY* (NEW

Some may still say: "Oh, yes they can. After all, there is the one chance!" Of course these people will still argue this point even if we were to reduce the time for throwing heads 100 times in succession to only 100 seconds, or to 50 seconds, or to ten seconds, or to one second. "After all, it is 'possible' that your thumb could, by some fantastically coordinated, adroit, lightning-fast feat, flip the coin 100 times in one second, obtain all heads and get the one chance in 10^{30}! (?)" they say. Apropos are the words of Saki: "When once you have taken the impossible into your calculations, its possibilities become practically limitless."

Where do we draw the line? If we are concerned about reality, we draw the line by believing the most probable will happen. We know that if we flip a coin once we will have a 50% chance of guessing which side will turn up. Who would care to stake something of significance, like say our life, that we could guess which side will turn up? If we flip the coin twice, the probability is one in four that heads will turn up both times, and three in four that it will not--which odds would you take? If we flipped the coin ten times, there would be one chance in about 1,000 that all the flips would result in heads, and 999 to 1,000 that there will be at least one tail in there to mess up the sequence. If the coin is flipped 100 times, there will be one chance in 10^{30} that the coins will turn up heads, and 999,999,999,999,999,999,999,999,999,999 to 1,000,000,-000,000,000,000,000,000,000,000 (10^{30}) that there will always be at least one tail turning up to squelch the run.

When trying to determine whether the desired results will happen, always consider that the fractions used in probabilities carry two stories with them. One tells you the chance of something happening, and the other tells you the chance that that same event will not happen; i.e., if the odds are one in ten (10%) that a certain event will occur, then likewise the odds are nine to ten (90%) that it will not.

Who could reasonably believe that a coin will turn up heads 100 times in succession, when the odds for it happening are:

$$\frac{1}{1,000,000,000,000,000,000,000,000,000,000} =$$
(.000000000000000000000000000001%)

and the probability that it won't is:

$$\frac{999,999,999,999,999,999,999,999,999,999}{1,000,000,000,000,000,000,000,000,000,000} =$$
(99.999999999999999999999999999%)

The probability that the event will not happen is what we

JERSEY: PRENTICE-HALL, 1965), P. 57.

must believe if we are concerned about being realistic. The
evolutionist, George Wald, has stated that a probability of 19,-
999/20,000 is "almost inevitable." This probability is 99.995%,
our probability of 99.99999999999999999999999999%, therefore,
must be virtual certainty.[23]

The laws of probability are proven and trustworthy. The
whole of science and every day practical living is based upon
the reliability of the probable happening and the improbable not.
One need do no more than be consistent with this accepted standard of reality when considering what to believe in relation to
the origin of life.

Probability of L-Proteins

Now let's turn to the contention that all L-amino acid proteins could come into existence by chance from a mixture of D-
and L-enantiomers and apply what we have learned from flipping
coins. It has been estimated that the simplest possible self-
replicating entity would contain 124 proteins of 400 amino acids
each.[24] In reality, the simplest known self-reproducing organism, the H39 strain of PPLO (mycoplasma), contains 625 proteins
of this size. Bacteria contain upwards of 2,000 (*E. coli* has
2,800) protein enzymes, and man is estimated to have at least
100,000 different proteins in his body. [25] What would be the
probability of one such protein, consisting of 400 L-amino acids,
coming into existence from a mixture of D- and L-forms?
1. There would be a 50% chance (1/2) of the L-form of each a-
   mino acid, except glycine which only exists in one form,
   linking up in the protein in preference to the D-form. (The
   computation is like calculating coin probabilities.)
2. If we deduct a proportionate fair share for glycine, (which
   you may recall exists in only one, not two, forms) say
   twenty, and work then with proteins of 380 (400-20) amino
   acids, then the probability of 380 amino acids of L-type
   linking up is: $1/2 \times 1/2 \times 1/2 \ldots 380$ times, or $1/2^{380} = 1/10^{114}$. (Fig. 21)

Of course, we must remember that the probability computation above is for just one protein. The simplest theoretical
living entity could not contain less than 124!

What would be the probability of 124 proteins coming into

23. *G. WALD: "THE ORIGIN OF LIFE," IN THE PHYSICS AND CHEMIS-
TRY OF LIFE (N. Y.: SIMON AND SCHUSTER, 1955), P. 12.*
24. *H. J. MOROWITZ: "BIOLOGICAL SELF REPLICATING SYSTEMS," IN
PROGRESS IN THEORETICAL BIOLOGY, 1(1967):52-57; J. F. COPPEDGE:
"PROBABILITY AND LEFT HANDED MOLECULES," IN CREATION RESEARCH
SOCIETY QUARTERLY, 8(1971):172.*
25. *H. J. MOROWITZ, (REF. 24) P. 54.*

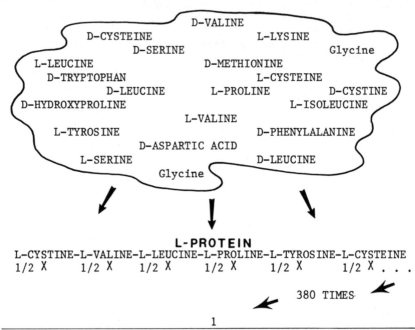

L-PROTEIN
L-CYSTINE-L-VALINE-L-LEUCINE-L-PROLINE-L-TYROSINE-L-CYSTEINE
1/2 X   1/2 X   1/2 X   1/2 X   1/2 X   1/2 X . . .

380 TIMES

$$\frac{1}{1,000,000,000,000,000,000,000,000,000,000,000,000,000,000,000,000,000,000,000,000,000,000,000,000,000,000,000,000,000,000,000,000,000,000,000,000,000,000,000,000,000,000,000}$$

Fig. **21** - L-Protein Probability
What is the probability of forming one 400 all L-amino acid pro-
tein from a milieu containing a mixture of D-and L-forms? Each
time an amino acid links, the probability that the amino acid will
be L is 1/2. (An exception for glycine must be made because it ex-
ists in only one form and its probability would be 1/1) Therefore,
the probability of forming the one protein would be $1/2^{380}$ (de-
ducting 20 for glycine), or, to the base ten would be $1/10^{114}$.
This is one chance in one quinto-sexdecillion.

existence by chance? It would be: $1/10^{114}$ X $1/10^{114}$ X $1/10^{114}$
. . . 124 times - $(1/10^{114})^{124} = 1/10^{14,136}$. Writing this number would take the space of about twelve pages with zeros!
From this, the convenience of superscript notation is obvious,
but remember not to be deceived by the real size of the numbers
represented.
      When we consider it is estimated there have only been 10^{52}
proteins ever in existence,[26] namely all the proteins that would

26. M. EDEN: "INADEQUACIES OF NEODARWINIAN EVOLUTION AS A SCI-
ENTIFIC THEORY," IN MATHEMATICAL CHALLENGES TO THE NEODARWINIAN

have been in all living organisms for the past ten billion years, according to evolutionary conclusions, then we see how extremely remote is the probability of one all L-amino acid protein coming into existence by chance $(1/10^{114})$, let alone 124 of them arising $(1/10^{14,136})$.

However, some might contend that perhaps there was a preference of L-amino acids for L-amino acids such that when linking up to make a protein, L-forms would "reject" the D-forms but "attract" the L-forms. Actually, we know that such preferential linking is not the case;[27] in fact, the opposite is known to be true--i.e., L-forms prefer D-forms in some instances.[28]

For the sake of argument, lets concede that perhaps the L-forms would prefer the L-forms on the order of 99%. In other words, instead of there being a 50% chance of the L-forms linking, there would be a 99% chance. How does this affect the probability of getting the 124 proteins of 380 L-amino acids? The computation would work out to approximately $1/10^{210}$, or one chance in 1,000,000,000,000,000,000,000,000,000,000,000,000,-000,000,000,000,000,000,000,000,000,000,000,000,000,000,000,-000,000,000,000,000,000,000,000,000,000,000,000,000,000,000,-000,000,000,000,000,000,000,000,000,000,000,000,000,000,000,-000,000,000,000,000,000,000,000,000! (Fig. 22)

Since the chance for the L-proteins characteristic of life coming into existence by chance is infinitely small $(1/10^{14,136})$, then the chance that they did not come into existence by chance is practical surety: 999 . . . for 14,133 more 9's/$10^{14,136}$.

We previously emphasized that probabilities tell two stories. One is the odds for an event happening, the other is the odds that the event will not happen. On the matter of origins, as we have agreed, there are only two possibilities. If we have shown the practical impossibility of the chance formation of L-proteins, therefore, logically, the opposite position, creation, becomes certainty according to this argument.

The creationist would approach the question of the origin of L-proteins in another slightly different way and come up with the same conclusion. We know it requires the sophisticated pre-existing machinery of the cell to form all L-proteins. Similarly it requires the sophisticated design, control, and intelligence of an experimental laboratory procedure to produce L-amino acids and proteins. If it takes intelligence to duplicate the processes accomplished by cells, namely, the formation of L-proteins, would it not require the same ingredient to form cells in the beginning?

INTERPRETATION OF EVOLUTION. EDS. P. S. MOORHEAD AND M. M. KAPLAN (PHILADELPHIA: THE WISTAR INSTITUTE, 1967), P. 7.
27. L. PAULING: *COLLEGE CHEMISTRY* (SAN FRANCISCO: W. H. FREEMAN, 1964), P. 731.
28. SHROEDER, EBERHARD AND KLAUS LUBKE: *THE PEPTIDES* (N. Y.: ACADEMIC, 1965), PP. 274, 275.

A

WHAT IS THE PROBABILITY OF FORMING ONE ALL L, 400 AMINO ACID PRO-
TEIN, FROM A 50% MIXTURE OF D- AND L-FORMS?
1. THE PROBABILITY OF EACH L LINKING IS ⟶ $1/2$
2. IF WE DEDUCT A FAIR SHARE FOR GLYCINE, SAY 20, THEN THE
   PROBABILITY WOULD BE:
   $1/2$ X $1/2$ X . . . FOR 380 TIMES(400-20) = $1/2^{380}$ = ⟶ $1/10^{114}$

B

WHAT IS THE PROBABILITY OF 124 SUCH PROTEINS, THE NUMBER NEEDED
FOR THE SIMPLEST POSSIBLE SELF-REPLICATING ENTITY, FORMING?
$1/10^{114}$(THE PROBABILITY OF ONE PROTEIN FORMING) X $1/10^{114}$ X
$1/10^{114}$ . . . 124 TIMES = $1/(10114)^{124}$ = ⟶ $1/10^{14,136}$

C

WHAT IS THE PROBABILITY OF 124 ALL L, 400 AMINO ACID PROTEINS FORM-
ING, IF THERE IS A 99% SURETY THAT L WILL PREFERENTIALLY LINK TO L?
1. THE PROBABILITY OF EACH L LINKING IS ⟶ $99/100$
2. THE PROBABILITY OF 380(400 - 20 GLYCINE) L-AMINO
   ACIDS LINKING IN SUCCESSION IS:

   .99 X .99 X .99 . . . 380 TIMES = $.99^{380}$ = ⟶ $1/10^{1.7}$

3. THE PROBABILITY OF 124 PROTEINS FORMING IS:

$1/10^{1.7}$ X $1/10^{1.7}$ . . . 124 TIMES = $1/(10^{1.7})^{124}$ = ⟶ $1/10^{210}$

*

Fig.22 - L - Proteins Probabilities

From an evolutionary viewpoint, the facts remain: amino
acids can form in the laboratory; amino acids, under certain
conditions, will be more L than D; amino acids can link together
in the laboratory to form proteins. None of these events require a divine hand, and all of them, at one time or another,
were thought impossible by creationists. It is, therefore, a
faith with no little basis to believe difficulties in evolutionary explanations will clear with further research.
So, in rebuttal to creationistic arguments from probabilities and L-amino acids, the evolutionist reasons:
1. If there is one chance, even if it is one in $10^{14,136}$, then
   L-proteins could still have formed in the primal brew.
2. Given enough time, the probability will increase.
3. Given the correct conditions, the odds might swing in favor
   of spontaneous L-protein synthesis.
4. A creationistic interpretation is premature and simply an
   expression of faith that future discovery will not vindicate

a naturalistic interpretation.

The creationist would counter by saying: number one conflicts with the law of probability which states that highly improbable events don't happen; and numbers two through four are simply expressions of faith in naturalistic philosophy, not evidences.

Keeping in mind the guidelines of our methodology--there are two possible positions, and only known and verified evidences count--we must decide which proposition is consistent with the evidences from probability calculations and stereochemistry.

Sequenced Proteins

The proteins of life are highly complex. They consist of from thousands to millions of individual atoms. For example, casein, a protein in milk that provides the basis for the formation of curds and cheese, has the chemical formula: $C_{708}H_{1130}O_{224}N_{180}S_4P_4$. The number associated with each letter indicates the number of atoms of each kind in one molecule of casein; e.g., C=carbon, and 708 indicates the number of carbon atoms in one of the casein proteins. Compare this chemical formula to the one for water--H_2O. A molecule of water contains three atoms whereas one of casein contains 2,250!

The protein, tryptophan synthetase A, has the chemical formula $C_{1289}N_{343}O_{375}S_8$ and contains a total of 2,015 atoms. To make lucidly clear the complex nature of the chemicals of life, note the detailed chemical handle for tryptophan A: Methionylglutaminylarginyltyrosylglutamylserylleucylphenylalanylalanylglutaminylleucyllysylglutamylarginyllysyglutamylglycylalanylphenylalanylvalylprolylphenylalanylvalylthreonylleucylglycylaspartylprolylglycylisoleucylglutamylglutaminylserylleucyllysylisoleucylaspartythreonylleucylisoleucylglutamylalanylglycylalanylaspartylalanylleucylglutamylleucylglycylisoleucylprolylphenylalanylserylaspartylprolylleucylalanylaspartylglycylprolylthreonylisoleucylglutaminylasparaginylalanylthreonylleucylarginylalanylphenylalanylalanylalanylglycylvalylthreonylprolylalanylglutaminylcysteinylphenylalanylglutamylmethionylleucylalanylleucylisoleucylarginylglutaminyllysylhistidylprolylthreonylisoleucylprolylisoleucylglycylleucylleucylmethionyltyrosylalanylasparaginylleucylvalylphenylalanylasparaginyllysylglycylisoleucylaspartylglutamylphenylalanyltyrosylalanylglutaminylcysteinylglutamyllysylvalylglycylvalylaspartylserylvalylleucylvalylalanylaspartylvalylprolylvalylglutaminylglutamylserylalanylprolylphenylalanylarginylglutaminylalanylalanylleucylarginylhistidylasparaginylvalylalanylprolylisoleucylphenylalanylisoleucylcysteinylprolylprolylaspartylalanylaspartylaspartylaspartylleucylleucylarginylglutaminylisoleucylalanylseryltyrosylglycylarginylglycyltyrosylthreonyltyrosylleucylleucylserylarginylalanylglycylvalylthreonyl-

glycylalanylglutamylasparaginylarginylalanylalanylleucylprolyl-
leucylasparaginylhistidylleucylvalylalanyllysylleucyllysylgluta-
myltyrosylasparaginylalanylalanylprolylprolylleucylglutaminyl-
glycylphenylalanylglycylisoleucylserylalanylprolylaspartylgluta-
minylvalyllysylalanylalanylisoleucylaspartylalanylglycylalanyla-
lanylglycylalanylisoleucylseryglycylserylalanylisoleucylvalyl-
lysylisoleucylisoleucylglutamylglutaminylhistidylasparaginyliso-
leucylglutamylprolylglutamyllysylmethionylleucylalancylalanyl-
leucyllysylvalylphenylalanylvalylglutaminylprolylmethionyllysyl-
alanylalanylthreonylarginylserine. (Whew! You might want to
check the spelling for me.)

In all proteins, the atoms (elements) whose relative a-
mounts are expressed in the chemical formula, are organized into
various amino acids which are, in turn, attached to one another
in a chain like pearls on a necklace. This is clearly seen by
studying the chemical name for tryptophan A above. The first
part of the name, Methionylglutaminylarginyl . . ., means L-
Methionine is attached to L-glutamic acid which is attached to
L-arginine. . . .

Normally the number of amino acids in a protein would exceed 500. But the number may range from 51 amino acids, in the
insulin molecule (the deficiency of which causes diabetes mel-
litus), to as many as 50,000.

The complexity of proteins depends upon more than the large
quantities of atoms they contain. Starches (a storage form of
sugar) and cellulose (the principle component of wood) also contain large quantities of atoms. But these large molecules are
not as diverse in activity as proteins are. The usefulness and
versatility of proteins depends primarily upon the sequential
arrangement of amino acids. A protein can consist of almost
countless arrangements of the   amino acids. On the other hand,
the large starch and cellulose molecules are made up of chains
consisting of only one, and sometimes two different molecular
species. The structure of cellulose would be something like:
aaaaaaaaaaaaaaaaaaaaa, where a is the repeating sugar molecule
of which cellulose is composed. Protein, however, can look
something like this: afioenvktudkgjqpeid, where each of the
letters represents one of the twenty amino acids.

If a molecule is composed of only one type of repeating
subunit, then the molecule can only be of one species, i.e.,
aaaaaaaaaaaa. Thus, cellulose is always cellulose and does not
have many forms and activities. If a molecule can be made up of
two different subunits, the arrangements could be: aa, bb, ab
or ba; if there are three subunits, the arrangements would be:
aaa, bbb, ccc, aab, aac, aba, aca, cab, bbc, etc., for 27 different arrangements and possible different molecules. The possible arrangements of the 20 different amino acids is almost
2,500 000,000,000,000,000 (25 X 10^{17}).

Protein molecules are always much larger that just 20 units
in length. A modest protein of 100 amino acids could be arranged in 10^{130} different sequences, and if one of every species

were put in a cube, the cube would measure 10^{18} light years on an edge. Just as a person who has a large vocabulary can express many different thoughts and ideas, proteins, with the many possible arrangements of the twenty amino acids, can perform many diverse functions.

To further emphasize the complexity of proteins in living systems, consider that a single hemoglobin molecule, the protein in our blood cells that transports oxygen from the lungs to the various tissues in the body, contains 574 amino acids. Each red cell in our blood, contains about 280 million molecules of hemoglobin, and it would take about 1000 red blood cells to cover the period at the end of this sentence.

If we alter the sequence of amino acids in hemoglobin by exchanging two valines for two glutamic acids--two in 574--sickle cell anemia, the dreaded disease of the Negro, results. The recipient of this condition could experience acute attacks of abdominal pain, pain in the joints, ulcers on the legs, abnormally shaped red blood cells that break open and lose their function, extreme anemia, and even death. All of this because two amino acids out of 574 have been exchanged! The proteins of life are not only highly complex, but also, as illustrated by sickle cell anemia, intricately organized and specific.

The highly specific nature of many proteins is dependent not only upon the optical activity and sequence of amino acids in the chain, but also upon the way in which the protein strand will fold and twist upon itself producing a distinctive three-dimensional globular arrangement, which effect is called the tertiary structure. This three-dimensional, tertiary configuration (deduced from x-ray diffraction studies), is crucial to many of life's proteins. (Fig. 23) Without the proper optical activity and sequence of the constituent amino acids, the three-dimensional folding of the protein chain would not be correct. If the tertiary structure is improper, the protein will be useless, inactive biologically.

Because amino acids can exist in two different forms (D or L), and proteins can be made up of different sequences of the 20 or so amino acids, the possible arrangements of amino acids in proteins is vastly huge: A 500 amino acid protein could exist in 10^{800} forms.[29]

But not just any of the 10^{800} arrangements of amino acids would make a functional protein with appropriate tertiary structure, any more than any random arrangement of lines, angles and letters could make a meaningful blueprint. Useful proteins must first of all contain only L-type amino acids, and secondly, only

---

29. *THIS NUMBER IS COMPUTED IN THE FOLLOWING MANNER: THE NUMBER OF POSSIBLE ENANTIOMERS WOULD BE $2^{500}(10^{150})$; THE NUMBER OF POSSIBLE ARRANGEMENTS OF THE 20 AMINO ACIDS WOULD BE 20^{500} (10^{650}); THE TOTAL POSSIBLE ARRANGEMENTS WOULD, THEREFORE, BE $10^{150} \times 10^{650} = 10^{800}$.*

Fig. **23** - Tertiary Structure

Proteins are specific because they possess all L-amino acids and non-random sequences of those amino acids. Some also fold into a specific three-dimensional configuration as illustrated here.

specific sequences of these L-amino acids.

The proteins of life are unique in that contained within their sequences of amino acids is information that dictates a specific three-dimensional structure which, in turn, accomplishes a specific, meaningful function for the organism. In other words, if we could translate proteins into English they would not read: idur iswThqp hhd divhsoop isettqqxnv u isYYop etzz . . . nonsen e; but rather would read something like this: The L-valine, L-serine, L-threonine and L-alanine at positions 330, 331, 332 and 333 will serve to catalyze electron transfer reactions that in turn allow the capture of energy from foods which can in turn be used to build more protein, etc.

So only a relatively few of the 10^{800} different sequences of our 500 unit protein would be useful biologically, that is, contain information relevant to living processes. This becomes manifestly clear when we consider, as mentioned before, the sum total of proteins calculated to have ever existed, given liberal evolutionary time assumptions and including not just different proteins but any protein, be they the same or not, is 10^{52}. (The actual number of different proteins in the sum total of all plants and animals in existence is 10^{12}.)

The probability of forming 124, 400 amino acid all L-proteins has been computed. But if we are to get a more realistic

picture of the probability of the proteins of our simple, hypothetical, 124-protein animalcule coming into existence by chance,
we must take into consideration the need for specific sequences
of amino acids.

Probability of Sequenced Proteins

What would be the probability of forming a specific sequence
of amino acids in one of the 124 proteins necessary for the simplest living organism?
The calculation would proceed as follows:
1. The probability of any one amino acid linking is 1/20, since
    there are only about 20 different amino acids.
2. Therefore, the probability of 400 amino acids linking in a
    specific meaningful sequence would be: 1/20 X 1/20 X 1/20 .
    . . 400 times = $1/20^{400}$ = $1/10^{520}$ (changing to the base 10).
    (Fig. 24)
This calculation would assume all L-amino acids.

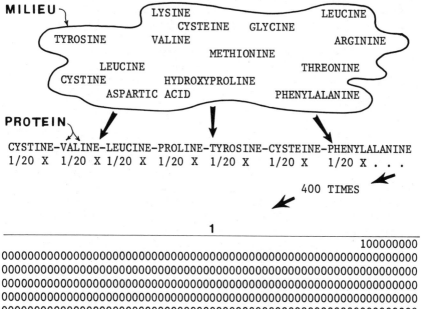

MILIEU

LYSINE   LEUCINE
CYSTEINE   GLYCINE
TYROSINE   VALINE   ARGININE
METHIONINE
LEUCINE   THREONINE
CYSTINE   HYDROXYPROLINE
ASPARTIC ACID   PHENYLALANINE

PROTEIN

CYSTINE-VALINE-LEUCINE-PROLINE-TYROSINE-CYSTEINE-PHENYLALANINE
1/20 X   1/20 X 1/20 X 1/20 X 1/20 X   1/20 X   1/20 X . . .

400 TIMES

1
‾‾‾‾‾‾‾‾‾‾‾‾‾‾
100000000
0000000000000000000000000000000000000000000000000000000000000000
0000000000000000000000000000000000000000000000000000000000000000
0000000000000000000000000000000000000000000000000000000000000000
0000000000000000000000000000000000000000000000000000000000000000
0000000000000000000000000000000000000000000000000000000000000000
0000000000000000000000000000000000000000000000000000000000000000
0000000000000000000000000000000000000000000000000000000000000000
0000000000000000000000000000000000000000000000000000000000000000
0000000000000000000000000000000000000000000000000000000000000000

Fig. **24** - Sequenced Protein Probability
The probability of forming one specific 400 amino acid protein is
$1/10^{520}$.

The probability of forming 124 of these sequenced proteins would be: $(1/10^{520})124 = 1/10^{64,480}$. (See Fig. 25) This total probability is meaningless however, unless we take into consideration the amount of time allowed for the chance to take place and the quantity of amino acids we would have to work with. Obviously, if there were only 124 X 400 (49,600) amino acids diluted by all of the oceans, and we allowed just one second for these to find each other and link up in a specific order to form 124 proteins, the probability would be infinitely less than $1/10^{64,480}$.

For those who like to think of the question of origins in terms of the universe, we'll consider quantities of amino acids and time on a huge scale. Let's assume all the stars in the universe (approximately 10^{25}) have one million "earths" revolving around them, and that each of these "earths" (10^{25} stars X 10^6 earths = 10^{31} earths) has bodies of water the same as our earth (10^{47} molecules). Let's make every molecule in every ocean of the 10,000,000,000,000,000,000,000,000,000,000 (10^{31}) hypothetical "earths" in the universe, an amino acid. (Most have estimated there could be about 10^{10} to 10^{13} planets suitable for life.[30] But it is not known for sure that there are any planets associated with the stars--a possible but disputable exception may be the so-called Van de Kamp's planet associated with Barnard's star.)

How probable would it then be to form 124 specific proteins if the total number of amino acids were linking up to form sets of 124 proteins, breaking up, and then recombining every second for ten billion years. That probability, given even these stupendous conditions, would be $1/10^{64,390}$. (Fig. 25)

Contemplate that! If it were necessary in the beginning to form 124 specifically sequenced very simple proteins of 400 amino acids each, given one million "earths" revolving around each of 10^{25} stars in the universe and making all of their associated seas comprised solely of amino acids, allowing 10^{73} proteins to form every second for ten billion years with a total of 10^{90} proteins obtaining, and giving no consideration to the need for the amino acids to be of only the L-type, the probability for such an occurrence is one chance in $10^{64,390}$ and $\frac{10^{64,390}-1 \text{ (64,390 nines)}}{10^{64,390}}$ that it would not! In other words, the proteins would not form. It is a practical impossibility according to the law of probability. (See ref. 22)

Total Protein Probability

This, in all fairness, is not the total story. The

---

30. G. WALD, (REF. 23) P. 25; H. SHAPELY: *VIEW FROM A DISTANT STAR* (N. Y.: BASIC, 1963)

𝒜

WHAT IS THE PROBABILITY OF FORMING 124 SPECIFICALLY SEQUENCED PROTEINS OF 400 AMINO ACIDS EACH?

1. THE PROBABILITY FOR EACH AMINO ACID IS ──────────► 1/20
2. THE PROBABILITY OF 400 SPECIFIC AMINO ACIDS LINKING IS: $1/20 \times 1/20 \ldots 400$ TIMES $= 1/20^{400} = $ ────► $1/10^{520}$
3. THE PROBABILITY OF 124 PROTEINS FORMING IS: $1/10^{520} \times 1/10^{520} \ldots 124$ TIMES $= 1/(10^{520})^{124} = $ ►$1/10^{64,480}$

ℬ

WHAT IS THE PROBABILITY OF FORMING 124 SPECIFICALLY SEQUENCED, 400 AMINO ACID PROTEINS, GIVEN 10 BILLION YEARS, MAKING EVERY MOLECULE IN THE OCEANS AMINO ACIDS, AND ALLOWING ALL OF THESE AMINO ACIDS TO LINK UP IN SETS OF 124 PROTEINS EVERY SECOND FOR THE DURATION OF THE 10 BILLION YEARS?

1. THE NUMBER OF SETS OF 124 PROTEINS FORMED PER SECOND IS: 10^{47}(MOLECULES IN OCEANS)$/10^{5}$(APPROXIMATE NUMBER OF AMINO ACIDS IN 124 PROTEINS) $= $ ──────────► 10^{42}
2. PROTEINS FORMED PER YEAR IS: 10^{7}(SECONDS IN ONE YEAR) $\times 10^{42} = $ ──────────► 10^{49}
3. PROTEINS FORMED IN 10 BILLION YEARS IS $10^{10} \times 10^{49} = $ ──► 10^{59}
4. THE PROBABILITY OF FORMING 124 PROTEINS IS: 10^{59}(TOTAL PROTEINS FORMED)$/10^{64,480}$(TOTAL POSSIBLE COMBINATIONS) $= $ ──────────► $1/10^{64,421}$

𝒞

WHAT WOULD BE THE PROBABILITY OF FORMING THESE 124 PROTEINS, GIVEN THE ABOVE CONDITIONS MULTIPLIED BY 10^{31}(THE TOTAL NUMBER OF "EARTHS" IN THE UNIVERSE IF EVERY STAR WAS ORBITED BY ONE MILLION "EARTHS")?

1. THE NUMBER OF SETS OF PROTEINS FORMED PER SECOND IS: 10^{78}(10^{31} "EARTHS" $\times 10^{47}$ OCEAN MOLECULES)$/10^{5}$(APPROXIMATE AMINO ACIDS IN 124 PROTEINS) $= $ ──────────► 10^{73}
2. THE PROBABILITY OF FORMING THE SPECIFIC 124 PROTEINS UNDER THESE CONDITIONS IS: 10^{90}($10^{73} \times 10^{17}$ SECONDS)$/10^{64,480} = $ ────► $1/10^{64,390}$

Fig. **25** - Sequenced Proteins Probabilities

---

assumption has been made in this calculation that all of the amino acids would be of the L-type. Even if the one chance in $10^{64,390}$ occurred (which of course is difficult to concede), and the amino acids were not L, all would be in vain. Any proteins forming would be useless biologically. So we must take into consideration the probability of the proteins consisting of all L-amino acids in addition to their having a proper sequence.

To determine the total probability of 124 proteins composed of specifically sequenced L-amino acids forming by chance, given the above described conditions, we simply multiply the probability of 124 specific proteins being properly sequenced

(1/10^{64,390}) times the probability of their being of the L-type (1/10^{14,046}).[31] The total would be 1/10^{78,436}. (Fig. 26) One chance in one followed by enough zeros to fill 75 pages. A trombone player in a telephone booth, with his mouth gagged, hands tied, his trombone slide welded stiff, and the whole of the telephone booth filled with hardened cement has more chance of playing a tune.

ŧotals

WHAT IS THE PROBABILITY OF 124 SPECIFICALLY SEQUENCED PROTEINS, CONSISTING OF 400 ALL L-AMINO ACIDS EACH, FORMING BY CHANCE, GIVEN EVERY MOLECULE IN EVERY OCEAN OF 10^{31} "EARTHS" BEING AN AMINO ACID, AND THESE LINKING UP IN SETS OF 124 PROTEINS EVERY SECOND FOR 10 BILLION YEARS?

1. THE PROBABILITY OF 124 SEQUENCED PROTEINS IS ——►1/10^{64,390}
2. THE PROBABILITY OF THESE PROTEINS CONSISTING OF ALL L-AMINO ACIDS IS ——————————————►1/10^{14,046}
3. THE TOTAL PROBABILITY WOULD BE:
   1/10^{64,390} X 1/10^{14,046} = ————————————————►1/10^{78,436}

*

Fig. **26** - Total Probabilities

However, the objection might be raised that computing the probability of forming just the one specific sequence of 124 proteins is not relevant to the origin of life. In other words, it may be argued that life could have arisen by starting sequences other than the one we have based our computation upon. This is true, but by the same token not just any sequence of amino acids could be relevant to life. Actually, almost all sequences would not be viable biologically, just as only a relatively few sequences of English letters (as compared to the total possible combinations) could form meaningful arrangements.

For example, the number of possible arrangements of letters to form a 50 word sentence is about 10^{210}, whereas the number of those arrangements that could carry useful meaning could be only at most a few thousand (10^3). The total possible arrangements

---

31. THE CHANCE OF 124 X 400 L-AMINO ACID PROTEINS FORMING IS 10^{14,136}. IF WE USE THE CONDITIONS FOR THE UNIVERSE OF 10^{25} STARS WITH 10^6 EARTHS AROUND EACH, THE OCEANS CONSISTING OF ALL AMINO ACIDS, AND THE PROTEINS FORMING AND REFORMING EVERY SECOND FOR TEN BILLION YEARS, 10^{90} SETS OF PROTEINS WOULD RESULT. THEREFORE, THE PROBABILITY OF FORMING THE 124 X 400 ALL L-AMINO ACID PROTEINS UNDER THESE CONDITIONS WOULD BE: 10^{90}/10^{14,136}, OR 1/10^{14,046}.

of our 124 proteins is $10^{64,390}$, and similarly only a few of those arrangements could be meaningful biologically. If we assumed all proteins that have ever been in existence (10^{52}) were different (there are believed to be only 10^{12} different proteins in the entire biological world), and any one of these could have been used for the origin of our first self-replicating entity, the probability of forming any of these would be $10^{50}(10^{52} - 124)/10^{64,390}$, or $1/10^{64,350}$. We have hardly made a dent!

From Probabilities to Where?

If chance alone is the guiding force for this first step of evolution, did the first step occur? In this calculation, vast time, plenty of suitable reagents and favorable conditions were granted. The event remained impossible according to the law of probability.

Some evolutionists believe these types of probabilistic inadequacies are not due to a failing of naturalistic philosophy, but rather due to a gap in present knowledge. They feel they have every reason to trust future discovery in clarifying and substantiating evolution by chance.

Others, actually most modern informed evolutionists, realize the inability of raw chance to account for the origin of proteins. Our probability calculations are not unique. Creationists have been making them for many years, and even evolutionists make similar calculations to demonstrate the inadequacies of chance.[32] Obviously then, one can believe in evolution and reject chance at the same time. How? Well, it is believed that evolution proceeds because of certain material biases and natural selection at the chemical level. In other words, evolutionists don't feel the naturalistic origin of life is akin to trying to build a complex structure from marbles, but rather like assembling a puzzle from puzzle pieces. Just as puzzle pieces predeterministically adjoin in only certain ways--they don't fit randomly--so too, the molecules of life fit together predeterministically due to their unique structures. Indeed, the sciences of biochemistry and molecular biology demonstrate that amino acids "like" to join together in preference

---

32. *THE FOLLOWING IS A SHORT LISTING OF REFERENCES CONTAINING SIMILAR CALCULATIONS: H. QUASTLER: THE EMERGENCE OF BIOLOGICAL ORGANIZATION (NEW HAVEN: YALE UNIVERSITY, 1964), PP. 6, 7; J. HUXLEY: EVOLUTION IN ACTION (N. Y.: NEW AMERICAN LIBRARY, 1953), P. 41; F. SALISBURY: "DOUBTS ABOUT THE MODERN SYNTHETIC THEORY OF EVOLUTION," IN AMERICAN BIOLOGY TEACHER, (SEPT. 1971), P. 336; H. MOROWITZ: ENERGY FLOW IN BIOLOGY (N. Y.: ACADEMIC PRESS, 1968), PP. 66, 67; H. BLUM: TIMES ARROW AND EVOLUTION (PRINCETON: PRINCETON U., 1968), P. 158.*

to joining with, say, nucleic acids; carbohydrates "like" to join together in preference to joining with, say lipids; . . . and so on for a whole array of biochemical biases. To be fair then, we should not quickly eliminate evolution because of unfavorable probability calculations but wait to see if evidence does demonstrate that life could have formed predeterministically. We will devote a later chapter to this concept of biochemical predestination.

The creationist says chance cannot account for life. Many evolutionists say it can. The probability calculations in this and the next chapter are simply meant to test the capabilities of raw chance. (However, you might note that we did calculate a 99% bias in the probability of forming 124 L-proteins--see Fig. 22)

You may recall the quotes in Chapter 3 where evolutionists stated that their position was secure because the only alternative, creation, was absurd. The creationist, using probabilities, reverses this logic with forceful vigor.

If the probability that proteins arose by chance is absurd ($1/10^{78,436}$), then the remaining position, creation becomes surety. The creationist says surety because the opposite of $1/10^{78,436}$ is nine followed by 78,435 more nines to $10^{78,436}$ that these biochemical events did not happen by chance.

During the course of a year, we are told, the odds for our becoming involved in an automobile accident resulting in death or severe injury is approximately 1/200. What if these odds were reversed, i.e., 199/200, how many would then lurch onto the highways? The risk would be far too great. Our highways would become bare, neighborhood streets quiet, the petroleum industry would go bankrupt, smog would wane, our economy would be catastrophically disrupted, and horse and buggies would become revitalized. All because we would believe 199/200 odds are a practical surety.

If this be true, then the odds $\dfrac{10^{78,436}-1 \ (78,436 \ nines)}{10^{78,436}}$

being termed a surety is an understatement. The creationist would say the probability that a creator, not chance, created the chemicals of life is, therefore, with no intent to be dogmatic(?), a certainty, necessity, certitude, positiveness, infallibility, reliableness, compulsion, inevitability and a fact, to say the least! Furthermore, the assertions of evolutionists about the chance spontaneous formation of the bare protein rudiments of life have been floccipaucinihilipilificated.[33] "Based upon what we know, which is, or course, all we have to work with, what other conclusion can be made?" the creationist urges.

On the other hand, as I have said, the evolutionist

---

33. *THIS WORD MEANS ESTIMATED AS WORTHLESS. I THOUGHT I'D NEVER GET A CHANCE TO USE IT.*

maintains that these probability calculations only show the inability of chance to account for life. They don't show that life did not evolve, only that RAW chance is not the mechanism for evolution. Rather than invoking a creator because of the inadequacy of chance, the evolutionist affirms his belief in biochemical predestination, and his trust that future discovery will elucidate a naturalistic interpretation.

ORIGIN
&
MODIFICATION
OF
DNA

The ability to reproduce is a unique, outstanding and essential characteristic of life. If the evolutionist is to describe life's spontaneous formation, he must include a naturalistic explanation of the origin of the reproductive capacity. On the other hand, the creationist must show the insufficiency of naturalism and the need to invoke supernatural intelligence.

Recent studies by scientists have revealed a catalog of data on the chemical mechanisms of reproduction. Included in their discoveries were the isolation of the chemical DNA (deoxyribonucleic acid) and the mechanism by which it functions in reproduction.

DNA is a chemical found in the nuclei of cells which carries the information of heredity. It is the substance of primary importance in the chromosomes and genes.

The DNA molecule is composed of many smaller molecules. There are phosphates, sugars (deoxyribose) and heterocyclic bases (adenine, guanine, cytosine, thymine). The structure of the molecule is described as a double stranded helix, or spiraled ladder, with sugars and phosphates alternating up and down each side of the ladder and bases hydrogen bonding to one another to form the rungs.

The nucleotide is the structural unit of DNA. Each nucleotide consists of a triplet of molecules: sugar, phosphate and base.

The heterocyclic bases that form the "rungs" of DNA are key to the molecule's vital role in reproduction and heredity. The base adenine always links to the base thymine, and vice versa; the base guanine always links to cytosine, and vice versa. One side of the "ladder," as a result of this obligatory base pairing, dictates the sequence of bases on the other side. (Fig. 27)

---

1. *J. A. V. BUTLER*: <u>*THE LIFE PROCESS*</u> *(LONDON: GEORGE ALLEN AND UNWIN, 1970), P. 54.*

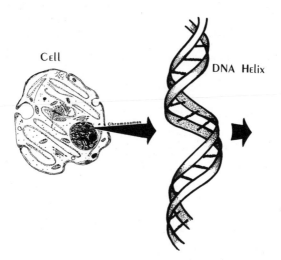

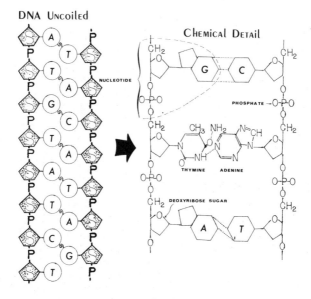

Fig. **27**- DNA Structure

DNA is a double-stranded helix found within the chromosomes of the nuclei of cells. The sides of the helix consist of alternating deoxyribose sugars and phosphates. The "rungs" of the helix are composed of heterocyclic purine and pyrimidine bases bonding to one another. Adenine will obligatorily attach to thymine, and guanine only attaches to cytosine. The triplet of molecules: sugar, phosphate and base, is termed a nucleotide.

When cells divide, the DNA molecule splits down the middle and each resultant single strand of DNA then duplicates the side that was lost. (Fig. 28) This process can occur at the amazing rate of 1,000 base pairs per second.

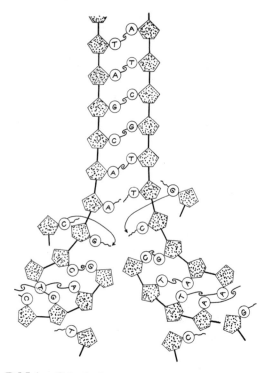

Fig. **28** - DNA Division

At cellular division, when DNA divides, complementary nucleotides replace those that are split away. In this drawing we can see the DNA double-stranded helix splitting down the middle. As the nucleotides that are split away are replaced according to obligatory base pairing(A-T; G-C), two new chains are formed which are identical in base sequence to the original molecule.

Duplication is made possible through obligatory base pairing. The end result of cellular division is two identical DNA helixes housed within the nuclei of two new daughter cells. (Some human cells will divide in this manner more than 50 times before they die. Every minute 3 billion cells die in our bodies and are replaced faithfully according to type.) Through obligatory base pairing.the unique DNA code of every individual is conserved within his cells. Since every individual comes from a single original cell composed of one half of the DNA from his mother and one half from his father, and every cell in a person's body is a product of the duplication of the DNA in that original cell, all cells, from the neurons in brain tissue to the epidermal cells on little pinky toes, contain the same sequence of DNA bases.

The human body is estimated to contain 100 trillion cells. The nucleus of each cell contains 46 chromosomes. If one were to count the number of DNA base pairs in the chromosomes of one cell, the number would compute to approximately 10 billion.[2] The sequence of these billions of bases provides the instructional code for heredity and also oversees many processes in metabolism.

All life, from bacteria to man, depends upon DNA. To say the least, DNA is a fantastic molecule. The mere arrangement of four bases into sequences analogous to sentences and paragraphs, and in quantities far exceeding the information content of several volumes of encyclopedias, dictates the millions of characteristics that differentiate the various kinds of life from one another, as well as the characteristics that make each individual unique within his own kind. Thus, DNA codes people, crabs, cows, ferns, moss, fish and clams, and provides uniqueness to each individual. For example, people are always identifiable as people and yet of the 3½ billion humans on earth, no two individuals have the same personality, features or fingerprints. What DNA dictates, by and large, is what we are.

On the molecular level, the arrangement of bases: A-T-C-T-G-G-G-T-C-T-A-A-T-A. . . for millions (splitting the DNA "ladder" down the middle and looking at one side), may code a turtle; while the sequence: T-G-C-T-C-A-A-G-A-G-T-G-C-C. . . for millions, may code an Einstein.

From the 1950's, when the Nobel prize winners, Watson and Crick, elucidated the structure of DNA and the mechanism by which it functions in reproduction and heredity, much progress has been made in the field of genetics and molecular biology. Application of this knowledge has been made on a practical level and, in addition, used by evolutionists and creationists to argue their respective sides.

Evolutionary Assertion

A couple of decades prior to Watson and Crick, Oparin, a Russian chemist, attempted to explain the chemical spontaneous generation of life. Oparin could not explain the origin of the reproductive capacity. This was simply because the details about DNA were not known. Now, with knowledge of DNA, evolutionists believe they have possible answers to the origin of life's reproductive capacity. They also assert, since all life contains

---

2. *H. BREMERMANN: "QUANTITATIVE ASPECTS OF GOAL-SEEKING SELF-ORGANIZING SYSTEMS," IN PROGRESS IN THEORETICAL BIOLOGY, ED. F.M. SNELL, 1 (1967):68.*

and is dependent upon DNA, that this constitutes evidence all life is related and has a common evolutionary ancestry.

Evolutionists contend that the various components of DNA (sugars, phosphates, bases) formed in the primitive oceans. These components of DNA then formed nucleotides which in turn linked into simple helixes. The DNA was then to have associated with protein and become encased within a membrane to ultimately become a living cell. Since the structure of an organism is dictated by the sequence of bases in DNA, and since it has been discovered that chemicals and various physical agents, like radiation, can alter the sequence of bases in the molecule, it is argued that upward evolution of life could easily occur, given time and selection of the most fit DNA alterations by nature:

PRIMITIVE OCEAN⟶SUGARS, PHOSPHATES, BASES ⟶NUCLEOTIDES ⟶

DNA HELIXES (+ PROTEIN + MEMBRANE AND OTHER NECESSITIES) ⟶

CELLS⟶DNA REARRANGEMENTS (MUTATIONS) ⟶COMPLEXIFICATION ⟶

MULTICELLULAR ORGANISMS ⟶INVERTEBRATES⟶FISH ⟶

AMPHIBIANS ⟶ REPTILES ⟶MAMMALS ⟶MORE TIME & MUTATIONAL DNA

REARRANGEMENTS ⟶MAN

This gradually unfolding evolutionary process advocated by Darwin is actually a philosophical exploitation of the ideas of Rene Descartes who wrote:

"The nature of physical things is much more easily conceived when they are beheld coming gradually into existence, than when they are only considered as produced at once in a finished and perfect state."

If this evolutionary sequence is correct, the case for evolution is proven. But hovering over this gradual progression lie the questions about chance and DNA. If life is to form, DNA must form; if life is to evolve, DNA must evolve. Can chance account for the formation and evolution of DNA? If chance can't, can other natural mechanisms account for DNA's origin and evolution?

If the evolutionist can prove the spontaneous generation of biologically meaningful DNA, then he has a case. If he cannot, he has a distinct problem on his hands. For the origin of the reproductive capacity is a central problem of origins. Without DNA there could be no reproduction, without reproduction there could be no natural selection or mutations. Without natural selection and mutations, the mechanism for evolutionary change is absent. If there is no mechanism for evolution there can be no evolution.

From an evolutionary standpoint, the questions at hand are:
1. Can the building blocks of DNA arise by chance?

2. Can the building blocks of DNA arrange themselves into codes?
3. Can coded DNA undergo spontaneous rearrangements resulting in new improved codes generating more and more complex organisms?
   Creationistic considerations will splinter from the consideration of these questions.

Forming the Letters

Scientists have been able to synthesize the building blocks of DNA, the letters, in the laboratory. This of course establishes the synthetic capabilities of the chemists, but whether the nucleotides of DNA could have repeated the laboratory process, spontaneously, is another matter.

Among the difficulties encountered in the proposition that DNA letters could have formed in the primitive milieu would be:
1. The sugars of DNA (deoxyribose) must be stereospecific, they must be D-forms. Spontaneous formation of sugars yields 50% mixtures of D-and L-forms. How from this mixture could DNA form, incorporating only the D-sugars?

PRIMEVAL MILIEU

50% D&L SUGARS ➤➤ **HOW?** ➤ **100%** D-DNA

2. Biopoiesis was to have occurred in a watery environment. The reactions combining nucleotides to form DNA chains are reversible. In the presence of water, the reactions would not proceed from the simple to the complex, but rather, from the complex to the simple.[3] (This matter will be discussed in detail in a later chapter.)

WATERY MILIEU

NUCLEOTIDES ⬅ ➤ DNA

3. The sugars of DNA would decompose in the presence of amino acids which are said to have been forming at the same time in the same oceans.[4]

3. *M.CALVIN: "CHEMICAL EVOLUTION," IN PROGRESS..., (REF.2) PP.19-23.*
4. *P.H.ABELSON:"CHEMICAL EVENTS ON THE PRIMITIVE EARTH," IN PROCEEDINGS OF THE NATIONAL ACADEMY OF SCIENCE,55(1966):1365.*

AMINO ACIDS + SUGARS ➡ DECOMPOSED SUGARS

4. The energy used to form DNA would have served much more readily to decompose it.[5] Other constituents of the early environment, like ultraviolet light, would have likewise degraded
DNA.[6]

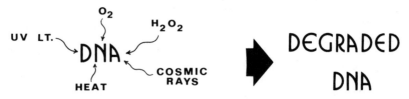

UV LT. → DNA ← O_2 / H_2O_2 / COSMIC RAYS / HEAT ➡ DEGRADED DNA

Does this exposé speak for a creationistic interpretation
then? Yes, if these impasses to the naturalistic formation of the
building blocks of DNA are immovable and if creation is the only
alternative.

Be this as it may, we can put aside all of these objections
to the chance formation of the building blocks of DNA. A more important question is whether the letters of DNA could arrange themselves into codes, sequences carrying information. Furthermore,
can codes improve through random rearrangements?

Special DNA Characteristics

To answer these questions we must first consider more detail
on the DNA molecule. DNA is a code, a language of the highest order. During the growth of the human embryo, the DNA in the zygote
(fertilized egg) provides a blueprint for the assembling of lifeless chemicals (biomonomers), provided by the mother's blood, into
complex structural and functional arrangements. DNA codes the formation of sequenced, all L-amino acid proteins, new DNA is synthesized to be placed in each new cell of the developing embryo, and
these and many more processes are timed, controlled and moderated
by the DNA and machinery of the cells.

Through the machinery of the cell, and the information embodied in DNA, life results, increases in complexity, and culmin-

---

5. D. HULL: "THERMODYNAMICS AND KINETICS OF SPONTANEOUS GENERA-
TION," IN NATURE, 186(1960):694.
6. R. TOCQUET: LIFE ON THE PLANETS (N.Y.: GROVE, 1962),P.28.

ates in the birth of the human--a staggeringly complex, ordered
biological machine. (Fig. 29)

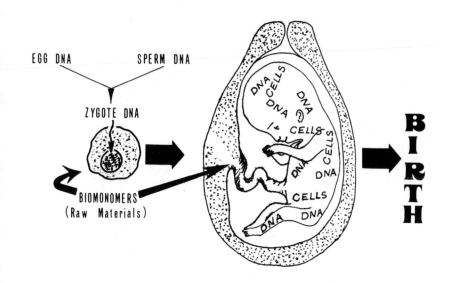

Fig. **29** - DNA Blueprint
*DNA, through the machinery of the cell, arranges lifeless and
random chemicals into highly ordered, complex structures. Here
we see the DNA received from parent sex cells coding the formation of a human through the use of the raw materials fed to the
infant via the mother's blood.*

Analogously we could compare DNA to blueprints for an automobile. An engineer is able to construct an automobile from raw
materials like iron, chrome, plastic and rubber, by reading and
applying the information in the prints. The raw materials for the
automobile would be analogous to the biomonomers (chemical building blocks of life), the blueprint would be analogous to DNA, the
engineer that reads the print and moderates the activity could be
compared to the machinery of the cell, or zygote, and the finished
automobile would be compared to the human at birth:

MODERATED BY THE

A - BLUEPRINT + RAW MATERIALS ——————— ENGINEER ————→ AUTOMOBILE
(IRON, CHROME,
PLASTIC, ETC.)

b - DNA + RAW MATERIALS ——————— CELL MODERATED ————→ HUMAN
(BIOMONOMERS)

The importance of recognizing that DNA is a code, a language carrying information, a blueprint, must be stressed. In any discussion of the molecule, one must of necessity describe its function in terms of the information it carries or in terms of the DNA base sequence language.

The quantities of information contained in living organisms is breathtaking. A one-celled bacterium, *E. coli,* is estimated to contain the equivalent of 100 million pages of *Encyclopedia Britannica.* Expressed in information science jargon, this would be the same as 10^{12} bits of information. In comparison, the total writings from classical Greek civilization is only 10^9 bits, and the largest libraries in the world: the British Museum, Oxford Bodleian Library, New York Public Library, Harvard Widener Library, and the Moscow Lenin Library have about ten million volumes, or 10^{13} bits![7]

The language of DNA is a molecular language, a language made up of nucleotide letters. Thus we have a language that has reached the smallest state. Bremermann says:

> "It is remarkable to realize that heredity information storage in the form of nucleotide sequences has reached the ultimate limit of miniaturization."[8]

It has even been postulated that the code on RNA (a molecule similar to DNA), or its encoded protein products, is responsible for memory.[9] This would mean the sequence of bases in RNA could be directly related to the letter sequence in human language, since, of course, we think and memorize with language. (Fig. 30)

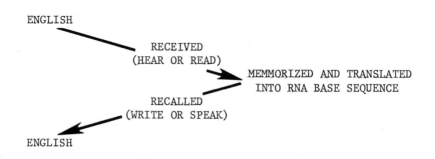

Fig. **30** -Nucleic Acid Language
DNA and RNA, both being nucleic acids, have the ability to be sequentially arranged to carry information. The language is a molecular one consisting of heterocyclic bases.

7. C. SAGAN: "THE ORIGIN OF LIFE," IN ENCYCLOPEDIA BRITANNICA,13 (1973):1083B;THE COSMIC CONNECTION(N.Y.:DELL,1973):236,237.
8. H. BREMERMANN, (REF. 2) P. 61.
9. B. W. AGRANOFF: "MEMORY AND PROTEIN SYNTHESIS," IN SCIENTIFIC AMERICAN, 216 (1967): 115-122.

Can information, codes, language, blueprints, of a meaningful decipherable nature arise by chance, given the basic letters? Simpson says:

"If evolution is to occur. . . Living things must be capable of acquiring new information, or alteration of their stored information. . ."[10]

DNA and Intelligence

Communication engineers and computer scientists have shown that information does not and cannot arise spontaneously.[11] It only arises as a result of the expenditure of energy and the action of intelligence.

Energy is needed to arrange letters, and intelligence is needed to direct their order, or sequence. Also, random rearrangements of the letters in an existing code always result in the scrambling and ultimate destruction of the code.

These scientifically established facts are nothing new. If one had a gunny sack full of lettered blocks and dumped the contents on the floor, then proceeded to kick them, mix them, roll in them, heat them, cool them, blow on them, look at them, and what have you, the sentence: "Randy loves Betty," would not result. The blocks were there, energy was there, but without concomitant intelligence, no information would arise.

If, on the other hand, one got down on his hands and knees and arranged (energy plus intelligence) the letters, the sentence: "Randy loves Betty" would not be at all surprising. If after this sequence (sentence) was arranged, one proceeded to randomly kick the blocks, would you expect the transformation of the sentence such that it would read: "Randy's platonic relationship with Betty transcends logic and proves to be an esoteric study"? Certainly not. Random disruption of the code would result in its destruction: "arsproeicdBoetRvostwpestciyypsc".

A- LETTERS + ENERGY + INTELLIGENCE ⟶ INFORMATION
B- NEVER: LETTERS + ENERGY ⟶ INFORMATION

*

A- INFORMATION + RANDOM REARRANGEMENT ⟶ RANDOM LETTERS
B- NEVER: INFORMATION + RANDOM REARRANGEMENT ⟶ IMPROVED INFORMATION

10. *G. G. SIMPSON: "THE NONPREVALENCE OF HUMANOIDS," IN SCIENCE, 143 (1964):772.*
11. *P. MOORHEAD AND M. KAPLAN, EDD.: MATHEMATICAL CHALLENGES TO THE NEO-DARWINIAN INTERPRETATION OF EVOLUTION (PHILADELPHIA: WISTAR INSTITUTE, 1967).*

These points are reasonable. As reasonable as knowing a ball thrown into the air will return to the ground, objects heavier than water will sink, oxygen is needed for combustion and love begets love. Likewise, the ordering of DNA letters into a code by random assortment is highly unlikely without the simultaneous application of intelligence.

A Jello Lesson

When one mixes gelatin, water and carrot shavings in a bowl and sets the mixture in the refrigerator, he is not surprised to later find that the mixture has changed from a liquid into a gel with the carrot shavings randomly dispersed throughout. This phenomenon is expected, it is a normal chemical process. The formation of biomonomers (DNA letters), as has been done in the laboratory by the "mixing" of C,H,O,N and P atoms, is not a great chemical surprise either--forgetting for the moment the difficulties we cited in their forming spontaneously.

However, if one puts the bowl of water, gelatin and carrot peelings in the refrigerator and later (hours or even millennia, it matters not) opens the door to find the liquid not only gelled, but molded into a highly elaborate, symmetrical structure, with carrot shavings arranged concentrically around the mold and bent into English letters describing the electrical, mechanical, mathematical and geometrical details necessary to allow one to build a computer system, we have an entirely different matter. Someone of a high caliber of intelligence got in the refrigerator when we weren't looking and did it. There is no other reasonable conclusion!

The information contained in DNA would make the information on the gel mold seem elementary by comparison. (The information content in a one-celled bacterium is, as you may recall, equivalent to 100 million pages of *Encyclopedia Britannica*.) What do we conclude about the origin of DNA? Did someone of extreme intelligence "get in there" and do it? The creationist would answer that the prodigious information riding on DNA is direct testimony for supernatural intelligence.

Computers, DNA and Time

In rebuttal, the evolutionist is quick to say that given enough time and random assortments of the DNA letters, the difficulties mentioned here are removed. Until recently, alluding to vast amounts of time would in effect remove the question from the realm of testability (other than through probability calculations) and, therefore, science itself.

Of late, however, large computers have been built that are able to iterate at speeds that would allow them to check the feasibility of building highly ordered molecules from random mixing of biomonomers. Schutzenberger, a computer scientist, in a paper delivered at a Wistar Institute of Anatomy and Biology Symposium, sheds light on the powers of time, nature and chance as related to spontaneous evolution:

> "A second point to which I would like to draw your attention is the fact that nowadays computers are operating within a range which is not entirely incommensurate with that dealt with in actual evolution theories. If a species breeds once a year, the number of cycles in a million years is about the same as that which one would obtain in a ten day computation which iterates a program whose duration is a hundredth of a second. . . Now we have less excuse for explaining away difficulties by invoking the unobservable effect of astronomical numbers of small variations."

Concerning the spontaneous improvement of the code through mutations and natural selection, he further states:

> "We believe that it is not conceivable. In fact, if we try to simulate such a situation by making changes randomly at the typographic level (by letters or by blocks, the size of the unit does not really matter), on computer programs we find that we have no chance (i.e. less than $1/10^{1000}$) even to see what the modified program would compute; it just jams."

> "Further, there is no chance (less than $1/10^{1000}$) to see this mechanism appear spontaneously and, if it did, even less for it to remain."[12]

Eden, a participant in the same symposium, compares DNA to a formal language and corroborates the fact that DNA codes could not evolve through random rearrangements:

> "No currently existing formal language can tolerate random changes in the symbol sequences which express its sentences. Meaning is invariably destroyed."[13]

Schutzenberger's conclusion, though an evolutionist, is:

> ". . . we believe that there is a considerable gap in the neo-Darwinian theory of evolution, and we believe this gap to be of such a nature that it cannot be bridged within the current conception of biology."[14]

Creationists sieze upon this information and assert that the "gap" in biological theory is easily filled by an intelligent cretor. Of necessity, they say, as shown by computer simulation, the formation of DNA demands not only letters and energy but intelligence. In the beginning there were not just atoms and energy, but

---

12. *M. P. SCHUTZENBERGER, (REF. 11) PP. 73-75.*
13. *M. EDEN: "INADEQUACIES OF NEO-DARWINIAN EVOLUTION AS A SCIENTIFIC THEORY," IN <u>MATH. CHALLENGES</u>. . . ,(REF. 11) P. 11.*
14. *M. P. SCHUTZENBERGER, (REF. 11) P. 75.*

there also must have been intelligence.

Professors Callender and Mathews discuss the formula for the measure of information content—$I = K \times$ logarithm base e X P (I is the information of one outcome in a situation which had P equally probable outcomes, K is an arbitrary constant and the logarithm is to the base e)—and the relationship of randomness to information content. They conclude information "never increases as a result of being communicated"; and comparing information content to the theory of heat (the authors compare the similarity in form of the above formula for information with the classical Boltzmann expression for heat distribution, or entropy: $s = k \ln W$), they say:

> "Thus entropy and information are strictly isomorphic quantities, though differing in 'sign', the first increasing and the second decreasing when randomness occurs."[15]

Therefore, since information cannot increase with randomness, and evolution is in large part based upon random mutations, we must at least be forced to do some heavy thinking on the notion of ascending evolutionary transformations produced through spontaneous randomly produced information increases. Furthermore, the total information represented throughout the animal and plant kingdoms could not be more than what was there in the beginning. For, to repeat, information does not increase through randomization.

The order in any system cannot exceed that which was put there in the first place. As Mora says:

> "The reaction product contains no more than the information put in . . . "[16]

The order characteristic of the molecules of life had to have been put there. Computers prove that time and chance can't account for biological design. Nature yields randomness and disorder; as far as we know, only intelligence can create coded order.

It is, therefore, little wonder that the evolutionist, Antonov, confesses:

> ". . . we have no unambiguous solution to the problem of the origin of DNA and its conversion into a hereditary substrate."[17]

The evolutionist proposes that DNA came into existence by chance, and through random rearrangements (mutations) increased in information to code increasingly complex forms of life. Countering this, the creationist says naturalism conflicts with facts.

15. H. L. CALLENDER AND D. H. MATHEWS: "HEAT, ENTROPY AND INFORMATION," IN ENCYCLOPEDIA BRITANNICA, 11(1973):258.
16. P. T. MORA: "THE FOLLY OF PROBABILITY," IN THE ORIGINS OF PREBIOLOGICAL SYSTEMS AND THEIR MOLECULAR MATRICES, ED.S.W. FOX (N.Y.: ACADEMIC,1965),PP. 41,42,49,61.
17. A.S. ANTONOV: "DNA: ORIGIN, EVOLUTION AND VARIABILITY," IN CHEMICAL EVOLUTION AND THE ORIGIN OF LIFE, EDD. R. BUVER AND C. PONNAMPERUMA (N.Y.: AMERICAN ELSEVIER, 1971), P. 422.

Two   Positions

In summary, the creationist says:
1. The formation of information demands intelligence.
2. DNA is information.
3. Therefore, DNA was formed by intelligence.
Also:
1. Random rearrangements in information result in loss of information content, never improvement.
2. DNA is information subject to random changes (mutation).
3. Random rearrangements in DNA would result in loss of DNA information content, not DNA improvement; it also follows that the total biological information extant today must be less, not more, than what was put (created) there in the beginning.

The evolutionist explains the data this way:
1. It is true that information normally demands intelligence for its formation, and random changes will normally destroy existing information, but--
2. Maybe DNA is not really information, perhaps processes were in operation in the past that we don't know about; who knows what vast time periods will produce; DNA may have been seeded here from another planet; perhaps our finite minds are incapable of understanding at this point in time; therefore--
3. There is no need to invoke a creator, for to do so would probably force us to repeat the mentality of those in the past who were always quick to insert a creator to fill the gaps in current naturalistic understandings. As new discoveries surface the creationist will have to intellectually retreat to the catacombs just as he always has.

We, the jurors, must decide which proposition comfortably fits the facts as we know them. Can the DNA within the biological world be accounted for by naturalistic mechanisms, or are we forced by current knowledge (science) to invoke a creator?

A   Built-in   Evolution   Preventative

It has recently been discovered that when DNA is injured by a mutagenic agent--its "letter" sequence is altered by x-rays, u-v light, etc.--the normal sequence is often restored by a biochemical first aid kit.

There are four different enzymes that serve to mend DNA whenever it is injured. For example, if the DNA base sequence is changed by a mutation from A-T-G-C to A-A-G-T, the aberrant sequence is enzymatically chiseled out and replaced by the original sequence. This mechanism is believed to be responsible for DNA being able to duplicate itself in cell division hundreds of millions of times with no alterations, no errors in the replication of the genes.[18] The DNA repair system is a quality control system.

There is a relationship between the longevity of an organism and the efficiency of the DNA repair system. Thus, long living man has a sophisticated repair system (not perfect, of course), and short living mice have cruder ones. Also, certain diseases are now being linked to disorders in the repair system, i.e., mutations not corrected result in disease.[19]

The coauthors, Hanawalt and Haynes, wrote:

"Thus the existence of quality control mechanisms in living cells may account in large part for the fact that 'like produces like' over many generations."

They further conclude:

"If the repair mechanism were too efficient, it might reduce the natural mutation frequency to such a low level that a population could become trapped in an evolutionary dead end."[20]

The evolutionist depends upon random mutational disruptions of DNA for biological improvement. Waddington wrote:

". . . we know of no way other than random mutation by which new hereditary variation comes into being."[21]

The evolutionist not only depends upon mutational disruptions but claims our very existence is accounted for by them. However, research now shows that existence, i.e., longevity and freedom from many diseases--life--depends upon a DNA repair system designed to prevent mutations--a sort of built in evolution preventative.

The creationist asks: "How can our existence be accounted for by mutations if our existence and sustenance depends upon the efficiency of a system specifically designed to prevent mutations?"

A counter to this argument might be that evolution is not prevented by, but, in fact, proceeds because of a tendency to select organisms with the best repair systems--those best suited for survival.

The creationist feels there is a paradox in this evolution-

18. A. M. SRB, ED.: GENES, ENZYMES AND POPULATIONS (N.Y.: PLENUM, 1973), PP. 223-235.
19. HART, R. AND SETLOW, R.: "CORRELATION BETWEEN DNA EXCISION REPAIR AND LIFE SPAN IN A NUMBER OF MAMMALIAN SPECIES," IN PROCEEDINGS OF THE NATIONAL ACADEMY OF SCIENCE,71(1974):2169; J. EPSTEIN: "RATE OF DNA REPAIR IN PROGERIC AND NORMAL FIBROBLASTS," IN PROCEEDINGS OF THE NATIONAL ACADEMY OF SCIENCE, 170 (1973): 977.
20. P. HANAWALT AND R. HAYNES: "THE REPAIR OF DNA," IN SCIENTIFIC AMERICAN, 216 (Feb. 1967), P. 36.
21. C. WADDINGTON: THE NATURE OF LIFE (N.Y.: ANTHENIUM, 1962), P. 98.

ary counter: How could evolution strive toward a state that would prevent itself? Would not the selection of the best DNA repair systems produce "evolutionary dead ends," as Hanawalt and Haynes said above? How could "A" get to "B" because of "C", if "B" prevents "C"? In other words, how long could one drive from car lot to car lot if each time he bought a new car he selected the one with the smallest gas tank--and finally one with no tank?

In summary, the creationist would insist that the DNA repair systems were functioning best when they were originally created and have since been perverted by mutations. The evolutionist alleges that the DNA repair systems were originally nonexistent and were developed because of mutations and selection.

We must adjudge.

Energy and Information Science

We know countless scientists have spent innumerable hours trying to unravel the code riding on DNA. If so much intelligently directed energy is necessary just to dissect and read the information and code, the creationist asks how much intelligence and energy was necessary to create it in the first place? He concludes that it must have been a staggering amount. Just as it requires more energy and intelligence to invent a complex machine than it does to simply disassemble one already built, so likewise, the energy spent unraveling DNA could not compare with that necessary for its original synthesis.

Through mathematical calculations, the information in a code can be quantified. The quantity of information thus calculated can then be related to units of energy. The more information content in a code, the more energy necessary to form it, i.e., energy is directly proportional to information content:

$$\text{INFORMATION CONTENT} = \frac{\text{ENERGY}}{1}$$

If one could quantitate the exact amount of information in a human, a calculation could be made to determine the amount of energy necessary to form the original human DNA code. Efforts are being made to determine information content in various organisms but science is still far from being able to probe into life with sufficient depth to get exact figures.

Let's venture into a calculation that will be far from precise but may allow us to see the general scope of energy necessary to author the equivalent of human DNA.

Bremermann has calculated the amount of information in the one-celled bacterium, *E. coli*, to be 10^{12} bits. (A bit is a unit of information.)[22] Sagan equates 10^{12} bits of information with 100 million pages of *Encyclopedia Britannica*.[23] (Elsewhere Sagan equates the information content of one human sperm to that in 133 volumes of *Webster's Unabridged (fine print) Dictionary*.)[24]

Humans contain about 1,000 different kinds of cells, with a total of 10^{14} cells in the entire body. Man, in addition to just the ability to reproduce and metabolize, like *E. coli*, has special sense organs of sight, hearing, taste, smell and touch, and mental capabilities riding upon ten billion neurons allowing memory and problem solving. Additionally, he has speech, the ability to perform complex voluntary and involuntary reflexes moderated by hormones and nerves, and several distinct organs with innate mechanisms for functional integration with themselves and other organs.

As an estimate, we'll assume that the production of man requires 10^8 times more bits of information than *E. coli*, or, 10^{20} (10^{12} X 10^8) bits. (It has been estimated that just behavioral characteristics in higher organisms require 10^5 bits, innate languages 10^3 bits and muscular movements 10^3 bits).[25]

If 10^{12} bits of information is equivalent to 10^8 pages of *Encyclopedia Britannica*, then 10^{20} bits would be equivalent to 10^{16} pages of *Encyclopedia Britannica* (10^{20} bits $\div 10^{12}$ bits = 10^8; x 10^8 pages = 10^{16} pages).

If we assume it would take 10 working days to produce one page of *Encyclopedia Britannica*, including research, writing, editing and revisions, then it would take 10^{17} days (10^{16} pp. x 10 days) to compose the equivalent of the information found in one human. (*Webster's Unabridged Dictionary* took 757 edit years to produce, not including the efforts of typists, printers, 200 consultants, photocopiers and clerics.)

These 10^{17} days, or 10^{15} years, dwarf the 10^{10} year estimate for the age of the universe.

An average man requires 50 Kilocalories of energy per hour. Figuring eight hour work days, the production of the information content in human DNA would require approximately 10^{20} BTU's of energy. P. C. Putman, in his book, *Energy in the Future*, computed the total amount of energy used by man from the first time he built a fire until 1950, as approximately 10^{20} BTU's. One would have to burn 380,000,000,000 tons of bituminous coal to yield this much energy, or drop one million atomic bombs of the size dropped on Nagasaki and Hiroshima.

Think of that, if we estimate the amount of human energy necessary to produce the information content encoded upon the DNA of one man, the energy necessary would be equivalent to one mil-

22. H. BREMERMANN, (REF. 2) P. 63.
23. C. SAGAN, (REF. 7) P. 1083B.
24. I. S. SHKLOVSKII & C. SAGAN: *INTELLIGENT LIFE IN THE UNIVERSE* (N.Y.: DELL, 1966), P. 197.
25. H. BREMERMANN, (REF. 2) PP. 64-75.

lion atomic bombs liberating 20,000 tons of TNT each!

If, in the process, our human DNA maker used ten sheets of paper daily he would consume enough paper which if stacked would reach one hundred billion miles beyond the sun! And if we weighed this paper, it would tip the scales at ten million million tons!

Further, if one pencil was used for every 10 days of work on this project, enough pencils would be used to fill 26 cubic miles. Or, put another way, if the pencils were placed end to end, they would have a total length equivalent to six million trips to the sun and back!

The controversy on energy and communication science is as follows: The evolutionist would maintain that any energy necessary to synthesize DNA could be amply supplied by the sun or any other "unintelligent" energy source. The creationist alleges that raw energy is not the only requirement; energy must be intelligently maneuvered to synthesize information, according to the principles of information science. Further, since it requires "intelligent energy" to dissect and read the information in DNA, the creationist stresses that the same ingredient would have been necessary to synthesize it in the beginning.

DNA Probabilities

Scientists are engaged in intense research trying to disclose the exact base sequences in specific genes. Investigators believe such knowledge would allow genetic engineering. Through manipulating the bases in genes, scientists hope to direct future evolution.

These noble aspirations, however, are spoiled by man's meager knowledge of DNA and the cell. Some of the intriguing and baffling problems before science are: What controls the timing of processes within the cell? How does DNA know when to begin cell division? What causes certain genes to be operative at just the right time in embryological development? What causes the replicating mechanism to go awry in cancerous cells? What is the mechanism of aging? These and many other questions remain largely unanswered.

The loopholes in our knowledge of DNA are many, but there is also much known about this giant molecule. One of the primary activities of DNA is the governing of protein synthesis. Proteins are, so to speak, the stuff of life. It is known that DNA within specific genes (*E. coli* has approximately 10,000 genes) dictates certain characteristics. For example, the genes controlling eye color code the formation of varying amounts of melanin pigment resulting in blue, brown, green, etc.

The mechanism by which DNA codes the formation of proteins has been worked out quite specifically: three DNA bases, in sequence, code one specific amino acid. Thus, in order to form a protein of 100 amino acids, 300 DNA bases are needed. (Fig. 31) Protein synthesis is extremely complex, and depends upon the integration of many complex chemicals such as transfer RNA, messenger RNA, ribosomal RNA and various enzymes (specialized proteins that catalyze chemical reactions).

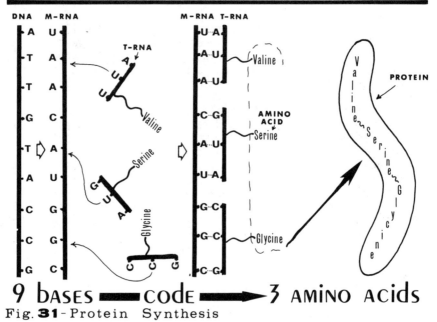

9 bASES ══════ CODE ═══════▶ 3 AMiNO AcidS

Fig. **31**- Protein Synthesis

DNA's role in protein synthesis begins with the coding of M-RNA (RNA is like DNA except the base uracil replaces thymine). M-RNA in turn pairs with T-RNA molecules. T-RNA contains three bases with an attached amino acid. Adjacent amino acids are enzymatically linked and "peel" off the T-RNAs as a protein.

What is known about DNA's role in the formation of proteins will aid us in computing the probability of a DNA molecule arising by chance. In our calculation we will determine the probability of forming sufficient DNA to code the proteins for the smallest self-replicating entity. We must first calculate the number of bases (nucleotides) necessary to code the proteins (124 proteins of 400 amino acids each).

The total number of amino acids in 124 proteins would be: 49,600 (124 x 400). Since three DNA bases are necessary to code one amino acid, the total number of DNA bases (nucleotides) necessary to code 49,600 amino acids would be: 49,600 x 3 = 148,800. (A living entity consisting of 124 proteins of 400 amino acids each is Dr. Morowitz's theoretical smallest organism. In reality, even the simple bacterium, *Escherichia coli*, the common intestinal inhabitant of man and animal, contains at least 3,000,000 DNA base pairs. Thus, it could manufacture 2,500 proteins of 400 amino acids each!)[26]

26. J. BUTLER, (REF. 1) P. 53, 54.

Given the conditions previously described for the chance formation of proteins in the universe, but making every molecule in all of the oceans a nucleotide rather than an amino acid, the probability of forming the one simple DNA molecule would be: $1/10^{89,190}$. (See Fig. 32)

This means $1/10^{89,190}$ DNA molecules, on the average, must form to provide the one chance of forming the specific DNA sequence necessary to code the 124 proteins. $10^{89,190}$ DNA's would weigh $10^{89,147}$ times more than the earth, and would certainly be sufficient to fill the universe many times over.[27] It is estimated that the total amount of DNA necessary to code 100 billion people could be contained in ½ of an aspirin tablet.[28] Surely, $10^{89,147}$ times the weight of the earth in DNA's is a stupendous amount and emphasizes how remote the chance is to form the one DNA molecule.

A quantity of DNA this colossal could never have formed, and so, by these calculations there would not even have been the one chance in $10^{89,190}$ to form the one specific DNA. Is the creationist taking undue liberty in asserting that DNA never did spontaneously arise?

Some, however, might argue this computation is too restrictive, i.e., more than just one DNA arrangement could have coded the first living organism. This is true, but we must emphasize that not just any sequence of DNA nucleotides could be relevant, any more than just any arrangement of letters could form meaningful sentences in any language. Let's deal with this legitimate argument.

If we assume there have been 10^{50} different and viable DNA'a ever in existence (in comparison you might recall there are beleived to be just 10^{12} different proteins in existence now and 10^{52} proteins--not necessarily different--that have ever existed) and compute the probability of forming any of these, the answer is: $10^{50}/10^{89,190} = 1/10^{89,140}$. In other words, if we take 10^{50} different arrangements of DNA and assume any one of these could have coded the first living organism, that organism, the DNA, by the law of probability would still never have arisen. (Fig. 32)

This is not to say evolutionists do not have rebuttals to these types of calculations. Our considerations to this point are meant only to dissect the notion of pure chance.

---

27. A) $10^{89,190}$ x $148,800$ (10^5 APPROXIMATELY--NUMBER OF NUCLEOTIDES
    IN EACH DNA) $=10^{89,195}$ (TOTAL NUCLEOTIDES)
    B) $10^{89,195} \div 10^{23}$ (NUMBER OF NUCLEOTIDES/MOLE) $=10^{89,172}$ (MOLES)
    C) $10^{89,172}$ x 300 GRAMS (10^2 APPROXIMATELY--NUMBER OF GRAMS/
    MOLE OF NUCLEOTIDES) $= 10^{89,174}$ GRAMS (TOTAL WEIGHT OF
    $10^{89,190}$ DNAs)
    D) $10^{89,174} \div 10^{27}$ GRAMS (APPROXIMATE WEIGHT OF THE EARTH) =
    $10^{89,147}$ TIMES LARGER THAN THE WEIGHT OF THE EARTH
28. A.MONTAGU: HUMAN HEREDITY (N.Y.: NEW AMERICAN LIBRARY,1963).P 25.

A WHAT IS THE PROBABILITY OF FORMING SUFFICIENT DNA TO CODE 124 PROTEINS OF 400 AMINO ACIDS EACH, GIVEN 10^{31} "EARTH" OCEANS OF NUCLEOTIDES, AND THESE NUCLEOTIDES LINKING TO FORM DNAS EVERY SECOND FOR 10 BILLION YEARS?

1 THE NUMBER OF NUCLEOTIDES NECESSARY TO CODE 124 PROTEINS OF 400 AMINO ACIDS EACH IS:

(PR) 124 X 400 X 3 (NUCLEOTIDES/AMINO ACID) = $\cdots\cdots\cdots$ 148,800

2 THE PROBABILITY OF FORMING THE ONE DNA STRAND IS:

1/4 X 1/4 . . . 148,800 TIMES = $1/4^{148,800}$ = $\cdots\cdots$ $1/10^{89,280}$

3 GIVEN THE ABOVE STATED CONDITIONS, THE AMOUNT OF DNA FORMING EVERY SECOND WOULD BE:

$\dfrac{10^{78}(10^{25} \text{ STARS X } 10^{6} \text{ "EARTHS" X } 10^{47} \text{ MOLECULES})}{10^{5}(\text{APPROXIMATE NUMBER OF NUCLEOTIDES IN ONE DNA})}$ = $\cdots\cdots$ 10^{73}

4 IN 10 BILLION YEARS (10^{17} SECONDS), THE NUMBER OF DNAS FORMED WOULD BE: 10^{17} X 10^{73} = $\cdots\cdots\cdots$ 10^{90}

5 SO, THE PROBABILITY OF FORMING THE ONE SPECIFIC DNA IS: $10^{90}/10^{89,280}$ = $\cdots\cdots\cdots\cdots$ $1/10^{89,190}$

B WHAT IS THE PROBABILITY OF FORMING ANY OF 10^{50} DIFFERENT DNA MOLECULES, GIVEN THE ABOVE CONDITIONS (10^{50} IS AN ESTIMATE OF THE TOTAL NUMBER OF DNA MOLECULES THOUGHT TO HAVE EVER EXISTED)?

*THE PROBABILITY WOULD BE: $10^{50}/10^{89,190}$ = $\cdots\cdots$ $1/10^{89,140}$

Fig. **32**-DNA Probabilities

DNA - Protein Totals

Actually, neither the probabilities computed for the spontaneous formation of proteins in our last chapter, nor the probabilities computed for the spontaneous formation of DNA, taken individually, give a true picture of the actual probability of forming life spontaneously. Life depends upon the simultaneous existence of DNA and protein.

Enzymes (proteins) are an absolute prerequisite to the linking of nucleotides into DNA helixes. Also, DNA is associated, necessarily, with nucleoproteins in the nucleus of cells. And, in addition, you may recall that the DNA repair systems are composed of enzymes.

If life evolved by chance, protein enzymes must have formed spontaneously before DNA in order to provide the crucial catalysis for nucleotide polymerization. On the other hand, though, functional enzymes could only have been produced by DNA. (In actuality it is believed proteins are older than nucleic acids because nucleic acids require phosphorus which would only have been supplied after the land masses had been eroded for some time.) Hence, we have the situation whereby DNA is dependent for its formation on the very chemicals it alone can produce:

1. Proteins depend upon DNA for their formation
2. But DNA cannot form and, therefore, exist without preexisting proteins.

Sagan called this dilemma a "biological treadmill."

The origin of life researcher, Fox, wrote:

"Some of the key questions of the origin of life concern the primordial sequence of nucleic acid, protein, and cell. Which came first? Whichever postulate has been considered has seemed to leave an unresolved question. One principal dilemma has comprised the two reflexive questions of how nucleic acids might have arisen without enzymes to make them or, alternatively, how enzymic protein might have arisen without nucleic acid to direct the sequence of monomers."[29]

The absolute interdependence between nucleic acids (DNA, RNA) and proteins is likewise confirmed in the following conversation between Buchanan and Haldane:

Dr. Buchanan: "But was the new RNA molecule being duplicated? Is this done in the presence or in the absence of an enzyme?"

Dr. Haldane: "Oh, in the presence, certainly. I don't see how it could be duplicated in the absence."[30]

The interdependence between DNA and proteins creates a seemingly insoluble problem for evolutionists:

1. The existence of (A) is necessary for the formation of (B)
2. But (A) can only exist if (B) has already formed
3. How then could (A) and (B) evolve independently

We have here, in chemical form, the old conundrum: which came first, the chicken or the egg.

If both sufficient DNA to code the 124 proteins, and sufficient protein (124) to house and catalyze the DNA independently evolved and subsequently associated together to form the first living entity, their individual probabilities must be multiplied.

The total probability would be: $1/10^{89,190}$ (the probability of forming the DNA) x $1/10^{78,436}$ (the probability of forming the 124 proteins) = $1/10^{167,626}$, assuming the previous described conditions--one million earths around every star in the universe, etc. This probability is essentially zero, i.e., the chance of forming 124-400 amino acid proteins and sufficient DNA to code that number of proteins, is zero. The origin of life researcher, Kaplan, said if the chance for the formation of life was $1/10^{130}$

29. *S. W. FOX AND OTHERS: "THE PRIMORDIAL SEQUENCE, RIBOSOMES, AND THE GENETIC CODE," IN CHEMICAL EVOLUTION...*, *(REF.17) P.252.*
30. *J. B. S. HALDANE: "DATA NEEDED FOR A BLUEPRINT OF THE FIRST ORGANISM," IN THE ORIGINS...*, *(REF. 16) P. 18; SEE ALSO R.W.KAPLAN:*

"One could conclude from this result that life could not have originated without a donor of information."[31]
Similarly, Borel concluded a probability of $1/10^{50}$ or less would never occur.[32] What then of our probability of $1/10^{167,626}$?
Just to write the number, $1/10^{167,626}$, would require 150 pages of solid zeros, or, about one-third of a mile string of them. To believe this improbability would occur is somewhat akin to hoping to throw tails with a two-headed coin, or hoping to throw tails twice in a row but only being given opportunity to throw the coin once.

> THE TOTAL PROBABILITY OF FORMING THE PROTEINS
> AND DNA FOR THE SMALLEST SELF-REPLICATING ENTITY,
> GIVEN ASTRONOMICALLY LARGE QUANTITIES OF REAGENTS
> AND TIME, IS:
> $$\frac{1}{10^{167,626}}$$

In considering similar probability figures for the origin of life, the evolutionist, Eden, states:
"It is our contention that if 'random' is given serious and crucial interpretation from a probabilistic point of view, the randomness postulate is highly implausible and that an adequate scientific theory of evolution must await the elucidation of new natural laws--physical, physico-chemical and biological."[33]
Known science, proven, workable and trustworthy science, is incapable of explaining the evolution of life, according to Eden. He awaits, as do many others who realize the difficulties in the random postulate, the future discovery of "new natural laws."
Most evolutionists have fallen from the random postulate to the notion that life is biochemically selected and predestined. In other words, they believe that life is the result of the outworking of the natural properties of matter and not dependent upon chance, as we mentioned in the previous chapter. Still others, like the famous astronomer, Sagan, still say:
"The evolution of life on Earth is a product of random events, chance mutations, and individually unlikely steps."[34]
However, biochemical natural selection and predestination is the

"THE PROBLEM OF CHANCE INFORMATION OF PROTOBIONTS BY RANDOM AGGRE-GATION OF MACROMOLECULES," IN CHEMICAL EVOLUTION..., (REF 17) P. 319.
31. R. W. KAPLAN,(REF. 30) PP. 320, 321.
32. E. BOREL: ELEMENTS OF THE THEORY OF PROBABILITY (NEW JERSEY: PRENTICE-HALL, 1965), P. 62.
33. M. EDEN, (REF. 13) P. 109.
34. C. SAGAN:THE COSMIC CONNECTION(N.Y.: DELL, 1973), P. 43.

more popular. This popular rebuttal to chance is the topic of our next chapter.

Could – Should Vs Can–Does

The creationist would say that evolution is not something we would expect. Spontaneous complexification is not something we could predict from any established principle or law in science. But, evolutionists will say, this does not deny that evolution could have occurred. In fact, don't there exist mounds of evidence from biopoiesis experiments, genetic mutations, fossils and natural selection that evolution has occurred, is occurring? Does this evidence not show DNA can form and complexify naturally?

In this chapter we have dealt with the question of whether DNA could and should form and complexify naturally, or whether it should be fixed and accounted for only by a supernatural agent. In later chapters we will see whether evidence actually shows that DNA can and does originate and complexify naturally, or can and does remain fixed and explicable only in supernatural terms.

BIOCHEMICAL
BIAS
7 &
CHEMICAL
NEO-DARWINISM

Probabilities speak decisively against the chance formation of life. Mora has stated:

> ". . . the presence of a living unit is exactly opposite to what we would expect on the basis of pure statistical and probability considerations."[1]

The evolutionist sees this problem and, if he excludes the creation alternative, reasons, "Since I know that life is here, the 'die' used for the naturalistic formation of life must have been weighted, lopsided. Ah, Yes, the chemicals that formed life must have had a natural attraction for one another just as magnets attract north to south and electricity attracts positive to negative. If magnets were randomly mixed they would not assort randomly like marbles, but would be influenced by natural magnetic forces and aggregate in a predictable orderly fashion. Probabilities are only valid if all possible outcomes are equally probable. The whole of biochemistry and thermodynamics points to the fact that not all reactions are equally possible. It is likely that chemicals were selected by one another and by the environment--a natural selection mechanism, Darwin's posit. Chemicals have preferences just as people do. Are people's actions random?".

Acceptance of the Counter

The following quotations will demonstrate this thinking and the modern swing away from double-crossing probabilities to biochemical bias and chemical natural selection:

A. I. Oparin:

> "It has now become quite clear that the origin of life

---

1. *P. T. MORA: "URGE AND MOLECULAR BIOLOGY," IN NATURE, 199 (1963):215.*

was not the result of some 'happy chance' as was thought
till quite recently, but a necessary stage in the evolution of matter. The origin of life is an inalienable
part of the general process of development of the universe and, in particular, the development of the earth."
Elsewhere he has also argued that exact knowledge of the conditions
in the early earth are not necessary to prove evolution, evidence
will come from chemical abilities themselves.[2]

H. Blum:
"Thus while referring to 'chance' as having contributed
to the origin of life--or having shaped subsequent evolutionary history--it should be recognized that the system under study is not a completely random one, but one
in which some events are more probable than others. The
cards are always dealt from a deck that is, to a greater
or less extent, stacked."[3]

J. Keosian:
"The materialist theory of the origin of life from inanimate beginnings recognizes the role of chance in the
interactions of matter in the universe, but views the
overall developments as in no way accidental; on the contrary, it is looked upon as inevitable, almost inexora-
ble, outcome of the emergence and operation of natural
laws."[4]

Elsewhere he wrote:
"Even if we were to accept the assumption that each of
these reactions pre-existed in the 'soup', the chance
assembly of all of them into a functioning unit is inconceivable. There is now every reason to believe that
life was an inevitable outcome of the gradual evolution
of matter and did not have to depend on improbable accidental occurences."[5]

L. Pauling and E. Zuckerkandl:
"It therefore seems safer to be among those who think
that the appearance and evolution of life on earth was
unavoidable . . . This does not mean that one should
deny the intervention of chance, provided the term is

2. *A. I. OPARIN: "PROBLEM OF THE ORIGIN OF LIFE: PRESENT STATE
AND PROSPECTS, " IN CHEMICAL EVOLUTION AND THE ORIGIN OF LIFE, EDS.
R. BUVER AND C. PONNAMPERUMA (N.Y.: AMERICAN ELSEVIER, 1971),
P. 3; LIFE: ITS NATURE, ORIGIN AND DEVELOPMENT (EDINBURGH: OLIVER
AND BOYD, 1967), P. 119.*
3. *H. BLUM: TIME'S ARROW AND EVOLUTION (PRINCETON: PRINCETON U.,
1968), P. 154.*
4. *J. KEOSIAN: "THE ORIGIN OF LIFE PROBLEM--A BRIEF CRITIQUE,"
IN MOLECULAR EVOLUTION: PREBIOLOGICAL AND BIOLOGICAL, EDS. D. L.
ROHLFING AND A. I. OPARIN (N.Y. : PLENUM PRESS, 1972), P. 14.*
5. *J. KEOSIAN: THE ORIGIN OF LIFE (N.Y. : REINHOLD, 1968) p. 78*

not misconstrued."[6]

Bernal:

"This answer would seem to me, combined with the knowledge that life is actually there, to lead to the conclusion that some sequences other than chance occurences must have led to the appearance of life as we know it."[7]

Scientists see the biases at the chemical level as being equivalent to natural selection on the species level. Darwin advanced natural selection as part of the mechanism by which organisms slowly ascended the evolutionary ladder. Assuming Darwin's ideas correct, molecular biologists then apply what they believe to be natural law (natural selection) to the sphere of chemical interactions, as can be seen by these quotations:

A. Szent-Gyorgyi:

"The usual answer to this question is that there was plenty of time to try everything. I could never accept this answer. Random shuttling of bricks will never build a castle or a Greek temple, however long the available time. A random process can build meaningful structures only if there is some kind of selection between meaningful and nonsense mutations."[8]

Orgel:

"It is very hard to avoid using words that suggest purpose when describing the wonderfully adapted structures that occur in the living world . . . Why are we tempted to use these 'loaded' words when describing what, after all, are only the consequences of errors in the process of nucleic acid replication? . . . Perhaps we should agree to use the verb 'to naturally select' in such situations."[9]

R. W. Kaplan:

"The apparatus must consist of a series of proteins as well as nucleic acids with the 'right' sequences. The only source of these functional patterns could have been chance, i.e. polymers with a large variety of random sequences, and selection of the right ones from this mass of random polymers by trial and error, i.e. Darwin's mechanism."[10]

6. L. PAULING AND E. ZUCKERKANDL: "CHANCE IN EVOLUTION--SOME PHILOSOPHICAL REMARKS," IN MOLECULAR EVOLUTION . . . ,(REF. 4) P. 126.
7. J.D. BERNAL IN THE ORIGINS OF PREBIOLOGICAL SYSTEMS AND THEIR MOLECULAR MATRICES, ED. S.W. FOX (N.Y. : ACADEMIC, 1965), P. 53.
8. A. SZENT-GYORGYI: "THE EVOLUTIONARY PARADOX AND BIOLOGICAL STABILITY," IN MOLECULAR EVOLUTION . . . ,(REF. 4) P. 111.
9. L.E. ORGEL: THE ORIGINS OF LIFE: MOLECULES AND NATURAL SELECTION (N.Y. : JOHN WILEY AND SONS, 1973), P. 182.
10. R. W. KAPLAN: "THE PROBLEM OF CHANCE IN FORMATION OF PROTOBIONTS BY RANDOM AGGREGATION OF MACROMOLECULES," IN CHEMICAL EVOLUTION . . . ,(REF. 2) P. 320.

The creationist challenges these escape routes of biochemical bias and natural selection. Are they legitimate or are they proposed simply to evade the carnivorous effect of probability calculations? First let's consider the notion of biochemical bias.

Biochemical Bias

There is no question but that molecules vary in their reactivities and that the spontaneous combination of biomonomers into polymers is not entirely random. Some molecules like to combine with certain kinds of molecules better than others. Thus, if molecule A prefers molecule B more than itself or molecules C and D; and C likes molecule D better than itself or A and D, and if we put all of these molecules in a bag and shake them, we would expect to get certain predictable combinations (A to B, C to D) rather than a random assortment. (Fig. 33)

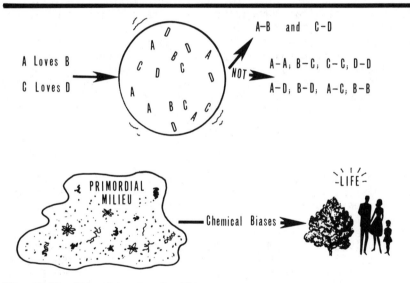

A Loves B

C Loves D

A-B and C-D

NOT → A-A; B-C; C-C; D-D

A-D; B-D; A-C; B-B

PRIMORDIAL MILIEU —— Chemical Biases ➤ LIFE

Fig. **33** – Biochemical Bias

*If molecule **A** prefers to link to molecule **B**, and molecule **C** prefers to link to molecule **D**, then if a batch of these is mixed, one would expect to obtain **A-B** and **C-D** combinations and not a random assortment of every possible combination. The evolutionist sees this as the way the chemicals that comprise life, and life itself, were originally formed, i.e., spontaneous generation was not a random event, rather a biased predestined process.*

Bias can overcome random arrangements only if the affinities are strongly preferential. In other words, A must really love B not just passively like it a little more than C or D. If A likes

B, but is promiscuous and will with little difficulty link to itself or C, or D, then the results of shaking the bag will closely
approximate randomness.

Do the submolecules of the large polymers of life show this
preferential love? Yes and no.

Yes, under appropriate conditions sugars, phosphates and
bases like--love--to form the nucleotide units of DNA; the heterocyclic base, guanine, loves to link with cytosine in preference
to adenine or thymine, and adenine loves thymine to the exclusion
of cytosine or quanine; amino acids love to form proteins; sugars
love to form polysaccharides; fatty acids love to link to glycerol
to form lipids. Thus, the essential constituents of life--nucleic
acids, proteins, carbohydrates and fats--love to form naturally.
Their formation has been observed over and over in the laboratory.
This is indeed a credit to the evolutionary argument. Many creationists in the past thought the formation of any of these chemicals of life outside of a living organism would be impossible.

No, to the question above, in that there are no molecular
preferences that are known to produce information like that found
riding on biological DNA and protein. The creationist would argue
that the evolutionist has merely shown that the chemicals of life
will form under "appropriate" artificial experimental conditions,
conditions of questionable relevancy to spontaneous origins. The
evolutionist has simply shown, so to speak, that letters can be
put on paper. The question is how do the letters order themselves
into sequences carrying information without intelligent manipulations? Put another way, the chemical biases the evolutionist
cites merely show that lettered beads can be put on a string.
These biases don't explain the real issue, i.e., how could the
beads automatically arrange themselves into codes and information?

In reality, no process is totally random. Even in our coin
flipping example heads could not have been perfectly weighted, air
movements could prejudice some throws, and the way in which we
held the coin would likewise influence the outcome. By actually
flipping the coin several thousand times we could determine by
the degree of variance from 50% heads to 50% tails, the degree of
bias involved. But such variance would only be a few percentage
points at the most. If the results showed 51% heads and 49% tails,
would it then be fair to conclude that we could throw 100% heads
and 0% tails? Certainly not. In like manner, the creationist
would ask if it is proper to extrapolate from small biases in chemical syntheses to cyclopedic arrangements of biomonomers?

Mora has synthesized sugars in the laboratory and found that
the polymers were entirely random and unlike the order found in
the large sugar molecules of life.[11] Schramm has found the sequence of spontaneously linked nucleotides are likewise completely

---

11. *P.T. MORA: "RANDOM POLYCONDENSATION OF SUGAR," IN THE ORI-
GINS . . . ,(REF. 7) P. 281-288.*

random.[12] And Fox has claimed certain degrees of order in proteinoids he has formed, yet the order therein is not meaningful
biologically nor found in sequences of amino acids from living
tissue.[13]

Aside from the fact that there is no evidence for bias producing codes and information, the creationist suggests that there
is a fallacy in even suggesting biochemical bias as the mechanism
originating life. He reminds us that life depends upon the sequence of repeating subunits. There are only four DNA letters,
how could molecular preferences dictate various sequences of these
four letters to form instructions for the myriads of different
functions within organisms? If there were preferences, then only
one word would repeat itself over and over. How could the repetition of one word yield the prodigious information found in even
a simple clam? If bias produced a sequence, it would produce only
one sequence, one monotonous simple organism. But life exists in
tremendous complexity and abundant structural and functional variations.

The same argument applies to proteins which are made up of
some 20 repeating subunits. If there were biochemical bias to the
degree that evolutionists would suggest, then all life should be
simple (although simplicity and life are opposites), and be similar or the same. But it is not.

The sequence of nucleotides in DNA and the sequence of amino
acids in proteins are sequences of language . . . language that
imparts meaningful information for the accomplishment of purposeful work.

If the letters of any language were prejudiced as to whom
they would associate with, then only one or a few words could be
spelled. For example, if the English letter C only liked E and
we shook a bag of letters, we could expect to get words with C
next to E like: "cell," or "accept," or "accelerate," but not
other words where C and E are not linked: "cattle," "cute," or
"chives." We see the possibilities becoming even more restricted
as we define other biases: A likes D, K likes O, M likes U. With
these biases we now cannot form such words as "know," "ominous,"
"asked," etc. If we were to continue with a description of biases,
our language would be restricted to only a few meaningful words
and several arrangements of letters that are not words,e.g. "KOMU,"
"DAOK," etc.

If we applied this thought to DNA formation and defined the
chemical biases as: adenine likes thymine on its right and guanine
on its left (T-A-G), guanine likes adenine on its right and cytosine on its left (A-G-C), cytosine likes (G-C-T) and thymine likes
(C-T-A); then a spontaneously formed DNA molecule would look like

12. *G. SCHRAMM: "SYNTHESIS OF NUCLEOSIDES AND POLYNUCLEOTIDES WITH
METAPHOSPHATE ESTERS," IN THE ORIGINS. . . ,(REF. 7) P. 305, 307.*
13. *H. H. PATTEE: "THE RECOGNITION OF HEREDITARY ORDER IN PRIM-
ITIVE CHEMICAL SYSTEMS," IN THE ORIGINS. . . ,(REF. 7) P. 399.*

this: A-G-C-T-A-G-C-T-A-G-C-T-A-G-C-T-A-G-C-T-etc. Rather boring, right? This is nothing but the repetition of one word. The sequence could hardly compare to the magnitude of the information in one bacterial cell--100 million pages of *Encyclopedia Britannica*
The sequence could hardly be considered information at all.

The creationist sees biochemical bias adding to, not relieving the evolutionist's dilemma:

1. If proteins and DNA molecules were formed by random processes (no biases) then no life could form--by the evolutionists own admission.
2. If DNA letters show preferences in the DNA chain and amino acids show preferences in proteins, then all DNA would be the same, and all protein would be the same. But life is diverse. Furthermore, the repetition of one or a few words could not account for the staggering complexity characteristic of all life.

The creationist raises other logical questions if the argument is advanced that the evolutionary urge lies within the molcules themselves: (1) From where would the atoms get the inherent ability, the "design" to evolve? (2) Why have the elements themselves not evolved, i.e., why do carbon atoms stay carbon atoms, and further, why do protons, neutrons and electrons not change? If evolution is a universal natural materialistic process, then no part of matter should be exempt from undergoing spontaneous complexification. (3) A well known principle in physics is the Heisenberg principle of uncertainty. The principle basically argues that the movement of electrons and atoms is a random process.[14] If the atom is governed by random processes, how could there be biochemical bias? If the law of the atom is randomness how can we cite the atom as the source of order?

Biochemical Neo-Darwinism

Some evolutionists would counterclaim that chemical bias only accounts for the building up of biochemicals, but that mutations and natural selection (neo-Darwinism) account for the development of information, higher organization and the great diversity among living forms. However, although this argument is usually advanced by the evolutionary physicist and chemist, it is rejected by evolutionists more familiar with the meanings of natural selection and mutation.

Dobzhansky, in speaking to a group of "origin of lifers," implored:

"Natural selection is differential reproduction, organ-

---

14. R. B. LINDSAY: "PHYSICS--TO WHAT EXTENT IS IT DETERMINISTIC?"
IN *AMERICAN SCIENTIST*, 56 (1968): 100.

ism perpetuation. In order to have natural selection, you have to have self-reproduction or self-replication and at least two distinct self-replicating units of entities . . . I would like to plead with you, simply, please realize you cannot use the words 'natural selection' loosely. Prebiological natural selection is a contradiction of terms."[15]

Gavaudan is also hesitant about applying natural selection to prebiological systems:

"But we have many doubts about the validity of the generalized application of the biological concept of natural selection to inanimate systems."[16]

And Mora also argues natural selection cannot apply to lifeless systems. He contends that at the molecular level there is only selection in the passive physico-chemical sense with the end result of--in the absence of reproductive ability--degradation.[17]

Blum concurs that natural selection cannot be given credit until reproduction is possible:

"The basis for evolution by natural selection should have been laid as soon as there was the possibility of persistent reproducible variations in pattern . . ."

To invoke natural selection prior to reproduction, according to Blum:

". . . postulates the prior existence of that for which the origin is sought."[18]

In other words, "chemical natural selection" begs the question.

Natural selection is the mechanism that "chooses" the most fit organisms in a particular environment to serve as progenitors for an adapted (more fit for survival) population. However, there can be no transmission of adapted "chosen" characteristics without reproduction. One chemical may be more fit than another in a particular environ, but its end result is degradation, dissolution, not the production of a population of more fit progeny that can perpetuate the beneficial characteristic.

The assumption is made that mutations and natural selection have caused the evolution of life from the cell to man. Then application is made of what is believed to be an all-pervading phenomenon--neo-Darwinism--to the molecular level. However, neo-Darwinism cannot operate on non-reproducing systems, by definition. The creationist alleges, as well as do many evolutionists, that invoking neo-Darwinism at the chemical level is, therefore, name dropping.

---

15. T. DOBZHANSKY IN *THE ORIGINS.* . . ,*(REF. 7) PP. 309, 310.*
16. P. GAVAUDAN: "THE GENETIC CODE AND THE ORIGIN OF LIFE," IN *CHEMICAL EVOLUTION.* . . ,*(REF. 2) P. 444.*
17. P.T. MORA: "URGE AND MOLECULAR BIOLOGY," IN *NATURE 199 (1963): 215.*
18. H. BLUM; (REF. 3) PP. 171, 165.

In spite of the adversities from probabilities and then from the notion of biochemical bias and chemical neo-Darwinism, evolutionists have much confidence that further reductionistic study will reveal an evolutionary explanation for the origin of life. Some evolutionists feel all problems dissipate with the insertion of enough time. There is almost a unanimous hesitancy to insert a creator in unexplainable holes when all the holes may represent is a present lack of knowledge.

Most everyone agrees that probabilistic considerations speak strongly against the formation of life. Nevertheless, life is here! Something has made probabilities look moronic. Was it time? Was it minute chemical abilities which we will elucidate with further reductionistic study? Or, was it an intelligent creator?

8 REDUCTIONISM

The purpose of science is to gain and apply knowledge. Usually, enlightment as to how this or that works is dependent upon a study of component parts. Thus we find knowledge and understanding increasing with the degree to which the scientist is able, either directly or indirectly, to observe the tiny, the miniscule, the itsy bitsy. Cadavers are dissected, tissues are sectioned for microscopic examination, individual cells are teased apart, inner microstructure is observed by electron microscopy, and laboratory analyses are performed on component chemicals.

We term the process by which science attempts to understand structure and how and why things work, through disassembling and examining the small, reductionism. Reductionism is largely responsible for the colossal amount of knowledge that has been stockpiled in the last century. As the technological means for exploring the diminutive increased, man's knowledge, understanding and command of the physical and biological worlds likewise grew.

For example, a real understanding of heredity was not attainable until scientists could fully apply reductionism: (1) The light microscope revealed the relationship of the chromosomes to cellular division; (2) Electron microscopy allowed visualization of genes and even DNA molecules within the chromosomes; (3) Chemical analyses, X-ray diffraction studies and various electronic analytical machines have revealed the specific structure of DNA, obligatory base pairing, and the roles of DNA, R-RNA, M-RNA, T-RNA, and various enzymes in genetics and heredity. Vague heredity terms like "unit" and "factor" were replaced with chemical jargon.

Is Life Reducible ?

This is all fine, you may say, but how does this commentary speak to the issue of origins? This way. Materialistic science attempts to use reductionism to explain the origin of life. Evolutionists are bent on demonstrating that life can be accounted for by a more complete and precise knowledge of the structure of, and the physical laws governing the small. As we noted in the previous chapter, any present difficulties in evolutionary interpretations are trusted to vanish upon further reductionistic study.

Keosian, puts it this way:

> "We have made a mystical concept of life . . . life is often looked upon as something more than the chemical systems that manifest the properties characterized by that term. This is a result of our holding tenaciously to old ways of thinking . . ."[1]

And, now, with a little embellishment from Gaylord Simpson:

> "There is no reason to postulate a miracle. Nor is it necessary to suppose that the origin of the processes of reproduction and mutation was anything but naturalistic. That is, study of these basic functions in existing organisms indicates that their novelty lay only in the organization or state of matter and its surroundings, and not in the rise of any new property or principle, physical or nonphysical. Once this point is established the origin of life is stripped of all real mystery . . ."[2]

Faith in reductionism is not without merit. Hasn't reductionism removed the mystical religious aura from fire, disease, anatomy, reproduction, physiology, chemistry and astronomy? Yes, it has. "Then likewise," the materialist argues, "cannot reductionism remove the question of the origin of life from the supernatural? Indeed, cannot life be accounted for by the laws governing the minute?"

The evolutionist argues that life does not transcend the laws of chemistry and physics and that life is, in fact, accounted for by these laws. He argues that life is merely physical, totally explainable in terms of natural spontaneous processes. If that be the case, then we could consider life a physical machine--it has all the properties of a machine plus some. If life is a machine, then arguments regarding a machine's origin can likewise apply to the origin of life.

Reductionism, however, is useful only for explaining how and why an existing machine operates and how it is structured. An understanding of the origin of the machine is not revealed through an uderstanding of its component parts or the laws governing those parts. Science describes structure and function, not origin, i.e., understanding the operation or structure of something does not tell us how it originally got there.

---

1. J. KEOSIAN: *THE ORIGIN OF LIFE* (N.Y.: REINHOLD, 1968), P. 88.
2. G. G. SIMPSON: *THE MEANING OF EVOLUTION* (N.Y.: YALE UNIVERSITY 1967), PP. 16, 17.

Speaking to this, Polanyi, a British scientist and philosopher, states:

> "Machines seem obviously irreducible, since they have comprehensive features that are not due to a spontaneous integration of physical and chemical forces. They do not come into being by physical-chemical equilibration, but are shaped by man."[3]

In other words, a machine operates consistent with physical laws, but is not accounted for by them. Man, mind, intelligence, are necessary for a machine's formation and thus account for its existence.

Life characteristically shows design, complexity, and, in addition, its component molecules carry information. As a book cannot be accounted for by a knowledge of constituent atoms, ink or cellulose, and a painting cannot be accounted for by its canvas and paint, and a song cannot be accounted for by its individual notes or the principles of musical notation, so DNA and life, it is argued, cannot be accounted for by an enumeration of, say, nucleotides and the chemical laws governing their interactions. A machine is more than a simple addition of the laws of physics, nuts, bolts, screws, grease and oil; and a book is much more than an addition of letters and paper; so life is much more than a simple addition of physical laws and atoms.

The molecular biologist, Mora, contends:

> ". . . the methods of (atomic) science are not sufficient, and they lead to contradiction when we try to explain the peculiar essence of living systems and when we consider a living system as a whole."[4]

And Wigner, in an article showing the impossibility of forming a self-reproducing unit through calculations based upon quantum mechanics, states:

> "The present writer has also been baffled by the miracle that there are organisms--that is, from the point of view of the physical scientist, structures--which, if brought into contact with certain nutrient materials, multiply, that is, produce further structures identical to themselves."

Wigner concludes that life is:

> ". . . a miracle from the point of view of the physical scientist . . ."[5]

Reasoning similarly, Lord Kelvin, the nineteenth century sci-

---

3. M. POLANYI: *"LIFE TRANSCENDING PHYSICS AND CHEMISTRY,"* IN <u>*CHEMICAL AND ENGINEERING NEWS*</u>, *45(1967): 57.*

4. P. T. MORA: *"URGE AND MOLECULAR BIOLOGY,"* IN <u>*NATURE*</u>, *199 (1963): 217.*

5. E. P. WIGNER: *"THE PROBABILITY OF A SELF-REPRODUCING UNIT,"* IN <u>*THE LOGIC OF PERSONAL KNOWLEDGE*</u> *(LONDON: ROUTLEDGE AND KEGAN PAUL, 1961), P. 231.*

entific great, wrote:

> "I need scarcely say that the beginning and the mainte-
> nance of life on earth is absolutely and infinitely be-
> yond the range of all sound speculation in dynamical
> science. The only contribution of dynamics to theoret-
> ical biology is absolute negation of automatic commence-
> ment or automatic maintenance of life."[6]

Kelvin said he was forced to this conclusion by his vigorous studies in physics.

(THE CREATIONIST ASKS, "WHAT BELONGS IN EACH BLANK: TIME,
(NATURE AND CHANCE, OR MIND AND INTELLIGENCE?"

1-NOVEL = GLUE + PAPER + INK + GRAMMAR + STYLE + _?_
2-SONG = NOTES + INK + PAPER + MUSIC NOTATION + _?_
3-MACHINE = METAL + NUTS + BOLTS + LAWS OF PHYSICS + _?_
4-PROTEIN = CARBON + HYDROGEN + OXYGEN + NITROGEN + ENERGY + _?_
5-DNA = SUGARS + PHOSPHATES + BASES + CHEMISTRY + _?_
6-LIFE = MOLECULES + ENERGY + CHEMICAL AND PHYSICAL LAWS + _?_

     To further illustrate the inability of reductionism to explain
origins, let's ask the question about the origin of a typewriter
and attempt an answer through reductionism: (1) First we look the
machine over, noticing its shape, screw holes, keys, knobs and e-
lectrical cord.   (2) We then remove the cover and note the positions and workings of the pulleys, springs, levers and motor. A
good understanding at this level requires schooling in physics,
and electrical and mechanical engineering. (3) A better understanding of electricity and physics requires delving into electronics. (4) To better understand the structure of the various metal,
plastic and rubber components requires expertise in chemistry.
(5) An adequate understanding of electronics and chemistry requires
knowledge of nuclear physics and quantum mechanics.
     At this point we have reached the limit of our reductionistic
abilities. We now, in hopes of understanding the origin of the
typewriter, find ourselves studying electrons, protons, neutrons
and nuclear forces. How now do we retrace our steps to the ques-

---

6. *LORD KELVIN (SIR WILLIAM THOMPSON): "ON THE AGE OF THE SUN'S
HEAT," IN* POPULAR LECTURES AND ADDRESSES *(LONDON: MACMILLAN, 1889),
P. 415.*

tion we set about answering? What does, say, the study of electron spin have to do with how the typewriter got its shape or why the particular relationships exist between the various levers, pulleys, wires, etc.? True, chemistry might explain the structure of the plastic on the keys or the bonding of the imprinted black letters on the white plastic, but how does this type of knowledge tell us why the letters are sequenced as they are on the keyboard--numbers consecutively arranged on the top keys, punctuation on the right hand keys, the sequence of all letters on essentially all type-writers being "Q"-"W"-"E"-"R"-"T"-etc.?

The attempt to explain origins through reductionism is some-what like trying to lift yourself by your own shoelaces. If we work our way back up through the steps we outlined above, the only way we can explain the orderly and purposeful arrangement of the components of the typewriter is to call in an added ingredient outside of chemistry and physics: an outside purposer, an intel-legence, an organizer--intelligence. (Fig. 34)

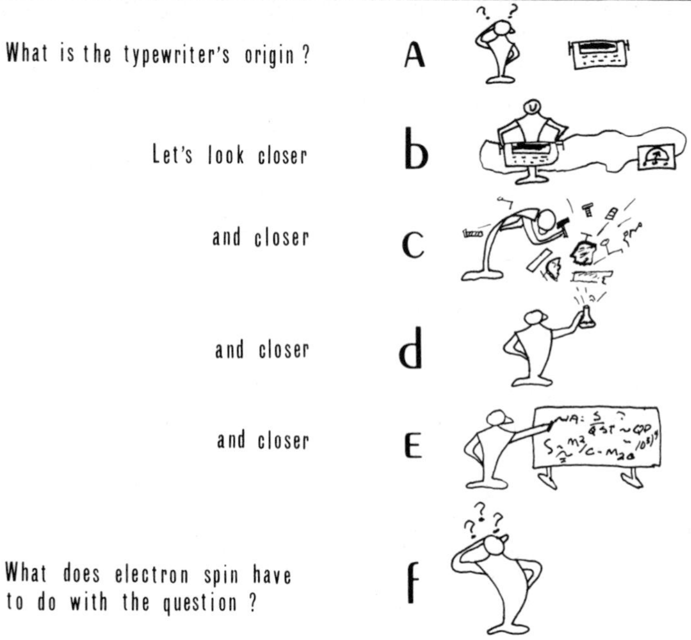

What is the typewriter's origin ?   **A**

Let's look closer   **b**

and closer   **c**

and closer   **d**

and closer   **E**

What does electron spin have to do with the question ?   **f**

Fig. **34**-Typewriter Reductionism
Can the origin of a typewriter be concluded from reductionism? Can the shape of the machine, or the relationships between the compo-nents, or the sequence of the keys be accounted for through nuclear physics or chemistry? Is not an outside organizer necessary? Can the same reasoning be applied to the question of the origin of life?

Life, life processes and machines are irreducible to chemistry and physics. By this argument, the origin of the design and
complexity characteristic of life,transcends physical laws. In
speaking of how reductionism led to the discovery of DNA, Polanyi
stated:

> "And at this point, strangely enough, the discovery of
> DNA, which is so widely thought to prove that life is
> mere chemistry, provides the missing link for proving
> the contrary."

Furthermore, he says:

> ". . . that the formation of a DNA molecule is embodied
> in the morphology of the corresponding offspring, assures
> us of the fact that this morphology is not the product
> of a chemical equilibration, but is designed by other
> than chemical forces."[7]

The creationist submits that the origin of the design Polanyi implies must be intelligent, it must have mind, will and personality.

In essence, then, the evolutionist looks to reductionism for
the naturalistic explanation for the origin of life; the creationist sees reductionism pointing to the need to invoke the supernatural to account for the origin of life.

Is Homo Humus ?

The creationist extrapolates from present cause and effect
relationships to conclude that life is miraculous. He reasons:
1. Machines are supernatural, i.e., their origin, their cause,
    cannot be explained by natural processes--artifacts do not a-
    rise spontaneously.
2. However, machines are not superhuman, i.e., their origin can
    be accounted for only by invoking intelligent men working with-
    in the framework of natural law.
3. Life is superhuman, i.e., its formation is beyond the capabil-
    ities of man.
4. Life is more complex than any machine (an artifact looks cruder
    and clumsier the closer it is viewed; life reveals continued
    order and beauty upon closer and closer scrutiny), therefore,
    if a machine is supernatural, then life must also be super-
    natural, i.e., its origin cannot be accounted for by natural
    processes.
5. Then life is a miracle, i.e., its origin is beyond the capac-
    ities of nature and beyond the intelligence of man.

So the creationist would stress that matter, nature, is simply a property of mind, and not the converse:

---

7. M. POLANYI, (REF. 3) P. 66.

What is matter? Never mind!
What is mind? No matter!

In other words, Homo is not humus.

On the other hand, the evolutionist asserts that matter comes prior to and is responsible for mind. But the creationist sees this as saying matter in chaos is superior to mind.

So, and we the jurors must decide: Is life a property of matter, or is matter simply a property of life? Can further reductionistic studies reveal the naturalistic mechanism for the origin of life and overcome probabilities? Does the complexity and design of life speak to its miraculous origin? Which extrapolation is most valid:

1. Reductionistic study has revealed an ocean of truth and in its wake caused the repeated retreat of religion, therefore, reductionism will ultimately explain the origin of life in naturalistic terms?

2. All complex machines transcend, defy being accounted for by physico-chemical explanations, therefore, life, a complex machine, must owe its existence to intelligence.

Staying in tune with our prescribed methodology, is creation or is evolution most consistent with the real world as we know it?

⟨9⟩ TIME

Evolutionists agree that the spontaneous origin of life is highly improbable from a pure statistical standpoint. But, say some, given sufficient time (an estimate of 50,000 years is needed for the rise of a single new species) and repeated trials the evolution of life becomes inevitable. The evolutionist, Wald, dismisses the objection that life could not evolve spontaneously, by asserting that this judgement is based upon the human scale of experience and does not take into consideration the vast geological time available for the process. He states:

> "Time is in fact the hero of the plot. The time with which we have to deal is of the order of two billion years. What we regard as impossible on the basis of human experience is meaningless here. Given so much time, the 'impossible' becomes possible, the possible probable, and the probable virtually certain. One has only to wait: time itself performs the miracles."[1]

The biologist, Leo Koch, agrees that given sufficient time,

> ". . . the highly improbable occurs regularly and indeed is inevitable."[2]

Urey argues:

> "However, the evolution from inanimate systems of biochemical compounds, e.g., the proteins, carbohydrates, enzymes and many others, of the intricate systems of reactions characteristic of living organisms, and the truly remarkable ability of molecules to reproduce themselves seems to those most expert in the field to be almost im-

---

1. G. WALD: "THE ORIGIN OF LIFE," IN THE PHYSICS AND CHEMISTRY OF LIFE (N.Y.: SIMON AND SCHUSTER, 1955), P. 12.
2. LEO KOCH: "VITALISTIC--MECHANISTIC CONTROVERSY," IN SCIENTIFIC MONTHLY, 85 (1957):250.

possible. Thus a time from the beginning of photosyn-
thesis of two billion years may help many to accept the
hypothesis of the spontaneous generation of life."[3]
Keosian summarizes the attitude of mechanists (evolutionary
materialists):
"The mechanists were not discouraged by the enormous span
of time required for this chance event. They point out
that, given enough time, the most improbable event becomes a statistical certainty."[4]
Blum wrote:
"The origin of life can be viewed properly only in the
perspective of an almost inconceivable extent of time."[5]
It is no secret that evolutionists worship at the shrine of
time. There is little difference between the evolutionist saying
"time did it" and the creationist saying "God did it." Time and
chance is a two-headed deity. Much scientific effort has been expended in an attempt to show that eons of time are available for
evolution. Man, the planets, the universe, the galaxies and matter
are labeled as vanishingly old by geological and radioactive dating
methods. Time is not spoken of in terms of mere decades or centuries, but as millions, sextillions, quintillions, "multiquad-
rupledoopleillions" and what have you. The evolutionist says
time is all that is needed to accomplish the spontaneous generation of life; the evolutionary physicists, geologists and paleontologists assure him he has plenty to work with.

Time and Probability

For the moment, let's grant the evolutionist the "multiquad-
rupledoopleillions" of years that he feels he has and needs. Does
time, as mentioned by Wald, "perform miracles?"
Time and repeated trials do indeed increase the probability
of improbable events. For example, as Wald brings out, if an
event's probability is 1/1000 and we have sufficient time to repeat
the attempts to obtain the one chance 1000 times, the probability
would increase to approximately 63/100.[6] The probability of each

---

3. *H. UREY: "ON THE EARLY CHEMICAL HISTORY OF THE EARTH AND THE
ORIGIN OF LIFE," IN PROCEEDINGS OF THE NATIONAL ACADEMY OF SCIENCE,
38 (1952):362.*
4. *J. KEOSIAN: THE ORIGIN OF LIFE (N.Y.: REINHOLD 1968), P. 10.*
5. *H. BLUM: TIME'S ARROW AND EVOLUTION (PRINCETON: PRINCETON U.,
1968), P. 151.*
6. *THIS PROBABILITY CALCULATION WOULD PROCEED IN THIS WAY.
SINCE THE CHANCE THAT THE EVENT WILL HAPPEN IS 1/1000, THEN THE
CHANCE THAT IT WON'T IS 999/1000. IF WE ATTEMPTED THE EVENT 1000
TIMES AND COMPUTED THE CHANCE OF NOT GETTING THE 1/1000 CHANCE,
WE WOULD MULTIPLY 999/1000 TIMES ITSELF 1000 TIMES, SINCE, IF WE*

138

attempt remains 1/1000 (since probabilities have no memory), but if the event is attempted often enough the total probability of obtaining the one chance is reduced.

If we threw a coin once, the probability of obtaining heads would be 1/2. If we threw it several times, the chance that we would get at least one head would be increased. This is logical. If someone told you you would receive a million dollars if you could flip a coin and get heads, and offered you the chance to either throw the coin once or one hundred times, which would you do? Of course, you would want to throw the coin one hundred times, since you know the chances (probability) of getting at least one head in one hundred tries is significantly greater than getting the head with only one flip.

Concerning the event whose probability is 1/1000, Wald goes on to show how that if the event were attempted 10,000 times, the probability of the event occuring would be increased to 19,999/ 20,000. The chance that the 1/1000 event will occur has thus become practically inevitable. The goddess of time has indeed performed a striking accomplishment.[7]

This argumentation might lead one to suspect that the improbability of life arising by chance could likewise be overcome by sufficient time. Precisely, this is what Wald and other evolutionists would contend.

Now the creationist steps in and says: "Just a minute, not everything is possible. Even given infinitely long spans of time, will time change rocks to gold, incandescent lights to stars, concrete to asphalt, fans to helicopters or phonograph records into books? Clearly, the line must be drawn somewhere."

How about the formation of life, is it really inevitable given the power of the time goddess?

Sagan would argue yes:

"For example, suppose the probability for the origin of the first self-replicating system in the primitive environment in any given year was 10^{-6}. Then the probability that the origin of life occurs in any given century in that era would have been $10^{-6} \times 10^2 = 10^{-4}$, a small number. But in 10^9 years, the probability becomes very close to one, and we may talk of the origin of life as a 'forced event'--that is, as a highly probable outcome of the chemical interactions on the primeval Earth."[8]

The creationist would echo back that a probability of 10^{-6} is unrealistically generous for the evolutionist. We considered in

WERE NOT TO GET THE 1/1000 CHANCE, WE MUST GET A SERIES OF 1000 OF THE 999/1000 CHANCES. THE PROBABILITY OF NOT GETTING THE 1/1000 CHANCE WITH 1000 TRIES WORKS OUT TO 37/100. THEREFORE, THE PROBABILITY THAT THE 1/1000 CHANCE WILL OCCUR IS THE OPPOSITE, OR 63/100.
7. G. WALD, (REF. 1) P. 12.
8. I. S. SHKLOVSKII, C. SAGAN: INTELLIGENT LIFE IN THE UNIVERSE (N.Y.: DELL, 1966), P. 227.

some detail the probabilities of simple chemical precursors arising spontaneously. Our $1/10^{167,126}$ is a far cry from Sagan's
$1/10^6$. Given unrealistically large time periods, lightning fast
combinations and recombinations, countless oceans of preformed
chemical building blocks, and other very liberal givens, nothing
of significance popped its head from the primordial slime. The
huge improbabilities remained. The chance that even the chemical
rudiments of life could form is so remote that time and countless
trials do not seem to dent the improbability. Time affects these
chances for the formation of life much like a hurdling flea with
a toothpick in hand worries the world's pole vault record holder,
or the increased obesity of a native in Haiti affects the balance
of the earth, its axis and rotations. So the creationist would
concede that time can increase the probability of certain improbable events but insist that time cannot make the impossible inevitable. He stresses that contending that time makes the formation
of life inevitable, based upon the probabilities of coin flippings
and events whose probabilities are merely 1/1000 (Wald), or $1/10^6$
(Sagan), is deception, argumentation from analogy and unjustified
extrapolation.

Oparin, an evolutionist, concurs by writing:
> "It is sometimes argued in speculative papers on the
> origin of life that highly improbable events (such as
> the spontaneous formation of a molecule of DNA and a
> molecule of DNA-polymerase in the same region of
> space and at the same time) become virtually inevitable
> over the vast stretches of geological time. No serious
> quantitative arguments, however, are given in support
> of such conclusions."[9]

Coppedge, a creationist, in his book on probabilities, argues that the time necessary to form one protein is commensurate
with the time necessary for an amoeba, crawling at the breathtaking speed of one inch per year, to move the entire mass of 10^{64}
universes the size of ours one atom at a time across a string
stretched the 30 billion light year diameter of the universe![10]

So, in essence, the question is whether the probability of
the spontaneous origin of life is something like $1/10^6$, or on the
order of, say, $1/10^{1,000}$. If the probability is $1/10^6$, and serious
quantitative arguments can support this, then, for sure, time will
do the rest. But if the probability is $1/10^{1,000}$, a practical
impossibility, then invoking time is merely a placebo. It is up
to us to decide whether to accept the spontaneous origin of life
as a probable or improbable event. Our calculations pointed to
improbabilities. As Oparin said above, "no serious quantitative
arguments" have supported chance origins as probable.

---

9. A. I. OPARIN: *LIFE: ITS NATURE, ORIGIN AND DEVELOPMENT* (ED-
INBURGH: OLIVER AND BOYD, 1961), P. 31.
10. J. COPPEDGE: *EVOLUTION: POSSIBLE OR IMPOSSIBLE* (GRAND RAPIDS:
ZONDERVAN, 1973), P. 120.

Time -- An Enemy of Biopoiesis ?

The biochemical reactions that were to have led to life are reversible. For example, in the reaction:

$$\text{A. Acid} + \text{A. Acid} \longleftrightarrow \text{PROTEIN} + H_2O$$

the reaction could go either to the right, toward synthesis (condensation), or to the left, dissociation (hydrolysis). The prevailing direction depends upon many factors such as energy input, and reactivities and concentrations of the reactants.

Most biochemical reactions outside of the body proceed very slowly toward synthesis, and very rapidly toward dissociation. Hull has calculated infinitely small concentrations (10^{-27}M for the amino acid glycine) that would result from reactions in the primitive earth and how the energy used to form the chemical precursors would more readily serve to their destruction--especially if subjected to time.[11]

In the body, protein enzymes catalyze the reactions to drive them toward synthesis. (Enzymes are known to catalyze as many as 1000 molecules per second.) At biopoiesis, with no enzymes available, the reactions would be in a state of back and forth flux, with the predominate pressure toward dissociation. In other words, amino acids don't normally spontaneously form from atoms and amino acids don't spontaneously form proteins, rather, proteins spontaneously degrade to amino acids, and amino acids degrade to atoms.

With time, no driving upward synthesis would result. If per chance some synthesis would occur, say a dipeptide (two amino acids linked), a tripeptide (three amino acids linked) or a polypeptide (many amino acids linked), time and the reversible reaction would cause their reversion to elementary precursors.

Wald sums up the difficulty:

> "In the vast majority of processes in which we are interested the point of equilibrium lies far over toward the side of dissolution. That is to say, spontaneous dissolution is much more probable, and hence proceeds much more rapidly, than spontaneous synthesis. . . The situation we must face is that of patient Penelope waiting for Odysseus, yet much worse: each night she

---

11. D. HULL: "THERMODYNAMICS AND KINETICS OF SPONTANEOUS GENERATION," IN NATURE 186(1960):693,694.

undid the weaving of the preceeding day, but here a
night could readily undo the work of a year or a century."

Wald sums up this difficulty by saying that he believes it to be
"the most stubborn problem that confronts us."[12]

Similarly, it is conceivable that wind might blow a pile of
toothpicks dumped from a picnic table into an arrangement resem-
bling a model airplane. Given enough time, it could happen. But
if that freak event does happen, would it remain if still subject
to time and gale winds? Would it even complexify? Isn't time
not only the creator, but more efficiently the enemy of the freak
event? Will time not surely destroy the order fortuitously created? The creationist asks: "How then can time be actually cited
as the very cause of the almost infinite complexity of life?"

If other impasses to the spontaneous generation of life were
removed, the equilibrium and reversible status of biopoietic reactions would remain as formidable inhibitory influences, especially if the reactions were subjected to the devastating effects
of sizable time periods.

Scientists are able to adjust concentrations and manipulate
their experimental models to accomplish in the laboratory what
would take spontaneous processes millions of years. In much the
same way, geneticists have millions of years at their disposal to
prove evolution by artificially increasing mutation rates. Evolutionists thus, in the laboratory, have all the time they want.[13]
The creationist would say: "Yes, and please note that given 'laboratory time,' evolutionists have not been able to form life irrespective of the relevancy of the conditions they use." The evolutionist would rejoinder: "Not yet, that is."

The Nature of Time

Just what exactly is time anyway? What is the substance of
this evolutionary goddess that is worshiped without restraint?
Time is not a quantity or entity unto itself. Can you touch it?
Can you feel it, package it, see it? Is not time only recognizable in relation to the running down of something. The spring of
a clock unwinds, runs-down, radioactive clocks decay, and with
time, rocks erode.

The creationist argues that time is only a measure of natural
decay. Time does not complexify, it does not originate or build
up anything without a predesigned "motor," rather, it dissipates,
degenerates, melts, dissolves and removes available energy.

Barnett wrote concerning the equivalence between randomness
and time:

---

12. *G. WALD*, *(REF. 1) P. 17.*
13. *A. I. OPARIN:* <u>*LIFE*</u> *. . . , (REF. 9) P. 284.*

"Time itself will come to an end. For entropy points
the direction of time. Entropy is the measure of randomness. When all system and order in the universe
have vanished, when randomness is at its maximum, and
entropy cannot be increased, when there is no longer
any sequence of cause and effect, in short when the universe has run down, there will be no direction to time--
there will be no time.[14]

The creationist would charge: "Can time start a clock, can
it wind it, can it yield perpetual motion or increase the complexity of anything by itself? The longer the time, the greater the
decay and the lesser the chance for any evolution whatever. Are
not 'evolution' and 'time' contradictions in terms? The evolutionist worshiping time, therefore, is like the Indian worshiping
Zor for rain, only to find out later that he had gotten some names
mixed up and Zor happened to be the sunshine God."

But certainly not all things decay. Machines, houses, cloth-
ing and other human artifacts are constantly being built up. Also, note the growth and complexification in the biological world.
We could measure time by these also.

Does the assembly line production of a car negate what has
been said about the degenerating effects of time? The car in its
production increases complexity because human intelligence is
acting in the process. The production of the automobile is not
natural, it is supernatural, it is human--the product of mind.
Left to nature, no car would ever arise, and, an existing car left
to time and nature corrodes and decays.

The creationist extrapolates: "Likewise, complexification
seen in the growth of organisms is a result of DNA information and
cellular design. Complexification, design and information always
result from the interference of mind, not the action of time. Besides, he reasons, biological growth is not natural, it is superhuman and supernatural--beyond the capabilities of humans or
nature. The question is, could time, prior to the existence of
information or design, complexify, build, create life?"

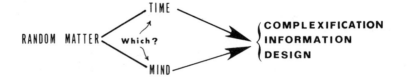

14. L. BARNETT: *THE UNIVERSE AND DR. EINSTEIN* (N.Y.: NEW AMER-
ICAN LIBRARY, 1957), P. 103.

The evolutionist cites chance, nature and time as the driving forces behind evolution. The creationist maintains that these forces all, without interference of mind, result in devolution, degradation, dissipation. Since the creationist feels that time, chance, and nature are insufficient causes for the origin and complexification of life, he sees evolution as a form of magic, a fairy tale under the guise of science. (Fig. 35)

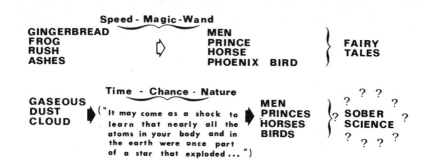

Fig. **35** - Gingerbread Men and Evolution

The creationist sees evolution as a fairy tale spread over millions of years, dubbed with the magical stardust of nature and chance, and then foisted on the public as sober science. (Quote from: K. F. Weaver:"The Incredible Universe," in National Geographic, 145 (1974):609; Diagram modified from D. Gish: Evolution--The Fossils Say No (San Diego: ICR, 1973), p. 5.) Is time, chance and nature sufficient cause for evolution, or are they magical causes?

On the other hand, the evolutionist sees creationism as a "cop out," a naive "God did it" cover-all for any problems in understanding the natural world. (Fig. 36)

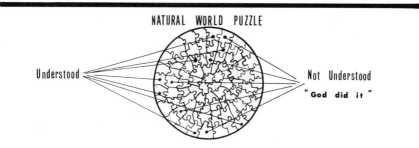

Fig. **36** - God of Gaps

The evolutionist sees creationists, historically and presently, as emotionalists anxious to insert a creator wherever a gap in naturalistic understanding exists--a created god of the gaps.

Is time sufficiently competent to account for the origin of life? In light of the evidences, in harmony with our methodology, we must decide whether time is consistent with a creationistic or evolutionary interpretation of origins.

Both evolutionists and creationists believe evolution is an impossibility if the universe is only a few thousand years old. There probably is no statement that could be made on the topic of origins which would meet with so much agreement from both sides. Setting aside the question of whether vast time is competent to propel evolution, we must query if vast time is indeed available. This subject is certainly not a closed issue as we shall see in the succeeding chapter.

YOUTH OR ANTIQUITY?

In the previous chapter the assumption was made that the evolutionist would have all the time to work with he wished. However, the amount of time available is a subject open to debate. The creationist, aside from arguing that time is not creative, would hold that the universe is not infinitely old.

Creation and evolution are at poles in their interpretations of time:

1. Evolutionism--the universe is infinitely old and life dates into the billions of years.

2. Creationism--the universe is youthful and life dates back only a few thousand years.

There are variances from these positions. I have chosen the traditional extremes. Most evolutionists hold quite closely to the notion of an infinite, or at least a vastly old universe. To most evolutionists, huge time and evolution are inseparable. Evolution is dependent upon time. On the other hand, creation, a miracle, is not at all dependent upon time. However, many creationists have veered considerably from the traditional creationistic view of time noted above. They have changed their position because of intense pressure from evolutionary scientific arguments for vast age. Some creationists now believe in the exact time scale advocated by the evolutionary proposition. Some think in terms of hundreds of thousands, or millions, but not billions. Others suggest that the universe is almost infinitely old but that life is relatively recent.

In this chapter we will attempt to answer the questions:

1. Are the universe and life ancient, or, by comparison, in their infancy?

2. Can we really know the answer?

Biases

The critical eye must be kept sharp when searching for truth on the subject of time dating methods. Time is admitted to be a crucial mechanism to evolutionism. Since many scientists assume the truth of evolution, we would expect their investigations to be prejudicial, i.e., if evolution is true, dating methods that support great ages must be true, dating methods that argue youth must be false.

In this regard, notice the comments by Weisz concerning the early aspirations of evolutionists:

"By this time (i.e. Pasteur's) the alternative to special creation, namely, the idea of continuity and historical succession, or evolution, had occurred to a number of thinkers. Some of these recognized that any concept of evolution demanded an earth of sufficiently great age, and they set out to estimate this age."[1]

Darwin was familiar with Kelvin's work and is noted as having said:

"I am greatly troubled at the short duration of the world according to Lord Kelvin, for I require for my theoretical views a very long period."[2]

Darwin also wrote in the conclusion to the second edition of the *Origin of Species*:

"The belief that species are immutable productions was almost unavoidable as long as the history of the world was thought to be of short duration . . . ."

Finally, Jastrow wrote concerning Darwin's dislike for Kelvin and the need for huge time in order for evolution to occur:

"Darwin developed a personal dislike for Kelvin calling him the 'odious specter' . . . Darwin was reassured by the geologists' new ideas on the age of the earth; he knew that enough time was available, and that was the secret strength of his theory . . . ages were great enough to give ample latitude to the geologists and the biologists for their explanations of the changes in the surface of the earth and the changes in the forms of the creatures that inhabit our planet."[3]

So it is obvious that prejudice has been at work in dating methods. The evolutionist is biased toward vast ages; the creationist is biased toward short earth history. What about the

1. P. WEISZ: *THE SCIENCE OF BIOLOGY* (N.Y.: MCGRAW-HILL, 1959), P. 636.
2. N. MACBETH: *DARWIN RETRIED* (BOSTON:GAMBIT, 1972), P. 109.
3. R. JASTROW: "HOW OLD IS THE UNIVERSE?" IN *NATURAL HISTORY*, 83 (1974):80-82.

dating methods themselves? Don't scientific dating methods prove
an earth history of millions or even billions of years? This is
practically the consensus, but is it true? Let's briefly examine
the methods.

Dating Assumptions

All dating methods designed to date objects beyond the point
of direct verification--beyond the time of historic man (three to
four thousand years B.C.)--are dependent upon a set of assumptions.
The evolutionist would be expected to play down the assumptions
used in his dating methods and headline the factualness of the
calculated huge age. The creationist would be expected to do the
same with calculated short age.

Direct your scrutinizing attention to the following dating
method:

1. According to Malthus, a political economist, population in-
    creases geometrically and each doubling requires an equiv-
    alent amount of time [4]:

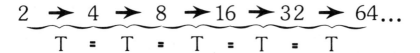

$$ 2 \rightarrow 4 \rightarrow 8 \rightarrow 16 \rightarrow 32 \rightarrow 64 \ldots $$
$$ T = T = T = T = T $$

2. Population increase, other than the present atypical increase,
    is of the order of one doubling every 150 years (figures for
    world populations between 1650 and 1950).[5]   This rate of in-
    crease takes into account deaths from disease, war, pestilence,
    etc.

3. The present world population is about 3.6 billion people.

4. When would the present world population have begun?
    a. 2-4-8-16-32-64 . . . . 3.6 billion = 31 doublings
    b. If one doubling takes 150 years, then 31 doublings would
        take: 31 X 150 = 4,650 years.

5. Therefore, the human race began approximately 4,650 years ago.[6]

---

4. *C. DARWIN: "POPULATION PROBLEMS," IN <u>BULLETIN OF THE ATOMIC
SCIENTISTS</u>, 114 (1958):322.*
5. *W. WEAVER: "PEOPLE, ENERGY AND FOOD," IN <u>SCIENTIFIC MONTHLY</u>,
78 (1954):359.*
6. *THIS CALCULATION IS WORKED OUT IN DETAIL IN: J.C.WHITCOMB &
H.M. MORRIS: <u>THE GENESIS FLOOD</u> (PHILADELPHIA: PRESBYTERIAN AND
REFORMED, 1970), PP. 396-398.*

6. If man's history goes back just 50,000 years (an extremely conservative evolutionary age), and population was doubling every 150 years, the original two would have doubled about 333 times up to now. Therefore, the earth should presently have 2^{333} people, or enough to cover this planet one thousand million miles deep with solid humanity!

Did you discern anything of note in this calculation? Did something about it bother you? It should have. Especially if I were to dogmatically assert the authenticity of the 4,650 year date. Why? Because, as you probably saw, there were key and questionable assumptions used in the calculation. For example, how do we know for sure that population always geometrically increases? How do we know that the 150 years per doubling is accurate throughout time? If these assumptions cannot be validated, could the conclusion based upon these assumptions be valid?

I use this calculation because of its shock valve. Its results are in striking contrast to dates we have been conditioned to accept. I have found that the presentation of this dating method is an effective tactic for awakening an audience that has been lulled to sleep. After the calculation is spread upon a blackboard you should see the hands fly up and hear the menacing questioning begin.

Hands also raise intimidatingly when other dating methods that testify to an age of the earth, solar system and life, on the order of thousands of years, rather than millions and billions, are discussed. Methods suggesting youth are admittedly based upon a set of assumptions which, of course, the evolutionist will--and should--quickly and anxiously point out.

Any dating method dealing with events in the remote past is like a chain. All of the links represent assumptions. The date that the links are fastened to will only be as strong as the weakest of the links. It is proper and necessary to examine the strength of links in dating methods that show youth, but, is it not also right and proper to do the same with dating methods that show vast antiquity? (Fig. 37)

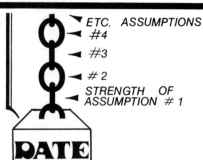

Fig. **37** - Dating Assumptions

The validity of any calculated date can be no stronger than the weakest assumption used in the calculation.

A common dating method that occasionally shows life to have great age, is the radiocarbon technique:

1. Radioactive carbon is formed from the action of cosmic rays on the nitrogen in the atmosphere.

2. C-14, in turn, combines with oxygen to form carbon dioxide which is then incorporated into plant and animal structures.

3. At death, no more C-14 is assimilated into tissues, and that present in organisms decays into nonradioactive materials.

4. Since the present level of C-14 in living tissue is known, and it is also known that 1/2 of the C-14 in a sample will decay in about 5,600 years, then to determine the age of a sample of organic material we simply measure the amount of C-14 left.[7]

For example, let's say the C-14 measured in a piece of bone is found to be 1.5 radioactive units (hypothetical units for this illustration). Since life today has an average of 24 radioactive units (hypothetical), and the animal from which the bone came likewise must have had 24 units at the moment of death, 22.5 radioactive units of C-14 have decayed (24U-1.5U=22.5U). One-half of C-14 will decay every 5,600 years (1/2 life). Therefore, C-14 has halved in quantity four times. The age of the sample would be: 4 halvings X 5,600 years = 22,400 years. (Fig. 38)

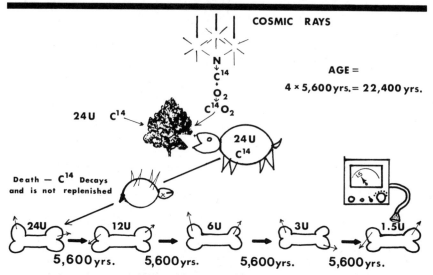

Fig. **38** - C-14 Dating Method
If we assume an equilibrium concentration of C-14 of 24 U, a bone found with 1.5 U would, therefore, be 22,400 years old.

7. W. F. LIBBY: <u>RADIOCARBON DATING</u> (CHICAGO: UNIVERSITY OF CHICAGO, 1952).

Can you see the assumptions in this method? They're there, oodles of them. Here are a few:

1. Since C-14 is formed as a result of cosmic ray influx, how do we know cosmic ray influx has always been constant, thus yielding a constant concentration of C-14 in the atmosphere over the time period in question?

2. A corollary of (1) is: Can we be sure that the concentration of C-14 in life is the same today as it has been in the past?

3. Has the 1/2 life of C-14 been accurately determined?

4. Has the decay of C-14 varied in rate?

5. Has there been contamination of the sample by extraneous C-14?

6. Has atmospheric nitrogen, the precursor to C-14, been constant?

7. Has any of the original C-14 been leached out by physical agencies?

8. Is the instrumentation precise and does the technique always yield uniform results?

That these C-14 assumptions are very real, and one is not just blowing hot air when he calls into question radioactively determined dates, we cite the critical words of the American specialist in varved clay chronology, Ernst Antevs:

"In appraising C-14 dates, it is essential always to discriminate between the C-14 age and the actual age of the sample. The laboratory analysis determines only the amount of radiocarbon present . . .. However, the laboratory analysis does not determine whether the radioactive carbon is all original or is in part secondary, intrusive, or whether the amount has been altered in still other irregular ways besides by natural decay."[8]

A laboratory at UCLA, under the direction of Libby, the Nobel prize winner for C-14 dating, issued the following statement:

"Recent elaborate studies have now demonstrated conclusively that the initial activity of C-14 samples and thus the rate of C-14 production has varied with time. Most recently the work of Suess (1965, *J. GEOPHYS. RESEARCH*, Vol. 70, pp. 5937, 5952) has clearly pointed out these variations."[9]

C. A. Reed writes similarly regarding the C-14 method:

"Although it was hailed as the answer to the prehistorian's prayer when it was first announced, there has been

8. E. ANTEVS: *"GEOLOGICAL TESTS OF THE VARVE AND RADIOCARBON CHRONOLOGIES," IN JOURNAL OF GEOLOGY*, 65(1957):129.

9. *"ON THE ACCURACY OF RADIOCARBON DATES," IN GEOCHRONICLE*, 2(1966).

increasing disillusion with the method because of the chronological uncertainties in some cases absurdities that would follow a strict adherence to published C-14 dates . . . What bids to become a classic example of 'C-14 irresponsibility' is the 6000 year spread of 11 determinations for Jarmo, a prehistoric village in north-eastern Iraq, which, on the basis of all archeological evidence, was not occupied for more than 500 consecutive years."[10]

Jueneman notes the possible influence of neutrino influx into our atmosphere and its subsequent absorption by elements causing their instability and decay. Since neutrino influx can vary, then radio-decay could likewise vary. He suggests, concerning the possibility of a large influx of neutrinos in the past, that this

". . . must have had the peculiar characteristic of re-setting all our atomic clocks. This would knock our C-14, potassium-argon, and uranium-lead dating measurements into a cocked hat! The age of prehistoric arti-facts, the age of the earth, and that of the universe would be thrown into doubt."[11]

One could rightly ask why we should believe dates that have not had their assumptions validated when so many dates that can be checked for accuracy are wrong, sometimes ludicrously so. For example:

1. Living mollusks (snails, etc.) have had their shells dated by the C-14 method up to 2,300 years.[12]

2. New wood from actively growing trees has been dated by the same method at 10,000 years![13]

3. Mortar from the Oxford Castle in England was assigned an age by C-14 of 7,370 years, but the castle was built only 785 years ago.[14]

4. Freshly killed seals have been dated at 1,300 years, and mum-ified seals dead no longer than 30 years have been dated up to 4,600 years.[15]

---

10. C. A. REED: "ANIMAL DOMESTICATION IN THE PREHISTORIC NEAR EAST," IN *SCIENCE*, 130 (1959):1630.
11. F. B. JUENEMAN IN *INDUSTRIAL RESEARCH*, 14 (1972):15.
12. M. KIETH AND G. ANDERSON: "RADIOCARBON DATING: FICTITIOUS RE-SULTS WITH MOLLUSK SHELLS," IN *SCIENCE*,141 (1963):634.
13. B. HUBER: "RECORDING GASEOUS EXCHANGE UNDER FIELD CONDITIONS," IN *THE PHYSIOLOGY OF FOREST TREES*, ED. K.V. THIMANN (N.Y.: RONALD, 1958).
14. E. A. VON FANGE: "TIME UPSIDE DOWN," IN *CREATION RESEARCH SO-CIETY QUARTERLY*,11 (1974):18.
15. W. DORT: "MUMMIFIED SEALS OF SOUTHERN VICTORIA LAND," IN *ANTARCTIC JOURNAL OF THE U.S.*, 6 (1971):210.

Hardly then is there reason for C-14 cynical cockiness.

Half-Life Assumption

The most basic assumption of not only the C-14 clock, but also of all other radioactive clocks (potassium-argon, uranium-lead,
thorium-lead, etc.) is that decay is constant and unaffected by
external influences. In other words, it is believed that once radioactive clocks are turned on they keep reliable time. But even
this most fundamental assumption is challengeable.

In the quote above, Jueneman suggests that the rate of neutrino influx into our atmosphere may alter the decay of radioactive
clocks. Actually, the decay of any radioactive mineral can be altered if the mineral is "energized" by being bombarded by high
energy particles from space (neutrinos, cosmic rays, etc.) or from
particles emitted from other radioactive minerals in close association. It has also been demonstrated that radio-decay can even be
altered by physical pressure and chemical combinations![16]

The nuclear physicists, Anderson and Spangler, wrote concerning their observations of the effect of electricity and other environmental influences on decay rate:

> "Under these conditions, one can reach only one reason-
> able conclusion--barring artifactuality, the detected
> emissions are not of the random expectation. The devia-
> tions (of decay rate) are a function of the environment
> . . . we are each convinced that the thesis of decay in-
> dependence and the thesis of 'decay constancy' needs
> considerable revision and reexamination . . . at a mini-
> mum, an unreliability factor must be incorporated into
> age dating calculations."[17]

Alterations in decay rate have been measured in modern laboratories. There is also evidence that decay rate has varied in
the past.

When radioactive elements decay in certain types of rocks,

16. "PRESSURE DEPENDENCE OF THE RADIO DECAY CONSTANT OF BERYLLIUM
7", IN SCIENCE, 181 (1973):1164; J. J. ANDERSON: "NON-POISSON
DISTRIBUTIONS OBSERVED DURING COUNTING OF CERTAIN CARBON-14
LABELED ORGANIC (SUB) MONOLAYERS," IN JOURNAL OF PHYSICAL CHEM-
ISTRY, 76 (1972):3604: H. W. JOHLIGE AND OTHERS: "DETERMINATION OF
THE RELATIVE ELECTRON DENSITY AT THE Be NUCLEUS IN DIFFERENT CHEM-
ICAL COMBINATIONS, MEASURED AS CHANGES IN THE ELECTRON-CAPTURE
HALF-LIFE OF ^7Be," IN PHYSICAL REVIEW C--NUCLEAR PHYSICS, 2 (1970):
1616; R. T. BAINBRIDGE AND OTHERS: "INFLUENCE OF THE CHEMICAL
STATE ON THE LIFETIME OF A NUCLEAR ISOMER, Tc^{99m}," IN PHYSICAL RE-
VIEW, 90 (1953):430. FURTHER REFERENCES ARE IN THESE ARTICLES.
17. J. ANDERSON AND G. SPANGLER: "RADIOMETRIC DATING: IS THE
'DECAY CONSTANT' CONSTANT," IN PENSÉE, 4 (FALL, 1974):34.

for example mica, the particles emitted from the nuclei produce a zone of discoloration known as pleochroic halo. This zone will vary depending upon decay rate. The faster the decay rate, the larger the halo. If decay rate is constant, then we would expect halos to remain constant for the same elements in identical rocks. Although this constancy is popularly believed to be the case, it simply is not true.

Gentry, in a paper presented to an annual meeting of physics teachers, said:

> "Halo radii and the Geiger-Nuttall law are studied carefully with the result that little or no justification is found for the usual arguments proving the stability of the decay constant over geological time from pleochroic halo data."[18]

Joly, from whom most of the data about pleochroic halos has come, concluded that halos do vary and that decay rate may also have varied.[19] The implications that Joly's varying halos have on dating methods is expressed by Kovarik:

> "His suggestion of varying rate of disintegration of uranium at various geological periods would, if correct, set aside all possibilities of age calculation by radioactivity methods."[20]

If decay rate can be changed by bombarding nuclei with high energy particles, if decay rate can change due to chemical combinations and physical pressure, and if there is halo evidence that decay rate has changed over geological time, then the assumption that decay rate does not change, or has not changed, is truly an assumption.

If decay rate can vary (picking just this one assumption common to radio-dating methods), how can we speak about the certainty of radio-time? Radioactive clocks can be no more accurate than man-made clocks which show evidence of having been tampered with: gear size changed, spring tension increased, hands manually advanced, etc. Certainly we could not depend upon a man-made clock showing evidences of such tampering. Similarly, neither can we depend upon radioactive clocks beyond the point that their assumptions can be checked.

The fact that most dates are not "scientific," has almost entirely slipped by the public. We are all guilty of simply assuming as true what others have written or told us about the age of the universe, earth and life.

---

18. R. V. GENTRY: "PLEOCHROIC HALOS AND THE AGE OF THE EARTH," IN *AMERICAN JOURNAL OF PHYSICS*, 33 (1965):878.

19. J. JOLY: "THE AGE OF THE EARTH," IN *NATURE*, 109 (1922):480; J. JOLY: "THE GENESIS OF PLEOCHROIC HALOS," IN *PHILOSOPHICAL TRANSACTIONS OF THE ROYAL SOCIETY OF LONDON--A*, 217 (1917):51.

20. A. F. KOVARIK: "CALCULATING THE AGE OF MINERALS FROM RADIOACTIVITY DATA AND PRINCIPLES," IN *BULLETIN #80 OF THE NATIONAL RESEARCH COUNCIL*, JUNE, 1931, P. 107.

Dating Errors

An analysis of essentially every assumption in every dating method taking us beyond a few thousand years surfaces evident weaknesses and unknowns. But to detail the assumptions and weaknesses in each method should not be necessary if one understands in principle the dependence of accurate time upon valid and verifiable assumptions. The further we go back in time, the older the clock, the less chance we have of substantiating these assumptions and the more likely it becomes that the clock has been tampered with or mechanically deranged.

The evidence that radioclocks have actually been deranged is clear from the many dating errors of objects of known age. We previously mentioned the 6,000 year spread of dates for Jarmo which was known to be inhabited for only 500 years, as well as other C-14 errors. Errors with the potassium and uranium methods are equally striking. For example, lava from Hawaiian and other volcanoes around the world that is known to have flowed within the last two hundred years has been dated by the potassium-argon and uranium-lead methods at thousands of millions of years![21] Surely this demonstrates that the assumptions used in dating techniques are not only truly assumptions, but often truly wrong.

Kerkut has also noted several disappointing errors in various dating results. Some examples are:

1. A deposit in the Colorado Caribou Mine dated by uranium-lead yielded an error of 700 million years.

2. Swedish kolm was dated by uranium-lead from 380 million years to 800 million years.

3. Potassium-argon methods have dated "Cambrian" rocks 200 million years older than a previous estimate.[22]

Read, in a presentation to a California State Board of Education Meeting, revealed the findings of his research in the scientific literature dealing with moon datings. Apollo sample material dated by uranium-thorium-lead, agglutinate, and potassium-argon methods gave ages from two million years to 28 billion years.[23]

21. FUNKHOUSER, BARNES, AND HAUGHTON: "THE PROBLEMS OF DATING VOLCANIC ROCKS BY THE POTASSIUM-ARGON METHOD," IN BULLETIN VOLCANOLOGIQUE, 29 (1966): 709; S. P. CLEMENTSON: "A CRITICAL EXAMINATION OF RADIOACTIVE DATING OF ROCK," IN CREATION RESEARCH SOCIETY QUARTERLY, 7 (1970): 137-141.
22. G. A. KERKUT: IMPLICATIONS OF EVOLUTION (N.Y.: PERGAMON, 1960), PP. 139,140.
23. PROCEEDINGS OF THE SECOND, THIRD AND FOURTH LUNAR CONFERENCES;

We can compare radioactive dating methods to the melting of an ice cube. If we know how fast ice cubes melt and we are presented with a tray of water that is to have been derived from ice, we could calculate how large the original ice cube was and how long it took to melt. But what if we don't know if all of the water we are presented with has come from ice? What if water was already present in the pan before the cube was put there to begin melting? Or what if water was added or removed from the pan during the course of the melting? What if we don't know if the ice cube was melting under the exact conditions we used to determine the rate of melting, i.e., what if the conditions were warmer, colder or windier than the conditions used to determine cube "half-life"? Are we sure that some of the ice did not sublimate, or some of the water in the pan evaporate? Was the water in this cube as pure as the water in the cube we determined cube "half-life" on?

On and on we could go. If one were to argue that the age of the pan could be absolutely determined by ice cube decay he would certainly be on tenuous grounds unless he could answer with certainty each of the questions raised above.

But these questions cannot be answered, or, if answers are available, the clock becomes suspect. For example, in the thorium-lead dating method, thorium is like the ice in our illustration and lead like the water. It has been shown that lead can be added to the clock by free neutron capture from the environment--like adding extraneous water to the tray in our "ice cube clock."[24] Thus, there is no guarantee that the lead measured has all been derived from decay of the thorium. In the potassium-argon clock the potassium is the "ice" and the argon the "water." It is known that the gas, argon, can be easily lost from the clock (giving an age too young), or it can be added (giving an age too old). And such additions and subtractions have been the case for, as mentioned previously, Hawaiian lava flows known to be less than 200 years old have been dated up to three billion years old![25]

Until the assumptions in a dating method are known and scrutinized, the calculated date cannot be given serious consideration. How many who decry the veracity of dates have actually checked out the strength of the links in the chain?

My objective here is to simply point out that tacit acceptance of any date found in bold black type is dangerous. Whether the

EARTH AND PLANETARY SCIENCE LETTERS, VOLUMES 14 AND 17; SCIENCE, VOL. 167; APOLLO 12 PRELIMINARY SCIENCE REPORT; CHART OF FINDINGS AND COMPLETE REFERENCES IN BIBLE-SCIENCE NEWSLETTER, 13 (1975)5.
24. *M. A. COOK: PREHISTORY AND EARTH MODELS (LONDON: MAX PARISH, 1960), PP. 53-60.*
25. *C. NOBLE AND J. NAUGHTON: "DEEP-OCEAN BASALTS: INERT GAS CONTENT AND UNCERTAINTIES IN AGE DATING," IN SCIENCE, 162 (1968): P.265; J. FUNKHOUSER AND J. NAUGHTON IN JOURNAL OF GEOPHYSICAL RESEARCH, 73(1968):4606;A. LAUGHLIN:"EXCESS RADIOGENIC ARGON IN PEGMATITE MINERALS," IN JOURNAL OF GEOPHYSICAL RESEARCH,74(1969):6684.*

date comes from an expert or not, until the assumptions are evaluated and substantiated the date is simply a hypothesis, a proposition, a guess.

Many dates going back about four or five thousand years can be validated by dendrochronological means (tree-ring dating, itself questionable in some instances) or historical means, i.e., archeological and astronomical. Every age beyond that time, be it for life, the earth or the universe, is based upon a set of assumptions that cannot be scientifically or historically substantiated. We say this for the simple reason that the means for checking the accuracy of assumptions--historic man, tree rings, etc.--only go back to about 3000 B.C. [26] Therefore, the resultant dates are similarly not substantiated and cannot be asserted as fact.

"Appearance" of Age

An assumption common to all dating methods showing ages of great antiquity, is that there was no creation nor non-uniform cataclysmic historic earth episodes. If either creation or catastrophies have occurred, then dating methods based on uniformity--all things are proceeding today exactly as they have in the past--are invalid.

For example, if the creation were a sudden complete creation, there would automatically have been the immediate appearance of age. If we looked at the creation one second after: Adam may have appeared a mature man of several years; trees chopped down may have contained several annual rings, or, if no rings, tree bulk would suggest great age; distant stars would have been created along with photons of light thus being immediately visible from earth (The argument that star distances in millions of light years imputes like age to the universe is founded upon a tenuous assumption, namely, the assumption that the universe is Einsteinian. Scientists at M.I.T. and the University of Connecticut have shown through Riemannian curved space astrophysics that "the time required to reach us from the most distant stars is only 15 years.");[27] rivers would contain water in their beds throughout their course; and substances containing radioactive materials may have contained both parent element and daughter decay products in proportions giving the appearance of age on the order of billions of years, yet actually being only one second old! Thus, implicit in creation is the

26.   W. F. LIBBY: "RADIOCARBON DATING," IN AMERICAN SCIENTIST, 44(1956):107.
27.   P. MOON AND D. SPENCER:"BINARY STARS AND THE VELOCITY OF LIGHT," IN JOURNAL OF THE OPTICAL SOCIETY OF AMERICA, 43(1953): 635.

appearance of an age beyond the real age.

Addressing himself to those theistic evolutionists who believe in the literalness of miracles but find it difficult to believe in a sudden complete creation with the appearance of age, the creationist asks, "Would not Jesus' creation of bread, fish, flesh and wine give the sudden appearance of age? Wouldn't it 'normally' require a long period of time for the growth, harvesting, preparation and baking of wheat into bread? Would it not 'normally' require a long period of time for fish eggs to incubate, hatch, mature and grow into adult fish? Does not the healing of any tissue require, 'normally,' quite some period of time for the elements of the inflammatory reaction to mend and regenerate tissue? Is not wine "normally' a product requiring time for the growth of grapes and the fermentation of its juices?"

Actually any miracle--which creation is--would give the appearance of age beyond that which would be required for the same event to happen naturally. Therefore, the belief in any miracle admits the belief in an aged creation.

Creationists say that actual evidence the creation was indeed sudden and complete comes from study of rapidly decaying radioactive elements and pleochroic halos. In this regard, Gentry said:

>"The half-life of polonium 214 is only 164 microseconds. According to one theory of the planet's origin, the earth cooled down from a hot gaseous mass and gradually solidified over a period of hundreds of millions of years. If this were so, polonium halos could not possibly have formed because all the polonium would have decayed soon after it was synthesized and would have been extinct when the crustal rocks formed. ... Unless the creation of the radioactivity and rocks were simultaneous there would be no picture--no variant pleochroic halos. Further, by virtue of the very short half-life, the radioactivity and formation of the rocks must be almost instantaneous."[28]

In further corroboration of the feasibility of a sudden creation, a recent article in *Scientific American* suggested that all heavy hydrogen was made in the first fifteen minutes of the "big bang" in the big bang model for the origin of the universe.[29] And Jastrow agreed with the "extraordinary conclusion that our world began at a definite moment and has not been here forever."[30]

---

28. R. V. GENTRY: "COSMOLOGY AND EARTH'S INVISIBLE REALM," IN *MEDICAL OPINION AND REVIEW*, 3(1967):65-79.

29. J. PASACHOFF AND W. FOWLER: "DEUTERIUM IN THE UNIVERSE," IN *SCIENTIFIC AMERICAN*, 230(MAY, 1974):108.

30. R. JASTROW: "HOW OLD IS THE UNIVERSE?" IN *NATURAL HISTORY*, 83(1974):83.

More evidence of a sudden and complete creation comes from the interdependency of chemicals, organs, cells and tissues in organisms. The creationist sees the interdependency of organisms one upon the other and upon the environment speaking for a sudden complete creation. If there indeed were a sudden creation, would this not affect traditional dating methods?

Furthermore, if there were a world-wide flood, as the creationist would attest, flood activity would raise havoc with dating methods by mixing radioactive elements and speeding sedimentary deposition. The preflood atmospheric water canopy would shield the earth from high energy rays and thus throw off radioactive datings that assume a uniform atmosphere throughout time, e.g., carbon-14 dating.

It follows from this that the only established, factual, substantiated, verified amount of time at our disposal is on the order of a few thousand years. Anyone who needs substantiated vast ages is simply out of business.

Methods Showing Youth

Up to this point, what has our discussion of dating methods established? Have we proven through our exposé of radioactive dating methods that the universe is young? No, we have simply shown that we can't be sure of any age dates. Assumptions are involved that don't allow us to prove youth or antiquity.

However, when dating methods harmonize in showing the earth to be billions of years old, is this not testimony for the earth's antiquity? So what if the methods have a margin of error of a few percent? If rocks are dated ten billion years old, doesn't a ten percent error still leave you with a rock billions, not thousands, of years old?

The reason many dating methods are concordant in showing vast ages is simply because dates that show concordant vast ages are selected. Methods arguing for youth are simply omitted. "This seems a little hard to swallow," says Joe Public. "You mean scientists pick the dates they like and reject others? I haven't even heard of a scientific dating method that says the earth is only a few thousand years old, or that animals, plants and man are likewise only newcomers."

The public has been mental-regulated to believe in vast ages. Where can one go in the literature to even find one credible dating method arguing for youth? Nevertheless, there are many such methods.

I make a listing below. Informed creationists argue these methods in rebuttal to evolutionary datings. All of the methods, however, are based upon a set of assumptions that cannot be substantiated throughout the time of their applicability. Nevertheless, the listing should impress upon us the point that youth can be argued with equal validity to antiquity.

1-OIL GUSHERS

Often, when drilling for oil, a resevoir is tapped that is under
such great pressure that an oil gusher (geyser) results. Studies of the permeability of the rocks surrounding the oil bed
show that any pressure built up should be dissipated, bled off
into surrounding rocks, within a few thousand years. The excessive pressures found within oil beds, therefore, refute the notion of their age being on the order of millions of years and
argue for the youthful age (less than about 10,000 years) of
the rock formations and the entrapped oil.[31] (Many C-14 datings
of oil argue similarly;[32] and the current oil pinch has even
resulted in some backyard experiments producing oil from garbage
in a matter of hours showing that oil in the earth could have
been made rapidly and recently.) (Fig. 39)

2-CARBON-14 DISINTEGRATION VERSUS PRODUCTION

Libby, the winner of the Nobel Prize for his work with
C-14, assumed a vast age for the earth. He assumed that cosmic
rays have been producing C-14 over a long enough period of time
so that the rate of production of C-14 would equal the rate of
disintegration throughout the time for which the method is applied.   Robert Whitelaw, a Nuclear Consultant and Professor
of Mechanical Engineering at Virginia Polytechnic Institute, has
made some interesting calculations based upon comparisons of C-
14 production and disintegration.[33] In reviewing the data from
the scientist Rubey,[34] he found the production rate of C-14 not
equal to disintegration. The significance of this is as follows: If 27 atoms/gm.-min. of C-14 are being produced (Rubey),
and C-14 is only decaying at an average rate of 16.1 dis./gm.-
min. (Libby), then this speaks to a recent turning on of the C-
14 clock--otherwise disintegration-production would be in equilibrium. In other words, if the C-14 clock were turned on 5,600
years ago (one half-life of C-14), there should be presently a
disintegration rate of C-14 equal to one-half the production
rate (27/2=13.5 dis./gm.-min.); if it were turned on 11,200
years ago (2 X 5,600 yrs.) the present disintegration rate

---

31. *M. COOK, (REF. 24) P. 341; P. DICKEY AND OTHERS: "ABNORMAL
PRESSURE IN DEEP WELLS OF SOUTHWESTERN LOUISIANA," IN SCIENCE,
160(1968):609.*
32. *SCIENCE, 116(1952):439,667.*
33. *R. L. WHITELAW: "RADIOCARBON CONFIRMS BIBLICAL CREATION,"
IN WHY NOT CREATION, ED. W. LAMMERTS (PHILADELPHIA: PRES-
BYTERIAN AND REFORMED, 1970), PP. 90-100.*
34. *W. W. RUBEY: "GEOLOGICAL EVIDENCE REGARDING THE SOURCE
OF THE EARTH'S HYDROSPHERE AND ATMOSPHERE," IN SCIENCE, 112
(1950):20.*

Fig. 39 - Oil Gusher

An early Oklahoma well explodes with pressure when an oil bed is tapped.

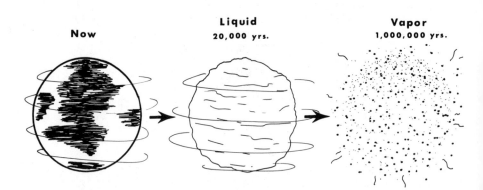

Fig. 40 - Magnetic Decay

If we extrapolate backwards from the rate of magnetic decay measured over the past 150 years, the earth would have been liquid 20,000 years ago, and vapor 1,000,000 years ago. The creationist feels that this means the earth could not be beyond a few thousand years old.

is approximately 16.1. Therefore, the clock should have begun between 5,600 years ago (13.5) and 11,200 years ago (20.25), or approximately 8,000 years ago.[35]

3-DECAY OF THE EARTH'S MAGNETIC MOMENT

Thomas Barnes, in a monograph, discusses the decay of the earth's magnetic field and the relation of magnetic decay to the origin and antiquity of the earth.[36] Based upon figures from 1835 to 1965, the half-life of the earth's magnetic field has been computed to be 1,400 years. Calculating the rate of decay of the magnetic field, and extrapolating backwards, the strength of the earth's field at any point in history can be computed. If we extrapolate to just 20,000 years, the Joule heat generated would probably liquify the earth. If we go back just one million years, the magnetic field would be 3×10^{215} Tesla, which is greater than the magnetism of all objects in the universe and would generate so much heat that the earth would vaporize! Therefore, according to this dating method, the earth cannot be millions or even tens of thousands of years old. Rather, the decay of the earth's magnetic moment speaks to (1) a creation of the earth; and (2) an age for the earth of less than 10,000 years. (We might also add that the magnetic field of the earth influences cosmic ray influx. The greater the magnetic field, the less the cosmic ray influx. Since the magnetic field was greater in the past, the cosmic ray dependent C-14 method would show ages for the past greater than what they are in reality.) (Fig. 40)

4-LARGE STARS

Some stars are so large and bright that it is concluded they could not have existed for billions of years, or even a few million years. Otherwise their initial mass would have been implausible.[37]

5-ATMOSPHERIC HELIUM

The radioactive elements, uranium and thorium, are continually

---

35. *FURTHER REFERENCES CONFIRMING THE DISEQUILIBRIUM BETWEEN C-14 PRODUCTION AND DISINTEGRATION: R. LINGENFELTER: "PRODUCTION OF C-14 BY COSMIC 8 RAY NEUTRONS," IN REVIEWS OF GEOPHYSICS, 1(1963):51; H. SUESS: "SECULAR VARIATIONS IN THE COSMIC RAY PRODUCED CARBON 14 IN THE ATMOSPHERE AND THEIR INTERPRETATIONS," IN JOURNAL OF GEOPHYSICAL RESEARCH, 70(1965):5947; JOURNAL OF GEOPHYSICAL RESEARCH, 74(1968):4529.*
36. *T. G. BARNES: ORIGIN AND DESTINY OF THE EARTH'S MAGNETIC FIELD (SAN DIEGO: ICR, 1973).*
37. *W. A. FOWLER: "FORMATION OF THE ELEMENTS," IN SCIENTIFIC*

Element	Concentration (mg/ml)	Residence Time (yrs.)	E.	C.	R.T.
Li	0.17	2×10^7	Cd	0.00011	5.0×10^5
Be	0.0000006	150	Sn	0.0008	1.0×10^5
Na	10,500	➤ 2.6×10^8	Sb	0.0005	3.5×10^5
Mg	1,350	4.5×10^7	Cs	0.0005	4.0×10^4
Al	0.01	100	Ba	0.03	8.4×10^4
Si	3.0	8.0×10^3	La	1.2×10^{-5}	440
K	380	1.1×10^7	Ce	5.2×10^{-6}	➤ 80
Ca	400	8.0×10^6	Pr	2.6×10^{-6}	320
Sc	0.00004	5.6×10^3	Nd	9.2×10^{-6}	270
Ti	0.001	160	Sm	1.7×10^{-6}	180
V	0.002	1.0×10^4	Eu	4.6×10^{-7}	300
Cr	0.00005	350	Gd	2.4×10^{-6}	260
Mn	0.002	1,400	Dy	2.9×10^{-6}	460
Fe	0.01	140	Ho	8.8×10^{-7}	530
Co	0.0001	1.8×10^4	Er	2.4×10^{-6}	690
Ni	0.002	1.8×10^4	Tm	5.2×10^{-7}	1,800
Cu	0.003	5.0×10^4	Yb	2.0×10^{-6}	530
Zn	0.01	1.8×10^5	Lu	4.8×10^{-7}	450
Ga	0.00003	1.4×10^3	W	0.0001	10^3
Ge	0.00006	7.0×10^3	Au	0.000004	5.6×10^5
Rb	0.12	2.7×10^5	Hg	0.00003	4.2×10^4
Sr	8.0	1.9×10^7	Pb	0.00003	2.0×10^3
Y	0.0003	7.5×10^3	Bi	0.00002	4.5×10^4
Nb	0.00001	300	Th	0.00005	350
Mo	0.01	5.0×10^5	U	0.003	5.0×10^5
Ag	0.00004	2.1×10^6			

Fig. 41- Ocean Dating

This chart, taken from the book, CHEMICAL OCEANOGRAPHY, depicts the residence times of various elements in the oceans. If the oceans were to be dated by these means, their age would calculate all the way from 80 years(Ce) to 2.6 billion years(Na). The creationist concludes that since these figures are based on uniformity(the past is exactly like the present), the discordant dates demonstrate: (1) uniformity is erroneous; (2) vast age or short age can be argued with equal "scientific uniformitarian" ease. (Courtesy of J. P. Riley)

decaying to form helium. If this decay has been going on for billions of years, the atmosphere should contain much more than the present 1.4 parts per million of helium. But it doesn't. In fact, since the present atmosphere contains 3.5×10^{15} grams of helium, and the rate of helium formation is about 3×10^{11} grams/yr., the earth's age, on this basis, would be about 10,000 years.[38]

6-DELTA FILLING

The Mississippi river dumps about 300 million cubic yards of sediment into the Gulf of Mexico each year. If that river were millions of years old, the Gulf would have been long since filled. By measuring the rate of growth of the delta (about 250 feet per year), its age calculates to about 4,000 years.

7-OCEAN CONCENTRATIONS

The uranium, sodium, nickel, magnesium, silicon, potassium, copper, gold, silver, mercury, lead, tin, aluminum, carbonate, sulfate, chlorine, calcium, lithium, titanium, chromium, manganese, iron, cobalt, zinc, rubidium, strontium, bismuth, thorium, antimony, tungsten, barium, molybdenum and bicarbonate concentrations (and many others) in the oceans are much less than would be expected if these elements and compounds were being added to the oceans at the present rate for thousands of millions of years. Some, for example nitrates and uranium, do not break down or recycle like salt. Their small concentrations are then taken as an accurate indicator that the oceans are a few thousand years old.[39] (Fig. 41)

8-EROSION

If erosion has been occurring for thousands of millions of years, why are there still sharp cliffs? Why have not the continents been leveled, the oceans filled and fossils dispersed?

MONTHLY, 84(1957):84.
38. B. MASON: PRINCIPLES OF GEOCHEMISTRY (N. Y.: JOHN WILEY 1952), P. 186; M. COOK, (REF.24) P. 340; M. COOK: "WHERE IS THE EARTH'S RADIOGENIC HELIUM," IN NATURE, 179(1957):213; H. FAUL: NUCLEAR GEOLOGY (N. Y.: JOHN WILEY, 1954).
39. M. COOK, (REF. 24) PP. 340, 341; CHEMICAL OCEANOGRAPHY, EDS. J. RILEY AND G. SKIRROW, VOL. 1 (N. Y.: ACADEMIC, 1965), PP. 164, 165; B. BOLIN: THE ATMOSPHERE AND THE SEA IN MOTION (N. Y.: ROCKEFELLER INSTITUTE, 1959), P. 155; L. SILLEN: "THE OCEAN AS A CHEMICAL SYSTEM," IN SCIENCE, 156(1967):1189.

9-HISTORY

If man has been here for millions of years, why do we only find records of man dating to about 3,000 B.C.? When such records are found, they reveal highly developed and sophisticated civilizations. Primitive civilizations are simply wreckages of "more highly developed societies forced through various circumstances to lead a much simpler, less-developed life."[40] (Fig. 42)

10-DENDROCHRONOLOGY

Some species of trees, for example bristlecone pines, are able to live thousands of years. There is apparently no reason why they could not live for tens of thousands of years yet all of them date less than about 6,000 years. (Fig. 43)

11-SEA OOZE

When plants and animals die in the sea, they build up an ooze on the floor of the oceans at the rate of about one inch every 10 to 5,000 years. When this ooze is measured, there is not nearly enough anywhere on the ocean floor to account for thousands of millions of years.

12-EARTH SPIN

The rotation of the earth is gradually slowing--losing time. A recent edition of *Popular Science* alluded to this in an article entitled, "The Riddle of the Leap Second."[41] The causes for this slowing are many, including gravitational drag forces exerted on the earth by the moon and sun. If the earth is billions of years old, and it has been slowing down uniformly through that time, the earth's present spin should be zero! Extrapolating backwards, the earth's spin billions of years ago would have been so great that the centrifugal force would pull the land masses to the equatorial regions and draw them out to a present day height of over 40 miles. The oceans would have been pushed to the poles and the overall shape of the earth changed from a sphere to a fat pancake.[42] But the earth is still spinning, its shape is spherical, its continents are not crowded to

40. *SCIENCE YEAR,* (1966), P. 256.
41. A. FISHER: "THE RIDDLE OF THE LEAP SECOND," IN *POPULAR SCIENCE,* 202(1973):110; SEE ALSO "TOWARDS A LONGER DAY," IN *TIME,* 87(FEB. 25, 1966):102.
42. THIS INFORMATION, IN PART, WAS TAKEN FROM T. BARNES' SUMMARY OF LORD KELVINS' ARGUMENTS AGAINST A VAST AGE OF THE EARTH

Fig.**42** - Oldest Writing (*top*)
The oldest writing, the forerunner of cuneiform, is the pictograph expression of Sumerian speech such as seen inscribed on the above tablet. The oldest tablets have been dated at 3,500 B.C. and were found in the Sumerian temple of Inanna.

Fig.**43** - Oldest Tree (*bottom*)
The oldest living thing is a Bristlecone pine(PINUS LONGALVA). The specimen designated WPN-114, growing in eastern Nevada, is 4,900 years old. (Nevada Dept. of Economic Development)

the equatorial regions and the oceans are not centered at the poles. What do we conclude? The earth is not billions of years old.

13-OCEAN SEDIMENT

There are about 28 billion tons of sediment added to the oceans each year.[43] If this process has been going on for billions of years, the continents en masse would have been eroded away hundreds of times and there would be a layer of sediment on the ocean bottom over 100 miles thick! But the ocean sediment is only an average of a few thousand feet thick and there is no evidence on the land surfaces that the continents have ever been eroded away even once.

14-VOLCANIC WATER AND ROCKS

If we assumed all of the water on this planet was produced through volcanic eruptions bringing water to the surface, by this means alone the present oceans would have been produced (even assuming no water to start with) in a much shorter time than evolutionists assume for the age of the earth. In like manner, if we extrapolate backwards billions of years using the present rate of rock accretion from volcanic activity, there would have been in the past a volume of rocks much larger than all of the rocks on all of the present continents.[44] (Fig. 44)

15-INFLUX OF COSMIC DUST

Cosmic dust is filtering down to the earth from interplanetary space and eventually into the oceans at a rate of about fourteen million tons per year.[45] The nickel content of this cosmic material is much higher than nickel concentration in earthly material. On this basis the amount of cosmic dust on the earth can be determined. If the earth has been here billions of years, there should be fifty or more feet of this dust on the earth or accounted for on the basis of nickel content in the ocean

IN T. G. BARNES: "PHYSICS: A CHALLENGE TO 'GEOLOGIC TIME'," IN ACTS AND FACTS, 3(JULY-AUGUST, 1974).
43. R. M. GARRELS AND F. T. MACKENZIE: EVOLUTION OF THE SEDI-MENTARY ROCKS (N. Y.: W. W. NORTON, 1971), PP. 102-111; ALSO SEE H. SVERDRUP AND OTHERS: THE OCEANS (N. Y.: PRENTICE-HALL, 1942).
44. J. WHITCOMB AND H. MORRIS: THE GENESIS FLOOD (PHILADEL-PHIA: PRESBYTERIAN AND REFORMED, 1970), PP. 387-391.
45. ISAAC ASIMOV: "14 MILLION TONS OF DUST PER YEAR," IN SCIENCE DIGEST, 45(1959):34,35.

Fig. **44**-Water and Rock Accretion *(top)*
An active Mexian volcanoe adds its measure of water and rock to the earth's surface.

Fig.**45** – Comet Decay *(bottom)*
Halley's comet is one of the many comets in the solar system which should not now exist if it has been orbiting the sun for millions of years.

sediments.[46] But there is only enough cosmic dust on the earth, or the moon for that matter, to account for a few thousand years of meteoritic dust influx.

16-COMET DECAY

Comets travel around the sun and are believed to be of the same age as the solar system. Each time a comet orbits it loses a certain amount of its mass through gravitational forces, tail formation, meteor stream production and radiative forces. There are numerous comets, both short and long period, traveling a-round the sun but no source of new comets is known. If the uni-verse is billions of years old, then these comets would have traveled many thousands of times around the sun and lost a huge amount of mass. Considering the size of comets today, their loss of mass per orbit, and extrapolating backwards billions, millions or even hundreds of thousands of years, their original mass would have had to have been several times that of the sun-- in which case the sun would have been orbiting the comets![47] Therefore, the existence of hundreds of comets in our solar system with closed elliptical orbits and random aphelia--proving they are not now being added by a particular source outside the solar system--suggests a youthful solar system. (Fig. 45)

17-MUTATION LOAD

Mutations accumulate by being added through time and passed from offspring to offspring. Most mutations remain buried within the genes, or are corrected by DNA repair systems. When mutations do show (phenotypically expressed), they are almost always harm-ful and are selected against. The more mutations do accumulate in populations, the greater the probability they will show up phenotypically and jeopardize the organisms. If life has been evolving for millions of years, there should presently be a huge accumulated mutation load in all organisms. But plants and ani-mals are thriving and are not in jeopardy from mutation loads. Therefore, it is reasoned, the biological world could not have vast antiquity.

18-POPULATION STATISTICS

Through the use of the following equation we can compute world

46. H. PETTERSSON: "COSMIC SPHERULES AND METEORITIC DUST," IN SCIENTIFIC AMERICAN, 202(1960):132.
47. R. A. LYTTLETON: MYSTERIES OF THE SOLAR SYSTEM (OXFORD: CLARENDON, 1968), P. 147.

population:[48]

$$P_n = \frac{2}{C-1} (C^{n-x+1})(C^x - 1)$$

P_n = World population after n generations
n = Number of generations
x = Life span in terms of generations
2C = Number of children per family

If a generation is 35 years, and each family has three children (there must be more than two, otherwise there would be zero population growth), and everyone, on the average, lives to the age of 35, how many people would be on earth after 52 generations (1,820 years)? In this case, 2C = 3, x = 1 and n = 52. If we plug these into the equation, the answer calculates to 4.34 billion people. On the other hand, using the same figures but calculating for 28,600 generations (one million years of evolutionary history), there would be 10^{5000} people! "Think of that," the creationist says, "reasonable figures show man's antiquity to be in terms of thousands of years; the same figures spread over a conservative estimate of evolutionary history (one million years) would infer a contemporary population on earth 10^{4900} times greater than could fit in the entire universe-- talk about crowded!"

19-STELLAR RADIATION

Small particles, called cosmic dust, exist in abundance in galactic space. Radiation from stars tends to push these particles out of the galaxy. If the universe is only a couple of million years old, calculations show that the galaxy should now be swept clean of dust. But the dust exists in abundance in interstellar space and there is no known source of any significant replenishment. From this, it is concluded that the galaxy must be young.[49] (Fig. 46)

20-COSMIC DUST VELOCITY

Stellar radiation exerts a pressure on cosmic dust accelerating

48. H. M. MORRIS: *"WORLD POPULATION AND BIBLE CHRONOLOGY,"* IN
SCIENTIFIC STUDIES IN SPECIAL CREATIONISM, ED. W. LAMMERTS
(PHILADELPHIA: PRESBYTERIAN AND REFORMED, 1971), PP. 198-205.
49. E. KRINOV: *PRINCIPLES OF METEORITICS* (N. Y.: PERGAMON,
1960), P. 506; H. ROBERTSON: *RELATIVITY AND COSMOLOGY* (PHILA-
DELPHIA: SAUNDERS, 1968), P. 115; DETAILS AND FURTHER REFER-
ENCES IN R. SAMEC: *"EFFECT OF RADIATION ON MICROMETEOROIDS, AND*

Fig. **46** – Nebular   Dust   (*top*)
The Orion Nebula contains vast amounts of gas and interstellar dust.   The presence of high concentrations of dust in the universe is an indicator of youth. (Courtesy American Museum Natural History

Fig. **47** – Surface   Crater   (*bottom*)
The Arizona meteor crater is 3/4 mile in diameter and 600 feet deep.   Most meteoritic materials and craters are confined to surface rocks--another indicator of youth.

it out of the galaxy. The older the galaxy, the faster the velocity of the particles. If the galaxy is billions of years
old, cosmic dust should now be moving at about 21,000,000 miles
per hour. If the galaxy is a few thousand years old, the particles should be moving only a few miles per hour. Observations
of interstellar cosmic dust show velocities of particles are almost static. Thus, the galaxy must be young according to this
dating method.[50]

21-POYNTING-ROBERTSON EFFECT

The solar drag force exerted upon micrometeoroids in the solar
system causes the particles to spiral into the sun. This is
called the Poynting-Robertson effect. The sun is thus vacuum
sweeping space at the rate of about 100,000 tons per day. If
the solar system is billions of years old, there should no longer
be any significant quantities of micrometeoroids since there is
no known source of significant replenishment. On the contrary,
however, the solar system is abundant in micrometeoroids. This
speaks for solar system youth.[51]

22-METEORITES

Virtually all meteorites that have bombarded the earth are found
in surface rocks. Furthermore, meteoritic craters are all dated
at a few thousand years. The creationist sees this as testimony that the earth is young and that layers of earthly rock
have not been building up over billions of years. Otherwise,
he reasons, meteorites would be found throughout the geological
record and in "older" rocks, and craters would be dated at millions of years as well as thousands.[52] (Fig. 47)

23-EARTH HEAT

The earth is slowly cooling. This cooling proceeds inward from

*EXISTENCE OF MICROMETEOROIDS AS EVIDENCE OF A YOUNG SOLAR SYS-
TEM," IN CREATION RESEARCH SOCIETY QUARTERLY, 12(JUNE, 1975):7.*
50. IBID.
*51. G. ABELL: EXPLORATION OF THE UNIVERSE (N. Y.: HOLT, RINE-
HART AND WINSTON, 1969), P. 364; J. POYNTING: "RADIATION PRES-
SURE," IN NATURE, 71(1905):377; R. SAMEC, (REF. 49).*
*52. B. MASON: METEORITES (N. Y.: JOHN WILEY, 1962), P.4; E.
KRINOV AND E. ANDERS IN THE MOON METEORITES AND COMETS, EDS. B.
MIDDLEHURST AND G. KUIPER (CHICAGO: UNIVERSITY OF CHICAGO,
1963), PP. 219, 406; FURTHER REFERENCES AND DETAILS IN P.
STEVENSON: "METEORITIC EVIDENCE FOR A YOUNG EARTH," IN CREATION
RESEARCH SOCIETY QUARTERLY, 12(JUNE, 1975):23.*

the surface in keeping with Stefan's law of radiation. Lord Kelvin, as early as the nineteenth century, calculated that the earth could not have a vast age of billions of years based upon considerations of the existing temperature gradient in the earth, the rate of cooling, and the assumption that the initial state of the earth could have been no hotter than "white hot."[53]

24-LUNAR INERT GASES

Samplings of the moon surface have revealed the presence of various inert gases. If the origin of these gases is due to solar wind of present-day intensity, it would require from 1,000 to 10,000 years to generate present lunar concentrations of, for example, Argon-36 and Krypton-84 (superman's nemesis).[54] If we assume uniformity, extrapolate backwards and assume the age of the moon can be based upon these inert gas concentrations, then the moon and perhaps the solar system would be only 1,000 to 10,-000 years old.

25-STALAGMITES AND STALACTITES

The formation of stalagmites and stalactites in caves has long been used to support great ages. The slow present-day growth rate of some of these structures, combined with the fact that some stalagmites and stalactites are huge, has led to the conclusion that huge spans of time were necessary for their formation. Thus, it is reasoned, the caves must be old and the earth must be old. But the rate of formation of these structures is dependent upon many variables such as water flow, temperature and lime concentrations. Some stalactites have been observed under modern-day bridges and tunnels several inches long. Their growth in some instances has even been measured at several cubic inches per year. Extremely rapid growth of a stalagmite in Carlsbad caverns is testified to by an encased bat.[55] The stalagmite grew so rapidly it was able to preserve the bat before decomposition! Thus stalactite and stalagmite growth can as well foster recent cave formation--and earth formation. (Fig. 48)

53. *LORD KELVIN: "ON THE AGE OF THE SUN'S HEAT," IN POPULAR LECTURES AND ADDRESSES (LONDON: MAC MILLAN, 1889), P. 415; SEE ALSO MATHEMATICAL AND PHYSICAL PAPERS (CAMBRIDGE: CAMBRIDGE UNIVERSITY, 1882).*
54. *D. HEYMANN AND OTHERS: "INERT GASES IN LUNAR SAMPLES," IN SCIENCE, 167(1970):557.*
55. *C. E. HENDRIX: THE CAVE BOOK (MASSACHUSETTS: EARTH SCIENCE, 1950), P. 26; M. SUTHERLAND: "CARLSBAD CAVERNS IN COLOR," IN NATIONAL GEOGRAPHIC, 104(OCT., 1953):442.*

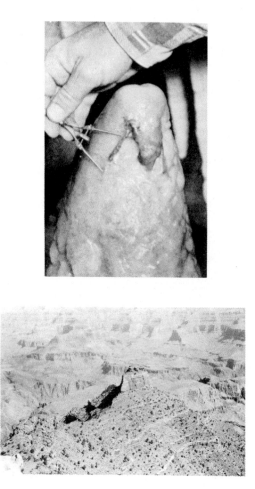

Fig. **48** – Bat in Stalagmite *(top)*
This stalagmite grew so rapidly that it cemented a bat that fell.
The feet are buried; the head hangs down; wing bones show up dark-
ly. (From 1953 National Geographic; courtesy "Tex" Helm)

Fig. **49** – Strata *(bottom)*
The even horizontal strata of Grand Canyon suggest rapid cyclic
depositions of the sedimentary materials forming the rocks.

26-TOPSOIL

The world-wide average depth of topsoil is about eight inches.
It has been calculated that it takes from 300 to 1,000 years to
build one inch of topsoil.[56] Thus, on this basis, the earth
could only be a few thousand years old.

27-GEOLOGICAL FEATURES

It is commonly assumed that the strata of the earth have been
built up over long stretches of time. It is likewise assumed
that the great canyons of the world were slowly cut through
hard rock or were otherwise formed slowly (some estimate 50 million years to erode one mile). The tremendous depth of the canyons could then be taken as an argument for vast time. However,
this lazy, rock-a-bye picture is contradicted by many facts and
phenomena which argue for the youthfulness of geological formations: (A) For example, sometimes deep rocks, even down to the
Cambrian, are in an unconsolidated state. If these rocks have
been lying under millions of tons of rocks for billions of years,
they would have long since been consolidated. (B) Many geological features can only be understood within the framework of catastrophy and rapidity. Some examples are fossils, coal and oil,
various sedimentary rocks like sandstones, shales, limestones,
conglomerates and dolostones, metals, and igneous rocks. The
earth is filled with thousands of cubic miles of these materials.
Many of these are not being formed at all today, dolostone, for
example, and the extent of all of them speaks to catastrophic
rapid processes. (C) Wherever the rocks of the earth are exposed, be it in the Grand Canyon or along a superhighway where
engineers have cut through hills, there appear flat horizontal
layers of sedimentary rocks. There is no uniformitarian blend-
ing of rocks into one another. In some cases, book-like terrac-
ing of strata extends to thousands of feet in thickness and is
spread over hundreds of miles, as far as the rocks and strata
are exposed. Yet, if these strata were built up gradually, each
layer would have been eroded to a more or less degree oblitera-
ting any horizontal continuity. Therefore, the creationist insists that the horizontal plates of strata must have been deposited rapidly in succession, one on the other without huge
time periods between depositions. (D) The meandering serpentine
course of many rivers and canyons, for example the SanJuan river
in Colorado, prove that the canyons were cut when the beds were

---

56. E. F. BLICK: "SECOND LAW OF THERMODYNAMICS AND LIVING
ORGANISMS," IN PAPER PRESENTED TO THE AMERICAN SOCIETY OF EN-
GINEERING EDUCATION, JUNE 18, 1974; J. C. TAYLOR: "LAWNS," IN
ONTARIO DEPARTMENT OF AGRICULTURE PUBLICATION, NO. 448, P. 5; A.
MICKEY: "MAN AND SOIL," IN INTERNATIONAL HARVESTER, 1945, P. 17.

still soft. Thus the canyons must have been carved rapidly,
another indication of geological youth.[57] (Figs. 49 and 50)

28-NIAGARA FALLS

The age of Niagara Falls can be calculated on the basis of the
rate at which its edge wears away. The French explorer, Henne-
pin, first mapped the falls in 1678. From then to 1842 the falls
wore away at the rate of about seven feet per year. Other, more
recent calculations show its rate to be 3.5 feet per year. Therefore, since the length of the gorge is about seven miles, the age
of the falls is between 5,000 and 10,000 years (seven miles divided by 3.5 or seven feet). (Fig. 51)

29-MOON RADIATIVE DUST

It is believed that the moon is the same age as the earth and the
rest of the solar system. R. A. Lyttleton, a highly respected
astronomer and consultant to the U.S. space program, wrote in
the mid-1950's:

> ". . . the lunar surface is exposed to direct sunlight,
> and strong ultra-violet light and X-rays can destroy
> the surface layers of exposed rock and reduce them to
> dust at the rate of a few ten-thousandths of an inch
> per year. But even this minute amount could during
> the age of the moon be sufficient to form a layer over
> it several miles deep."

Now, if we take the "few ten-thousandths of an inch per year"
to mean three or four ten-thousandths of an inch per year at the
minimum, the moon would have upwards of 20 to 60 miles of dust on
it from these radiative forces (not even considering meteoritic
dust) if the moon were really five or ten billion years old! But
it doesn't. It doesn't have 60 miles, 30 miles, 15, 5 or 1 mile.
It doesn't have 1,000 feet, 100 feet or even 10 feet. It has
only a thin veneer of dust. In arguing this same point, the
creationist, Professor Slusher, facetiously asked: "Is the Mar-
tian Mining Company loading this dust up and carting it away or
what?" So what can we conclude? Namely this. We can argue
scientifically that the moon is young because the dust found on
it would only take a few thousand years to be produced. On the
other hand, if the tables were turned and the moon did actually
have miles of dust on it, you can be sure that the evolutionist

---

57. *J. C. WHITCOMB AND H. M. MORRIS:* THE GENESIS FLOOD (PHILA-
DELPHIA: PRESBYTERIAN AND REFORMED, 1970), P. 155; SEE ALSO
SCIENTIFIC CREATIONISM, ED. H. M. MORRIS (SAN DIEGO: CREATION-
LIFE, 1974), PP. 91-130; J. SCHULTZ AND A. CLEAVES: GEOLOGY IN
ENGINEERING (N. Y.: JOHN WILEY, 1955), P. 153.

Fig. **50** – Fossils (*top*)
This piece of sedimentary rock is composed almost entirely of
fossil brachiopods. Huge fossil beds around the world speak to
rapid formation of rocks. (Courtesy of R. Cranson)

Fig. **51** – Niagara Falls (*bottom*)
The edge of Niagara Falls wears away at a rate which would form
the seven mile gorge in about 5,000 to 10,000 years. (Courtesy
of S. Rathbun)

would proclaim this as "scientific proof" of the moon's great antiquity. But the tables are not turned, so the creationist asks, "Why not believe the moon is young?"[58]

30-HYDROGEN IN THE UNIVERSE

Hydrogen is constantly being converted into helium throughout the universe. On the other hand, hydrogen cannot be produced in any significant quantity through the conversion of other elements. If the universe were vastly old, there should now be little hydrogen in it.   Fred Hoyle, a professor of astronomy, says, "the universe consists almost entirely of hydrogen." Therefore, since we have absolutely no evidence of hydrogen genesis, the high concentration of hydrogen in the universe speaks to a youthful universe. Hoyle concludes (although he is here attempting to lay the groundwork for his continuous, not special, creation hypothesis):

> "How comes it then that the universe consists almost
> entirely of hydrogen? If matter was infinitely old,
> this would be quite impossible. So we see that the
> universe being what it is, the creation issue simply
> cannot be dodged."[59]

31-MOON RADIATION

Apollo lunar material was found to be high in radioactivity. It is suggested that if the moon were very old--millions of years-- it would be intensely hot, or even melting from the heat of radiation. But the moon is rigid, and some argue the moon has a cool interior. This rigidity and relative coolness of the moon speaks for its youth--less than 50,000 years old.[60]

32-SHORT-LIVED LUNAR ISOTOPES

Short-lived U-236 and Th-230 isotopes found in lunar materials are taken as testimony for youth. If the moon were of great age, the short-lived isotopes would have long since decayed and thus be presently absent. Yet they are not absent, they are in

58. *R. A. LYTTLETON: THE MODERN UNIVERSE (N. Y.: HARPER, 1956),
P. 72.*
59. *F. HOYLE: THE NATURE OF THE UNIVERSE (N. Y.: HARPER, 1960),
P. 125.*
60. *PROCEEDINGS OF THE FOURTH LUNAR SCIENCE CONFERENCE,
3(1973):2515; SCIENCE, 176(1972):975; 181(1973):49; NATURE,
230(1971):359; JOURNAL OF GEOPHYSICAL RESEARCH 76(1971):5947;
FURTHER REFERENCES IN J. READ'S PRESENTATION TO THE CALIFORNIA*

relative abundance. Thus, according to this method, the age of
the moon should be spoken of in terms of thousands of years, not
millions or billions.[61]

33-ATMOSPHERIC OXYGEN

If the earth were barren of vegetation, and the atmosphere was
without oxygen, and suddenly vegetation was created to cover the
earth, the amount of time necessary to generate present levels
of atmospheric oxygen would be 5,000 years. According to this
calculation, creation could have been 5,000 years ago.[62]

Conclusion

The universe and life can be made to look imperceptibly old
by certain radiodating techniques, star distance calculations,
rate of expansion of the universe, sedimentation buildup, rates
of erosion, and many other methods. These various methods can
be found detailed in practically any modern scientific work dealing with earth history. Discussions of dating methods showing
youth are virtually absent from the scientific literature. For
this reason the above listing was made. It is apparent that if
we assume uniformity, namely that processes and conditions have
always been as they are now, "legitimate scientific" dating
methods based upon this assumption can be used to give dates for
the same objects from a few thousand to several billion years.
This throws uniformity itself into question, i.e., if the
assumption of uniformity leads to contradictions--youth and antiquity for the same sample--the assumption must not be correct.
However, this merely belabors the point I have tried to emphasize throughout the chapter: scientific dating techniques rest
upon a series of assumptions which usually cannot be validated.
Where does this leave us? We have a draw. The creationist
has faith his scientific dating method assumptions are valid;
the evolutionist has faith his scientific dating method assumptions are valid.
The evolutionist believes he has the edge because the majority of the scientific community backs him.

*STATE BOARD OF EDUCATION, MAY 8, 1975, REPRODUCED IN BIBLE-
SCIENCE NEWSLETTER,13(1975):5.*
*61. PROCEEDINGS OF THE SECOND LUNAR SCIENCE CONFERENCE,
2(1971):1571; PROCEEDINGS OF THE THIRD LUNAR SCIENCE CONFERENCE,
2(1972):1636; LUNAR SCIENCE IV(1973):239, 634; FURTHER REFEREN-
CES IN J. READ'S PRESENTATION . . . IBID.*
*62. G. EHRENSVARD: LIFE: ORIGIN AND DEVELOPMENT (CHICAGO:
UNIVERSITY OF CHICAGO, 1962), P. 135.*

The creationist believes he has the edge because his methods operate over a shorter time and, like a clock, are less likely to malfunction than a method, or clock, operating for billions of years. Similarly, since any scientific dating method must extrapolate backwards from knowns established for only about the last 100 or less years, extrapolations from these knowns to billions of years is less likely to be accurate than an extrapolation to a few thousand years.

Pure probability considerations speak against evolution. The argument of vast time is practically a litany used by evolutionists to overcome probability difficulties. In this and the previous chapter we attempted to deal with the capabilities and quantity of time. Does time in capacity or amount solve the conclusions from probabilities? Does the evidence support creation or evolution? Who has the faith resting on the more solid evidence?

⑾ BIOGENESIS

Prior to the time of the Italian physician Redi (1688), life was popularly believed to emerge spontaneously from lifeless decaying matter. The idea was held by such notable figures as Newton, Aristotle, Harvey, Thales, Plato, Epicurus, Democritus, Goethe, Copernicus, Galileo, Bacon, Hegel and Schelling.[1] This belief, known as spontaneous generation, gave rise to such novel notions as the origin of geese from barnacles, mice from dirty undergarments and bees from dead calves, and drew its credibility from observations. Banana peels do appear to yield fruit flies and manure does appear to yield maggots. It was a scientific hypothesis.

Spontaneous Generation Disproved

Spontaneous generation was discredited because seekers of truth bothered to look beyond the surface. Redi, Spallanzani (1780) and Pasteur (1860) devised various experiments to check the validity of the hypothesis. In essence, their experiments were designed to see if life truely came from matter itself, or whether it resulted from biological contamination.

These experimenters found that when matter was presterilized and sealed off from the environment, no life arose. (Fig. 52) The work of these three men plus that of the pathologist Rudolf Virchow (1858), who showed that cells do not arise from amorphous exudate, but rather from preexisting cells, and the labors of countless scientists in all of the various disciplines of biology since, have established the law of biogenesis--life springs from

---

1. A. I. OPARIN: *LIFE: ITS NATURE, ORIGIN AND DEVELOPMENT* (EDINBURGH: OLIVER AND BOYD, 1961), P. 13.

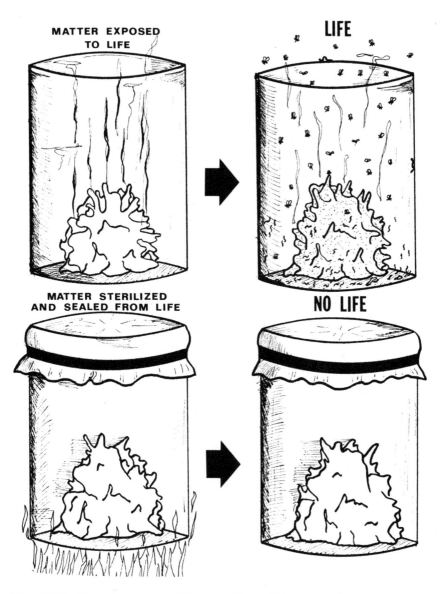

Fig. **52**-Spontaneous Generation Disproved

Organic material exposed to bacteria, fly eggs, fungal spores, etc., may generate populations of life. Superficially it appears as though life is coming from the matter itself. However, as shown by Redi, Pasteur and Spallanzani, if matter is sterilized and then sealed from possible biological contamination, no life arises. Thus, there is no spontaneous generation, only biological reproduction according to kind--biogenesis.

preexisting life.

Aside from proscribing the spontaneous formation of life, the law of biogenesis dictates that life will only perpetuate its own kind and type. The law was set forth many years ago, even before modern evolutionary thought was well established, and remains affirmed to this day. Actually, creationistic argumentation attempts precise confirmation and reiteration of the law of biogenesis. The law cancels the possibility of the chance spontaneous formation of life and also negates proposed evolutionary transformations of one kind of organism into another.

Biogenesis Vs Evolution

The experiments and scientific methodology of Redi, Pasteur and Spallanzani are held in very high esteem by the scientific community. The overturning of the spontaneous generation hypothesis is taught to students world over to demonstrate modern, rational, experimental science. The *Encyclopedia Britannica* states concerning Rudolf Virchow:

> "His aphorism 'omnis cellula e cellula' (every cell arises from a pre-existing cell) ranks with Pasteur's 'omne vivum e vivo' (every living thing arises from a preexisting living thing) among the most revolutionary generalizations of biology."[2]

A student learns the historical greatness of these facts from his natural science teacher on one day in class, but on the next, so to speak, is taught spontaneous generation as a truth concerning the origin of life. (Fig. 53) The terminology is changed from spontaneous generation to biopoiesis, abiogenesis, biochemical predestination, mutations and natural selection, and the event is removed to the remote past, but the meaning remains.

The creationist is quick to remind evolutionists that biopoiesis and evolution describe events that stand in stark naked contradiction to an established law. The law of biogenesis says life arises only from preexisting life, biopoiesis says life sprang from dead chemicals; evolution states that life forms give rise to new, improved and different life forms, the law of biogenesis says that kinds only reproduce their own kinds.

Evolutionists are not oblivious to this law. They simply question it. They say that spontaneous generation was disproved under the conditions of the experimental models of Pasteur, Redi and Spallanzani. This, they contend, does not preclude the spontaneous formation of life under different conditions.

To this, the creationist replies that even given the artifi-

---

2. *E. H. ACKERKNECHT: "RUDOLF VIRCHOW," IN ENCYCLOPEDIA BRITAN-NICA, 23(1973):35.*

Fig. 53 Educational Paradox

Students the world over are taught the historical and scientific greatness of the disproof of spontaneous generation and the establishment of the law of biogenesis. Creationists boil when these educators then, with no compunction, dogmatically assert to these same students the fact of spontaneous generation as the mechanism by which life arose.

cial conditions and intelligent maneuverings of biopoiesis experiments, life has still not "spontaneously" generated. To argue that biogenesis is not a law because of what might be accomplished in the future is simply a statement of faith. Similarly any law could be "invalidated." Until such time as life is observed to spontaneously generate, the creationist insists the law of biogenesis stands!

The evolutionist would counter by pleading that the so-called law of biogenesis was "established" when science was in its infancy. Rather than a law, biogenesis could better be termed a naive generalization. "You say that life only springs from life? Well, Mr. Creationist, what is 'life?' Are proteins alive? How about viruses or crystals? Are DNA molecules or coacervates alive? All of these can be formed in the laboratory, you know. If they are 'alive' then biogenesis is refuted. If you don't know or can't decide if these substances are alive, if you have trouble defining life, does this not speak to the continuum from life to non-life? Indeed, is 'life' not just a stage in the complexification of matter?" (Our next chapter will deal with the controversy over life's definition.)

The evolutionist suggests that the whole reason life is not spontaneously generating now is because the conditions are not right. Any organic molecules that might form are either oxidized by present oxidizing conditions or preyed upon by already existing life. Given the proper conditions, it is believed, the conditions existing at the time life originally arose, life will spontaneously form.

Biogenesis a Principle ?

Some try to circumvent the contradictions between biogenesis and evolution by stating that the work of Pasteur and others revealed a "principle," not a law. Thus, you will find in various biology texts and dictionaries the "principle" of biogenesis, not the law of.

A popular dictionary of biology states under the entry "Biogenesis, Principle of," the following:

"The biological rule that a living thing can originate only from a parent or parents on the whole similar to itself. It denies spontaneous generation . . ."

Furthermore, it goes on to say of this "principle":

". . . it may possibly need further qualification in the case of the simpler viruses, which it has been suggested may arise from normal constituents of cells."[3]

The possible exception noted by these authors is probably a reference to the Kornberg virus experiments (see chapter 15).

---

3. *M. ABERCROMBIE, C. HICKMAN AND M. JOHNSON: A DICTIONARY OF BIOLOGY (BALTIMORE: PENGUIN, 1961), P. 33.*

However, the creationist avers, Kornberg's work is not counter to the law of biogenesis. The ingredients used by Kornberg were from living cells, and certainly Kornberg was alive. Thus, even if we considered a virus alive, its production (a virus was not produced by Kornberg, only the DNA was) by life--Kornberg--and from parts derived from life, simply substantiates the law of biogenesis, i.e., life only can arise from preexisting life.

The creationist sees no difference between asserting that frogs come from algae, bears from berries, flies from fruit, maggots from manure, geese from barnacles and cells from exudate, and the assertion that cells come from viruses, or carbon, or nitrogen, or sulfur, or hydrogen, or water, or from a thick slimy broth with all of these admixed.

The "principle" nomenclature is forced from a realization of the implications of biogenesis as a law on evolution, not because contradictions to the law have been found. When the scientific method was discussed we learned that a law is established when a theory is time tested and proven universally true. Thus, the laws of heredity, first conceived by Gregor Mendel in about 1850, are proven laws because they are always true, they give predictable results. The law of biogenesis finds its starting foundation in the work of Francesco Redi in the 1600's. Since that time the hypothesis of biogenesis has known no exceptions and proves perfectly predictable (assuming "life" can be defined). How can biogenesis be termed any less than a law?

The creationist follows up on this pleading that creationism says the exact same thing the law does: life must come from life, and life will reproduce only according to its kinds. So the creationist sees the law of biogenesis, the formulation of which is extolled by evolutionists the world over as a model for the vindication of truth, as nothing but a restatement of the creation proposition! (Fig. 54)

"Then, if the events described by the biogenetic law are the same as those described by the creation proposition, is the creationist's stand merely a proposition?" he asks. "Are not things equal to the same things, equal to each other?"

1 BIOGENESIS DEMANDS THAT ALL LIFE SPRING FROM PREEXISTING LIFE AND REPRODUCE ACCORDING TO KIND AND TYPE.

2 CREATION DEMANDS THAT ALL LIFE SPRING FROM PREEXISTING LIFE AND REPRODUCE ACCORDING TO KIND AND TYPE.

3 THEREFORE, BIOGENESIS EQUALS THE CREATION PROPOSITION.

4 BIOGENESIS IS A LAW.

5 THEREFORE, CREATION IS A LAW?

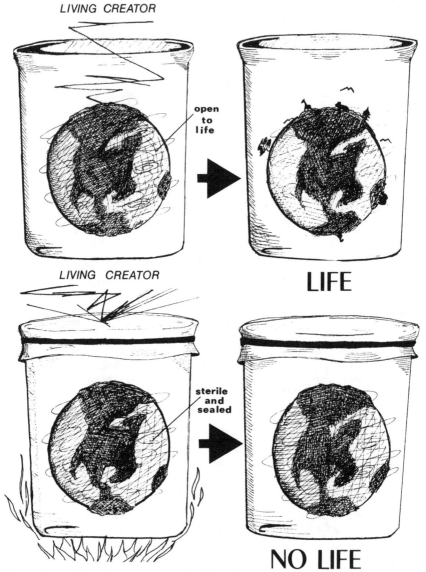

Fig. **54** - Biogenesis and Origins

According to the law of biogenesis, life cannot spring from life-less matter. Therefore, the creationist reasons, if the primordial earth were exposed to a living creator, life could arise. If there were no living creator, or his creative power was restricted from the earth, no life could have arisen. The creationist sees this as indirect proof for the existence of a creator.

Biogenesis Vs Creator

The evolutionist asks: "If life only comes from preexisting life, where did a creator come from? Furthermore, if life can only reproduce according to its kind, why is the creator different from his progeny?"

The creationist would say that these questions are interesting but that they do not reflect on the fundamental issue of whether life originated by chance or design. The law of biogenesis clearly precludes the chance origin and transmutation of life. The only alternative explanation is creation. Therefore, having established that there is a creator, we have answered the question concerning the origin of life. Subsequent questions about the creator do not reflect upon his reality.

With this understanding--that biogenesis has negated spontaneous generation and validated creation--the creationist would proceed to answer the "peripheral"questions about the relationship of biogenesis to the creator himself. The evolutionist, of course, does not see these questions as peripheral. If creationists force biogenesis on evolutionists, then evolutionists can return the favor.

The creationist answers the first question--if life only comes from life, where does a creator come from?-- this way. Biogenesis forbids life from arising from nonlife. The law does not mean that life must come from a preexisting life form other than itself. Asexual organisms are eternal in the sense that when they reproduce they divide in half making the progeny the parents and vice versa. The biogenetic law is not violated by these organisms because life is arising from life even though the preexisting life is one with offspring. An eternal creator having an existence extending into infinity, a life continuum, does not ring out of tune with the biogenetic law. Only if the creator arose from lifeless matter would the law be violated. Biogenesis forces the belief in infinite life.

To be sure, the concept of a living being that knows of no beginning is sufficient to "blow one's mind," yet so is the thought of infinity. Those who reject a creator because they cannot "visualize" an eternal being, usually, and glibly so, accept infinity as true and even presume to understand it. Yet who can mentally digest the infinite? No one can. Our minds are finite, by definition unable to grasp the infinite. But this does not deny the possibility of infinity in time, in space or embodied in a creator. A pet dog cannot conceive of mathematics, does that mean mathematics doesn't exist? Just because we cannot fully understand the nature of an eternal being does not mean he can't exist. And besides, materialists do not have the upper hand in this matter, for they are forced to believe in their infinite gods of matter and energy.

The creationist would answer the second question--if life can only reproduce according to kind, why is the creator different from his progeny?--this way. When life reproduces, the progeny are according to the kind dictated by the information inscribed on the DNA of the parents. Likewise, it could be argued that when life was created, the created kinds would take the form dictated by the will of the living creator. Thus, biological reproduction is according to the kind dictated by the instinctive "will" of DNA; creation is production according to the kind willed by the creator's mind. Created kinds will only be "according to the kind" predetermined by the creator.

Creator Transcends Created

Although these answers are often given, the creationist feels he need not directly answer the two questions raised above at all. Why? Because the biogenetic law need not apply to the creator. The biogenetic law is as much a part of the creation as are the plants and animals. Thus, the biogenetic law would apply to the created world, not to the creator. So just as a creator would not necessarily have to eat, sleep and drink, he likewise would not be rigidly subject to the biogenetic law. By definition, a creator can transcend the laws imposed upon his creation.

Similarly, an engineer who has created an engine that can only operate through the combustion of gasoline has, in effect, created not only the engine, but the "law of gasoline usage." Can we turn this "law" then back upon the engineer and ask why he does not consume gasoline? Or should we deny his existence because he does not consume gasoline?

To presume that a being with creative power equalling the task of producing the vast universe would be limited by his created laws is contradictory and inconsistent. By definition creation is not reproduction. Creation is not subject to the restrictions of biological reproduction. To reason that biogenesis must apply to the creator is naturalistic reasoning. Since biogenesis refutes naturalism, how could naturalistic thinking then invalidate the creator? A creator is not naturalistic, he is supernaturalistic and is consequently not bound and restricted by the natural world and its laws.

Knowledge of the creator is necessarily limited by our own finite minds, by what we can deduce from the created world, or by what he would choose to reveal to us by revelation. Biogenesis establishes that there is a creator by negating spontaneous generation. Subsequent questions about his exact nature, construct, purposes or longevity do not cancel his reality, creationists insist

In summary, we can see that the creationist takes the biogenetic law as proof of his position and as disproof of evolution. The evolutionist attempts to controvert this challenge by (1) maintaining biogenesis is inconsistent with a creator; (2) attesting that biogenesis is only valid under certain conditions; and (3) alleging there is no real distinction between life and non-life.

We must decide. We must openly weigh the arguments and choose the proposition most consistent with the facts. If you feel unqualified at this point, our next few chapters will bear upon the arguments and counterarguments given here and will help us in this decision.

12 $\Big\{$ IS LIFE DEFINABLE ?

The subject we have been pursuing concerns the origin of "life." We speak of life as if it were something apart from the material. Is life unique, or is it merely another form of matter itself?

Evolutionists argue that it is very difficult to define life. They then insist that the confusion in defining life, in clearly setting it apart from the physical world, actually shows its continuous nature with the inorganic lifeless world. Life is understood to be simply a degree of complexification of matter. Life is not thought of as "originating." Defining life is thought of as putting artificial constraints upon something that is a part of a material continuum.

Bernal, of McGill University puts it:

"Life can be thought of as water kept at the right temperature in the right atmosphere in the right light for a long enough period of time."[1]

Keosian takes this position:

"Where does life fit into this progression? Nowhere. It makes little sense to attempt to squeeze anywhere into this gradual scheme sequence of stages to matter a nebulous undefinable something called 'life', which presumably breaks this gradual sequence abruptly into two groups--inanimate and living."[2]

Elsewhere he remarks regarding the difficulty in defining life:

"This marked lack of success is a measure of proof that matter goes through a continuous hierarchy of

---

1. N. J. BERRILL: YOU AND THE UNIVERSE (N. Y.: DODD, MEAD, 1958), P. 117.
2. J. KEOSIAN: THE ORIGIN OF LIFE (N. Y.: REINHOLD, 1968), P. 89.

increasingly complex stages, and that there is indeed
one evolution, the evolution of matter, even to the
level of reasoning power."[3]
    To be sure, if life is not unique, there would be no prob-
lem in accounting for it--philosophically at least. If evolution is simply change, and life is simply a change from a more
simple material state, then evolution is true and life is accounted for by it.

Gap, or No Gap ?

    If life is simply a stage of matter, a stage in the material
evolutionary continuum, the creationist challenges the evolutionist to show him the links leading to life. Scientists have
been able to form the building blocks of life, but the missing
links between building blocks and the complexity characteristic
of life are numerous.
    Evolutionists themselves recognize this and lament the gap
between the living and the dead as the unsolved mystery of the
origin of life: ·
    Butler:
        ". . . the gap between a rich organic environment with
        all the necessary precursors, including even polypep-
        tides and nucleic acids, and the simplest organized
        life, remains immense . . . even the simplest complete
        organisms we know of today are almost unbelievably com-
        plex. It is difficult to visualize the steps by which
        they may have originated because the various processes
        which occur in them are interdependent; none can func-
        tion without the others."[4]
    Orgel:
        "The major intellectual problem presented by the ori-
        gins of life is concerned with the next stage, the
        evolution of biological organization. How did a com-
        plex self-replicating organism evolve from an unorgan-
        ized mixture of polymeric molecules? Little experi-
        mental evidence is available, so one is forced to
        attempt a speculative reconstruction of this phase in
        the origins of life."[5]
    Mednikov:
        "At present there are grounds to suggest several ex-
        perimentally different ways of emergence of low

---

3. *J. KEOSIAN, (REF. 2) P. 90.*
4. *J. BUTLER: THE LIFE PROCESS (LONDON: GEORGE ALLEN AND
UNWIN, 1970), PP. 185, 188, 189.*
5. *L. E. ORGEL: THE ORIGINS OF LIFE: MOLECULES AND NATURAL
SELECTION (N. Y.: JOHN WILEY, 1973), P. 230.*

192

molecular predecessors of life (amino acids and
nucleotides). Less is known about the second stage,
i.e. that from the 'primary broth' to coacervate or
the microsphere. As to the third stage, from coacervate to the protocell, we can offer little more than
speculations."[6]

Oparin:
"But the problem at present is not so much how this
primordial soup has arisen, but rather how from this
originally sterile primordial soup arose the original
living organisms."[7]

Simpson:
"If atoms of hydrogen and oxygen come together under
certain simple and common conditions of energy, they
always deterministically combine to form water. Formation of more complex molecules requires correspond-
ingly more complex concatenations of circumstances
but is still deterministic in what seems to be a com-
paratively simple way . . . It is still a far cry
from the essential preliminary formation of proteins,
nucleic acids, and other large organic molecules to
their organization into a system alive in the full
sense of the word . . . It requires an attitude of
faith to assume that the acquisition of organic adaptability was deterministic or inevitable to the same
degree or even in the same sense in which that was
probably true of the preceeding, more simply chemical
origin of the necessary macromolecules . . . The further organization of these molecules into cellular
life would seem, on the face of it, to have a far
different, very much lower order of probability. It
is not impossible, because we know it did happen at
least once."[8]

If life is not different, how did the term ever arise? Is
the science of biology really the science of physics? Are persons born? Are they alive? Do they die? Or, is there no such
thing as "death" because there is no such thing as "life?"

If we are to attempt a definition of life, we must describe
the gap between the chemicals that comprise life, and "life" the
organism. In other words, since even the evolutionist sees a

6. B. MEDNIKOV: "THE ORIGIN OF RIBOSOMES AND THE EVOLUTION OF
R-RNA," IN CHEMICAL EVOLUTION AND THE ORIGIN OF LIFE, EDS. R.
BUVER AND C. PONNAMPERUMA (N. Y.: AMERICAN ELSEVIER, 1971),
P. 425.
7. A. I. OPARIN: "HISTORY OF THE SUBJECT MATTER OF THE CONFER-
ENCE," IN THE ORIGINS OF PREBIOLOGICAL SYSTEMS AND THEIR MOLECU-
LAR MATRICES, ED. S. W. FOX (N. Y.: ACADEMIC, 1965), P. 95.
8. G. G. SIMPSON: "THE NONPREVALENCE OF HUMANOIDS," IN SCIENCE,
143(1964):771,772.

gap, a definition of the uniqueness of life must lie with a description of the gap. Is life merely a higher degree of complexity, or what?

Mora feels that:

> ". . . the most important and peculiar attribute of the living, is the relentless striving to survive, to absorb, to expand, to dominate."[9]

The German scientist, Schramm, in a similar vein says:

> "In my opinion the most fundamental property of a living organism is its ability to multiply."[10]

And Pattee, in another way, states:

> ". . . the constraints of living matter must contain their own descriptions."[11]

Mora, elsewhere, defines life as having a characteristic "urge." He states further that life reproduces, is ordered, nonrandom and contains a specific sequence of molecules carrying a specific message dictating, moderating and controlling the "urge."[12]

Ah, yes, maybe that's it. Life is the result of the specific code inherent within its large polymers! But could that be all? Is a bare DNA molecule with a specific code alive?

To answer this question I will digress to a discussion of viruses, the ultramicroscopic particles that many believe demonstrate the continuum between the living and the non-living.

Virus Life Cycle

Evolutionists cite viruses, or some virus-like particle, as the final precursors to the cell.[13] At first glance this seems to be a reasonable assertion, but is it? The answer lies with understanding the virus life cycle.

The virus is an obligate parasite. It is absolutely dependent upon the cell for its survival. The majority of viruses are composed primarily of DNA or RNA surrounded by a protein coat. Viruses attach themselves to a suitable host cell and inject their DNA into the cytoplasm of the cell. In turn, the injected DNA perverts the reproductive machinery of the cell

9. P. T. MORA: "URGE AND MOLECULAR BIOLOGY," IN *NATURE*, 199 (1963):212.

10. G. SCHRAMM: "SYNTHESIS OF NUCLEOSIDES AND POLYNUCLEOTIDES WITH METAPHOSPHATE ESTERS," IN *THE ORIGINS*. . .(REF. 7) P. 299.

11. H. PATTEE: "THE RECOGNITION OF DESCRIPTION AND FUNCTION IN CHEMICAL REACTION NETWORKS," IN *CHEMICAL EVOLUTION* . . . (REF. 6) P. 45.

12. P. T. MORA: "THE FOLLY OF PROBABILITY," IN *THE ORIGINS* . . . (REF. 7) P. 41.

13. R. TOCQUET: *LIFE ON THE PLANETS* (N.Y.: GROVE, 1962), P. 43.

such that the cell no longer produces cells, but rather, viruses. The viruses thus formed are then released and proceed to parasitize other host cells. (Fig. 55) Some viruses, for example the T₂ bacteriophage, can produce 200 progeny in 20 minutes in this manner.[14]

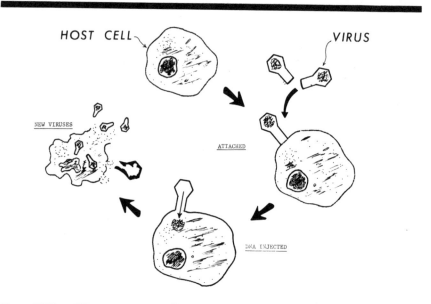

Fig. 55 - Virus Life Cycle

Viruses are obligate parasites. They attach to suitable host cells, inject their nucleic acid, and then monopolize the machinery of the cell to the end of reproducing new viruses. Could a virus or a virus-like particle predate the cell? Do viruses exhibit the characteristic reproductive independency of life?

The question: Could viruses precede the cell by thousands or millions of years to serve as evolutionary precursors? Well, the virus is dependent upon the machinery of the cell for its reproduction. It cannot procreate without the simultaneous existence of the cell. Therefore, the cell either existed before the virus, or they both sprang into existence at the same time. Thus, regarding the spontaneous formation of viral particles, Wolfhard Weidel says:

> ". . . that particle would have remained lonely and forever forgotten without the simultaneous presence of living cells."[15]

14. P. T. MORA: "URGE . . .," (REF. 9) P. 213.
15. WOLFHARD WEIDEL: VIRUSES (ANN ARBOR: UNIVERSITY OF MICHIGAN, 1959), P. 154.

Most evolutionists concede the point that viruses as we know them could not have predated the cell. Consequently they propose an "ultravirus" or virus-like particle.[16] In any case, they are still only talking about protein and nucleic acid (DNA or RNA) in combination, which is something far less than a cell. Without its own machinery, a "virus-like particle" would of necessity demand the concomitant sophisticated machinery of a cell for survival.

Life: DNA Plus

DNA and proteins of the complexity found in life, as well as viruses, are only produced and sustained through the sophisticated machinery of the cell. The creationist challenges: "So, given DNA, proteins and viruses, could life form? How could it? As is evident from the life cycle of viruses, which contain both complex proteins and DNA (or RNA), anything less than a fully formed cell is dependent upon the simultaneous existence of a cell. Further, we know the removal of about any part of a cell destroys the cell. It follows from this, that anything simpler than a cell could not survive. If precursors to life did not survive, did not exist, then life could not exist. But it does. Therefore, spontaneous generation could not be true," he reasons.

Could we say that DNA is life, that it possesses the characteristic "urge?" No. Neither DNA nor DNA plus protein mean life. DNA is not even a self-replicating molecule as is so commonly parroted. Rather, DNA is obligatorily parasitic upon the machinery of the cell for the accomplishment of its many functions.

The first living entity would have probably required, in addition to DNA: carbohydrates, lipids, coenzymes, high energy phosphates, hormones, carotenoids, alkaloids, RNA, the correct pH, a lipid cell membrane with pores just the right diameter to allow the passage of substances in and out, an endoplasmic reticulum for protein synthesis and intracellular transportation, transfer RNA, ribosomal RNA, messenger RNA, Golgi sacs for the synthesis and packaging of glycoproteins, hundreds of mitochondria to supply the energy needs of the cell, lysosomes for housing digestive enzymes, ribosomes by the thousands for protein production, centrioles to aid in cellular division, a nuclear membrane to house the chromosomes and nucleoli for producing RNA-protein complexes.[17] (Fig. 56)

A living cell is a staggeringly complex machine. It consists of thousands of organelles (small organ-like structures such as mitochondria and ribosomes) and myriads of diverse chemicals all beautifully orchestrated and functioning in a mutually beneficial and orderly fashion. (Fig. 57) But even complexity does not guar-

---

16. R. TOCQUET, (REF. 13) P. 43.
17. L. MARGULUS: "MICROBIAL EVOLUTION ON THE EARLY EARTH," IN *CHEMICAL EVOLUTION* . . .,(REF. 6) P. 481.

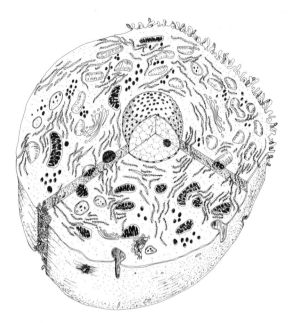

Fig. **56** Living Cell

antee life, for if the cell could not find food it would die.
Therefore, food, a packaged form of energy must be present and in
available form. The cell, on the other hand, needs just the right
kind of chemical apparatuses to breakdown, store and utilize the
food, plus an appropriate means of eliminating the toxic end products of metabolism.

　　The authors of the book, *Enzymes*, speak to the problems posed
by imagining life forming through gradual complexification:

> "Let us now suppose that in some way proteins did come
> into existence; even if they had enzymatic properties
> there is no reason why their activities should be re-
> lated, and it is highly improbable that they would form
> a continuous chain such as we have seen is necessary for
> the trapping of energy and its utilization for the bio-
> synthetic reactions which constitute life. Yet the oc-
> curence of a single gap would prevent the development of
> the system . . . The inherent instability of the vital
> mechanism is also a difficulty, since it requires a con-
> tinuous supply of available energy to maintain it. Un-
> til a complete functional system is produced, capable of
> producing the energy for its own maintenance, it might
> have a strong tendency to disintegrate, as do living
> cells as we know them when the energy supply is cut off
> . . .Thus the whole subject of the origin of enzymes,
> like that of the origin of life, which is essentially

the same thing, bristles with difficulties. We may surely say of the advent of enzymes, as Hopkins said of the
advent of life, that it was 'the most improbable and the
most significant event in the history of the universe'."[18]

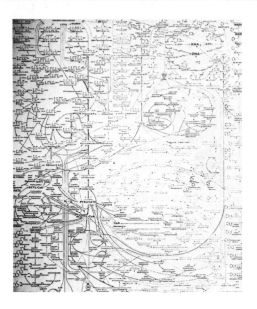

Fig. **57** - Biochemical   Interdependency
*Within the tissues of life are an infinite-like array of chemical
pathways. Life results from synchronization of complex chemistry
and not from the isolated independent action of any of life's
parts (note arrows).*

The evolutionist, Robert Tocquet, also corroborates statements
here about the complexity and interdependency in living organisms:
"Living matter is, therefore, a highly organized system,
'an extremely well-ordered state,' to use the term of
Professor Schrodinger, presenting a complicated and precise architecture, yet capable of adjustment in the process of assimilation. Each of its elements taken alone
is not the bearer of life, but taken together they are
living. If they dissociate, life vanishes."[19]
Blum writes in a similar vein:
"In all modern organisms energy metabolism is so closely

18. M. DIXON AND E. WEBB: *ENZYMES* (N.Y.: ACADEMIC, 1964), PP.
668, 669.
19. R. TOCQUET, (REF. 13) P. 29.

198

dependent upon the existence of proteins, catalysis by
enzymes being an intimate part, that it is difficult to
see how they could have evolved separately . . . The
riddle seems to be: How, when no life existed, did substances come into being which today are absolutely essential to living systems yet which can only be formed
by those systems . . . although it may be obvious that
the gene could not have arisen before there existed complex molecules, how can it be decided whether or not
such molecules arose before the initiation of life itself?"[20]

Life, in the absence of interdependency and complexity, is un-
heard of. Life rides upon complexity, not on DNA alone, nor on
protein, a membrane or organelles alone.

So then, what is life? Incorporating the ideas we have discussed: Life is a code describing an urge for self maintenance and
perpetuation in combination with a mechanism and machinery that
allows the independent expression of that code. This is consistent with the understanding of the authors, Anthony and Kolthoff,
who wrote, and I paraphrase, "life means self-maintenance and self-
reproduction."[21]

On the other hand, anything less than life cannot sustain or
perpetuate itself without the concomitant existence of life. Non-
living matter may accrete, or "grow," such as is the case with
crystals, or the building of polymers in the laboratory, but these
processes will not continue beyond a point. There is no continuous functional drive to a higher level of complexity. The fate
of anything less than life is degradation, dissolution, destruction and return to randomization. Non-life reaches a stalemate,
an equilibrium, a static state; life has continual direction and
progressive urge. (Fig. 58)

The scientist, Sinnott, wrote of life, it:
". . . stands in direct opposition to the behavior of
lifeless matter. The latter moves toward ever greater
randomness . . . A living organism, on the contrary,
draws out from its chaotic environment particular substances and builds them into a system of ever greater
and more organized complexity, thus steadily decreasing
the randomness of matter. An organism is not an aggregate, but an integrate . . . Life is organization."[22]

20. H. BLUM: TIME'S ARROW AND EVOLUTION (PRINCETON: PRINCETON
UNIVERSITY, 1968), PP. 160, 164, 171.
21. C. P. ANTHONY AND N. J. KOLTHOFF: TEXTBOOK OF ANATOMY AND
PHYSIOLOGY (ST. LOUIS: MOSBY, 1971), P. 3.
22. E. W. SINNOTT: TWO ROADS TO TRUTH (N.Y.: VIKING, 1953) P. 131.

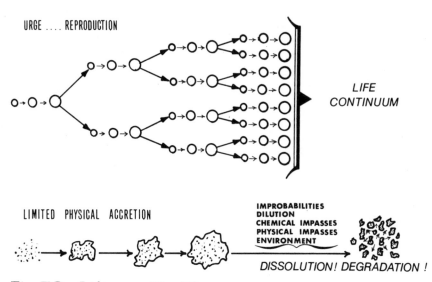

URGE .... REPRODUCTION

LIFE CONTINUUM

LIMITED PHYSICAL ACCRETION

IMPROBABILITIES
DILUTION
CHEMICAL IMPASSES
PHYSICAL IMPASSES
ENVIRONMENT

DISSOLUTION! DEGRADATION !

Fig. 58 Life vs Nonlife
Life is unique in that it contains information describing an urge for self-maintenance and reproduction, in combination with a mechanism and machinery that allows the independent expression of that information--top drawing. Every spontaneous process, in the absence of life, experiences only limited accretion and ultimate dissolution--bottom drawing. (Modified from D. T. Gish: SPECULATIONS AND EXPERIMENTS RELATED TO THEORIES ON THE ORIGIN OF LIFE (San Diego: ICR, 1972).)

One must wonder why, if life is simply a property of matter, is "life" restricted to a time and place? Why is life not all pervasive as is the physical law of gravity, for example? Why are the unique characteristics of life only there when the living is alive? Is life really a property of matter, or is matter a property of life? Is man really more than the $5.60 worth of material he is composed of?

Haldane, an evolutionist, argues:

> "If the minimal organism involves not only the code for its one or more proteins, but also twenty types of soluble RNA, one for each amino acid and the equivalent of ribosomal RNA, our descendents may be able to make one, but we must give up the idea that such an organism could have been produced in the past, except by a similar pre-existing organism or by an agent, natural or supernatural, at least as intelligent as ourselves, and with a good deal more knowledge."[23]

23. *J. HALDANE: "DATA NEEDED FOR A BLUEPRINT OF THE FIRST ORGANISM," IN* THE ORIGINS *. . .,(REF. 7) P.12*

Haldane is not here abdicating his evolutionary position, yet he is unusually open and fair in admitting the difficulties in envisoning a chemical evolutionary progression culminating in life. Other evolutionists would take issue with the need for all of the materials Haldane suggests might be necessary for the minimal organism. They suggest further knowledge will one day allow us to define, if not make, organisms that could serve as the intermediaries between complex chemicals and life.

For our part, we must decide, based upon the evidence we have, whether life is a property of matter, or matter a property of life. In the preceding chapter we discussed the law of biogenesis which says life cannot spring from non-life. If there is really no such thing as "life," then the law cannot be used to refute spontaneous generation. If there is such a thing as "life," if it can be definitionally set apart from the material, then the law stands and spontaneous generation remains in violation.

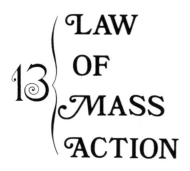

13 { LAW OF MASS ACTION

The chapters on the origin of DNA and protein assumed no difficulties would be encountered in spontaneously forming the respective biomonomers (building blocks). The assumption was also made that the biomonomers would link (polymerize) into giant protein and DNA polymers with ease. To this point we have primarily concerned ourselves with the sequences in protein and DNA, i.e., what could account for all L-proteins? what could account for the information riding on the sequences in DNA and protein? can existing DNA within organisms be modified and complexify? etc.

In this chapter and the next, we will consider questions regarding the mechanics of the formation of biomonomers and polymers. The evolutionary model must demonstrate that natural processes can account for biomonomers and subsequent polymerization of these into chains. The evolutionist must advance natural mechanisms and a natural environmental setting for their spontaneous formation. The creationist must sit back and watch, challenging the evolutionary proofs that are pleaded. If the mechanism and evidence used to demonstrate naturalistic origins are credible, then the evolutionist has a feather in his cap. If the creationist can show that naturalism is inadequate, then, since life with all of its complex biochemicals is here, he could argue the need for a supernatural agent to account for it. If his case is unsatisfactory, the evolutionist could counter by expressing trust that future discovery and thought will vindicate his position. The creationist would, in turn, object to the evolutionist expressing faith in future discovery to justify belief in evolution, and contend that even if biomonomers could form, they could not link into information carrying sequences. And on and on the controversy would go.

We must listen intently and critically as we continue to ask ourselves: Where does the evidence fit best, under creation, or under evolution?

From the Water or "Sky"?

Let's examine the controversy over the formation of biochemical polymers from biomonomers. Adler said: "Life began in water, probably over two billion years ago."[1] Given this watery slime of antiquity, will the biomonomers of proteins (amino acids), the biomonomers of DNA (nucleotides), the biomonomers of polysaccharides (sugars), or the biomonomers of lipids (glycerol and fatty acids) link up into increasingly complex polymers? (In the subsequent discussion we will focus on protein formation, but what is said will apply as well to DNA, polysaccharides and lipids since they all polymerize by a similar chemical process.)

Let's assume there was a brew of 100% L-amino acids (forgetting the difficulties in this as discussed previously) in the oceans of the primordial earth. What would happen given these watery conditions?

Amino acids participate in the following general reaction:

Amino Acid + Amino Acid ⟷ Protein + Water

This reaction is reversible, as you may note by the double arrows. The amino acids may combine (condensation) to form protein and water, or the protein may react with water (hydrolysis) and revert back to the constituent amino acids. Actually, neither reaction occurs at the exclusion of the other. Rather, the reaction is in equilibrium--a state of dynamic back and forth flux.

Many factors, such as the conditions employed, chemical reactivities, and relative amounts of each of the reactants influence the direction in which a reversible reaction will predominate. If we assumed the conditions for the early earth postulated by evolutionists, which way would the reaction predominate: to the right--formation of protein, or to the left--formation of amino acids? The reaction to the left, the formation of amino acids, would prevail.

This is true because the direction in which a reversible reaction will go depends to a large extent upon the relative quantities of the chemicals on each side of the equation. The more opportunity chemical reagents on one side of the reaction have to "bump" into one another, the greater are the chances they will react. If there is an abundance of amino acids, then the reaction should proceed primarily to the right because the amino acids on the left are "bumping" into each other with greater frequency than

---

1. *IRVING ADLER: HOW LIFE BEGAN (N.Y.: NEW AMERICAN LIBRARY, 1957) P. 55.*

are the protein and water molecules on the right. On the other
hand, if there is an abundance of protein or water, then the reaction will proceed primarily to the left because the protein and
water are "bumping" into each other with greater frequency than
are the amino acids on the left. This chemical principle is known
as the law of mass action and is summarized:

Smaller Number of Molecules $\rightleftharpoons$ Larger Number of Molecules

Stated still another way, if a reaction can proceed in either
direction, that is, if it is reversible, it will predominate in
the direction from highest concentration to lowest concentration--
assuming adequate and appropriate energy is present.
So what about the evolutionist's argument that life began in
the water? Well, excess water would prevent the formation of protein, as well as lipids, nucleic acids and polysaccharides.(Fig.59)
In other words, although some protein would form, the law of mass
action would immediately become operative upon it. The protein
would react with the abundant water and hydrolyze back into the
original amino acids:

Amino Acid + Amino Acid $\rightleftharpoons$ Protein + Excess Water

Recognize that we're only talking about two amino acids linking. Imagine the problems involved in trying to hook up hundreds
or thousands into the proteins characteristic of life. The simple
chains of two and three amino acids would dissociate into their
constituent amino acids as soon as they would form. Never would
they hang around long enough to form the long complex chains characteristic of the proteins of life.
Keosian has said:
> "Dehydration (condensation) reactions are thermodynami-
> cally forbidden in the presence of excess water."[2]

Blum wrote:
> "It is commonly assumed today that life arose in the o-
> ceans . . . But even if this soup contained a goodly con-
> centration of amino acids, the chances of their forming
> spontaneously into long chains would seem remote. Other
> things being equal, a dilute hot soup would seem a most
> unlikely place for the first polypeptides to appear . . .
> The chances of forming tripeptides would be about one-
> hundreth that of forming dipeptides, and the probability
> of forming a polypeptide of only ten amino acid units
> would be something like $1/10^{20}$. The spontaneous forma-

---

2. *J. KEOSIAN: THE ORIGIN OF LIFE (N.Y.: REINHOLD, 1968), P. 74.*

tion of a polypeptide of the size of the smallest known
proteins seems beyond all probability."[3]

Polemics on Polymer Origins

The creationist says, following upon this, that the law of mass
action and an aqueous primal earth are a formidable dam to naturalistic formation of polymers. The evolutionist counters by arguing
that evidence the dam can be broken is provided in the chemists'
laboratory. The polymers found in life can be formed in the lab,
why, given similar conditions,could they not be formed in the primordial earth, he reasons. Further, the body is mostly water yet
it forms protein. Why couldn't the primal earth do the same?

When proteins are synthesized in the laboratory, the reaction
is "pushed" to the right by supplying sufficient energy and removing water as soon as it is formed. The reaction must be "hot and
dry" (Fox).[4] The removal of water and the addition of large quantities of amino acids result in the chemicals on the left side being more abundant than those on the right. Thus, under these conditions, mass action would force the reaction to the right, that
is, toward the formation of proteins.

Mora has described the needs of a reversible reaction in this
way:

> "To keep a reaction going according to the law of mass
> action, there must be a continuous supply of energy and
> of selected matter (molecules) and a continuous process
> of elimination of the reaction products."[5]

However, is the ability of chemists to force the reaction to
the right under designed and controlled conditions support for the
thesis that synthesis could occur spontaneously in the primordial
oceans? The creationist would claim the experimental formation of
proteins simply shows the need for a synthesizer, a designer, without which no synthesis would take place. Chance and inherent chemical forces and abilities are not the primary driving cause of synthetic experiments in the laboratory, the intelligent designer is!
The chemist has inserted the extra ingredient--mind, the creationist would insist.

Organisms are predominantly water yet they are veritable factories of protein polymers. Is this not testimony that polymers
could form spontaneously in the early oceans? The human body is

3. H. F. BLUM: *TIME'S ARROW AND EVOLUTION* (PRINCETON: PRINCETON
UNIVERSITY, 1968): 158
4. S. FOX IN *THE ORIGINS OF PREBIOLOGICAL SYSTEMS AND THEIR MO-
LECULAR MATRICES*, ED. S. W. FOX (N.Y.: ACADEMIC, 1965), P. 378.
5. P. MORA: "THE FOLLY OF PROBABILITY," IN *THE ORIGINS* . . .,
(REF. 4) P. 43.

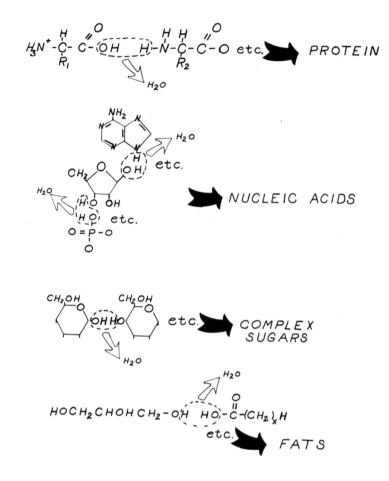

Fig. **59** – Condensation Reactions

The chemical reactions that form proteins, nucleic acids (DNA, RNA), complex sugars (polysaccharides) and fats (lipids) are known as condensation reactions. As the polymers are built up from subunits (e.g., proteins from amino acids), water is liberated. After the water is released the subunits join: the C=O of one amino acid will attach to the N of the next amino acid. These condensation reactions are reversible and in the presence of excess water (the primitive oceans?) will proceed from the complex to the simple rather than from the simple to the complex:

SUBUNITS ⟷ POLYMER + H_2O (EXCESS)

approximately 60% water, but the body is not a primordial soup with processes randomly directed. Living organisms are highly integrated and elaborately constructed synthetic laboratories. Inherent in living organisms is the ability to initiate, catalyze and control chemical reactions. Just as the chemist is able to manipulate and control his experiments in order to drive the reactions in the direction desired, likewise the machinery of the body can manipulate chemical processes. In this case, the law of mass action is "postponed" by the biological machinery much like the law of gravity is "postponed" by the machinery of an elevator.

The question before us is how did the synthetic laboratories embodied in living organisms come into being in the first place? The creationist would argue that the ability of chemists and living cells to form proteins is beside the point. The issue is the formation of protein prior to the existence of human chemists or living biochemical factories. Besides, the creationist maintains, designed experiments demonstrate that the proteins of life could be generated by design--the application of intelligence exogenous to the synthesis.

Not with protein synthesis do the problems posed by the law of mass action stop. Most of the crucial reactions necessary for the building up of living tissue are condensation reactions. As mentioned earlier, fats, complex sugars and nucleic acids (DNA, RNA) are polymerized via the liberation of water. (See Fig. 59) So these chemicals as well as proteins could not arise spontaneously from the watery milieu assumed by evolutionists. Excess water would drive the reactions to the left, that is, toward the simplest units rather than toward complex polymers.

But evolutionists are not without additional answers to the objections raised by mass action. Several have suggested different means by which polymers could form in the early earth. Some deny that life originated in the oceans.

Blum, after considering the improbabilities of polymer formation in a primal "hot soup," says:

> "Of course, one may imagine that the first polypeptides were formed in relatively non-aqueous media. It has long been a laboratory practice to carry out such reactions in solvents other than water."[6]

Sydney Fox has postulated the formation of proteins in the hot and dry environs envisioned on the edges of volcanoes. Bernal has suggested that the syntheses proceeded on clay or mineral catalysts. Melvin Calvin proposes the condensing agent, dicyanamide (DCDA), as the savior to the formation of proteins. Schramm believes phosphorus pentoxide in ether would have promoted protein formation. Others have suggested polymerization through the intermediate of hydrogen cyanide.

To be sure, there is no lack of laboratory explanations for

---

6. *H. BLUM, (REF. 3) PP. 158,159.*

the formation of the chemicals of life on the early earth. However, do these explanations support the thesis of spontaneous origins, or do they simply demonstrate the expertise of chemists in the laboratory? The relevancy of each scientist's pet model to actual early earth conditions is the subject of heated debate even in "origin-of-lifer" circles.

In Fox's model the volcanic heat used to form proteins would more readily function to degrade them.[7] Schramm's phosphorus pentoxide in ether model is of questionable relevancy to earthly conditions now or in the past. Bernal's clays could only form miniscule amounts of products. The hydrogen cyanide model demands an atmosphere of ammonia which is contradicted by the geological evidence.[8] And Calvin's dicyanamide model uses excess amino acids to drive the reaction to the right, and acid pH, yet the primitive geological picture points to an alkaline (opposite of acid) environment with no chemist present to add the excess of amino acids. The complexity of the molecules formed by these various proposals is only faintly suggestive of the giant information carrying molecules of life, e.g., Calvin's dicyanamide forms only four unit "proteins."

Arguments Summarized

In summary, how does the controversy stand on the question of the origin of the polymers of life?
(A) The evolutionist believes that the chain-like polymers of life could have originated prebiotically through natural processes. He reasons, contemplating the similarity between the sea and living watery protoplasm, the ancestral cradle must be the primordial seas. The ability of watery protoplasm to synthesize these molecules is taken as testimonial to the verity of this belief. He also gives credence to extrapolations from laboratory productions of protein strands, polynucleotides, etc. The laboratory conditions are suggested to portray on a small scale the larger early earth scenario. If difficulties in any of these naturalistic conditions surface, faith is expressed they will clear with further research and thought. Invoking the supernatural would be premature and reminiscent of the naive mentality of ages past, e.g., when the inability to form any organic compounds outside the body was taken as proof for a creator.
(B) The creationist would suggest that the failure to explain the natural origin of life's giant polymers in a credible

---

7. *C. SAGAN IN* THE ORIGINS *. . . ,(REF. 4) P. 374-377.*
8. *P. H. ABELSON: "CHEMICAL EVENTS ON THE PRIMITIVE EARTH," IN* PROCEEDINGS OF THE NATIONAL ACADEMY OF SCIENCE, *55 (1966): 1365-1369.*

fashion points to the need to invoke an other than natural agency (supernatural) to account for their existence. Since the notion of life beginning in water is negated by the law of mass action and based upon the argument that similarity proves relationship (the similarity between sea water and tissue fluids is understood to mean tissues are related to the sea--have come from the sea), he concludes (1) life could not have begun in the water and (2) the argument that similarity points to relationship is invalid. He feels designed laboratory experiments point not to naturalistic extrapolations, but to the need to invoke the added ingredient--intelligence. Therefore, the origin of life would depend upon preexisting intelligence. Even if the results of experimental models are allowed, their relevancy to early earth conditions is of questionable feasibility. Additionally, unjustifiably huge extrapolations are necessary to conclude anything about origins from them. The creationist also pleads that the evolutionist's faith in future naturalistic discoveries is perhaps logical but certainly not a scientific basis for belief in naturalistic interpretations of origins <u>now</u>. If naturalists contend their position is true because of what is known now, how can what is unknown, i.e., faith in future discovery, be used to substantiate the belief?

We the jurors must weigh the two arguments within the context of the methodological guidelines we have agreed upon. Based upon evidence we know to be true, can we best extrapolate to the evolutionary or to the creationistic interpretation?

14 { PRIMITIVE ENVIRONMENT

The primordial earth is viewed by evolutionists as a hot ball that gradually cooled over eons of time. With the formation of the crust and the oceans, the earth's forte was then the spontaneous generation of life. An atmosphere was formed, lightning bolts struck, and to these amenities it is suggested we **owe homage for our** existence.

There have been many experiments that attempt duplication of the speculated primordial conditions. The results have been, to say the least, most exciting to evolutionists. The products obtained in these experiments have included the organic building blocks of life! Have creationists been given the coup de grace? Do these results constitute proof that life could or did arise spontaneously?

In this chapter we will closely examine the speculated early earth conditions. In the next we will scrutinize biopoiesis (spontaneous generation) experiments.

Oxygen

A significant difficulty in the spontaneous generation of the chemical precursors to life concerns the composition and nature of the primitive environment. For example, it is well known that the chemicals of life will decompose in the presence of atmospheric oxygen.[1] Oparin, in discussing the conditions to be employed in experiments designed to demonstrate biopoiesis, confirms the hostility of present conditions:

---

1. *P. H. ABELSON: "SOME ASPECTS OF PALEOBIOCHEMISTRY," IN ANNALS OF THE NEW YORK ACADEMY OF SCIENCE, 69(1957):281.*

"First of all, we saw that the present atmosphere, with
its ozone screen and highly oxidizing conditions, is not
a suitable guide for gas-phase simulation experiments."[2]
This sensitivity of biochemicals to oxygen is cited as one of the
main reasons why life is not spontaneously forming now.

The chemicals of life are predominantly in a reduced state,
the opposite of oxidized. If these chemicals are exposed to oxygen or oxidizing conditions, they lose their necessary reduced
state and decompose to their member chemicals, namely, into carbon dioxide, water and nitrogen. (It is startling to realize that
we are living in an atmosphere containing this poisonous gas, oxygen. And not only are we living in it but we are breathing it
and depending upon it for our very existence!) This is much the
same as paper will burn (decompose) when exposed to heat and oxygen. Consequently, the evolutionist reasons, "since life is here,
and it therefore must have evolved, the primitive atmosphere must
have been a reducing one, not an oxidizing one."

The assertion that the primitive earth had a reducing atmosphere is an assumption forced by knowledge that the chemicals of
life could not have evolved in an oxidizing atmosphere.[3] A reducing atmosphere is not an induction forced from observations.
Harold Urey makes this clear in speaking to the difficulty of biopoiesis in an oxidizing atmosphere:

"This problem practically disappears if Oparin's assumptions in regard to the early reducing character of the
atmosphere are adopted."[4]

Urey, a pioneer in biopoiesis research, simply assumes a reducing
atmosphere as proposed by the earlier work of the Russian evolutionary biochemist, Oparin.

Urey and Oparin are not alone in their assumption of a reducing early atmosphere. The biochemists, Steinman and Kenyon, summarize the situation:

". . . conclusions have been disputed to some extent,
but there is general agreement at least among 'origin
of lifers' on major points such as the virtual absence
of molecular oxygen in the primitive secondary atmosphere."[5]

There are evidences that chemists can cite to argue for the
notion that the primeval earth had a reducing atmosphere, but all

---

2. *A. I. OPARIN: LIFE: ITS NATURE, ORIGIN AND DEVELOPMENT
(EDINBURGH: OLIVER AND BOYD, 1961), P. 118.*
3. *T. LOEBSACK: OUR ATMOSPHERE (N.Y.: NEW AMERICAN LIBRARY, 1961)
PP. 17, 22; H. UREY: "ON THE EARLY CHEMICAL HISTORY OF THE EARTH
AND THE ORIGIN OF LIFE," IN PROCEEDINGS OF THE NATIONAL ACADEMY
OF SCIENCE, 38(1952):352*
4. *H. UREY, (REF. 3) P. 352.*
5. *A. I. OPARIN, (REF. 2) P. 34.*

of them fall short of being unequivocal. The experimenter, Stanley Miller, states regarding the arguments for a reducing atmosphere:
> "These ideas are of course speculation, for we do not know that the earth had a reducing atmosphere when it was formed."[6]

The evidence that speaks for an early atmosphere containing oxygen is usually ignored. Davidson delivered an address at a symposium on the evolution of the earth's atmosphere and argued that the earth's atmosphere was always essentially as it is today:
> "These observations based on the stratigraphical record contradict the belief that a primeval reducing atmosphere persisted for much of Pre-Cambrian time."[7]

Urey himself has noted that early rocks have iron in them in an oxidized state (ferric oxide).[8] If iron is oxidized in the rocks supposedly dating to the time of biopoiesis, then the implication is that oxygen may have been there to do the oxidizing.

Also, if water is acted upon by radiation from the sun or by electrical discharges in the atmosphere, it will dissociate into hydrogen and oxygen. Thus, Brinkman argues:
> "Appreciable oxygen concentrations might have evolved in the earth's atmosphere before the evolution of widespread photosynthesizing (oxygen producing) organisms. It does not seem that early evolution could have proceeded in such an atmosphere."[9]

The oxygen formed by the photolysis of water could also combine with hydrogen to form peroxides which are particularly destructive to biochemicals.[10]

So there are many evidences that argue directly for an early oxidizing atmosphere. The belief that early conditions were reducing is, therefore, truly an assumption.

The problems facing spontaneous origins are not solved simply by postulating a reducing atmosphere (methane, carbon monoxide, hydrogen, ammonia, nitrogen, water) rather than an oxidizing atmosphere (carbon dioxide, water, nitrogen, oxygen). If we dismiss the evidence cited above that militates against an early reducing atmosphere, concede a reducing atmosphere, we find ourselves still faced with tremendous problems.

---

6. *S. L. MILLER: "PRODUCTION OF SOME ORGANIC COMPOUNDS UNDER POSSIBLE PRIMITIVE CONDITIONS," IN JOURNAL OF THE AMERICAL CHEMICAL SOCIETY, 77 (1955): 2351.*

7. *C. F. DAVIDSON: "GEOCHEMICAL ASPECTS OF ATMOSPHERIC EVOLUTION," IN PROCEEDINGS OF THE NATIONAL ACADEMY OF SCIENCE, 53(1956):1203.*

8. *H. UREY, (REF. 3) P. 360, 361.*

9. *R. T. BRINKMAN: "DISSOCIATION OF WATER VAPOR AND EVOLUTION OF OXYGEN IN THE TERRESTRIAL ATMOSPHERE," IN JOURNAL OF GEOPHYSICAL RESEARCH, 74 (1969):5366.*

10. *A. SZUTKA: "PROBABLE SYNTHESIS OF PORPHYRIN-LIKE SUBSTANCES DURING CHEMICAL EVOLUTION," IN THE ORIGINS OF PREBIOLOGICAL SYS-*

Ultraviolet Light

For the moment, let's assume a reducing early atmosphere. Without oxygen in the early atmosphere, ozone, the gas produced by oxygen and found surrounding the earth about 15 to 30 miles high, would likewise not have been present. Ozone shields the earth from ultraviolet rays. Ultraviolet rays, if permitted to reach the earth in significant quantities, could destroy the chemicals of life just as decisively as could oxygen.[11] In fact, if the ozone shield in our present atmosphere were removed, most organisms would expire in less than an hour--many within one second![12] (It is the presence of these rays in outer space that makes the idea of life being seeded here by cosmic spores implausible.)

Thus we have the conundrum: If oxygen were in the primitive atmosphere, life could not have arisen because the chemical precursors would have been destroyed through oxidation; if oxygen were not in the primitive atmosphere, then neither would have been ozone, and if ozone were not present to shield the chemical precursors of life from ultraviolet light, life could not have arisen. The evolutionist is in the position of "not being able to live with it, and not being able to live without it!" (Fig. 60)

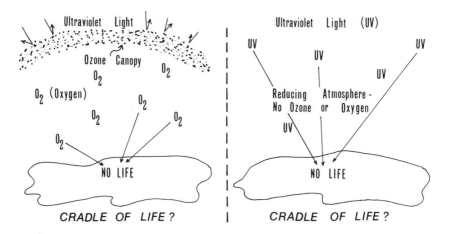

Fig. **60** - Atmospheric Puzzle

TEMS AND THEIR MOLECULAR MATRICES, ED. S. W. FOX(N.Y.: ACADEMIC, 1965), P. 243.
11. R. TOCQUET: LIFE ON THE PLANETS (N.Y.: GROVE, 1962), PP. 22,23.
12. C. SAGAN: "PRIMORDIAL ULTRAVIOLET SYNTHESIS OF NUCLEOSIDE PHOSPHATES," IN THE ORIGINS . . .,(REF. 10) P. 212; ALSO SEE HIS ARTICLE IN ENCYCLOPEDIA BRITANNICA, 13(1973):1083L.

Protein Growth Dead – Ended

The primitive oceans would have contained not only water, but simple organic molecules like aldehydes and amines in far greater abundance than the more complex amino acids. The water, as mentioned in Chapter 13, would hydrolyze proteins. Additionally, the aldehydes and amines will react with amino acids to render them unsuitable for building amino acid chains (proteins)--in effect, they "dead-end" protein growth. Building amino acid chains in the early ocean would be like trying to build a stack of blocks by removing items randomly from a box that contained a far greater number of balls than blocks: if ever we did get a few blocks stacked, the odds would be greatly in favor of our next grab into the box yielding a ball which would end the series of blocks.

Trop and Shaki, of Bar-Ilan University in Israel, have calculated the probability of forming one protein of 100 amino acids as a random product built from a milieu of amino acids and other simpler organic compounds (carboxyl acids, aldehydes and simple amines) to be $1/10^{157}$. This probability is so remote that Trop and Shaki concluded that no proteins of this size could ever have been produced on the earth even given the vast time periods evolutionists argue for.[13] (Similar application of this calculation could be made to show the implausibility of ever forming any complex biochemical chains like DNA or RNA.)

Nitrogen Concentrations

The materialist needs an ancient milieu rich in organic molecules in order for them to join together and form the giant molecules of life. When we calculated the probabilities for forming proteins and DNA, we substituted for every molecule of water in the earth's hydrosphere, amino acids and nucleotides respectively. But a concentration of this magnitude is clearly infeasible. In reality, evidence suggests that the concentrations of the subunits could never have been significant at all in the early earth.

Gish, a biochemist, has made an interesting calculation relevant to early earth concentrations of nitrogen containing molecules (most biochemicals contain nitrogen).[14] He calculated that if all of the nitrogen in the atmosphere, less that rendered unavailable for molecule building by ultraviolet light, were spread

---

13. *M. TROP AND A. SHAKI: "IS MOLECULAR EVOLUTION OF PROTEINS POSSIBLE?" IN CREATION RESEARCH SOCIETY QUARTERLY, 11(1974):28,29.*
14. *D. GISH: SPECULATIONS AND EXPERIMENTS RELATED TO THEORIES ON THE ORIGIN OF LIFE--A CRITIQUE (SAN DIEGO: ICR, 1972), P. 11.*

between 1000 different biochemicals (five unit proteins alone could exist in almost a million different arrangements), the concentration of any one species would be 0.0000002 molar. To express Gish's figure in a different way we could say that if one of the 1000 molecules was a nucleotide, that nucleotide would have to hunt through about one million different molecules before it could find another nucleotide to link to (irrespective of whether the linking would result in the appropriate sequence). Thus, the concentration of any one chemical species would be too low to generate the more complex molecules necessary for life.

Phosphorus Concentrations

Similar observations have been made regarding the availability of phosphorus. Phosphorus is necessary for the formation of the phosphates in the DNA chain and for the formation of high energy compounds which are used in numerous biochemical transformations. Bernal has argued that the phosphorus concentration under primitive earth conditions would have been so low that life could not have evolved.[15] (This is not saying that he or most of those quoted herein do not believe life evolved.) Ponnamperuma and Sagan have shown that adenosine triphosphate (high energy phosphate) could not form in prebiological conditions.[16] Schwartz maintains that all suggestions on the origin and role of phosphates in biopoiesis are implausible geologically (not relevant to early earth conditions).[17]

Hull's Testimony

Hull has made calculations that imply even greater difficulties for the biochemist who needs a concentrated primeval ocean of organic chemicals. Given the primitive environment described by Urey and Miller, Hull calculated that the reversible reaction that forms the amino acid glycine would only yield a 10^{-27} molar concentration.[18] This would mean that glycine would have to hunt though approximately 10^{29} other molecules before it could find

15. J. BERNAL IN THE ORIGINS . . .,(REF. 10) P. 236.
16. C. SAGAN AND C. PONNAMPERUMA IN THE ORIGINS . . .,(REF. 10) P. 275.
17. A. W. SCHWARTZ: "THE SOURCES OF PHOSPHORUS IN THE PRIMITIVE EARTH--AN INQUIRY," IN MOLECULAR EVOLUTION: PREBIOLOGICAL AND BIOLOGICAL, EDS. D. L. ROHLFING AND A. I. OPARIN (N.Y.: PLENUM,1972), P. 129.
18. D. HULL: "THERMODYNAMICS AND KINETICS OF SPONTANEOUS GENERATION," IN NATURE, 186(1960):693,694.

another glycine to link to. Imagine, if we substituted people
for molecules, having to find a friend in a crowd of people 100,
000,000,000,000,000,000 times greater than the earth's population (10^{-27} molar)!

Hull has made similar calculations for more complex amino
acids (glycine is the simplest) and found that even smaller concentrations would obtain. As the complexity of the molecule to
be formed increases, its yield decreases. The concentration of
glucose would be 10^{-134} molar.[19] This almost infinitely dilute
solution of sugar would mean that a sugar molecule would have to
hunt through 10^{136} other molecules to find another sugar molecule
to begin building a polysaccharide. Translated into the situation where a person is looking for a friend in a crowd, the friend
would have to look through a crowd larger than could be contained
in a cube measuring 87 quadrillion light years on an edge!

The energy sources that are cited by evolutionists as the
driving force for the reactions yielding biochemicals, often serve
more readily to destroy the products than to create them. Hull
calculates that ultraviolet light would destroy glycine as soon
as it would form. The larger molecules, proteins, sugars, fats,
etc., would be even more efficiently destroyed by the energy in
the primitive environment. As complexity increases (1) reaction
yield decreases, (2) stability against heat decreases, and (3) the
molecules become more susceptible to ultraviolet ray decomposition.[20]

Hull concludes from his data:

"Consideration of other sources of energy, although they
are very much weaker than the ultraviolet radiation,
leads to similar conclusions. Thus ionizing radiation
may form complex products from simple reactants, but
the more complex and highly organized compounds are more
vulnerable to the same agent than their simple precursors. G-values of the order of unity are found for the
decomposition of proteins by radiation; whereas the formation of protein by radiation has not been observed.

"The conclusion from these arguments presents the most
serious obstacle, if indeed it is not fatal, to the theory of spontaneous generation. First, thermodynamic
calculations predict vanishingly small concentrations
of even the simplest organic compounds. Secondly, the
reactions that are invoked to synthesize such compounds
are seen to be much more effective in decomposing them.

"The physical chemist, guided by the proved principles
of chemical thermodynamics and kinetics, cannot offer

---

19. *D. HULL, (REF. 18) PP. 693,694.*
20. *IBID*

any encouragement to the biochemist who needs an ocean full of organic compounds to form even lifeless coacervates."[21]

Other researchers have made similar conclusions about the hostility of the early environment to biopoiesis.

Oparin:

"Numerous calculations of a thermodynamic equilibrium, which would occur when the organic substances dissolved in the primordial hydrosphere were irradiated with ultraviolet or were provided with some other energy sources show that no primeval broth could exist there, since under ultraviolet light, decomposition processes prevail over synthetic ones."[22]

Dayhoff has calculated that the concentration of organic substances in the atmosphere could be only insignificant.[23] And Szutka has likewise concluded that ultraviolet light would prevent the formation of larger molecules in the primitive earth.[24]

Keosian observes:

"With few exceptions, the simulated primitive earth conditions employed by investigators are harsh; not only inimical to present living things, but destructive to polymeric substances . . . The first organism, it is claimed, had to hide from the very elements that led to its creation, for it is generally agreed that atmospheric conditions on the primitive earth, especially the high flux of energetic ultra-violet rays, would destroy any form of life."[25]

If life is to have spontaneously evolved, each progressive step must be compatible with the conditions that brought it about. But we have seen that what little product could be formed is destroyed by the very agency that created it. Thus, an upward progressive complexification (without even considering the necessity of forming sequences carrying information) is contradicted; and devolution, degradation, dissolution, and decomposition are much more probable.

The Evolutionary Counter

It is suggested that the atmosphere changed suddenly from reducing to oxidizing simultaneous with the origin of life. In this

---

21.   IBID
22.   A. OPARIN: "PROBLEM OF THE ORIGIN OF LIFE: PRESENT STATE AND PROSPECTS," IN CHEMICAL EVOLUTION AND THE ORIGIN OF LIFE, EDS. R. BUVER AND C. PONNAMPERUMA (N.Y.: AMERICAN ELSEVIER, 1971), P.6.
23.   A. OPARIN, (REF. 22) P. 6.
24.   A. SZUTKA IN THE ORIGINS . . .,(REF. 10) P. 243.
25.   J. KEOSIAN: THE ORIGIN OF LIFE (N.Y.: REINHOLD 1968), PP. 63,77,78.

way, evolutionists say, life would have been protected from ultraviolet light by the ozone canopy formed from the oxygen, and
the evolved life forms would have had oxygen with which to re-
spire.

Sagan discusses the change from reducing to oxidizing conditions:

> "At that time, the 'free' production of organic matter
> by ultraviolet light was effectively turned off and a
> premium was placed on alternative energy utilization
> mechanisms. This was a major evolutionary crisis. I
> find it remarkable that any organism survived it."[26]

Sagan's amazement is warranted for several reasons. For example, organisms that cannot live in the presence of free oxygen
(obligate anaerobic bacteria) would have been destroyed with a
"sudden" change from reducing to oxidizing conditions. Furthermore, even if all of the plants presently on this planet were
there in the beginning to produce oxygen, a "sudden" genesis of
oxygen to a level comparable to present day concentrations would
require 5,000 years.[27]   However, plants were not there,
and even if they were they could not survive without concomitant
oxygen for their own cellular respiration.

Scientists are not to be found without explanations though.
There are investigators who have tried to overstep the difficulty
encountered by ultraviolet light in an oxygen free atmosphere by
suggesting that life was spontaneously generated under a protective shield of several feet of water.[28] On the other hand, some
have tried to overcome the problem of mass action (protein synthesis being thwarted in a watery environment) by proposing the spontaneous formation of proteins on dry rocks and clays.

A summary of explanations is interesting. It has been shown
that life could not form in the presence of an atmosphere containing oxygen, so life must have formed in a reducing atmosphere.
Yet that couldn't be, since living organisms need oxygen to survive, and without atmospheric oxygen there would not be an ozone
canopy to shield the fragile chemicals of life from ultraviolet
light. Therefore, life must have formed under the protective
shield of several feet of water. But if the chemical precursors
to life were under several feet of water, what would supply the
chemicals with the necessary energy to react and form more complex molecules, and how could proteins be formed if water favors
their dissociation rather than their synthesis? Furthermore, what
would prevent currents within the water from bringing the chemical
precursors to the surface where they would meet their demise from

---

26. C. SAGAN IN *THE ORIGINS* . . ., (REF. 10), P. 253.
27. G. EHRENSVARD: *LIFE: ORIGIN AND DEVELOPMENT* (CHICAGO: UNIVER-
SITY OF CHICAGO,1962), P. 135.
28. G. WALD: "THE ORIGIN OF LIFE," IN *THE PHYSICS AND CHEMISTRY
OF LIFE* (N.Y.: SIMON AND SCHUSTER, 1955), P. 25.

the action of the ultraviolet rays? It must be, therefore, that the biochemicals were formed on dry clays and rocks, but if that were so then we're back to the original problem of the chemicals being exposed either to the destructive powers of oxygen (oxidizing atmosphere) or ultraviolet light (reducing atmosphere), etc., etc., etc. And round and round and round we go, where we stop nobody knows!

The materialist has trouble explaining the chance formation of life because life and its environment is a highly ordered integrated system. The present ecological crises testify to the highly tuned and integrated nature of the life-environment system. Just as it would be difficult to explain how a complex machine could operate with vital gears, circuits, pulleys and levers missing or defective, so it is difficult to explain the piecemeal formation of the life-environment system on this planet.

The creationist sees the inability of evolutionists to explain a feasible chemical evolution, as testimony for a real lack of evidence for evolution. The dynamic, integrated, life-environment systems, the creationist says, speaks for an intelligent creator. The evolutionist, however, might suggest that even if all of the evidence for evolution was shown impotent, then this would simply mean we have not yet found the right evidence.

We must decide: (1) Does the inability to explain a feasible abiogenesis in the early environment argue for the fact that it never did occur? (2) Does this deficiency in the evolutionary explanation point us to creation? (3) Does the integration between life and its environment force us to believe a sudden coming into existence of both the environment and life--a creation? (4) Do weaknesses in evolutionary explanations simply show the need for more research?

15 ⎰ BIOPOIESIS
⎱ EXPERIMENTS

The origin of life is a subject of intense research. In
the early 1900's, Oparin and Haldane pioneered research in
biopoiesis. Today there are several laboratories around the
globe set aside for the express purpose of investigating the
origin of life. It is not uncommon to read of the accomplishments of these "origin-of-lifers" in the local newspaper.
Often they are credited with discoveries that imply to the
reader that man is able to synthesize life in the laboratory.
It is commonly held that the accomplishments of researchers
have discredited the notion of creation.
    Laboratory experimentation allows men to come the closest
to direct visual, repeatable proof of spontaneous origins,
and disproof of creation. Since chemical evolution depends
upon entirely natural forces, an examination of these forces
in the laboratory could make or break abiogenesis (biopoiesis,
spontaneous generation, chemical evolution). On the other hand,
the laboratory proof of creation is impossible because creation,
of course, depends upon a supernatural agent, and laboratory
procedures are performed by natural human agents. But creation
can be disproved in the laboratory by the proof of the alternative.
    However, laboratory "proofs" or "disproofs" must be
qualified. Any "proof" or "disproof" would be circumstantial
in that conditions used in any experiment could not be proven
to be the exact conditions extant at the time of the origin
of life. Nevertheless, if scientists were able to create life,
the argument that a supernatural agent is an absolute necessity,
could be dismissed.
    We will discuss the more significant experiments, their
legitimacy, value and pertinence. Origin of life experimentation can basically be divided into two categories. The first
involves laboratory duplication of primitive earth conditions;

the second involves dissections of organisms and subsequent artificial duplication of life processes through the use of dissected parts.

Miller – Urey Duplication

The most widely acclaimed experimental model is that of Miller and Urey. Urey, as we noted in the previous chapter, assumed a reducing atmosphere in the early earth. He also argued that the atmosphere would have contained abundant amounts of ammonia, methane, hydrogen and water vapor. The Miller-Urey spark discharge tube was designed to determine if organic compounds could be produced by discharging sparks (simulated early earth lightning) into this postulated atmosphere. (Fig. 61)

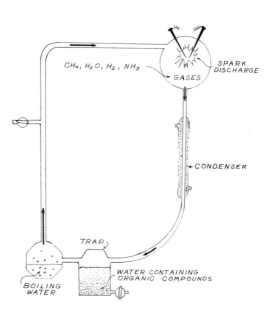

Fig. **61**-Spark Discharge Apparatus

In the Miller-Urey apparatus, the gases, methane, water, hydrogen and ammonia are subjected to spark discharges. These gases were supposedly the major gases of the primitive earth's atmosphere. The spark discharges are suggested to simulate lightning bolts. The products of the spark move into a trap as it is believed the early organic chemicals would have fallen into the oceans.

Miller's work with the discharge tube, along with the work of several others using similar devices, has shown conclusively that organic compounds can be artificially formed. A vast list of chemicals have been produced, including amino acids, DNA components and various other organic substances.[1]

That these experimental results constitute proof life could spontaneously arise is specious. The relevancy of the Miller-Urey model is also open to debate.

The following list describes some of the common objections to the Miller-Urey model:

A. The concentrations of methane and ammonia were chosen to approximate the constituents of the amino acid glycine. No evidence forces the use of this concentration, rather, it is chosen with the express intent to produce organic molecules, not mimic early earth conditions. If the concentrations of methane and ammonia were high, no amino acids would obtain.[2]

B. A methane-ammonia reducing atmosphere would be highly toxic to life.

C. The geochemist, Abelson, states: "The hypothesis of an early methane-ammonia atmosphere is found to be without solid foundation and indeed is contradicted." He makes this conclusion because (1) ultraviolet light would destroy ammonia more rapidly than it could be formed; and (2) if methane were in abundance in the early atmosphere, older sedimentary rocks should contain significant amounts of organic material, but they don't; and (3) evidence indicates that heavy gases like xenon and krypton escaped from the primitive atmosphere, therefore, so would the lighter methane and ammonia gases have escaped. This knowledge excludes the possibility of a dense methane-ammonia early atmosphere. Abelson has his own ideas as to how life arose (volcanic outgassing), but concludes about the Miller-Urey model: "What is the evidence for a primitive methane-ammonia atmosphere on earth? The answer is that there is no evidence for it, but much against it."[3] Others have made similar negative conclusions about the feasibility of a methane-ammonia atmosphere.[4]

D. The Miller apparatus is designed to produce. If the products

1. J. KEOSIAN: *THE ORIGIN OF LIFE* (N.Y.: REINHOLD, 1968), PP. 32-38.
2. P. ABELSON: "SOME ASPECTS OF PALEOBIOCHEMISTRY," IN *ANNALS OF THE NEW YORK ACADEMY OF SCIENCE*, 69(1957):275.
3. P. ABELSON: "CHEMICAL EVENTS ON THE PRIMITIVE EARTH," IN *PROCEEDINGS OF THE NATIONAL ACADEMY OF SCIENCE*, 55(1966):1365.
4. M. STUDIER, R. HAYATSU AND E. ANDERS: "ORGANIC COMPOUNDS IN CARBONACEOUS CHONDRITES," IN *SCIENCE*, 149(1965):1455-1459; W. RUBEY: "GEOLOGIC HISTORY OF SEAWATER," IN *BULLETIN OF THE GEOLOGICAL SOCIETY OF AMERICA*, 62(1951):1111-1148.

formed in the spark-discharge tube were not removed from the energy used to form them, they would be more readily degraded than synthesized.

Science News reported that the scientist, Arrhenius, "contends that if actual lightning struck rather than the fairly mild discharges used by Miller, any organics that happened to be present could not have survived."[5]

Miller himself admits in this regard: "Most of the photochemical reactions at these low wavelengths would have taken place in the upper atmosphere. The compounds so formed would have absorbed at longer wavelengths and therefore might have been decomposed by this ultraviolet light before reaching the oceans."[6]

Oparin believes: "The significant accumulation of organic substances, sometimes rather complicated ones, in such experiments is related to their removal from the sphere of action of the energy source which caused their formation . . . For instance, in Miller's experiments, amino acids which have been formed in an electric discharge, have rapidly moved from the site of their formation and accumulated in an adjoining vessel."[7]

But substances formed in the atmosphere could not rapidly leave their sphere of formation for, as Hull states, it takes three years to move from the stratosphere to the surface. Hull's conclusion regarding the Miller apparatus is: "They have merely used the well-known principle of increasing the yield of a reaction by selectively removing the product from the reaction mixture. The mere fact that a chemist can carry out an organic synthesis in the laboratory does not prove that the same synthesis will occur in the atmosphere or open sea without the chemist."[8]

E. The experiments have provided only the building blocks of life, never the highly ordered, information carrying, optically active (D or L) molecules characteristics of life--let alone anything even suggestive of a living entity.

5. *SCIENCE NEWS* (DEC. 1, 1973):340.
6. S. L. MILLER AND H. C. UREY: "ORGANIC COMPOUND SYNTHESIS ON THE PRIMITIVE EARTH," IN *SCIENCE*, 130(1959):247.
7. A. I. OPARIN: "PROBLEM OF THE ORIGIN OF LIFE: PRESENT STATE AND PROSPECTS," IN *CHEMICAL EVOLUTION AND THE ORIGIN OF LIFE*, EDS. R. BUVER AND C. PONNAMPERUMA (N.Y.: AMERICAN ELSELVIER, 1971), P. 6.
8. D. HULL: "THERMODYNAMICS AND KINETICS OF SPONTANEOUS GENERATION," IN *NATURE*, 186(1960):693,694.

There are many more problems with the Miller-Urey model that are shared among all origin of life experiments. We will forestall their discussion to consider them after we examine the Fox model.

Fox   Duplication

Sydney Fox and coworkers have suggested a model to explain the formation of proteins and other complex organic molecules on the early earth. The model is ingenious and is receiving much

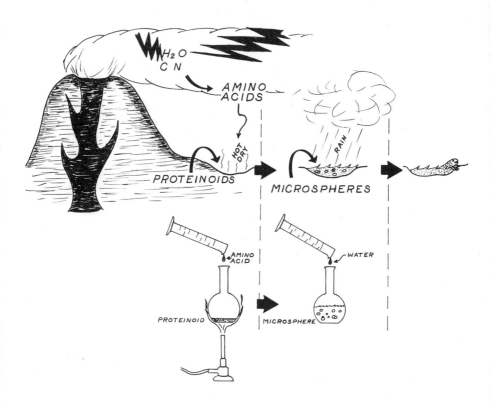

Fig. **62**- Fox   Model

The Fox experiments are illustrated in the bottom two drawings. Fox believes this process, by the sequence seen in the top drawings, occurred in the primeval earth.

acclaim. Fox heats a dry mixture of L-amino acids and obtains chains of amino acids which he calls proteinoids, or thermal pan-polymers. He then puts these polymers into water, and there they aggregate into small spherules which he terms microspheres. Fox is very enthusiasic about this model because he believes it explains the spontaneous origin of not only proteins, but also cell-like precursors that could serve as prebiological systems. He also feels the model is relevant to the conditions in the early earth: amino acids formed in the atmosphere could settle out on the hot and dry environs of volcano edges, polymerize, and subsequently be washed by rain into pools of water where they would in turn form microspheres and ultimately complexify into life itself. (Fig. 62)

Fox feels that proteinoids have most of the qualities of biological proteins. He has reported that proteinoids have cata-lytic ability(suggestive of enzymes), some antigenicity, and are not entirely random in their sequences.[9]

Microspheres are reported to have many of the qualities of living organisms: osmotic phenomena, budding abilities like yeast cells, septate division, aggregation into groups and chains similar to bacteria, internal granular appearance, double-layered outer membrane, non-random movement of internal particles similar to cytoplasmic streaming, blastula-like appearance, rouleaux form-ation like red blood cells, Gram staining like bacteria, molecular communication, growth and catalytic activity. (Fig. 63)

Photographs of microspheres and coacervates (Oparin's term-inology for a similar structure)showing these "life-like" charac-teristics abound in the literature.[10] Freshman college students are even making these structures in their basic science courses. (Fig. 64)

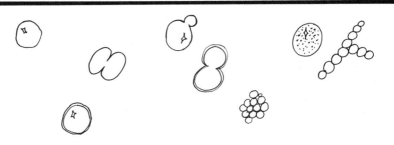

Fig. **63** - Microsphere Forms

These drawings represent the various "life-like" forms microspheres can take. The twin forms seen here, and "microsphere division" are generally produced by pressing on the microscope cover slip.

9. S. W. FOX AND K. HARADA: "THE THERMAL COPOLYMERIZATION OF AMINO ACIDS COMMON TO PROTEIN," IN JOURNAL OF THE AMERICAN CHEMICAL SOCIETY, 82(1960):3745-3751.
10. J. KEOSIAN, (REF. 1) P. 47.

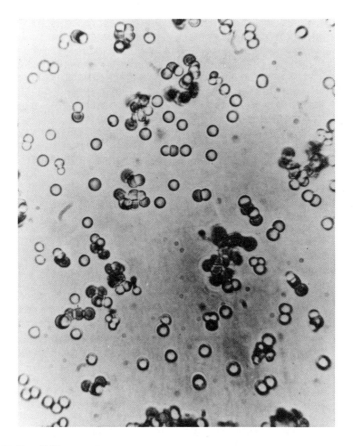

Fig. 64 - Microspheres
This is a photograph of microspheres magnified X 450. Many of the forms drawn in Fig. 63 can be seen here. (Courtesy of S.W.Fox)

As with the Miller-Urey proposal, Fox's model, although attractive, has come under much attack by critical scientific eyes. Let's scrutinize the proteinoid theory of the origin of life.

A. We learned from our study of the law of mass action that proteins could not form in the presence of excess water. Fox knows this also. He suggests that proteins formed on the hot and dry environs of volcano edges and lava flows. Such conditions seem very unlikely, or at least rare in an environment subject to frequent rains--an environmental condition that Fox also argues for.

B. Temperatures as high as 1000°C are used by Fox in his experiments. This heat would quickly destroy many amino acids, especially the sensitive molecules of threonine, serine and cysteine. Likewise this heat would destroy any protein forming. (Protein enzymes will degrade in temperatures as low as $60^{\circ}C$, and all contemporary life would expire at $150^{\circ}C$.)

C. Fox is not oblivious to these problems. However, he has suggested that the series of events he is able to accomplish in the laboratory would have likewise occurred on the primitive earth. He suggests a watery atmosphere in which amino acids are formed, a hot dry locale on volcano edges for the synthesis of proteins, and periodic rains to quickly wash the products away from the heat into pools of water. There the proteinoids would concentrate to form microspheres.

He suggests that there would have been this succession of events over and over again on the early earth: Amino acids formed in a watery atmosphere; proteins formed in the absence of water; microspheres formed in the presence of water. (See Fig. 62) Vallentyne, Miller and Urey feel that the Fox model is irrelevant to what could have happened on the early earth.[11] Sagan writes: "This sequence may be convenient in the laboratory; whether it occurs frequently in nature is less clear." Sagan maintains that the temperatures used in the Fox experiments would pyrolyze (heat destruction) amino acids, depolymerize proteins and degrade microspheres.[12]

D. Fox argues that the proteinoids he has formed have "qualitatively virtually all of the properties of contemporary protein."[13] This may be true, but so does a junkyard by the presence of iron, glass, plastic and chrome have the "qualities" of an automobile; and a field of cotton has the "qualities" of a nicely tailored London cotton suit; and a box of erector set components has the "qualities" of a draw bridge made of these components. The proteins of life are unique because of their structure and their information carrying sequence. They have certain qualities shared by proteinoids it is true, but biological proteins are quantitatively different in these qualities much the same as the literary work of a two year old differs from that of a Pulitzer prize winner.

Here are further reasons why the proteinoid theory is questioned:

---

11. J. VALLENTYNE IN THE ORIGINS OF PREBIOLOGICAL SYSTEMS AND THEIR MOLECULAR MATRICES, ED. S. W. FOX (N.Y.: ACADEMIC, 1965), P. 379; S. L. MILLER AND H. C. UREY: "THE ORIGIN OF LIFE," IN SCIENCE, 130(1959):1622-1624.

12. C. SAGAN IN THE ORIGINS . . ., (REF. 11) PP. 374-377.

13. S. W. FOX: "THE PROTEINOID THEORY OF THE ORIGIN OF LIFE AND COMPETING CONCEPTS," IN AMERICAN BIOLOGY TEACHER, 36(1974):172.

1. The concentration of proteinoids formed spontaneously (assuming any would form at all) would be too low.[14]
2. All L-amino acid proteinoids are not formed spontaneously.
3. Any catalytic ability possessed by proteinoids is not due to a specific structure, but rather due to certain active amino acids, (added by the experimenter) spread randomly through the polymer.
4. Proteinoids lack tertiary structure.
5. No information conveying sequence is found in proteinoids, they are essentially random.[15]
6. The amino acids, aspartic acid and glutamic acid, are found in far larger proportions in proteinoids than in biological protein; cystine, serine and threonine are found in only trace amounts in proteinoids, yet are abundant in biological proteins.[16]
7. The overall simplicity of proteinoids and the lack of any rational mechanism by which they could complexify to the status of biological proteins makes them of dubious relevancy to the origin of the proteins of life. Thus, even Fox honestly admits: "Proteinoid is, however, not identical to contemporary protein."[17]

E. Microspheres (Fox) and coacervates (Oparin) are cited as the intermediary step between dispersed chemicals and isolated biological systems. It is within these prebiological systems that evolution is believed to have proceeded upward to the cell. The main drawing card for microspheres is that they are attributed with life-like characteristics, i.e., budding, membranes, division, growth, etc. Microspheres have also come under scientific attack:

1. Microspheres contain none of the complex biochemicals found in life--unless such chemicals are added to the medium whereupon they may be absorbed into the spheres like a napkin absorbs. If the sphere then takes on the properties of the chemical absorbed, is the sphere then life-like? Could we consider a napkin alive if it absorbed similar substances?

   Growth in coacervates and microspheres is also a physical process. As the spheres absorb, they increase in mass. But, of course, a napkin will increase in mass as it absorbs spilt milk--is it then considered life-like?

14. C. SAGAN, (REF. 12) P. 377.
15. S. L. MILLER AND H. C. UREY, (REF. 6) P. 1624.
16. S. W. FOX AND K. HARADA, (REF. 9) PP. 3745-3751; S.W.FOX, K. HARADA, K. WOODS AND C.R. WINDSOR IN *ARCHIVES OF BIOCHEMISTRY AND BIOPHYSICS*, 102 (1963):439.
17. S. W. FOX: "THE EVOLUTIONARY SIGNIFICANCE OF PHASE-SEPARATED MICROSYSTEMS," REPRINT OF *INTERNATIONAL MOSCOW SEMINAR*, AUG. 2, 1974, P. 13.

2. Microspheres and coacervates are extremely fragile. Fox even says microspheres "can be redissolved by warming the microscope slides."[18] Any complexity that may develop within microspheres would be lost upon a slight bump in the road, e.g., "warming" (Fox).

   Smith and Bellware suggest that microspheres increase in complexity as they are repeatedly dehydrated and hydrated (dilution destroys microspheres), i.e., formed and destroyed.[19] The complexity that they speak of must surely be only a superficial physical complexity, not the orderly type characteristic of life. It would seem that high degrees of order could never be accomplished through repeated destructions. Order achieved at any level would be vitiated each time the microspheres would dissolve. How could the order of a preceeding stage be remembered and built upon in the succeeding stage if between the two stages everything was randomly dispersed?

3. Microspheres and coacervates contain none (setting aside superficialities) of the dynamic and structural characteristics of cells. Any property shown by these structures is a pure physical phenomenon, as Oparin cautions.[20] Asserting that these tiny spheres are life-like is no more valid than proclaiming that oil droplets in a mixed decanter of vinegar and oil salad dressing are life-like because they are round, small and are seen to move in the liquid.

   The claim that microspheres have "membranes" is no more true than suggesting the separation between oil and vinegar in the shelved decanter is a "membrane". The order of complexity in microsphere membranes is similar to the vinegar-oil phase separation. The membranes encasing living cells, on the other hand, are elaborately complex structures.[21] Cell membranes are so complex that thousands upon thousands of man-hours have been spent just trying to understand their structural detail.

A car eats food in the form of gas, is it therefore alive? A pile of sand grows as more is added, is it alive? A drop of

---

18. S. W. FOX: "THE THEORY OF MACROMOLECULAR AND CELLULAR ORIGINS," IN *NATURE*, 205(1965):336.

19. A. E. SMITH AND F. T. BELLWARE: "DEHYDRATION AND REHYDRATION IN A PREBIOLOGICAL SYSTEM," IN *SCIENCE*, 152(1966):362,363.

20. A. I. OPARIN IN *THE ORIGINS* . . ., (REF. 11) P. 357.

21. H. HOLTER: "HOW THINGS GET INTO CELLS," IN *SCIENTIFIC AMERICAN*, 205(1961):167-180; M. AND L. HOKIN: "THE CHEMISTRY OF CELL MEMBRANES," IN *SCIENTIFIC AMERICAN*, 213(1965):78-86.

mercury will divide when it is thrown to the floor, is it
therefore alive? Glue in tannic acid will form a membrane, grow
as a result of osmosis and divide, is the glue alive?

Life means information content, a definitive structure, the
ability to seek out and consume food, expel wastes, metabolize,
regulate activities and reproduce. Microspheres and coacervates
perform none of these functions.

The claim that the Fox model proves life can form spontaneously is premature to many scientists. Perhaps the Chinese
proverb is aptly applied here: "The man who eagerly awaits the
arrival of a friend should not mistake the beating of his own
heart for the thumping hooves of the approaching horse."

Other Duplication Problems

There are other experimental models for the origin of life
besides the two we have discussed. Most of the experiments are
modifications of the Miller-Urey type. The apparatus is changed
somewhat to increase yield, and other energy sources have been
used besides electrical discharges, for example: ultrasonics,
hypersonics, radiation, sun, heat, artificial light, ultraviolet
light, gamma radiation and even bullets shot into pools of
reagents.[22]   All of the experiments that pursue the objective of duplicating early earth conditions in hopes of observing
the spontaneous formation of life share certain common
deficiencies.

Abelson lists five major factors--usually not taken into
consideration in the experimental models--that would limit the
kinds of compounds that might accumulate in the primitive
oceans:[23]

1. There are serious limitations on what can be made by
   inorganic means.
2. All organic material degrades spontaneously with time.
3. Most of the substances suggested to be precursors of
   life would be destroyed by the prevalent radiation in
   the early earth.
4. Many products formed in the ocean would be removed and
   rendered inactive as precipitates, e.g., fatty acids
   would combine with magnesium or calcium; and arginine,
   an amino acid, chlorophyll and porphyrins would be
   absorbed on clays.
5. Many of the chemicals would react with other chemicals
   to form nonuseful, nonbiological products. For example,
   sugars and amino acids would be chemically incompatible.

---

22. J. *KEOSIAN*, *(REF. 1) PP. 28,68.*
23. P. *ABELSON IN* <u>*PROCEEDINGS*</u> . . ., *(REF. 3) P. 1369.*

In the experimental models, the scientists usually start with pure reagents (Fox begins with L-amino acids and no sugars are present). They adjust the temperature, regulate the pH and make other maneuverings to insure success. Would the primitive oceans have been so benevolent toward these processes?

Another more general deficiency can be noted by examining carefully the following quote from Keosian's book, *The Origin of Life:*

> "In general an investigator takes substances which he assumes were the precursors of primitive organic compounds and places them in an apparatus designed to similate and maintain presumed primitive earth conditions."[24]

Did you notice the phrases: "substances which he assumes," and "presumed primitive earth conditions?" This makes manifestly clear the point we made in the chapter on methodology, that is, the question of the origin of life is not a scientific question.

Even if experimenters were able to create conditions which resulted in the spontaneous formation of life, as we said earlier, the answer of origins would still not be answered. Why? Because the conditions and materials employed are not known to have been common with the conditions and materials at the time of the origin of life. Thus it is impossible to do as Sagan says we can: "duplicate primitive conditions."[25]

Keosian states:

> "There is no general agreement on what represents primitive earth conditions . . ."[26]

It is for this reason, as Oparin admits:

> "The degree to which experimental conditions actually simulate primitive earth conditions is very often the subject of considerable controversy among workers in the field."[27]

Without exact knowledge of the conditions to be duplicated, experiments on the origin of life are certainly not science, rather, as Mora states:

> "Such experiments are no more than exercises in organic chemistry."[28]

This brings us to the next deficiency common to duplication experiments.

The creationist alleges that intelligent meddling in experiments designed to show the spontaneous formation of life

---

24. *J. KEOSIAN, (REF. 1) P. 27.*
25. *C. SAGAN: THE COSMIC CONNECTION (N.Y.: DELL, 1973), P. 3.*
26. *J. KEOSIAN, (REF. 1) P. 27.*
27. *A. I. OPARIN: LIFE: ITS NATURE, ORIGIN AND DEVELOPMENT (EDINBURGH: OLIVER AND BOYD, 1961), P. 33.*
28. *P. MORA: "THE FOLLY OF PROBABILITY," IN THE ORIGINS . . ., (REF. 11) P. 41.*

actually demonstrates the need for intelligent interference
when life originally did arise. Thus, even if life were synthesized in the laboratory, without exact duplication of primitive earth conditions, what would be proven? The creationist
sees this as proof that life will not arise without the added
ingredient--mind? (Fig. 65) The evolutionist objects to this
creationist conclusion because it precludes the possibility that
any experimental work could support evolution, since experimental investigation, by definition, requires an intelligent
investigator.

from <u>The Creation Evolution Controversy</u> by R L Wysong © 1976

Fig. **65** - The Experimental Paradox

Many scientists, for example, Oparin, argue that exact
conditions are not necessary to demonstrate the spontaneous
origin of life. Evidence, he says, will result from the chemical abilities themselves.[29] Fox goes further and argues that
his experiments have actually shown the predeterministic
abilities of chemicals.

Arguing against the creationistic position, he states:

"In my view, the most fundamental argument for not
including creationist overviews in biology textbooks
is that the science alone is sufficient to explain in
outline what is and has been going on, plus the
subtle specificities in the vast array of the biological realm. No additional agent need be invoked to
explain an evolutionary sequence that is proving to
be self-generating at every stage that has been
studied."[30]

"Self-generating" he says, but creationists would come back
and say: "Notice this description of one of his 'typical panpolymerization experiments'":

"Typical Panpolymerization - Ten grams of L-glutamic
acid was heated at 175-180° until molten (about 30
min.) after which period it had been largely converted
to the lactam. At this time, 10 g. of DL-aspartic
acid and 5 g. of the mixture of the sixteen basic and
neutral (BN) amino acids were added. The solution was
then maintained at 170° ± 2° under an atmosphere of
nitrogen for varying periods of time. Within a period
of a few hours considerable gas had been evolved, and
the color of the liquid changed to amber. The
vitreous mixture was rubbed vigorously with 75 ml. of
water, which converted it to a yellow-brown granular
precipitate. After overnight standing, the solid was
separated by filtration. This was washed with 50 ml.
of ethanol, and as substance S dialytically washed in
moving Multidialyzers in water for 4 days, the water
being changed thrice daily. The term dialytic washing indicates dialytic treatment of a suspension. In
some preparations, the solid was dissolved completely
in sodium bicarbonate solution and then dialyzed. The
dialysis sacs were made of cellulose tubing, 27/32 in.,
to contain 50 ml. The nondiffusible material was
ninhydrin-negative before the fourth day. The non-
aqueous contents of the dialysis sac were mainly solid
A and a soluble fraction B recovered as solid by con-

---

29. *A. I. OPARIN, (REF. 27) P. 119.*
30. *S. W. FOX: "THE PROTEINOID THEORY OF THE ORIGIN OF LIFE
AND COMPETING CONCEPTS," IN THE AMERICAN BIOLOGY TEACHER,
36(1974):172.*

centration in a vacuum desiccator. The mother liquor of S was also dialyzed for 4 days, and then dried to give additional solid C."[31]

"Spontaneous" Televisions

Investigators examine the intricate structural details of life. Amino acids fit together to make proteins, sugars link up to form polysaccharides and DNA nucleotides combine together to form chains. Then, in the laboratory, they produce the same arrangements by artificial means, namely, proteins, DNA chains, etc; primitive earth conditions are postulated to accomplish the same events performed in the laboratory, and the pronouncement is made: "Life is purely the result of spontaneous chemical processes."

The creationist says: "Could I not argue the same about the origin of a portable television set I find left behind on a deserted beach? If I have never seen such a machine before, and know not its origin, I could reason, being a materialist, that it originated by natural causes. To 'prove' this, I take the set to my laboratory and disassemble it. I notice during my investigation that there are certain biases, e.g., metal screws will only enter holes if turned in a clockwise fashion, only certain resistors will fit in particular impressions in the circuitry board, the glass on the front of the set can only be placed in position if its longest edge is kept horizontal to the set.

"I make certain chemical analyses and find that the melted plastic is not as miscible with the cardboard insulation as it is with itself; that right-handed screws can be made by forming molds and pouring molten iron into them; that solder will only bond the metal parts, not the plastic, wood or paper parts. In other words, the arrangements I see within the set are 'self-dictating'. With the appropriate conditions and materials I find that I can observe the "spontaneous" generation of each of the components of the set.

"Aha! The television set is the product of the natural outworking of the properties of the atoms of which it is composed. A creator? Bah! Humbug! I can create a television set in the laboratory! But, someone says, 'There was no laboratory on the beach.' Getting a little cocky, I say: 'Nature is the laboratory. The atoms themselves possess the intrinsic abilities to combine in the arrangements we see in the television set. What probably happened was that the mountain east of the beach was once a volcano. When it was spewing out lava several multi-

31. *S. W. FOX AND K. HARADA IN* JOURNAL A.C.S., *(REF.9) P. 3745.*

quadrupledoopleillion years ago, the stage was set for the formation of the television set. While the lava flows were still
hot, meteorites made impressions in them of various configurations. When the lava hardened, then molten iron, plastics, etc.,
came from reactions in the atmosphere under conditions similar
to what I had in the laboratory, and from fissures in the earth,
to fill these impressions.'

"'When it rained, there would be differential shrinking of
the lava molds from the hardened materials within--a perfectly
natural physical process. The molded product, let's say a screw,
would then loosen from the mold and be shook out of it by earth
tremors (very common in the early earth). The screw would roll
down the hill, by gravity--again just a natural process--and
bounce into the appropriate holes in the television chassis which
had similarly been formed and was sitting on the beach at the
bottom of the mountain. Of course, there was some measure of
chance in these processes, for example, those screws rolling
counterclockwise would not fit whereas those rolling clockwise
would. But since the holes in the chasis were biased such that
they could only receive a screw rolling in the clockwise direction, sooner or later such a screw would roll into place. The
screws were thus selected--you know, natural selection. Probability has little to do with such events though; the properties
of the components themselves, their biases and their selection
override any improbabilities that might be imagined!

"Duplication experiments are designed to produce, not mimic
what might have been plausible conditions at the time of the
origin of life. Of course amino acids can link together, they
must be able to since life is filled with millions of them
linked together in proteins. Of course nucleotides can form
chains, they must be able to, since all life contains and produces such chains constantly! The question is not whether these
chemicals can be made to form outside of the biological machine,
but, whether such processes would occur naturally."

The Seashore Experiment

Keosian says, concerning origin of life experiments:
"For reasons of expediency, all employ apparatus which
too greatly confines the reactants and products, a
condition which can greatly alter the course of reactions and the nature and amount of end-products."[32]
Then why not simply make a large vat, supply an atmosphere, ocean,

---

32. J. KEOSIAN: "THE ORIGIN OF LIFE PROBLEM--A CRITIQUE," IN
MOLECULAR EVOLUTION: PREBIOLOGICAL AND BIOLOGICAL, EDS.
D. L. ROHLFING AND A. I. OPARIN (N.Y.: PLENUM, 1972), P. 18.

seashore, chemicals, bombard it with energy, let it rock gently, and then see what happens? This is being seriously considered by some because of the questionable relevancy of the various experimental models. But it is not done. Why?

Steinmann and Kenyon have suggested such a seashore-like experiment, but reject its feasibility because they would not know "what one should look for." However, "not knowing what to look for" does not prevent them from advocating experiments like these of Miller, Urey and Fox. This is because these experiments are designed to produce a product. Thus one knows what to look for.

Steinmann and Kenyon advocate biochemical predestination and rule out the notion of probability as having a role in the origin of life. Then, in discussing a seashore model which would most closely approximate real earthly natural conditions, they state:

> ". . . if we have the phenomenal luck of finding a
> fully developed organism arising in such a simulation
> experiment."[33]

Luck? What does luck have to do with it? Is life, or is it not the inevitable consequence of matter?

A "seashore" model experiment would do much toward quieting the nagging creationists and scientists picking bones with the various experimental models, or, it would silence the bragadoccio of abiogenists. The experiment should be performed.

Dissections and Recombinations

The second general class of experimentation involves dissecting living organisms and then recombining the chemicals thus derived. Scientists (Kornberg, Ochoa, Goulian, Sinsheimer, Khorana and others) have been able, through years of devoted study of living organisms, their anatomy, physiology and biochemistry, to disassemble simple life forms like viruses, put the extracted DNA in a testube along with appropriate enzymes and DNA nucleotides, then observe the resultant replication of the DNA molecule. (Fig. 66) This is in turn heralded in the local newspaper as "Man creates life in testube." Then, to the uninformed, this somewhat sloppy piece of propaganda constitutes proof that there is no God and that chance evolution is an established fact.

The creationist counters by asking: "Is one the creator of a novel if he simply copies an existing one? Is one the creator of an art masterpiece if he traces what already exists on

33. *D. H. KENYON AND G. STEINMANN: BIOCHEMICAL PREDESTINATION (N.Y.: MCGRAW HILL, 1969), PP. 31,36,37.*

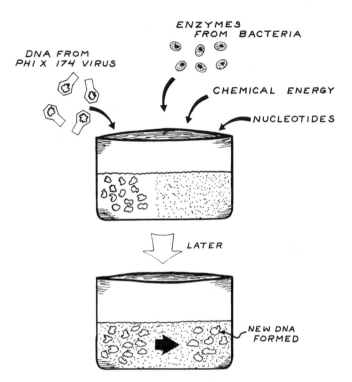

ENZYMES FROM BACTERIA

DNA FROM PHI X 174 VIRUS

CHEMICAL ENERGY

NUCLEOTIDES

LATER

NEW DNA FORMED

Fig. 66 – Kornberg   Experiment

Kornberg, Goulian and Sinsheimer, in 1968, performed an experiment in which millions of DNA molecules from the PHi X 174 virus were combined with the enzymes DNA ligase and DNA polymerase from bacteria that are the natural host of PHi X 174. Nucleotides and chemical energy were also added. The circular DNA from PHi X 174 was replicated, the virus with intact protein coat was not produced.

another's canvas? Is one the creator of a concerto if he simply follows the music that has already been written by another? No! He is simply a copycat.

"Likewise, the heralding of the scientist as the creator of life, when in fact he has simply copied and used parts of living organisms in his experiment, is misrepresentation. He is simply walking a path the creator has already cleared. To decry that these experiments either prove evolution or negate the existence of a creator is absurd.

"The intelligence expended by the scientist just to unravel the secrets of life shows the necessity for intelligence at the beginning of life. To advocate that the formation of life in the testube would cancel out a creator is no more true than asserting that the art tracer, novel copier and concerto duplicator, cancel the existence of the original artists."

Ferreting out truth demands that we realize the difference between circumstantial, speculative, subjective, tendentious, persuasive evidence, on the one hand, and demonstrable, coercive, empirical, compulsive, laboratory evidence, on the other. The conclusions based upon experiments related to the origin of life can only be considered totally honest if the assumptions used in the work are appropriately used as qualifiers. However, quite often this honest approach is not used. As a result, we often hear or read statements about these experiments proving the chance origin of life but no mention is made of the basic assumptions used in the work.

Scientists working in this area of research are fully aware of their assumptions and the inadequacies of their experimental models. Most will openly admit limitations, but maintain further study and research will vindicate evolution. This belief is fine, as long as the experimenter does not forget the highly speculative nature of his work and propose prejudiced conclusions as scientific facts to the public for tacit acceptance.

The Creationistic Counter

The creationist admits science has performed remarkable laboratory feats in origin of life research. However, he rejects the evidence from biopoiesis experiments as irrelevant to the spontaneous origin of life for the following general reasons:

1. The conditions and materials used in the experiments are speculated.
2. Substances derived from life, not from spontaneous processes, are used in many of the experiments.
3. There is intelligent maneuvering of the experiments to obtain preconceived products. Conditions that may be relevant geologically are omitted if they might vitiate the goal of the experiment.
4. Only the chemical building blocks of life have been formed, never the information-carrying and orderly-arranged sequences found in, and indeed, characteristic of life.
5. The need to insert massive amounts of brain power just to unravel the secrets of life and produce experimental conditions allowing the formation of just the building blocks of life, the creationist says speaks to the need for intelligence in the beginning, not spontaneity.

What could the materialist do to prove his case, the evolutionist may say. He could never prove it in the scientific methodological sense, but he could lend considerable credibility to his position if he would simply try to duplicate early earth conditions as faithfully as possible, let the chemicals react--keeping his clammy little hands out of the pot--then see what obtains. This could be the only experimental model relevant to the origin of life. "Let the materialist try this, then," the creationist says, "we'll talk about results."

Additionally, the creationist feels biopoiesis experimentation is all rather ironical. Scientists are spending millions of intellectual man-hours trying to produce the various chemical components of life and sapping tax dollars by the millions to finance their effort. It is obvious, to the creationist at least, that if scientists were to produce all of these chemicals (in "origin of life" relevant or irrelevant conditions), and even in the correct relationships with the degree of complexity seen in living cells, no life would result. How do we know? Because we have abundant free test material. That material is the world of the dead.

Examine cadavers in morgues, blood and guts in slaughter houses, canned and frozen meat and vegetables in grocery stores or pickled bologna at meat markets. All of this material already contains the ingredients scientists are trying to produce. These dead products, if fresh, contain cells, enzymes, DNA, nuclei, cell walls, etc., etc. . . . but they are dead! And they remain dead regardless of the amount of stirring, irradiating, cooling, heating, burning or squashing. No amount of blind energy or added ingredients will ever rejuvenate the cells in pickled bologna, frozen broccoli or fresh chicken gizzards, the creationist insists.

The creationist concludes: "Is not the hope to produce life by arriving at proper chemicals and chemical relationships in experiments a rather bizarre aspiration? It is futile. The trillions of organisms that die and have remained dead stand as solemn proof that life is a unique supernatural quality not reproducible by the puny efforts of men wistfully reaching like moths for the stars."

The evolutionist is not particularly dismayed by the creationist flying all of these objections in his face. "After all, creationists once thought it futile to attempt the formation of proteins and other organic compounds in the laboratory. Well, we formed them with time and effort. Likewise, with more time and effort life will be synthesized in the laboratory both in relevant and irrelevant early earth model conditions," the evolutionist retorts with confidence.

16ࠀTHERMODYNAMICS

The laws of thermodynamics are among the most important in all of science. The science of thermodynamics involves study of energy transformations and the relationship between heat and work. Besides the far-reaching practical uses of the science, both creationists and evolutionists have used thermodynamics to bolster their respective sides.

First Law of Thermodynamics

The first law simply states that energy can neither be created nor destroyed. Energy may be changed from one form into another, but the total amount remains unchanged. Einstein showed that matter is just another form of energy: the two are equal as expressed by the equation: $E = MC^2$. The release of destructive energy by atomic bombs demonstrates that matter can be transformed into energy on a sudden, colossal scale. We might restate the first law then in this way: the sum total of energy, including its form in matter, can neither be created nor destroyed.

How do our two propositions on origins measure up to this law? The evolutionist applies reductionism to nature. He explains that all entities have ultimately sprung from a parent of smaller stature and less complexity. Thus, man has come from primate, which has in turn come from mammal, which has come from reptile, which has come from amphibian, which has come from fish . . . protozoa . . . DNA . . . protein . . . nucleotides . . . amino acids . . . atoms . . . protons . . . neutrons . . . electrons . . . 0. The finale of evolutionary reductionism is zero--all things originally have come from nothing.

This zero state, Isaac Asimov ponders in the following quote: "Where did the substance of the universe come from? . . .

239

If 0 equals (+1) + (-1), then something which is 0 might just as well become +1 and -1. Perhaps in an infinite sea of nothingness, globs of positive and negative energy in equal-sized pairs are constantly forming, and after passing through evolutionary changes, combining once more and vanishing. We are in one of these globs between nothing and nothing and wondering about it."[1]

The astronomer, Professor Fred Hoyle, suggests that matter is continually being created. He hypothesizes that throughout the vast reaches of space, matter is simply "blooping" into existence here and "blooping" into existence there. He says:

"The total rate for the observable Universe alone is about a hundred million, million, million, million, million, tons per second."[2]

The evolutionist asserts that the evolutionary process was in accord with natural law, and, in fact, natural law is held to be the initiator and sustainer of the process. Evolution is spoken of as being "natural." Yet the evolutionary mechanism demands the initial creation of matter and energy from nothing. (Some, however, believe that matter has always existed.) The first law of thermodynamics indicates that just can't happen naturally. Energy can neither be created, nor destroyed:

$$0 \xrightarrow{\quad\times\quad} ENERGY \quad \& \quad MATTER \xrightarrow{\qquad} LIFE$$

$$\underset{First \quad Law}{\uparrow No!}$$

The creationist's proposition, on the other hand, is not "natural"--it is supernatural. As a consequence, the first law of thermodynamics need not apply pre-creation. In other words, the first law would be a creation that would begin with creation.

Other creationists would plead that even if applied, the first law does not contradict creation. The creator is described as infinite, timeless (free from decay) and containing the potential to create the universe. With his infinite power he created matter, according to the creationist. Then at creation he merely externalized a part of himself. Energy was not created, it was simply transformed. So the first law is not violated, i.e., energy was neither created nor destroyed:

$$CREATOR \xrightarrow{\quad\quad} ENERGY \quad TRANSFORMED \xrightarrow{\qquad} ENERGY, MATTER$$

$$\underset{First \quad Law}{\uparrow ok} \qquad\qquad LIFE$$

The two propositions for the origin of matter are contrasted

1. I. ASIMOV: "WHAT IS BEYOND THE UNIVERSE?" IN *SCIENCE DIGEST*, 69 (1971):69.
2. F. HOYLE: *THE NATURE OF THE UNIVERSE* (N.Y.: HARPER, 1960), P. 126.

in this way:
1. Evolution describes everything as ultimately coming from nothing in the beginning.
2. Creation describes everything as being in the beginning from
   which a part subsequently sprung.
   The evolutionist is unable to account for the origin of matter (the atoms of which form the molecules that comprise living
tissue) through natural law. The first law of thermodynamics is
a natural law that says very simply: energy (matter) cannot be
naturally created from nothing.
   Some evolutionists, to circumvent this problem, state that
matter and energy have always existed. Furthermore, they suggest
that this energy and matter inevitably transformed itself into the
universe and biological world by chance. By invoking infinite
matter the evolutionist may have side-stepped the first law of
thermodynamics--just as the creationist does by advancing an infinite creator--but he then finds himself wide-open for an upper-
cut from the creationistic use of the second law of thermodynamics.

Second Law Defined

   The first law of thermodynamics speaks to the quantitative
conservation of energy. The second law (entropy principle) concerns the qualitative degeneration of energy. The ultimate consequence of the second law upon the universe is to be what has
been termed "heat death." In the end, the universe is to be completely random. All energy will be leveled out. No energy gra-
dients will be available for the accomplishment of work, and beauty and order will be lost to a uniform, bleak, blah cold.
   Basically the second law says three things:
1. Systems will tend toward the most probable state.
2. Systems will tend toward the most random state.
3. Systems will increase entropy, where entropy is a measure of
   the availability of energy to do useful work.
   Professor Greene said of the second law:
      "It is a very broad and very general law, and because
      its applications are so varied it may be stated in a
      great variety of ways."[3]
   In its practical and basic sense (as opposed to its theoretical sense, or merely its description of heat flow) the second
law says the above three listed things. These three, in essence,
say one thing. That is, spontaneity causes degradation.
   Julian Huxley, taking the second law as testimony against
the idea of purpose in the universe, has said essentially the same

---

3. E. S. GREENE: PRINCIPLES OF PHYSICS (NEW JERSEY: PRENTICE-
HALL, 1962), P. 310.

thing:

> "Nowhere in all its vast extent is there any trace of
> purpose, or even of prospective significance. It is im-
> pelled from behind by blind physical forces, a gigantic
> and chaotic jazz dance of particles and radiations, in
> which the only over-all tendency we have so far been
> able to detect is that summarized in the Second Law of
> Thermodynamics--the tendency to run down."[4]

Lincoln Barnett wrote:

> "Although it is true that the amount of matter in the
> universe is perpetually changing, the change appears
> to be mainly in one direction--toward dissolution. All
> the phenomena of nature, visible and invisible, within
> the atom and in the outer space, indicate that the sub-
> stance and energy of the universe are inexorably dif-
> fusing like vapor through the insatiable void. The sun
> is slowly but surely burning out, the stars are dying
> embers, and everywhere in the cosmos heat is turning to
> cold, matter is dissolving into radiation, and energy
> is being dissipated into empty space.
>
> "The universe is thus progressing toward an ultimate
> 'heat-death' or as it is technically defined, a condi-
> tion of 'maximum entropy.' When the universe reaches
> this state some billions of years from now all the proc-
> esses of nature will cease. All space will be at the
> same temperature. No energy can be used because all of
> it will be uniformly distributed through the cosmos.
> There will be no light, no life, no warmth--nothing but
> perpetual and irrevocable stagnation. . . . And there
> is no way of avoiding this destiny. For the fateful
> principle known as the Second Law of Thermodynamcs,
> which stands today as the principle pillar of classical
> physics left intact by the march of science, proclaims
> that the fundamental processes of nature are irreversi-
> ble. Nature moves just one way."[5]

H. Morowitz likewise wrote:

> "For not only is man himself a part of nature, a naked
> ape in the current idiom, but he is a naked ape in a
> universe that is decaying to a homogenized nothingness."[6]

Sir Arthur Eddington described the second law as "time's arrow." This implies that the second law points the direction of
all material events in time. Blum has written a book around this

---

4. J. HUXLEY: *EVOLUTION IN ACTION* (N.Y.: NEW AMERICAN LIBRARY,
1953), PP. 11,12.
5. L. BARNETT: *THE UNIVERSE AND DR. EINSTEIN* (N.Y.: NEW AMERICAN
LIBRARY, 1957), PP. 102,103.
6. H. MOROWITZ: "BIOLOGY AS A COSMOLOGICAL SCIENCE," IN *MAIN CUR-
RENTS IN MODERN THOUGHT*, 28(1972):151.

theme, entitled: *Time's Arrow and Evolution*. Therein, Blum states:

> ". . . all real processes tend to go toward a condition of greater probability . . . increase in randomness may be taken as a measure of direction in time. . . . The second law of thermodynamics predicts that a system left to itself will, in the course of time, go toward greater disorder."[7]

As with all laws, thermodynamics works within the confines of certain conditions. Thermodynamics distinguishes between open and closed systems. An open thermodynamic system exchanges heat, light or matter with its surroundings. A closed thermodynamic system does not exchange energy with its surroundings. The universe is believed to be a closed system going toward "heat death," but parts of the universe are open and thus able to exchange energy. It is said that a system within the universe that increases order always does so at the expense of a greater decrease in order in another system. The result of the exchange is a net decrease in order (increased entropy) for the universe. (Fig. 67)

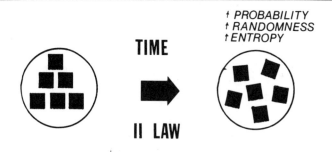

↑ PROBABILITY
↑ RANDOMNESS
↑ ENTROPY

TIME

II LAW

Fig. **67** - The Second Law

The above two circles represent a closed(no energy exchanges with the outside) thermodynamic system. The blocks represent the degree of order therein. The second law of thermodynamics says that all systems will spontaneously tend toward the state of greatest probability, greatest randomization and highest entropy.

In a universe moving toward the oblivion of "heat death," life seems to be an anachronism. Note the growth, the systematic increase in order in an embryo, the energizing of protoplasm to accomplish useful work, and the building up of highly improbable biochemicals. Do not these processes confute the second law? No, for scientists tell us that living systems are not closed systems. Therefore, it is reasoned, the ordering in life must be at the ex-

7. H. BLUM: *TIME'S ARROW AND EVOLUTION* (PRINCETON: PRINCETON UNIVERSITY, 1968), PP. 5,192,201.

pense of a greater disordering elsewhere: The energy utilized by animals and plants comes from the sun which is in turn continually running down, becoming disordered (entropy increase).

If the decreased entropy and high orderliness of life is accounted for solely on the basis of open system thermodynamics, you might ask why other open systems don't likewise experience such ordering? In other words, why don't battered Volkswagons in junkyards order themselves into shiny new Cadillacs? A junkyard is an open system. Why don't heaps of solder, resistors, circuitry boards and plastic in an open thermodynamic system form television sets? These and essentially all other physical systems, open or not, are experiencing constant deterioration not self improvement. In this regard Lindsay wrote:

"There is a general natural tendency of all observed systems to go from order to disorder, reflecting dissipation of energy available for future transformation-- the law of increasing entropy."[8]

The second law, by its refusal to allow perfect efficiency, is the nemesis of those trying to build perpetual motion machines, i.e., in any process energy will be lost to a state where it cannot be reutilized for useful work.

Why is it that life--one-billionth part of the weight of the earth--appears to complexify while the rest of the physical world runs down? Is it really because life is an open system? This does not seem to be a satisfactory answer. The physical world runs down yet it is an open system. Furthermore, all organisms die, i.e., run down, lose organization, yet life is an open system.

One of the reasons for the seeming biological anachronism is that life increases order not only because of outside energy input (an open system), but also because of design, a preexisting metabolic motor, complexity, DNA. Recognizing the uniqueness of life as compared to other systems, Sagan, an evolutionist, stated:

"It is not known whether open-system thermodynamic processes in the absence of replication are capable of leading to the sorts of complexity that characterize biological systems."[9]

Mora concludes that life can be defined as a continuous decrease in entropy (increased order).[10] Immediate reversal of this process occurs upon "death." Mora argues that life, therefore, is unique and stands apart from a physical world which characteristically will always spontaneously increase entropy (decrease order). In other words, Mora asks, why, if life is merely defin-

8. R. B. LINDSAY: "PHYSICS--TO WHAT EXTENT IS IT DETERMINISTIC," IN *AMERICAN SCIENTIST*, 56(1968):100.

9. C. SAGAN: "THE DEFINITION OF LIFE," IN *ENCYCLOPEDIA BRITANNICA*, 13(1973):1083A.

10. P. T. MORA: "URGE AND MOLECULAR BIOLOGY," IN *NATURE*, 199 (1963):216.

able in terms of physics and chemistry, does life experience the constant decrease in entropy and hold this unique ability only so long as the organism is alive.[11]

In the process of trying to finance my schooling I once had occasion to work at a production facility that packaged caulking compounds. Another worker and I would operate a machine that automatically filled and crimped aluminum tubes. One of us would insert the empty tubes into the machine, the other would remove the filled tubes from the other end of the machine and place them in boxes. This was our plight eight hours a day, five days a week for several months--sounds like fascinating work, right?

Anyway, the machine operated by electricity; energy was pumped into it so it was an open thermodynamic system. We never questioned the fact that if the cord were unplugged, the machine would no longer be able to do its job even though it was still operable.

We also knew that if we would place the end of an electrical cord in a barrel of aluminum tubes and caulking compound, that even though energy was flowing into the barrel (an open system) the tubes would not fill uniformly and be crimped. Neatly filled and crimped tubes were clearly a result of energy and the machine's design. (Actually we never really thought this one through, our minds were blank most of the time: put a tube in, take a tube out, put a tube in, take a tube out. . . .)

In principle, this illustrates the situation with life. Neither open system thermodynamics nor the organization in life independently account for systematic biological ordering. They are both necessary. The uniqueness of life, however, is not due to open system thermodynamics, but rather to life's inherent structural mechanism that allows the channelling of energy into useful processes. Life simply "postpones" the second law with respect to biological processes much the same as the law of gravity is "postponed" by a rocket ship.

Blum made note of how a photosynthetic microorganism, if exposed to sunlight, water, CO_2, and certain inorganic ions, would soon reproduce itself many times over. It appears as though the system is increasing order by assembling light rays, random ions and CO_2 molecules into microorganisms. However, Blum continues to explain that the source of the energy for the ordering is the sun, and the sun is losing order at the expense of the new microorganisms gaining it. Thus, if the sun-earth system were summated, there would be a net loss of organization, i.e., more organization is lost by the sun than is gained by new microorganisms--the second law is not violated. Although this might explain somewhat the relationship between the second law and life, it does not really illustrate the problem of the origin of organization. Blum

11. P. T. MORA: "THE FOLLY OF PROBABILITY," IN THE ORIGINS OF PREBIOLOGICAL SYSTEMS AND THEIR MOLECULAR MATRICES, ED. S. W. FOX (N.Y.: ACADEMIC, 1965), P. 43.

reasons:

> "In each of these cases we have deliberately introduced the pattern of that organization into the system when we seeded it with a microorganism, and as a result there has been a quantitative increase in the organization of the system as a whole. But there is no evidence of a qualitative increase in organization--no introduction of new pattern--so these examples tell us nothing about how organization originates."[12]

In other words, an outside energy source, an open system, may tell us why organization can repeat itself, in this case microorganism reproduction, but energy itself does not answer the question of how the original organization got there, or how more organization could be added.

This brings us to the second reason that life appears to be a thermodynamic anachronism: Life is not really increasing qualitatively in complexity. Adult organisms are nothing but the expression of the genes, the preexistent order in DNA. Any order in the adult was already in the genes of the parents. So, for example, as man grows from sex cells, to zygote, through embryological stages, to birth, through infancy, adolescence and puberty, to adulthood, no complexity beyond what was already present in the genes occurs. Similarly, a house is no more complex than its blueprints.

Actually, rather than life complexifying as it grows and ages, it is actually becoming disordered. The random effects of mutations, disease, wear and tear and imperfect healing of lesions, result in the adult being less ordered than the original genetic blueprints. Continued time wears down biological organization until finally death results. Then decomposition swiftly sets in producing random dust--maximum entropy finally wins out.

In summary, we could say the second law causes universal decay and disordering except when the system is open to outside organization and energy. If organization is imparted from one system to another, there will be a net loss of organization--looking at the two systems as one--because it is impossible for the exchange to be perfect, i.e., some order will be transformed to disorder. (Fig. 68)

We are now left with an important question. How did life arise without the preexistence of genetic order? This is a topic of heated debate.

Evolution and the Second Law

The spontaneous formation and evolutionary development of

---

12. H. BLUM, (REF. 7) P. 191.

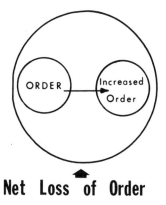

Net Loss of Order

Fig. **68** - Net Result
Everything is running down. Even if order in one place is used to increase order in another, the transformation, summated, results in a net decrease in order.

life seems, at first glance at least, to be clearly against the second law. Evolution means the accumulation of improbabilities, decreased entropy and order from disorder, whereas the second law says the opposite should happen.

Lacey and Mullins write:

"This direction in evolution can thus also be character-ized by an increase in complexity and independence of the environment."[13]

Oparin remarks:

". . . any transition from one stage of biopoiesis to the next usually entails the growth of a complex and organized system. After the second law of thermodynam-ics a reverse decomposition process is much more prob-able than the direct synthetic one."[14]

Materialists see this problem. Some argue that life itself clearly demonstrates that the second law need not always apply. The growth, development and ordering in living organisms are taken as evidence that life could have evolved. Life, they argue, is an open system draining energy and order from its surroundings for its own use and complexification.

In other words, the contrariness of life to the deteriorating

13. *J. C. LACEY, JR. AND D. W. MULLINS, JR.: "PROTEINS AND NUCLEIC ACIDS IN PREBIOTIC EVOLUTION," IN MOLECULAR EVOLUTION: PREBIOLOG-ICAL AND BIOLOGICAL, EDS. D. L. ROHLFING AND A. I. OPARIN (N.Y.: PLENUM, 1972), P. 172.*
14. *A. I. OPARIN: "PROBLEM OF THE ORIGIN OF LIFE: PRESENT STATE AND PROSPECTS," IN CHEMICAL EVOLUTION AND THE ORIGIN OF LIFE, EDS. R. BUVER AND C. PONNAMPERUMA (N.Y.: AMERICAN ELSEVIER, 1971), P. 6.*

effect of the second law is due supposedly to life being an open system. Likewise, it is reasoned, at the time of biopoiesis such spontaneous ordering could occur because the primordial slime was also an open system--the seas were subjected to lightning flashes, heat, cosmic and ultraviolet rays.. . . . Therefore, the materialist argues, the deteriorating effect of the second law need not apply to an open biopoietic system, just as it does not apply to growing complexifying organisms today.

However, as shown above, the uniqueness of life is not due to open-system thermodynamics, it is due to the design, the metabolic mechanism within protoplasm. Life overcomes the disordering effects of the second law because of preexisting order. It is no more valid to argue that random inorganic chemicals plus energy could form the complexity of living tissue because living tissue plus energy is able to form ordered materials, than for me to have argued that scrap pieces of metal and energy could form a packaging machine because the machine plus energy was able to produce an ordered product in the form of uniformly filled and neatly crimped tubes. Similarly, a rocket does not overcome gravity because of energy, it overcomes it because the design of the rocket correctly controls the use of energy.

Once order is present, its subsequent use of thermodynamic systems to produce order is easily understood. The question before us is how did life get here in the first place when there was no preexisting machine? (Fig. 69) To argue that life processes today demonstrate how life could have gotten here in the beginning is begging the question. The evolutionist portrays the early earth as a random and chaotic world devoid of life, mind, and design. From this state of rigor mortis was to have sprung the metabolic machinery of life.

Could Both be Universal ?

The deteriorating effects of the second law of thermodynamics apply to the universe as a whole and its component parts. The law was concluded and proven on components of the universe and is found to rigorously apply to all observed systems.

Albert Einstein was struck by the pervading truth of the second law and concluded:

> "Classical thermodynamics . . . is the only physical theory of universal content concerning which I am convinced that, within the framework of applicability of its basic concepts, it will never be overthrown."[15]

There have been many laws on the shelves of the scientific market that have been discarded. Some feel that there are no

---

15. CITED BY M. J. KLEIN: "THERMODYNAMICS IN EINSTEIN'S UNIVERSE," IN SCIENCE, 157(1967):509.

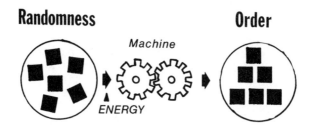

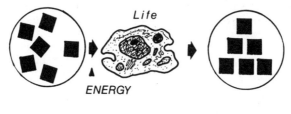

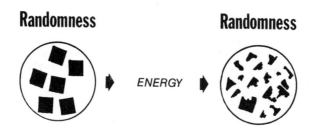

Fig. **69** - Open Thermodynamic Systems

*The three circles on the left represent random arrangements of
building blocks. In the top drawing, if the blocks are acted
upon by energy(an open system) and a machine, order can result.
In like manner, in the second drawing, random chemicals acted
upon by energy(open system) and the living machine, can also
create ordered products. If the random building blocks in the
third drawing are only acted upon by energy(open system), apart
from a machine, increased randomness will result, not order.
Does "open-system thermodynamics" solve the problem of spontaneously forming the complexity of life? Does not "raw energy"
only expedite the removal of whatever order exists?*

"fixed" scientific laws since they come and go like will-o'-the-wisps. But there are some laws that have never known of exceptions. Among these are the laws of thermodynamics. Concerning the second law of thermodynamics, the authors of the textbook, *Thermodynamics*, wrote:

"The second law of thermodynamics not only is a principle of wide reaching scope and application, but also is one which has never failed to satisfy the severest test of experiment. The numerous quantitative relations derived from this law have been subjected to more and more accurate experimental investigation without the detection of the slightest inaccuracy."[16]

The British astronomer, Arthur Eddington, believes the second law to be the most binding in nature. He says theories cannot be easily dislodged, however,

"...if your theory is found to be against the second law of thermodynamics I can give you no hope; there is nothing for it but to collapse in deepest humiliation."[17]

Evolutionists contend that there must be 1,000,000 technical civilizations in our galaxy.[18] So the supposed spontaneous formation of life is certainly not a negligible fluctuation in the universe. Actually, like the second law, evolution is spoken of as a universal process.

Julian Huxley described evolution in this way:

"Evolution in the extended sense can be defined as a directional and essentially irreversible process occuring in time, which in its course gives rise to an increase of variety and an increasingly high level of organization in its products. Our present knowledge indeed forces us to the view that the whole of reality is evolution--a single process of self-transformation."[19]

In agreement with Huxley, Dubos wrote:

"Most enlightened persons now accept as a fact that everything in the cosmos--from heavenly bodies to human beings--has developed and continues to develop through evolutionary processes."[20]

The geneticist, Dobzhansky, concluded:

"Evolution comprises all the stages of the development

---

16. *G. N. LEWIS AND M. RANDALL: THERMODYNAMICS (N.Y.: MCGRAW-HILL, 1961), P. 87.*
17. *A. S. EDDINGTON: THE NATURE OF THE PHYSICAL WORLD (N.Y.: MACMILLAN, 1930), P. 74.*
18. *C. SAGAN: "INTELLIGENT LIFE BEYOND THE SOLAR SYSTEM," IN ENCYCLOPEDIA BRITANNICA, 13(1973):1087.*
19. *J. HUXLEY: "EVOLUTION IN GENETICS," IN WHAT IS MAN, ED. J. R. NEWMAN (N.Y.: SIMON AND SCHUSTER, 1955), P. 278.*
20. *RENE DUBOS: "HUMANISTIC BIOLOGY," IN AMERICAN SCIENTIST, 53(1965):6.*

of the universe: the cosmic, biological, and human or cultural developments."[21]

The creationist sees a contradiction here. Evolution means spontaneous disorder to order, the second law means spontaneous order to disorder. He wonders how both processes could be universal in their effects. The creationist reasons that since the second law has been proven true, and evolution is merely a proposition, then the second law would oppose, yes, prevent evolution. Besides, isn't it obvious to anyone that things don't automatically complexify but rather do the opposite, become scrambled? Evolutionary complexification is not observed, second law disordering is.

On the other hand, the evolutionist charges that the creationist is abusing the second law. He feels the creationist has not taken into account the capabilities of open-system thermodynamics. Evolutionists are not ignoramuses. It is safe to say that practically all modern-day thermodynamicists are evolutionists. If the second law means you can't go from disorder to order, how can thermodynamicists believe in evolution and continue to receive a paycheck? The answer: by invoking open thermodynamic systems.

Since it is thermodynamically possible for entropy in a non-isolated system to decrease, evolutionists see evolution proceeding through the selection of these entropy reversals. Blum contends that when evolution is viewed in the perspective of the earth-sun system, thermodynamics pointed evolution, not prevented it. This belief led him to the title of his book: *Time's Arrow and Evolution*. In the same vein, Jungck wrote:

". . . entropy will not be the nemesis of evolution; on the contrary, the selection of entropy-driven processes in biological systems has been responsible for the evolution of the sophisticated organization of contemporary biota."[22]

The various biochemical systems in organisms are found to be thermodynamically favored ones. If the reactions that occur in organisms are thermodynamically favored, preferred, how can it be against thermodynamics for the biochemical systems to have evolved?

Open to What ?

According to the evolutionist, the prebiological world of chemicals was one of chaos, randomness, disorder. From this scenario life was to have evolved--disorder was transformed into or-

---

21. T. DOBZHANSKY: "CHANGING MAN," IN *SCIENCE*, 155(1967):409.
22. J. R. JUNGCK: "THERMODYNAMICS OF SELF ASSEMBLY: AN EMPIRICAL EXAMPLE RELATING TO ENTROPY AND EVOLUTION," IN *MOLECULAR EVOLUTION* . . .,(REF. 13) P. 107.

der. The process is believed to be consistent with the second
law because the earth is an open system receiving energy from the
sun.

On the other hand, the creationist believes that although it
is theoretically possible for order to be derived from disorder
in an open system, the practical and empirical application of the
second law would forbid continued transformations from disorder
to order regardless of whether the system was open or not. All
observed cases of order being derived from disorder demand a motor, a machine, preexistent order of a magnitude at least as great
as that which is produced. Evolution does not invoke a preexistent machine to account for the order of life, the creationist does
invoke a preexistent order, a creator.

In contrast, then, evolutionists reconcile the second law
with evolution by invoking an earth-system open to the energy from
the sun; the creationist says energy is incompetent to create the
order seen in life and alternatively invokes an earth-system open
to a creator.

Thermodynamic Debating

With this general background on the meaning of the second law,
and with an understanding of the positions both sides take, let's
listen in on a creation-evolution thermodynamic debate.

Creationist: "Where is the precedent? Where is one, just
one, observed example of random chemicals possessing high entropy
(randomness), spontaneously (in the absence of a motor or machine)
ordering themselves into anything even remotely akin to the simplest form of life? There are no examples. Even making a system
as open as possible (but not interjecting intelligence), no complexity even approaching the order characteristic of life occurs.

"A heap of chrome, steel, rubber and plastic sitting in an
open field is an 'open system' by the materialists definition, for
the heap is subject to outside energy sources such as wind, sunlight, heat and cold. (In actuality there is no truly closed system; all systems are effected by outside energy to some degree.)
But would we expect, even think of this heap transforming itself
into a Rolls Royce because of open-system thermodynamics? If anything, we would guess that what order was there would become even
more randomized. The metal would corrode, the rubber disintegrate
and the plastic slowly erode.

"All observations confirm the inability of randomness to
transform itself (open or closed system, it makes no difference)
into high order."

Evolutionist: "This does not mean evolution is a thermodynamic impossibility."

Creationist: "Probabilities for the formation of simple proteins and DNA confirm the infeasibility--impossibility--of deriv-

ing order from disorder. Henry Bent, a chemist, calculated on the basis of the second law that the chance for a reversal of entropy such that one calorie could be converted completely into work is comparable to the odds for a group of monkeys randomly punching at typewriters to 'produce Shakespeare's works 15 quadrillion times in succession without error.'[23]

"So when you cite open-system thermodynamics as the savior to the evolutionary scheme, you are concentrating on and putting your faith, hope and trust in impossible probabilities. You are hoping for the accumulation of improbabilities when the second law clearly means that systems, especially if given long periods of time, will form the most probable state. The most probable state is certainly not the accumulation of infinite improbabilities."

Evolutionist: "Look here, isn't crystal formation the spontaneous formation of order? Does this not prove that the order characteristic of life could also spontaneously form?"

Creationist: "To extrapolate from crystal formation to life formation is like assuming that a nine second 100 yard dasher proves that runners can also break the sound barrier!

"Crystal ordering is the result of the 'information' riding upon atoms, their electrical characteristics and spatial configurations. When atoms form crystals the full potential of their information is realized. There is here a translation of order into order, not a conversion of disorder to order. Similarly, a tree is no greater than its seed. The effect, therefore, is not greater than its cause. A crystal is dead-ended and does not progress to a higher level let alone toward anything akin to the complexity of life. So crystal growth is in full accord with the law that order can only result from preexistent order. The final nail is driven in the coffin of your objection when I ask: 'Where do atoms get the order that enables them to form crystals?'"

Evolutionist: "I challenge you to demonstrate through mathematical calculations the impossibility of evolution occurring in an open system. But this you know you can't do, or, if you do, I'll show you that your computation does not assume the appropriate conditions."

Creationist: "In other words, you're telling me there is no conflict between evolution and the second law in 'theory.' In like manner, however, there is no theoretical conflict between the second law and the proposition that an automobile can spontaneously form from a heap of scrap metal. All one has to do is assume the appropriate conditions, e.g., an assembly line, blueprints, engineers, etc.!

"The authors of *The Mathematics of Physics and Chemistry*, wrote of the second law that entropy was equivalent and propor-

---

23. S. W. ANGRIST: "PERPETUAL MOTION MACHINES," IN *SCIENTIFIC AMERICAN*, 218(1968):120,121.

tional to the logarithm of the probability.[24] In other words,
the more improbable the event--the higher the exponent of the de-
nominator--the more likely it is that the event will not occur.
Furthermore, events will progress toward the most probable states
just as events will progress toward the states of greatest entropy.
Earlier in this book the probability of forming DNA and proteins
was calculated. That probability, even giving unreasonably huge
concessions to you worked out to $1/10^{167,126}$. The second law then
reaffirms my previous assertion that the primeval tub of dumb,
blind, amorphous, higgledy-piggledy, scrambled molecules would not
spontaneously form life. It is against reason, probabilities,
chemistry, physics and the second law.

"I am not alone in disbelieving the thermodynamic feasibility
of evolution. Addressing himself to the mechanical view of life,
Gray made the following comments in the highly respected British
journal, *Nature*: 'Let us look for a moment at the theory of the
evolution of animate from inanimate matter. From a biological
point of view it seems at first sight reasonable.. . . As a physical phenomenon it is undoubtedly "possible" for a living organism
to have been evolved . . . it is also possible for a stone to leap
spontaneously from the surface of the earth . . . we assume the
improbable events do not in fact occur. On this arbitrary but effective basis rests most, if not all, the laws of physics and chemistry which we apply to the study of living matter.. . . Would any
serious credence be given to the suggestion that a motor-car or
even a footprint on the sands came spontaneously into existence
without the intervention of directive forces? Why, then, should
we accept the spontaneous origin of living matter? . . . Biology
itself provides not one shred of observational evidence to support
the spontaneous origin of living matter . . . if these intermediate stages occurred they must be classified as miracles, not as
"natural" events . . . all systems appear to move toward the state
of greatest probability.. . . Is there any evidence which suggests
that, within the physical world, a dynamic machine has spontaneously come into existence?. . . the spontaneous origin of living
matter seems to be a negation of the principles which underlie scientific thought . . . From this point of view the spontaneous origin of living from inanimate matter must be regarded as a highly
improbable event, and as such can be assumed not to have occurred.'"[25]

Evolutionist: "Now you're trying to convince me with expert
testimonials."

Creationist: "No, I just think Gray sums up nicely the point
I'm trying to make--highly ordered systems just don't come from
disorder automatically."

---

24. H. MARGENAU AND G. MURPHY: *THE MATHEMATICS OF CHEMISTRY AND
PHYSICS* (N.Y.: VON NOSTRAND, 1943), P. 435.
25. J. GRAY: "THE MECHANICAL VIEW OF LIFE," IN *NATURE*, 132(1933):
661-664.

Evolutionist: "Then I must repeat, all you have to do is describe the correct conditions, and order can come from disorder."

Creationist: "Well then, what would be the right conditions? The only fruitful conditions you could suggest would be those existing within the confines of living material. So you've taken me full circle. The formation (spontaneously?) of life demands the conditions of life. Or, put another way, if we have life we have life! You've explained nothing."

Evolutionist: "Now don't get too cocky. If you take water from Africa and simply change its position by moving it to the North Pole, it will change from random water molecules to ordered ice crystals. You see, you can't conceive of life forming spontaneously because you have not envisioned it occurring in the right situation. In the right situation, as with water ordering itself into ice, the formation of life will not only be thermodynamically favored, but the event will also be highly probable."

Creationist: "Is the formation of ice from water a valid basis for believing the most orderly entity in the universe, life, will form spontaneously from a chaotic chemical pool?"

Evolutionist: "I think so. It may be circumstantial evidence but it does establish a precedent."

Creationist: "Let's be more realistic. Let me return a question. We'll grant the ice cubes, but what would you think if the water we transport from Africa not only crystallized but ordered itself into a four-storied compartmentalized igloo? Do you believe this would happen?"

Evolutionist: "No."

Creationist: "Then what scientific principle or law forces you to this conclusion?"

Evolutionist: "The second law."

Creationist: "Then if the second law forces disbelief in spontaneous igloos, even given an open system, how can we then believe the almost infinitely less possible spontaneous open system formation of life? Why can we not cite the second law as reason for rejecting spontaneous formation?"

Evolutionist: "Simply because different chemical systems would be involved. Your analogy doesn't prove anything."

Creationist: "I think we could make any similar analogy and you would agree that the second law prevents spontaneous order. It is your bias that prevents you from reaching the same conclusion on the origin of life.

"Let me ask you another question. Do you believe that the universe is progressing downhill toward total randomization, the heat death?"

Evolutionist: "Yes."

Creationist: "Can you prove that the universe is a closed system?"

Evolutionist: "No."

Creationist: "This is interesting, for if you believe the universe is running down, not evolving, and yet you cannot prove that the system is closed, where is your ammunition to scathe me when I argue that the molecules in the primitive oceans were running down, losing order, not evolving, even though the system may have been open?

"Really, your criticism of my use of thermodynamics to refute evolution lies only with theoretical computations. If forced to retire your pen and point a finger to actual experimental or other observational support for your criticisms, you're pathetically lost. The anemia in the bag of evidences for evolution is vividly portrayed by the modern vogue pro-evolution arguments. You have left the field and laboratory and now feverishly, in collaboration with slide rules and banks of computers, grind out abstract esoteric mathematical formulas and calculations in an effort to prove your case. In other words, rather than demonstrate within the laboratory or field, the feasibility of evolution, you hand me something like:

$$\triangle S_{TU} = \triangle S_E + \triangle S_S = -\triangle H_S \big/ T + \triangle S_S \ldots$$

Who would dare question this?!

"The prolific science writer, Isaac Asimov, an evolutionist like you, said in regard to theoretical ideas on the second law: 'Using Clausius' term, we can say concisely: In any spontaneous process, entropy either does not change (under ideal cases) or it increases (in real cases). Forgetting the ideal, we can just take it for granted that in the real world about us entropy always increases.'[26]

"Science means observation, and we have never seen the spontaneous origin of order beyond that which was already present in one form or another. There must be a reason for this. That reason is the second law."

Evolutionist: "I believe the prerequisite order resided within the molecules themselves, just like you argued crystals result from the order within atoms."

Creationist: "This is simply a guess on your part. Where is the evidence? Abstract formulas show only that evolution could occur, not that it has or would. Similar arguments could prove anything will happen. We don't--you don't--normally believe in what could happen; we believe what would and should happen.

"I think your open-system argument catches you in its backlash. Let me try to make my point again with you. Listen to this conversation between us.

> I say: 'The second law contradicts evolution.'
> You say: 'I'm sorry, but you're mistaken.'
> I say: 'Does not the second law argue against spontaneous ordering?'
> You say: 'No, this is where you betray your misunderstanding. If the system were open, life could

26. I. ASIMOV: *LIFE AND ENERGY* (N.Y.: DOUBLEDAY, 1962) PP. 57,58.

form and there would be no conflict with the
second law. You've restricted your interpretation of the second law to closed systems;
the primitive oceans were open.'

I say: 'Would it be in accord with theoretical thermodynamic calculations for a Cadillac to spontaneously form from a heap of metal?'

You say: 'Yes, if the system were open.'

I say: 'Practically speaking, would you believe that
a Cadillac would form from the heap of scrap
even if the pile were an open system?'

You say: 'No.'

I say: 'What scientific principle or law forces you
to this answer?'

You say: (after a long hesitation and many gulps) 'The
second law.'

I say: 'You have contradicted yourself. You have
criticized me for citing the second law as a
reason for disbelief in the spontaneous formation of life yet you have cited the second
law as a reason for not believing in the spontaneous formation of a car, an almost infinitely more probable event.'

"Since there is no precedent for order of the magnitude found
in life, or order even close to that, appearing spontaneously in
either open or closed system thermodynamics; and since the deteriorating effects of the second law are clearly observed everywhere,
then the deteriorating effects of the second law would have acted
upon the chemicals in your alleged fertile primitive oceans.

"Left to themselves and the mindless efforts of 'open-system
energy,' the chemical precursors of life would never have done the
improbable, decreased entropy or increased order. The second law
says it just won't done ain't gonna happen. Also, is not the contention that chaos forms order a flagrant contradiction of not only
the second law, but the principle of cause and effect, i.e., an
effect, in this case order, cannot be greater than its cause --
chaos? Your evolutionary proposition has 'collapsed in deepest
humiliation' (Eddington). But life is here! Are we not forced
to find an agency competent to produce it?"

Evolutionist: "Do I get three guesses as to what you think
that agency is?"

Creationist: "Let me continue. There is a very real dis-
crepancy between the natural laws and your proposed chance origin
of life. Speaking to this, Tocquet, himself an evolutionist,
states: 'It (life) creates a systematic accumulation of asymmetry
(order) in such a way that its evolution is contrary to that of
the physical world. It appears, therefore, that life cannot be
considered as completely identified with the physical world about
it.'[27]

---

27. R. TOCQUET: *LIFE ON THE PLANETS* (N.Y.: GROVE, 1962), P. 31.

"The second law shows that life is beyond-, over-, super-natural. Then we must look beyond the natural for the cause of life. The magnitude of the design in life convincingly forces us to implicate intelligence as the cause for the formation of life. A machine does not form spontaneously from its component atoms, be they subject to open or closed thermodynamics. The machine is ordered by intelligence. No human made machine can compare to the metabolic motor of life. Therefore, mind, for a certainty, was necessary to account for life.

"I agree that the thermodynamic system at the origin of life was open. Open, yes, but not in the inept sense that you describe. Rather, it was 'open' to the creative power of a creator. Anything less than that is unreasonable, unscientific and impotent." (Fig. 70)

Evolutionist: "I knew it. Everytime man is unable to totally understand something in the natural world, you can count on creationists to say this gap in knowledge constitutes proof for a creator. You may have shown the sufficiency of creation, and perhaps some insufficiencies of evolution, but you have not proven the necessity of your proposition in an absolute sense. Why be so dogmatic?"

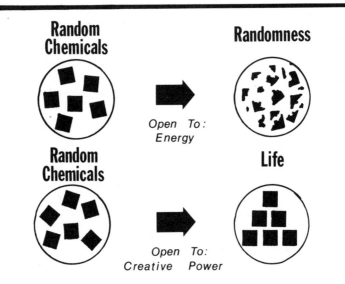

Random Chemicals

Randomness

Open To: Energy

Random Chemicals

Life

Open To: Creative Power

Fig. **70** - Competent " Openness "
The creationist believes that if the earth was only open to energy in the beginning, that whatever order was there would have been lost. The creationist invokes an open system, but open to a creator. Order of the degree found in life, he feels, could only be accounted for by a super-mind.

Creationist: "All I can do is deal with what evidence we have. That evidence, it seems to me, clearly points to the error in evolution and the correctness of creation. All man is capable of doing is proving sufficiency or insufficiency. Man never proves anything in an absolute sense. Why do you expect me to do it here? Why not at least believe the proposition that is most sufficient and hold it in abeyance for further corroboration or refutation?

"Another point I want to make is that the second law not only contradicts spontaneous origins, but also contradicts evolutionary transformations. Evolution of the species means constant and steady increase in order and complexity--the amoeba to man idea. The second law says no such thing can occur spontaneously..

"If I am just spouting off steam by making these statements, then show me any spontaneous process in nature that accomplishes what you argue occurred, occurs and will occur in evolution:
1. To substantiate the notion of spontaneous generation, cite an example of atoms and energy spontaneously (without utilizing concurrent machines, life or intelligence) ordering themselves and decreasing entropy to the degree seen in life.
2. To substantiate the notion of evolutionary transformations, cite an example in which random energy will spontaneously increase the order of an existing order similar to the increase that would have been necessary for the transformation of, say reptiles to birds or primates to men.

"You will not do this though. You can't! The second law won't let you. But you will continue in arrogance deriding my understanding of the second law and blowing forth braggadocio about what occurred in the past and what you hope to do in the future, but remain silent about what you have actually observed or done."

Evolutionist: "May I get a word in edgeways here?"

Creationist: "In a minute. While I'm wound up let me reiterate a couple of points. Isaac Asimov, an evolutionist, wrote: 'In fact, if we are not dealing with the imaginary constructions of the theoretical physicist but with reality itself, it becomes difficult to imagine a truly closed system. The outside environment always has some effect and must be included.'[28] So I am out of line in suggesting that the practical application of the second law confutes evolution even though the system was open?

"You confuse quantity of energy with quality of energy--the abilities of energy. The question is not whether the earth was open in the beginning to sufficient quantities of energy, but rather, whether it was open to sufficient energy abilities and qualities. In other words, could there have been in the beginning a quality of energy that endowed itself with the ability to organize and order molecules into life? The second law would

---

28. *I. ASIMOV: LIFE AND ENERGY (N.Y.: DOUBLEDAY, 1962), P.59.*

contend that what quality was there would be lost, not that it would upgrade and improve itself.

"You claim that creationists lack competency to speak on the relationship between origins and the second law. What must we say then of Lord Kelvin, the very founder of the law? Certainly he was a competent thermodynamicist and note what he said:

> "The only contribution of dynamics to theoretical biology is absolute negation of automatic commencement or automatic maintenance of life."[29]

Evolutionist: "I wish to close by repeating a point I have continued to make throughout our debate. Calculations can be made to show that evolution, given the right conditions, is thermodynamically possible. If this be true, which you even admit, then I don't see how we could exclude evolution on the basis of the second law. I see our present inability to completely understand how life thermodynamically could have evolved, not automatically calling up a creator, but rather pointing to the need for further research. It's as simple as that."

Origin of the Universe

The second law, as pointed out above, is driving the universe to a heat death. In the end there will be maximum entropy and randomness. All physical systems will be in the state of greatest probability. What this means is, at present, things are more ordered, more improbable, and have a lower entropy than they will be tomorrow, a year from now and a thousand years from now. But this also means that in the past, systems must have had a lower entropy, less randomness and greater improbability than now. If we went back in time far enough we should reach the point of minimum entropy, maximum orderliness and greatest improbability. From this point everything proceeded to decay, much as a clock wound up slowly unwinds.

This reasoning is somewhat of a take-off from one of Thomas Aquinas' five theological proofs. The Aquinas argument of "gradation" states that the concepts of qualitative degrees—"more," "less," etc.—imply the reality of a maximum. In our case, the second law describes the qualitative changes of "more ordered" and "less ordered." Therefore, the future will bring maximum disorder and the past must have held maximum order.

Then, from the standpoint of the universe, we're faced with a point in time when the clock was wound up—a process clearly

29. LORD KELVIN: "ON THE AGE OF THE SUN'S HEAT," IN POPULAR LECTURES AND ADDRESSES (LONDON: MACMILLAN, 1889), P. 415.

in defiance of the deteriorating pressure of the second law. What could wind up matter, energy, the universe, to a perfectly ordered state?

Lincoln Barnett, in the book, *The Universe and Dr. Einstein*, wrote:

> "Everything indeed, everything visible in nature or established in theory, suggests that the universe is implacably progressing toward final darkness and decay.
>
> "There is an important philosophical corollary to this view. For if the universe is running down and nature's processes are proceeding in just one direction, the inescapable inference is that everything had a beginning: somehow and sometime the cosmic processes were started, the stellar fires ignited, and the whole vast pageant of the universe brought into being . . . So all the evidence that points to the ultimate annihilation of the universe points just as definitely to an inception fixed in time."[30]

Since the universe is believed to be a closed system, an open system does not provide an escape clause for this materialistic dilemma. Does the original perfect order, minimum entropy and hugely improbable status of the universe demand a competent cause? What could have been the cause?

The creationist says: "Would not a perfect mind with infinite capabilities be competent? What else could? Is it not universally true that what comes prior and originates, or causes, is superior to the effect produced? Is not the beaver greater than his dam, a man greater than his machine? Nothing within the natural world could spontaneously yield the pristine perfect physical order--the condition extant when the universe was wound up. (Fig. 71)

The evolutionist, at the opposite pole, contends that nothing outside of the matter and energy of the universe would have been necessary. The material universe, so to speak, was self propogated.

A Double-cross for Naturalists

Evolution is said to be not only self (natural)-improving, but self (natural)-creating and self (natural)-sustaining. The very laws within which the materialist restricts his thinking, the creationist maintains, refute the naturalistic position:
1. The second law points to a time when the universe was wound

---

30. L. BARNETT, (REF. 5) PP. 105,106.

262

CAUSE ?   **II LAW**

PERFECT ORDER   **NOW**   **HEAT DEATH**

Fig. **71** - In the Beginning
*The second law points to the ultimate heat death of the universe.
A frequently overlooked corollary to the second law is the notion
that the universe must have had a beginning. If the end product
of the second law is perfect disordering, then at the beginning
the universe must have been perfectly ordered. The initial
perfect ordering of the universe cannot be accounted for by natural laws--the second law would deny the possibility of any such
ordering. Therefore, the creationist sees us faced with the need
to implicate the SUPERnatural.*

up--created--yet the second law says that no winding up can
occur, everything must wind down.
2. Evolution is spoken of as a universal natural process by
which matter is ordered, pushed to low entropy and huge
improbabilities. However, the second law of thermodynamics,
a natural law, defies such spontaneous ordering.
3. Reductionism, a philosophy based upon naturalism, leads to
a point at which there was nothing from which everything
subsequently sprung. Yet the first law negates the natural
creation of matter or energy.
Creationists also feel theirs is the best scientific model.
They stress: "The utility of any scientific model is gauged by
its ability to predict. It would be virtually impossible to
predict the two laws of thermodynamics starting from the assumption
that evolution is true. On the other hand, the two laws are predicted and demanded by the creation model, i.e., creation is a
past completed event with no current creation being accomplished
--the first law; the physical world, since the creation should
be static or qualitatively degenerating--the second law."

Does Thermodynamics Point to the Supernatural ?

The creationist asserts that natural processes cannot

account for either the origin of matter, or the origin of life. He maintains that a study of the laws of thermodynamics demonstrates the need to subscribe to the supernatural to account for origins:

1. The second law points to a time in the past when the universe, matter, was wound up--created in a perfect state. Yet the second law would deny the possibility of a natural winding up. Therefore, a supernatural explanation is needed to account for the origin of the universe.
2. The second law would prevent any spontaneous origin of, or complexification of life. But since life is here, it must be accounted for. If natural processes do not account for the origin of life, then supernatural processes must be invoked.
3. The naturalistic philosophy of reductionism would have us believe everything has come ultimately from nothing. The first law of thermodynamics denies the possibility of the natural creation of matter and energy. But since matter must have begun, according to the second law, its beginning must lie with a supernatural agent.

The creationist charges: "The materialist is left with infinite energy as the sole cause of the tremendous complexity in the universe. But energy, according to their own natural laws, which say energy erodes, decays, disorders, is incapable of performing the task. However, they continue to cling to this infinite impotent god of energy and scoff at and impugn the intellectuality of creationists who believe in an infinite, but competent creator. In so doing they violate the scientific and universally applicable principles of cause and effect, i.e., an effect can not be greater than its cause. One does not have to stir his grey matter too much to see that the panorama of creation is an effect far greater than an amorphic chaos of energy and atoms cause. Evolution is, therefore, a thermodynamic and logical felony."

The evolutionist is not without a retort. His counterarguments could be summarized:

1. As to the argument based upon extrapolating backwards from the second law, realize that this is truly an extrapolation. Any extrapolation from present processes--the way we see the second law operating now--removes any conclusion from fact and renders it guess. We don't know the second law has always operated on the universe as it does now. Therefore, we can't prove the universe was initially "perfect."
2. Any argument that assumes the universe to be closed is specious. Many modern astrophysicists believe that the universe is open and could have been wound up at the expense of outside energy and order. The conslusion that the universe was initially more ordered than it is now simply forces us to invoke an outside agency . . . not necessarily an intelligent creator.

On and on the debate goes. With openness and honesty we must listen and decide.

17 { FIXITY VS TRANSFORMATIONS

Beginning with this chapter we will broaden the scope of our discussion by going beyond chemistry and the question of origins, to the biological level and the controversy on fixity versus transformations. This will take us into the fields of genetics, paleontology, geology, embryology and other disciplines that bear on the controversy. To this point we have, in somewhat of a theoretical fashion, talked about whether organisms should evolve or stay fixed. Now, however, we will concern ourselves more with not whether they should, but whether organisms actually have evolved in the amoeba to man sense, or whether they actually have remained fixed in the creationist kind sense.

If we are to talk about biological change, we must talk genetics. If we are to talk about genetics, we must ultimately talk about DNA. In our previous chapters we have dealt with three questions about DNA:

1. Can the building blocks of DNA arise by chance?
2. Can the building blocks of DNA arrange themselves into sequences of information?
3. Can encoded DNA undergo spontaneous rearrangements resulting in new improved sequences generating more and more complex organisms?

The creationist feels the answers are, respectively, no, no, no. The creationist predicts that evolution could not occur, and avers that there is no real evidence at any level in support of it. He insists that there is no feasible spontaneous mechanism to form or transform this molecule of heredity. Chiding the evolutionist, he asserts: "Evolution is like a shiny dragster that appears very fast and impressive on the outside. When inspected closely, however, this dragster proves to be without an engine, drive train, steering mechanism, wheels, fuel system or starting capabilities. Any claim about the dragster winning the Indianapolis 500 is absurd. Although evolution is superficially

cute, it has no depth, no mechanism to propel it. Any claim
about evolution 'winning' the origin and complexification of
life must be equally absurd."
    The evolutionist believes the answers to the above questions
are, respectively, yes, yes, and to question number three, an
especially big yes! He rests confident that the evidence from
laboratory and field genetics, and the fossil record, will
silence the nagging whine of creationists and clear the air of
their intellectual halitosis. (Before proceeding into this and
subsequent chapters it would be well to review the discussion in
Chapter 4 on definitions to get clearly in mind what is meant
by creationistic fixity and evolutionary transformations.)

Lamarckism

    A prerequisite to change in organisms is a mechanism to
produce that change. If evolution is to occur, some offspring
must vary from their parents to such an extent that nature can
select the most fit. The exact mechanism producing genetic
change has been the subject of intense debate for the last 100
years.
    During the nineteenth century practically all scientists
believed the theory of acquired characteristics. This theory,
as advanced by the frenchman, Jean de Lamarck, attributed to
environment and individual need, the driving force for evolutionary changes. Lamarck's contention was that changes forced
upon the parents by environmental pressures would be inherited
by the offspring. Consequently, it was thought that the reason
giraffes have long necks is because they "needed" them to reach
higher into the trees to gather food. Constant stretching of
their necks was to have resulted in longer necks, and this change
was supposedly, in turn, passed on to the offspring. It follows
from this theory that a blacksmith's child should have more
strongly developed arms than an average sissy; and a musician's
child should be more musically inclined than the run-of-the-mill
yokel.
    This theory seemed reasonable and was popularly believed
(even Darwin was a disciple of Lamarck).[1] Could it stand the
test of experimentation? About the end of the nineteenth century,
August Weismann cut the tails off 20 generations of mice and
found the progeny stubbornly continuing to be born with tails.
His experiments, and those of many others since, proved that
changes in the soma (the body as opposed to the sex cells) would
not provide the impetus for change in offspring.

---

1. *J. BARZUN: DARWIN, MARX AND WAGNER--CRITIQUE OF HERITAGE
(N.Y.: DOUBLEDAY, 1958), PP. 34,35; M. GARDNER: GREAT ESSAYS
IN SCIENCE (N.Y.: POCKET BOOKS, 1957), PP. 1,2.*

By the 1930's the Lamarckian idea of inheritance of acquired characteristics had been discarded by the scientific community in favor of modern Mendelian genetics. However, Lamarckism was revitalized in the political ideologies of Marx and Engels. To them, inheritance of acquired characteristics could provide the justification for class struggles and the means for social change. The Russian, Lysenko, was dubbed the high priest of Lamarckism and Russian biology dictator. Finally, in the mid-1960's, the last vestige of Lamarckism died when Russia officially dismissed it as unsound and unscientific.

The problem with Lamarckism is that it overlooks the fact now established that genes and their contained DNA must experience alterations before any changes can be transmitted to the offspring. If one attempts to grow a tree by planting bark, wood chips or leaves, he fails. He must plant the seed if he is to be successful. If an automobile engine needs a tune-up, timing and starting problems will not be solved by washing and waxing the body. You need to open the hood and work on the fuel and electrical systems. If a pet has accidently consumed rat poison, grooming and brushing Fifi won't help. Only the antidote, Vitamin K, will. Likewise, if offspring are to be altered from the parents, the seeds, the sex cells, the genes, chromosomes, DNA, the blueprint that dictates the characteristics of offspring, must be changed. Endless skin tattooing, limb amputations, weight lifting exercises or development of musical and other artistic skills by the parents, will not affect the offspring inscribed upon the DNA within the parent's sex cells.

Mutation   Theory

At the turn of the century, Hugo DeVries observed sudden changes in the offspring of evening primroses and called such sports mutants. DeVries did not understand mutations to mean what modern genetics does (a change in DNA or chromosomes), but nonetheless he was the one to coin the term and direct attention to the germ cells as the means through which alterations occur and are transmitted. Mutations generally result from an alteration of DNA letter sequence in the genes, gross changes in chromosomes (inversion, translocation), or change in number of chromosomes (polyploidy, haploidy). In any case, the end result of a mutation is an alteration in genetic information. (Mutations can also occur in somatic cells, but in this case only those cells derived from the mutated cell through cellular division inherit the alteration. This type of mutation is not sexually heritable, and thus not important to evolution.)

The proposed mechanism for the evolutionary changes from amoeba to man center upon chance DNA alterations (mutations), natural selection and time. DNA is the blueprint of the form

life takes. It seems convincingly reasonable that one simply
need alter the blueprint and life will transform. In turn, it
is said, nature will select those altered forms most fit for the
environment to serve as progenitors for modified new populations.
Given time and countless chance alterations in the DNA code, nature should then have myriads of different life forms from which
to choose. It is in this way that most evolutionists explain
the biological world we see about us today. Sagan, for example,
says we do not have organisms with wheels because earth is too
bumpy. He then goes on: "We can very well imagine another planet
with enormous long stretches of smooth lava fields in which
wheeled organisms are abundant."[2]
There are a variety of evolutionary opinions as to what
exactly mutations are, how they are produced, and the degree with
which they are capable of producing evolutionary change. Some
believe most of the sports that are called mutants are actually
only the expression of hidden genes that have always been present. There is even a renegade scientific faction that insists
that the coding capabilities are found not in the nucleus of
cells, but in the cell body, the cytoplasm. Therefore, mutations
would be cytoplasmic not nuclear. The evolutionist, Goldschmidt,
has a following that maintains evolution could never proceed
through small mutations accumulating over vast stretches of time.
They have formulated the "hopeful monster" theory which envisions
evolution by leaps and bounds. Instead of mutations causing a
slightly longer arm, or the slow regression of a fin, Goldschmidt's
megaevolution would produce changes something like frogs from
fish eggs, snakes from frog eggs and birds from snake eggs.(Fig. 72)
One thing is certain, if evolution is to occur, there must
be mutations to supply genetic changes. There seems general a-
greement on this.
Mayr wrote:
> "It must not be forgotten that mutation is the ultimate
> source of all genetic variation found in natural popu-
> lations and the only new material available for natural
> selection to work on."[3]
Dobzhansky wrote:
> "The process of mutation is the only known source of
> the new materials of genetic variability, and hence
> of evolution."[4]

Mutations   Harmful

Surprisingly, there is a consensus among evolutionists that

2. C. SAGAN: <u>THE COSMIC CONNECTION</u> (N. Y.: DELL, 1973), P. 42.
3. E. MAYR: <u>POPULATIONS, SPECIES AND EVOLUTION</u> (MASS.: HARVARD
    U., 1970), P. 102.
4. T. DOBZHANSKY IN <u>AMERICAN SCIENTIST</u>, 45(1957):385.

268

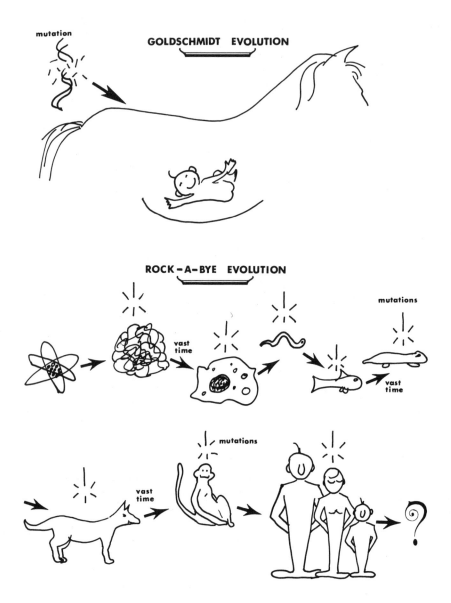

Fig. **72** - Evolution by Mutations

There is general agreement that evolution could not occur without mutations. One school of thought envisions evolution proceeding by leaps--Goldschmidt's hopeful monster theory. The other school sees evolution proceeding very slowly through unlimited small variations--rock-a-bye evolution.

mutations are practically universally harmful. Crow states:
" . . . we could still be sure on theoretical grounds
that mutants would usually be detrimental. For a mutation is a random change of a highly organized, reasonably smoothly functioning human body. A random
change in the highly integrated system of chemical
processes which constitute life is certain to impair--
just as a random interchange of connections in a television set is not likely to improve the picture."[5]

Julian Huxley remarks:
"One would expect that any interference with such a
complicated piece of chemical machinery as the genetic
constitution would result in damage. And, in fact,
this is so: the great majority of mutant genes are
harmful in their effects on the organism."[6]

Muller, the winner of the Nobel prize for his work with mutations, corroborates this view:
"It is entirely in line with the accidental nature of
mutations that extensive tests have agreed in showing
the vast majority of them detrimental to the organism
in its job of surviving and reproducing, just as changes accidently introduced into any artificial mechanism
are predominantly harmful to its useful operation . . .
good ones are so rare that we can consider them all
bad."[7]

Theodosius Dobzhansky, a staunch evolutionist, draws the
conclusion from his research:
"Most mutants which arise in any organism are more or
less disadvantageous to their possessors. The classical
mutants obtained in *Drosophila* (fruit fly) show deterioration, breakdown, and disappearance of some
organs."[8]

The author of, *The Mystery of Heredity*, concludes:
"We have to face one particular fact, one so peculiar
that in the opinion of some people it makes nonsense
of the whole theory of evolution: Although the biological theory calls for incorporation of beneficial
variants in the living populations, a vast majority of
the mutants observed in any organism are detrimental to
welfare. Some are lethal, causing incurable diseases

5. *J. F. CROW: "GENETIC EFFECTS OF RADIATION," IN BULLETIN OF
THE ATOMIC SCIENTISTS, 14(1958):19,20.*
6. *J. HUXLEY: EVOLUTION IN ACTION (N. Y.: NEW AMERICAN
LIBRARY, 1953), P. 37.*
7. *H. J. MULLER: "HOW RADIATION CHANGES THE GENETIC CONSTITU-
TION," IN BULLETIN OF THE ATOMIC SCIENTISTS, 11(1955):331; TIME
MAGAZINE, NOV. 11, 1946, P. 96.*
8. *T. DOBZHANSKY: EVOLUTION, GENETICS AND MAN (N. Y.: WILEY,
1955), P. 105.*

or fatal deaths; others are sub-lethal killing off or incapacitating most of the carriers but allowing some to escape; still others are sub-vital, damaging health, resistance or vigor in a variety of ways."[9]

C. P. Martin of McGill University adds:

"The mass of evidence shows that all, or almost all, known mutations are unmistakably pathological and the few remaining ones are highly suspect . . . all mutations seem to be of the nature of injuries that, to some extent, impair the fertility and viability of the affected organisms . . . The impaired stamina of present-day domestic breeds is shown by their inability to survive in natural environments . . . Resistance to disease conferred by some mutations in an unusual environment is no evidence that they are not injuries, for injured organisms are sometimes more viable than normal ones in exceptional environments."[10]

Ernst Mayr wrote:

" . . . it is a considerable strain on one's credulity to assume that finely balanced systems such as certain sense organs (the eye of vertebrates, or the bird's feather) could be improved by random mutations. This is even more true of some ecological chain relationships (the famous Yucca moth case, and so forth). However, the objectors to random mutations have so far been unable to advance any alternative explanation that was supported by substantial evidence."[11]

Finally, we will quote Heribert Nilsson:

"A review of known facts about their ability to survive has led to no other conclusion than that they are always constitutionally weaker than their parent form or species, and in a population with free competition they are eliminated . . . Therefore they are never found in nature (e.g. not a single one of the several hundreds of *Drosophila* mutations), and therefore, they are able to appear only in the favorable environment of the experimental field or laboratory . . ."[12]

Fruitage of Mutations

In the book, *Human Heredity*, by the evolutionist, Ashley

9. J. J. FRIED: *THE MYSTERY OF HEREDITY* (N.Y.: JOHN DAY, 1971), PP. 135, 136.
10. C. P. MARTIN: "A NON-GENETICIST LOOKS AT EVOLUTION," IN *AMERICAN SCIENTIST*, 41(1953):103.
11. E. MAYR: *SYSTEMATICS AND THE ORIGIN OF SPECIES* (N.Y.: COLUMBIA U. 1942), P. 296.
12. H. NILSSON: *SYNTHETISCHE ARTBILDUNG* (LUND, SWEDEN: GLEERUP, 1954), P. 1186.

Montagu, the inherited disorders of man are extensively listed
in an appendix. Some of the conditions noted are congenital
(stemming from intrauterine causes) and some are genetic. What
is most striking from this listing is the obvious absence of any
character that could be considered clearly of benefit to the recipient. The maladies, most of which have been caused by mutations, are listed by organ systems. The following is a short
list of some of the conditions he cites: asthma, oral gangrene
(acatalasia), various anemias, arteriosclerosis, congenital
heart anomalies (persistent right aortic arch, ductus arteriosis,
septal defects, etc.), varicose veins (phlebectasia), arthritis,
clubfoot, bunion (hallux valgus), hip dislocation, flat foot
(pes planus), rickets, cleft spinal column (spina bifida), deaf-
mutism, albinism, cataracts, glaucoma, vision abnormalities,
finger and toe abnormalities, kidney disfunction, absence of
uterus, goiter, excess fluid on the brain or in it (hydrocephalus),
microcephaly, emphysema, gout, retardation, muscular dystrophy,
paralysis, cretinism, mongolism, schizophrenia, eczema, tooth
decay, cleft palate, harelip, breast cancer, leprosy disposition,
absence of teeth, lack of resistance, and predisposition to
tuberculosis.[13]

Dobzhansky wrote:
>"A majority of mutations, both those arising in lab-
>oratories and those stored in natural populations pro-
>duce deteriorations of the viability, hereditary disease
>and monstrosities. Such changes it would seem, can
>hardly serve as evolutionary building blocks."[14]

Thompson stated, regarding mutations, in the introduction to
The Origin of Species:
>"If we say that it is only by chance that they are use-
>ful, we are still speaking too leniently. In general,
>they are useless, detrimental or lethal."[15]

There are numerous examples of freakish mutations in the biological world. There are two-headed fish, one-eyed fish, Siamese
twins, bull dog calves and thousands of artificially produced
fruit fly monstrosities. Mutations of this type, and those listed
by Montagu above, seem obviously not beneficial. But hasn't man
produced improved varieties?

Yes, man has produced through mutations and carefully controlled selection, "improved" organisms that benefit man. Seedless
grapes, for example, are easier for people to eat, but hardly
would seedlessness help the grape in the wild. A short crooked-
legged sheep, the Ancon breed, produced through genetic manipulations, is unable to jump fences and maintains weight better than

13. *A. MONTAGU: HUMAN HEREDITY (N.Y.: WORLD,1963), PP. 346-374.*
14. *T. DOBZHANSKY: GENETICS AND THE ORIGIN OF SPECIES (N.Y.: COLUMBIA U. 1951), P. 73.*
15. *W. R. THOMPSON: "INTRODUCTION TO THE ORIGIN OF SPECIES," IN C. DARWIN: ORIGIN OF SPECIES (N.Y.: DUTTON, 1956).*

the normal more ambulatory breeds. However, the fertility of this ram is markedly reduced, and hardly would the mutated weakened legs aid the ram in escaping from predators in the wild state. All mutants, as Nilsson and others implied above, are weakened for existence in the wild state; mutant "improvements" seem to be only in reference to their value to man.

Rarity of Mutations

Estimates of the incidence of gene mutations vary widely but agree in attesting to mutation rarity. (This is probably due primarily to the DNA repair systems mentioned in Chapter 6.) Huxley estimates a mutation rate of one in 100,000. Simpson assumes a rate of one in 10,000. Ayala estimates a rate of one mutation/10,000 to one/1,000,000 per gene per generation. Waddington guesses a rate of once in a million animals or once in a million lifetimes. Others have proposed one mutation per 100,000 generations; a stability of human genes for 2,500,000 years; and a mutation rate such that only one cell in 10,000 to one in 10 billion mutates.[16]

Simpson calculated, based upon a mutation rate of .00001, that the probability of five mutations in the same nucleus would be $1/10^{22}$. Further, he reasoned,

"With an average effective breeding population of 100 million individuals and an average length of generation of one day, again extremely favorable postulates, such an event would be expected only once in 274 billion years, or about a hundred times the probable age of the earth."

Simpson concludes from this:

". . . unless there is an unknown factor tremendously increasing the chance of simultaneous mutations, such a process has played no part whatever in evolution."[17]

All of this negativism is not to be taken to mean evolutionists have dropped their belief in evolution by mutations. Montagu, in the same book where he lists extensively the harmful mutations we cited above, expresses the belief that mutations and natural selection have provided the mechanism for the rise of man from ape-like ancestors.

Dobzhansky, after discussing the harmful effects of mutations wrote:

16. J. HUXLEY, (REF. 6) P. 42; G. G. SIMPSON: THE MAJOR FEATURES OF EVOLUTION (N.Y.: COLUMBIA UNIVERSITY 1953), P. 96; F. AYALA IN PHILOSOPHY OF SCIENCE, 37(1970):3; WATCHTOWER BIBLE AND TRACT SOCIETY: DID MAN GET HERE BY EVOLUTION OR CREATION? (N.Y.: WATCHTOWER, 1967), P. 61; E. SHUTE: FLAWS IN THE THEORY OF EVOLUTION (NEW JERSEY: CRAIG, 1961), P. 31.
17. G. G. SIMPSON: THE MAJOR FEATURES OF EVOLUTION (N.Y.: COLUMBIA UNIVERSITY, 1953), P. 96.

"This is not inconsistent with the recognition that useful mutations did occur in the evolutionary line which produced man, for otherwise, obviously, mankind would not be here."[18]

Mutations are generally harmful, it is agreed. However, evolutionists believe if the right mutation is in the right environment it may actually benefit the organism. For example, sickle-cell anemia causes nothing but problems to people in North America, but the recipient of the mutation in Africa is more fit for survival because the disease confers resistance to malaria.

Creationists react by saying the evolutionist is not concerned about the facts, but only intent on keeping his proposition inviolate and sacrosanct. If mutations are in part the mechanism for evolution, is not evolution suspect if its mechanism is? Creationists see the belief in beneficial mutations as only a product of the a priori assumption of evolution: since life is here, life evolved; since life could not have evolved without beneficial mutations, there must have been beneficial mutations. Evolutionists simply exclude the possibility that evolution could be wrong and that creation is a viable alternative.

As for the sickle-cell anemia argument, the creationist maintains that the recipient is still diseased. Sickle-cell anemia is compatible with life only if one sickle-cell gene is present. If babies are homozygous--carrying two sickle-cell genes--they die. As sickle-cell genes build up in a population, therefore, the chances for homozygosity increase and the whole population becomes jeopardized. The creationist insists that the empirical evidence speaks nothing at all positive for mutations.

Evolutionists continue to hold that any evidence that mutations can be beneficial at all is at least circumstantial proof that evolution could occur. When given vast populations and huge gene pools spread over eons of time, evolutionists believe they can justifiably extrapolate to the larger changes necessary for evolution in the amoeba to man sense.

Increased Mutation Rate and Time

Simpson, quoted above, used vast quantities of organisms in his calculations and even time beyond the largest estimates for the age of the universe and nothing evolutionarily good happened.

Increasing the quantity of mutations and the time for them to occur has not proven to be the panacea for the evolutionary dilemma. X-rays are known to increase the mutation rate in fruit flies by as much as 15,000%,[19] yet no new kind of organism or even a new

---

18. *T. DOBZHANSKY: MANKIND EVOLVING (NEW HAVEN: YALE UNIVERSITY, 1962), P. 140.*
19. *E. J. GARDNER: PRINCIPLES OF GENETICS (N.Y.: WILEY, 1964) P. 180.*

functioning organ have been generated. From the early 1900's, beginning with the work of T. H. Morgan, until now, millions of fruit flies have been irradiated and observed. Scientists have tortured this pathetic little creature beyond imagination and hovered over it for decades waiting for the expected transformations. The net results are an embarrassment. There were big-winged, small-winged, wrinkled-winged and no-winged fruit flies; small-bodied, large-bodied and no-bodied fruit flies; short-legged, long-legged and no-legged fruit flies; red-eyed, speckeled-eyed, leg in place of an eye and no-eyed fruit flies; many-bristled and scantily-bristled fruit flies; and often, more than not, sterile and dead fruit flies.

Man was able to catalyze the fruit fly evolutionary process such that what has been seen to occur in Drosophila (fruit fly) is the equivalent of many millions of years of normal mutations and evolution. And since the average fruit fly generation is about 12 days, what was seen in fruit flies was what could be expected in millions of years of human evolution. What was the net result? Experimenters began with fruit flies and they ended with the same-- fruit flies. Any significant variations caused death, sterility or reversion after a few generations to the original wild type. For example, bristles numbered from 25 to 56 in mutants, but after a few generations all would revert to the original 36.[20]

Another problem in the time-numbers explanation for evolution through mutations is that such mutants as leg in place of an eye fruit flies and wingless bats are produced suddenly. Why the need for citing vast time periods to substantiate the origin of organs? Such argumentation ascribes to the past that which can't be observed today, and consequently removes the whole question about the abilities of mutations from testability.

Another ideal test material for checking the abilities of mutations over time and through large populations is bacteria and protozoa. For almost seventy years the major pathogenic bacteria have been identified, cultured, isolated and observed. Many factors, such as radiation, heat, antibiotics and various chemicals can cause bacterial mutations. In spite of the ease with which they mutate, and the fact that about 75% of all life forms are bacteria, and that bacteria are supposed to be almost three billion years old, and that if left to reproduce unhindered for a day and a half would cover the entire earth to a thickness of over a foot, no new forms have arisen! New strains, varieties and antibiotic resistant "sports" have emerged, but these are all still clearly identifiable with the basic types known and identified for the past seventy years. The same holds true for the fecund protozoa.

Lammerts, a botanist, concluded from his work in which he increased mutation rate in roses:

20. N. MACBETH: "THE QUESTION: DARWINISM REVISITED," IN YALE REVIEW, JUNE, 1967, PP. 622-623.

"Mutations can alter only the various phases of the basic varietal pattern expression; the pattern itself is not changed. Truly unique and outstanding varieties such as Peach, Charlotte, Armstrong, or Queen Elizabeth would never result from the accumulation of mutations . . . Here was the first disappointment for evolution-minded biologists, for most mutations were harmful. In fact, only about one in a thousand seemed to be even neutral or showed slight advantage under laboratory methods of nutrient agar culture. . . clear-cut cases of obviously advantageous mutations simply do not occur . . . neutron irradiation of axillary leaf buds, or 'budding eyes' of roses, was a highly effective way of obtaining mutations. In fact, more mutations were obtained by the irradiation of 50 rose 'budding eyes' than one could find in a field of a million rose plants in a whole life-time of patient searching for sports . . . An interesting feature of this work is . . . all, without exception were weaker than the variety originally irradiated."[21]

Hypocrisy ?

One of the main mutagenic agents is radiation: x-rays, neutron radiation and gamma rays. Rate of mutations is almost directly proportional to radiation. When the atomic bombs were dropped on Japan during World War II, did the radiation result in improved men, plants and animals? Most think not. Changes were seriously detrimental, as evidenced by the increased incidence of leukemia, or even lethal.

On the other hand, a possibility, though difficult to prove, evolutionists might contend that the lightning fast comeback and advanced and aggressive technology of Japan after the war, making Japan one of the greatest trade powers, was due to beneficial mutations received from the bombs. It's doubtful that Japanese scientists, at least, are convinced sufficiently of this to thank the Americans for the radiation.

Consider this also. Why are you meticulously covered by lead apparel when being x-rayed? Is it not to prevent exposure to radiation and its effect, mutations? Additionally, there are many chemicals that have mutagenic effects such as mustard gas, epoxides, urethan, hydrogen peroxide, and various drugs, for example, thalidomide. Are not these chemicals feared? Are they not removed from

21. *W. E. LAMMERTS: "PLANNED INDUCTION OF COMMERCIALLY DESIRABLE VARIATION OF ROSES BY NEUTRON RADIATION," IN SCIENTIFIC STUDIES IN SPECIAL CREATION, ED. W. LAMMERTS (GRAND RAPIDS: BAKER, 1971), P. 278; W. E. LAMMERTS IN WHY NOT CREATION (GRAND RAPIDS: BAKER, 1970), PP. 300-302.*

the commercial market? Extremists tell us we should even fear the radiation from luminous wristwatches.

Radiation is also known to produce cancer, leukemia, heart disease and arteriosclerosis. Mutations reduce longevity in mice and in men.[22] Thus the longevity of radiologists is about five years less than the average. Medical schools teach that all radiation is to be feared. There is no threshold below which radiation is safe.

Gardner states:

"There is reason to believe, however, that exposure to high energy irradiations of any kind, and at any dosage level, is potentially harmful. Mutations are generally proportional to the dosage and the effect is cumulative."[23]

What is the point of all this. Mutations are clearly a negative force. In practice, scientists as well as the rest of the educated public fear mutations and the polluting agents that induce them.But evolution demands pollution: the pollution of radiation and other physical and chemical mutagens.

The creationist sees this as rather ironic: "If the evidence unanimously points to the deleterious effects of mutations, and man in practice (as opposed to just belief) fears, respects and avoids mutagenic agents, is this not sufficient to negate the proposition that mutations provided the mechanism for the spontaneous appearance of the whole biological world? Yet the world in general espouses faith that mutations, the phenomenon feared because of its negative force, provides the positive force for evolving new, improved, more perfected organisms. The evolutionist has equated a minus with a plus! Should the inquirer believe the facts, the evidence, the actions and practices of scientists, or should he believe the pious and prejudiced propaganda they vent?" (Fig. 73)

Natural Selection

Evolutionists say, after listening to the above arguments, that we have omitted the fact that evolution proceeded because of mutations and natural selection. To this the creationist argues that nature cannot select what is not produced. No matter how long you hold out your hand for a loaf of bread, if all that is available is rock, that is all you will ever receive. Mutations produce nothing that would improve an organism for the wild, so nothing of value is offered for nature to select. What is offered is degenerate and therefore becomes the prey of selection.

Caullery, in commenting upon mutations, said in agreement:

---

22. H. J. CURTIS: "BIOLOGICAL MECHANISMS UNDERLYING THE AGING PROCESS," IN SCIENCE, 141 (1963):686-694.
23. E. J. GARDNER, (REF. 19) P. 192.

"SO, YOU SEE, IT IS TO EVOLUTION THROUGH MUTATIONS THAT WE OWE OUR EXISTENCE!"

VS

A-Bomb

DANGER: FALLOUT

DANGER: MUTAGENIC DRUG

DANGER: X-RAY SCATTER

Fig. **73** - Mutation   Paradox

Why, if mutations produce the beneficial changes necessary for evolution, are mutations feared? Why is the public protected from mutagenic agents? Creationists see evolutionists holding a hypocritical double standard on this matter.

". . . almost all are degenerate in kind and would there-
fore be rapidly eliminated by natural selection."[24]
(We will discuss natural selection in detail in the chapter on neo-
Darwinism.)

Evolutionists know that mutations are almost always detrimental. They take refuge in the qualifier, "almost." A few good
ones are all that are believed to be needed to generate selected
populations and spearhead evolution.

Fixity ?

H. Graham Cannon reveals:
> "A fact that has been obvious for many years is that
> Mendelian mutations deal only with changes in existing
> characters . . . No experiment has produced progeny
> that show entirely new functioning organs. And yet it
> is the appearance of new characters in organisms which
> marks the boundaries of the major steps in the evolution-
> ary scale."[25]

Creationists say this is exactly what is expected based upon
study of DNA. Not only should mutations be harmful, but they should
be incapable of creating new information which in turn results in
new kinds of organisms or organs. This explains why the biological world is heterogenous, i.e., there are "distinct" demarcations
between the various kinds of animals and plants. There are hundreds of varieties of fruit flies that have resulted from variations in existing characteristics like eye color and wing length,
but they all remain identifiable as fruit flies. Mutations seem
to only remove, relocate, multiply or vary the size and color of
existing organs. There are about 200 varieties of dogs but they
are all dogs. There are about 500 varieties of sweet peas developed since the 1700's, but they are all sweet peas. Studies in
"evolution" always, characteristically, begin and end with the
same organism. Creationists see "evolution" studies as studies
of simple genetic variation within the basic kinds.

Evolutionists feel quite differently. I recently had occasion
to view a film designed to document the fact of evolution through
the mechanism of neo-Darwinism (mutations and natural selection).
The late Julian Huxley introduced the film by stating: "All biologists accept the fact of evolution just as all astronomers and
physicists accept the idea that the earth revolves around the sun
and not vice versa."[26] Well, with this said, the film proceeded

24. M. CAULLERY: <u>GENETICS AND HEREDITY</u> (N.Y.: WALKER, 1964) P. 10.
25. H. G. CANNON: <u>THE EVOLUTION OF LIVING THINGS</u> (MANCHESTER:
MANCHESTER UNIVERSITY, 1958).
26. "NATURAL SELECTION," ENCYCLOPEDIA BRITANNICA FILM #2140.

for the next fifteen minutes to show: (1) how melanic moths can adapt by changing color; (2) how mosquitoes can produce offspring resistant to the action of DDT; (3) how mimulus plants can adapt to altitudes. This evidence is taken as proof that the mechanism of mutations and natural selection can work. Given this, given time, evolution in the broader sense should occur.

Creationists do not see the evidence cited here as by any means sobering proof of the fact of evolution. Does this documentation of evolution through the transformation of moths into moths, mimulus into mimulus and mosquito into mosquito force the belief in evolution (from "amoeba to man") as decisively as astronomical evidence forces the belief in a heliocentric universe?

The fossil record shows a remarkable absence of transitional forms between the various fauna and flora.(See Fig.75) Why is life not homogenous today with myriads of intergrading forms making classification impossible? (This is a point which Darwin himself could not understand: *Origin of Species*, Chapter 6) Furthermore, why was life not homogenous in the past? Should not life abound with partially formed organs: 20% feather, 80% scale; 75% wing, 25% leg; 60% foot, 40% fin; 12% flower, 88% spore; 17% hoof, 83% toes; etc. If life today is experiencing evolution in action, where are the new nascent organs?

The evolutionary literature is filled with graphical trees showing the evolutionary descent of plants and animals. (Fig. 74)

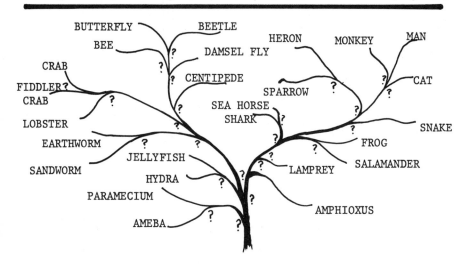

Fig. **74** - Evolutionary Tree
This evolutionary tree is designed to show family relationships and the common ancestry of all organisms. However, the connections between the twigs and branches, branches and limbs, and limbs and trunk are speculative. (From I. Adler: HOW LIFE BEGAN, 1957)

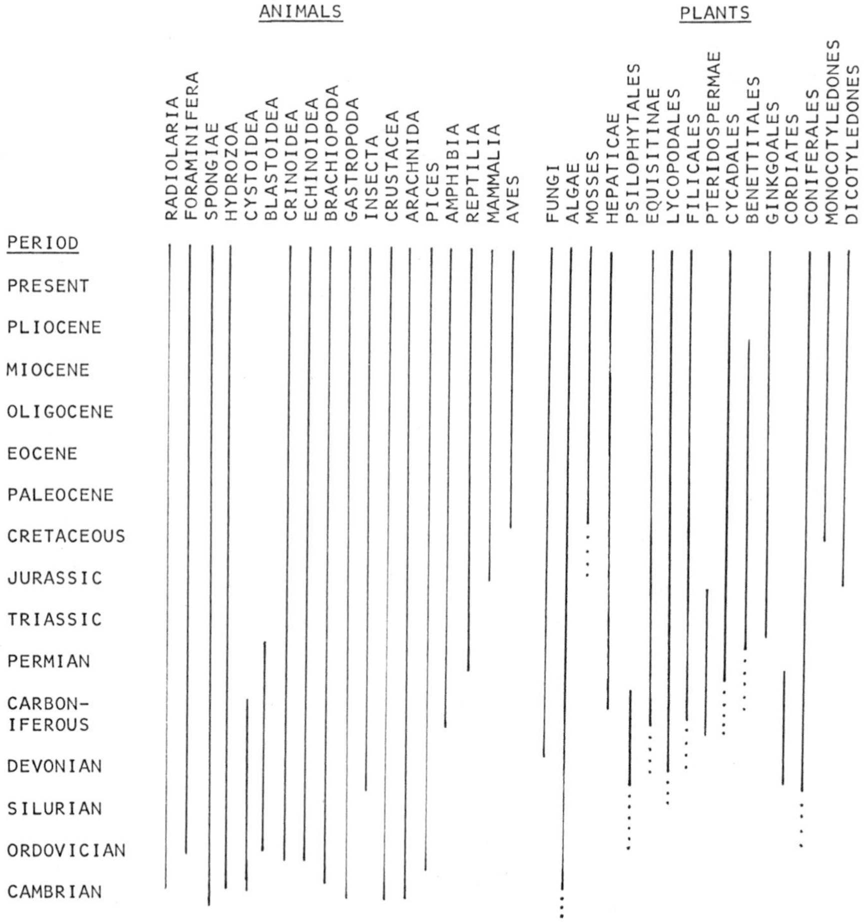

Fig. 75 - Fossil Record

The above vertical lines depict the existence of fossil forms of each of the major groups of plants and animals as they exist in the various geological strata. There is a noted absence of interconnecting forms (evolutionary tree branches), and the fossils appear "suddenly" at the Cambrian. (From W. Harland: THE FOSSIL RECORD)

All the limbs are shown attached to the larger branches which are in turn attached to the trunk. But in actuality, reality, factuality, apart from guesswork, there are no attachments of the twigs to the branches, branches to the limbs, or limbs to the trunk. Transitional forms between the higher categories don't exist today, nor are they evidenced in the fossil record. All major divisions of the plant and animal kingdoms have separate and distinct ancestries. Histories are not interconnected on one big grandiose tree, but appear more like distinct and separately planted twigs.(Fig. 75)

Testimonials to No Transitions

The suggestion that transitional forms have not been found is strange in light of popular opinion. I will list statements below by scientists--all evolutionists as far as I know--corroborating the absence of evidence demonstrating evolutionary histories. These statements tend to refute the assertion implied by evolutionary trees, namely that all life is related by common ancestry.

Theodore Delevoryas, in his book on plant fossils, states that the various groups of plants are without previous phylogenies (evolutionary histories).[27] Arnold wrote in his text on paleobotany: "It has long been hoped that extinct plants will ultimately reveal some of the stages through which existing groups have passed during the course of their development, but it must be freely admitted that this aspiration has been fulfilled to a very slight extent, even though paleobotanical research has been in progress for more than a hundred years. As yet we have not been able to trace the phylogenetic history of a single group of modern plants from its beginning to the present."[28] And E. H. Corner surprisingly writes: ". . . I still think that to the unprejudiced, the fossil record of plants is in favor of special creation."[29]

The microbial physiologist, Andre Lwoff, states that the ancestry of the metazoa (many-celled organisms) "is a baffling mystery."[30]

Marsland, in his biology text, wrote: "Not much definite information is available in regard to the evolutionary origin of the Platyhelminthes." (flatworms)[31]

27. T. DELEVORYAS: *MORPHOLOGY AND THE EVOLUTION OF FOSSIL PLANTS* (N.Y.: HOLT, RINEHART AND WINSTON, 1962).
28. C. A. ARNOLD: *AN INTRODUCTION TO PALEOBOTANY* (N.Y.: MCGRAW-HILL, 1947), P. 7.
29. E. J. H. CORNER: *EVOLUTION IN CONTEMPORARY BOTANICAL THOUGHT*, EDS. A. M. MACLEOD AND L. S. COBLEY (CHICAGO: QUADRUPLE, 1961).
30. *BIOCHEMISTRY AND PHYSIOLOGY OF PROTOZOA*, ED. ANDRE LWOFF (N.Y.: ACADEMIC, 1951), P. 35.
31. D. MARSLAND: *PRINCIPLES OF BIOLOGY* (N.Y.: HOLT, RINEHART AND WINSTON, 1957), P. 560.

Edward Baker, of Duke University, says that the phylogeny of mites and ticks is "Obscure."[32]

G. Robson, of the British Museum, concedes concerning the origin of snails, clams and squids, that at present the "question is unsettled."[33]

E. Dodson, a zoologist, laments concerning the ancestry of the sea urchins, sand dollars and star fishes, that the fossil record "does not throw light upon the origin of the phylum, nor upon its possible relations to other phyla."[34]

H. Smith, of New York University, admits in regards to evolutionary history of vertebrates, that "the gap remains unbridged and the best place to start the evolution of the vertebrates is in the imagination."[35]

J. Norman, of the British Museum, penned concerning the geological record of the fishes, that fossils have "provided no evidence as to the origin of fishes."[36] And Ommanney feels the 100 million year gap between fish and their supposed evolutionary ancestors "will probably never be filled."[37]

A. J. Marshall is here quoted: "The origin of birds is largely a matter of deduction. There is no fossil of the stages through which the remarkable change from reptile to bird was achieved."[38] (The ability to fly supposedly evolved four times independently: in the birds, the mammals-bats, the insects and the extinct pterosaur reptiles. Yet not one piece of fossil evidence has surfaced showing the evolution of the flying ability.)

C. Pope wrote in regards to snakes: "Their family tree is still adorned with question marks rather than branches."[39]

R. Haines said of rodents: ". . . the question of their origin must be left open."[40]

T. Storer, a zoologist, admitted: "The real origin of horses is unknown"[41]

R. Andrews notes that there is no general agreement as to where true men developed, and further adds: "Each authority has

32. E. BAKER: AN INTRODUCTION TO ACAROLOGY (N.Y.: MACMILLAN, 1952), P. 34.

33. G. ROBSON IN ENCYCLOPEDIA BRITANNICA, 15(1957):677.

34. E. DODSON: A TEXTBOOK OF EVOLUTION (PHILADELPHIA: SAUNDERS, 1952), P. 181.

35. H. SMITH: FROM FISH TO PHILOSOPHER (N.Y.: LITTLE BROWN, 1953), P. 26.

36. J. NORMAN : A HISTORY OF FISHES (N.Y.: HILL AND WANG, 1963), P. 296.

37. F. D. OMMANNEY: THE FISHES (N.Y.: TIME, 1964), P. 60.

38. BIOLOGY AND COMPARATIVE PHYSIOLOGY OF BIRDS, ED. A. J. MARSHALL (N.Y.: ACADEMIC, 1960), P. 1.

39. C. POPE: THE GREAT SNAKES (N.Y.: A. KNOPF, 1961), P. 164.

40. R. HAINES: "ARBOREAL OR TERRESTRIAL ANCESTRIAL ANCESTRY OF PLACENTAL MAMMALS?" IN QUARTERLY REVIEW OF BIOLOGY, 33(1958):19.

41. T. STORER: GENERAL ZOOLOGY (N.Y.: MCGRAW HILL, 1957), P. 216.

his own theory for which he will fight like a mother for her child."[42]

Substantiating the more universal nature of the lack of evidence for intermediates are the following quotations:

Heribert Nilsson:

"It may be firmly maintained that it is not even possible to make a caricature of an evolution out of paleo-biological facts. The fossil material is now so complete that it has been possible to construct new classes, and the lack of transitional series cannot be explained as being due to the scarcity of material. The deficiencies are real, they will never be filled."[43]

(Douglas Dewar, puts it this way: "The gaps are gone, but the links remain--missing.")

G. G. Simpson:

"This regular absence of transitional forms is not confined to mammals, but is an almost universal phenomenon, as has long been noted by paleontologists."[44]

Jean Rostand:

"The theory of evolution . . . presents only fallacious solutions to the problem of the nature of evolutionary transformations . . . perhaps we are now in a worse position than in 1859 because we have searched for one century and we have the impression that the different hypotheses are now exhausted. Presently, nature appears to be more steady, more firm and more refractory to changes than we thought . . . The world supposed by transformation is a phantasmagoric, surrealistic world . . . Personally I believe this phantasmagoria has existed before the calm and stable reality that we now observe in the nature."[45]

E. L. Core:

"We do not actually know the phylogenetic history of any group of plants and animals."[46]

W. R. Thompson:

"What the available data indicated was a remarkable absence of the many intermediate forms required by the theory; the absence of the primitive types that should have existed in the strata regarded as the most ancient;

42. R. ANDREWS: *MEET YOUR ANCESTORS* (N.Y.: VIKING, 1956), P. 27.
43. QUOTED IN A. C. CUSTANCE: *THE EARTH BEFORE MAN* (OTTAWA: DOORWAY PAPERS).
44. G. G. SIMPSON: *TEMPO AND MODE OF EVOLUTION* (N.Y.: COLUMBIA U., 1944), P. 106.
45. ROSTAND, 1972, QUOTED IN J. GARRIDO: "EVOLUTION AND MOLECULAR BIOLOGY," IN *CREATION RESEARCH SOCIETY QUARTERLY*, 10(1973):168.
46. E. CORE: *GENERAL BIOLOGY* (N.Y.: WILEY, 1961), P. 299.

and the sudden appearance of the principle taxonomic groups . . . the position is not notably different today. The modern Darwinian paleontologists are obliged, just like their predecessors and like Darwin, to water down the facts with subsidiary hypotheses which however plausible are in the nature of things unverifiable."[47]

A. Clark:

". . . throughout the fossil record these major groups remain essentially unchanged . . . No matter how far back we go in the fossil record of previous animal life upon the earth, we find no trace of any animal forms which are intermediate between the various major groups or phyla . . . Since we have not the slightest evidence, either among the living or the fossil animals, of any intermediate types following the major groups, it is a fair supposition that there never have been any such intergrading types."[48]

D. D. Davis wrote of suggested accumulations of adaptive changes:

"Unfortunately there is in general little evidence on this point in the fossil record, for intermediate evolutionary forms representative of this phenomenon are extremely rare (a situation bringing smug satisfaction to the anti-evolutionist) . . . 'Links' are missing just where we most fervently desire them, and it is all too probable that many 'links' will continue to be missing."[49]

G. G. Simpson, quoted above, wrote elsewhere:

"There remains, however, the point that for the still higher categories discontinuity of appearance in the record is not only frequent but also systematic. Some break in continuity always occurs in categories from orders upwards, at least, although the break may not be large or appear significant to most students."[50]

T. N. George, in his article summarizing fossil evidences, said:

"The fossil record nevertheless continues to be composed mainly of gaps."[51]

47. W. R. THOMPSON, (REF. 15).
48. A. H. CLARK: THE NEW EVOLUTION: ZOOGENESIS, ED. A. H. CLARK (BALTIMORE: WILLIAMS AND WILKINS, 1930), PP. 100,189,196.
49. D. D. DAVIS: "COMPARATIVE ANATOMY AND THE EVOLUTION OF THE VERTEBRATES," IN GENETICS, PALEONTOLOGY AND EVOLUTION, EDS., G. JEPSEN, E. MAYR AND G. SIMPSON (NEW JERSEY: PRINCETON U., 1949), P. 114.
50. G. G. SIMPSON, (REF. 17) P. 366.
51. T. N. GEORGE: "FOSSILS IN EVOLUTIONARY PERSPECTIVE," IN SCIENCE PROGRESS, 48(1960):3.

Additionally, we'll quote the words of N. D. Newell writing
under the subheading, "Systematic Gaps in the Record":
"The second kind of paleontological break is systematic. That is, it reflects a genuine deficiency of the
record not dependent on insufficient collecting or
chance factors of sedimentation. The earliest members
of higher categories, phyla, classes, orders and super-
families generally have most of the basic characteristics of those categories rather than dominantly
ancestral characters. Thus, the higher categories tend
to be separated sharply from other related groups with
little or no tendency for intergradation. The meaning of this morphological isolation of higher categories has troubled students of the fossil record and was
explained by Pre-Darwinian paleontologists as indica-
tive of special creation."[52]
G. A. Kerkut is an evolutionist in the Department of Physiology and Biochemistry at the University of Southhampton. In
1960 he wrote a book entitled: *The Implications of Evolution.*
Therein he documents the weakness of the amoeba to man thesis
(monophyletic evolution) and opts for the polyphyletic explanation of origins, i.e., he believes the evidence militates
against the idea that modern forms of life have all arisen from
one original germ and supports the notion that modern organisms
sprung from many separate and distinct precursors--many separate
twigs rather than the one tree idea.
This polyphyletic explanation is somewhat consistent with
the creation model in that, for example, dogs and horses would
each have separate genetic histories and would not be genetically
or evolutionarily related.
Kerkut in no way attempts to support creation, but his conclusions and arguments imply that the creation model (polyphyletic origins) is the more reasonable of the two explanations of
origins. Therefore, considering that Kerkut is a highly respected scientist and is not writing with the special bias of a
creationist, his exposé is most forceful. I will here quote
several of his remarks on evolutionary attitudes and his conclusions on amoeba to man evolution. Kerkut's arguments and
conclusions are drawn from not only fossils, but biochemistry,
comparative anatomy, embryology, vestigial organs, genetics and
classification. His is a sobering testimony to no transitions.
Commenting on the seven basic assumptions of evolution
Kerkut begins:
". . . these assumptions by their nature are not
capable of experimental verification . . . It is
therefore a matter of faith on the part of the biolo-

---

52. *N. D. NEWELL: "THE NATURE OF THE FOSSIL RECORD," IN PRO-
CEEDINGS OF THE AMERICAN PHILOSOPHICAL SOCIETY, 103(1959):267.*

gist that biogenesis (spontaneous generation) did occur and he can choose whatever method of biogenesis happens to suit him personally . . . From our limited experience it is clear that the biochemical systems within protoplasm are not uniform, i.e. there is no established biochemical unity . . . We have as yet no definite evidence about the way in which the Viruses, Bacteria or Protozoa are interrelated . . . The precise relationship of the four classes of Protozoa is uncertain . . . The Viruses, Rickettsiae, Bacteria and Protozoa are all quite distinct from one another and their interrelationship is anything but clear and certain . . . What conclusion can be drawn concerning the possible relationship between the Protozoa and Metazoa? The only thing that is certain is that at present we do not know this relationship . . . We can, if we like, believe that one or other of the various theories is the more correct, but we have no real evidence . . . they do indicate that the difference between the coelenterates and the sponges are quite considerable and basic. It is thus doubtful if there is any close relationship between these two groups. It is also impossible to state whether the sponges arose earlier than the coelenterates . . . Our conclusion, therefore, is that the situation is not at all clear . . . it is difficult to tell which are the most primitive from amongst the Porifera, Mesozoa, Coelenterata, Ctenophora or Platyhelminthia and it is not possible to decide the precise inter-relationship of these groups . . . Thus though one can arrange a series . . . there is no historical justification for either such series . . . We still know very little about the primitive anthozoans but it requires a lot of imagination to bridge the gap between the Antipatharia and the Protozoa . . . There is no clear indication that the ctenophores either gave rise to or were derived from the Turbellaria . . . It would appear that the relationship between the various invertebrate phyla is a very tenuous one . . . Though it is useful to consider that the relationships determined by comparative anatomy and embryology give proof of a monophyletic origin of the major phyla, this can only be done by leaving out much of the available information . . . It is a matter of faith that the textbook pictures (of horse evolution) are true, or even that they are the best representations of the truth that are available to us at the present time . . . In effect, much of the evolution of the major groups of animals has to be taken on trust . . . Of course one can say that the small observable changes in modern species may be the sort of thing that lead to all the major changes, but what right have we to make such an extrapolation? . . . it is premature, not to say arrogant, on our part if we make any dogmatic assertion as to the mode of evolution of the major branches of the animal kingdom . . . I think that the attempt to explain all living forms in terms of an evolution from a unique source, though a brave and valid attempt, is one that is premature and not satisfactorily supported by present-day evidence."[53]

Fixity Through Time

Surely, if evolution occurs, we would not expect to find evidences of the immutability of organisms over vast stretches of time. Animals and plants that exist now should be new evolved forms. Ancestral fossils should not look like modern day forms. If mutations have occured through time to the degree necessary to form the panorama of biota we see today, then how could animals and plants resist change throughout the same period of time that huge evolutionary transformations were to have occured?

But organisms whose ancestry can be checked by fossils show fixity through time. I will list below a scattering of fossil finds and the evolutionary date affixed to them. Each of these fossils have look-a-like modern-day counterparts:

1. Bat, "50 million years old"[54] (Fig. 76)
2. Tuatara (beakhead), "135 million years old"[55] (Fig. 77)
3. Neopilina (deep-sea mollusk), "500 million years old"[56] (Fig. 78)
4. Cockroach, "250 million years old"[57] (Fig. 79)
5. Dragonfly, "170 million years old"[58]
6. Starfish, "500 million years old"[59] (Fig. 80)
7. Bacteria, "600 million years old"[60]
8. Metasequoia tree, "60 million years old"[61] (Fig. 81)

53. *G. KERKUT: IMPLICATIONS OF EVOLUTION (N.Y.: PERGAMON, 1960).*
54. *G. L. JEPSEN: "EARLY EOCENE BAT FROM WYOMING," IN SCIENCE 154(1966):1333.*
55. *C. M. BOGERT: "THE TUATARA: WHY IS IT A LONE SURVIVOR?" IN SCIENTIFIC MONTHLY, 76(1953):165.*
56. *N. AND R. MCWHIRTER: GUINESS BOOK OF WORLD RECORDS (N.Y.: STERLING, 1973), P. 89.*
57. *C. T. BRUES: "INSECTS IN AMBER," IN SCIENTIFIC AMERICAN, 185 (1951):57.*
58. *"THE DRAGONFLY: FOSSIL ON WINGS," IN SCIENCE DIGEST, 49(1961):6*
59. *B. NELSON: AFTER ITS KIND (MINNEAPOLIS: BETHANY, 1967), QUOTE FROM SMITHSONIAN INSTITUTE BULLETIN 88.*
60. *N. AND R. MCWHIRTER, (REF. 56) P. 97.*
61. *R. CHANEY: "METASEQUOIA DISCOVERY," IN AMERICAN*

9. Ginkgo tree, "200 million years old"[62] (Fig. 82)
10. Cycad tree, "225 million years old"[63] (Fig. 83)
    (Other plant examples: Switch-pine and
    Turnip-pine--"250 million years old;"
    clubmosses, horsetails, ferns, liverworts,
    mosses, hornworts--"400 million years old;"
    algae--"600 million years old")
11. Coelacanth fish, "50 million years old"[64] (Fig. 84)
12. Apus(crustacean), "180 million years old"[65]
13. Shark, "181 million years old" (Fig. 85)
14. Nautilus(mollusk), "100 million years old"
15. Sea lily (echinoderm), "160 million years old" (Fig. 86)
16. Sea urchin, "100 million years old"
17. Spirula(squid), "200 million years old" (Fig. 87)
18. Vampyroteuthis(squid-octopus), "100 million years old"[66]
    (Fig. 88)

Fig. 76-Fossil   Bat
*This fossil bat, ICARONYCYERIS INDEX, looks essentially identical
to contemporary bats even though supposedly 50 million years old.
Preservation in this Eocene rock is remarkable. Bones as fine as
human hair are preserved.(Courtesy Princeton Museum Nat. History)*

SCIENTIST, 36(1948):490.
62. T. DELEVORYAS, (REF. 27) P. 134.
63. W. L. STOKES: *ESSENTIALS OF EARTH HISTORY* (NEW JERSEY: PREN-
TICE HALL, 1960), P. 266.
64. *LIFE*, APRIL 3, 1939, P. 26.
65. *THE INTERNATIONAL WILDLIFE ENCYCLOPEDIA*, EDS. M. AND R. BURTON
(N.Y.: MARSHALL CAVENDISH, 1969), P. 75.
66. J. COOK AND W. WISNER: *THE NIGHTMARE WORLD OF THE SHARK* (N.Y.:
DODD, 1968), P. 12; C. IDYLL: *ABYSS--THE DEEP SEA AND THE CREATURES
THAT LIVE IN IT* (N.Y.: CROWELL, 1971), PP. 232-253.

Fig. **77** - Tuatara (top)
This large lizardlike reptile found in New Zealand looks identical to specimens supposedly 135 million years old. The tuatara is the only extant rhynchocephalian. (Courtesy Wolfe worldwide films)

Fig. **78** - Neopilina (bottom)
This mollusk, NEOPILINA GALATHEA, thought to be neither clam nor snail, looks identical to fossil representatives supposedly 500 million years old. (Galathea expedition)

Fig. **79** - Fossil   Insects   (top)
*The fossil cockroaches(1,2), the spider(3) and the myriopod--
centipede-millipede--(4), all look essentially identical to modern
forms even though these rocks are believed to be "hundreds of
millions of years old." (Courtesy American Museum Nat. History)*

Fig. **80** - Fossil   Starfish   (bottom)
*This fossil starfish found in Jurassic rock in the Black Hills of
South Dakota, reckoned "hundreds of millions of years old," seems
identical to modern specimens. (Courtesy American Museum Nat. History*

Fig. **81** - Metasequoia   (left)
This tree, METASEQUOIA GLYPTOSTROBOIDES, a deciduous conifer, prior to 1945 was found only as a fossil in Mesozoic strata "60 million years old." This specimen is one of several on the Michigan State University Campus.

Fig. **82** - Ginkgo   (right)
This Ginkgo tree, with its distinctive leaves in fan shape, grows on the M.S.U. campus and looks identical to fossils "200 million years old."   (Complete with Wysong clan)

Fig. **83** - Cycad (top)
This Cycad tree has remained unchanged for over "200 million years" according to evolutionists. (Ambassador College Photo)

Fig. **84** - Coelacanth   (bottom)
The Coelacanth, once thought to be a fossil link between fish and amphibian, and extinct some 90 to 400 million years ago, has been found live off the coast of Africa at depths to 1,640 feet. These specimens look exactly like their fossil remains. (Ambassador Photo)

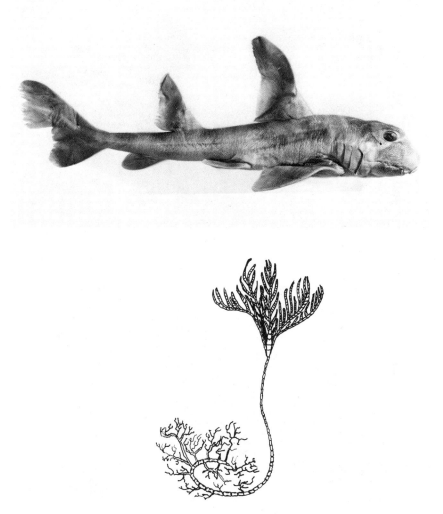

Fig. 85 - Port Jackson Shark (top)
The Port Jackson Shark, HETERODONTUS JAPONICUS, is believed to have remained unchanged for "181 million years," according to evolutionists. Likewise, the cow shark has been traced back "166 million years" and the cat shark "136 million years." (Courtesy of American Museum of Nat. History)

Fig. 86 - Sea Lily (bottom)
This sea lily RHIZOCRINUS LOFOTENSIS, not a plant but an animal, is identical with fossils "160 million years old."

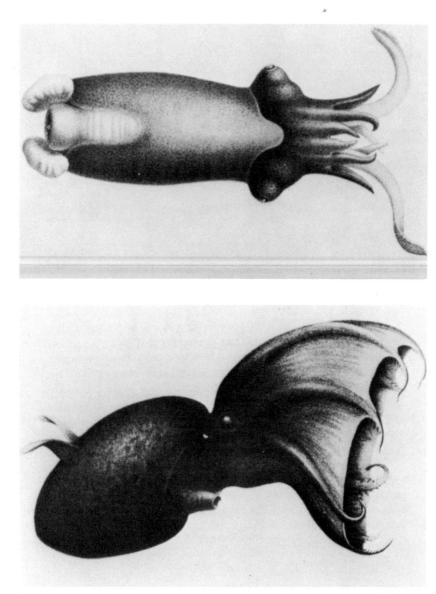

Fig. **87** - Spirula   (top)
*Spirula, a deep-sea "squid," is the only living representative of
the belemnite group--"200 million years old." (Valdivia expedition)*

Fig. **88** - Vampyroteuthis   (bottom)
*VAMPYROTEUTHIS INFERNALIS is neither octopus nor squid. This deep-
sea creature hasn't changed for "100 million years." (Valdivia)*

Proposed Transitional Forms

Due to the striking absence of transitional forms, there has been and is much fraud perpetrated to fill the gaps. Various schematics in books and displays in museums show neat progressive evolutionary chains and trees of men from primates, bats from rodents, lizards from snakes, and horses from four-toed, shin-high, rabbit-like creatures. From these displays it would appear that the case for evolution is victorious. However, more often than not, the trees turn out to be a facade, only a veneer of proof. Let's examine some of the more common examples.

● NEBRASKA MAN

Hesperopithecus haroldcookii, alias Nebraska man, was discovered in 1922 by--you guessed it--Harold Cook. A find of a single molar fossilized tooth was the basis for this reconstruction believed to be half-man and half-ape. *The Illustrated London News* of that year spread a painting of hairy, stooped, Mr. and Mrs. Hesperopithecus across two pages complete with an "authentic" environmental setting. This "authentic, genuine, impeccable" link had to be abandoned when later it was discovered that the lone tooth used for the reconstruction belonged to an extinct pig! Nebraska man was judged authentic by evolutionists of that time and aged at one million years. Nebraska man was also used in the famous Scopes trial to berate the "ignorant" creationist, Bryan. Even though the evidence was available to discredit the reconstruction,

Fig. **89** - Nebraska   Man

Nebraska man was appealed to as an authentic link for many years. For example, S. E. Winbolt, in the Pelican Book Series book, *Britain B.C.*, alluded to Nebraska man as a genuine link in 1943! Evidently some feel the reconstruction is correct, the environmental setting is correct, the stooped shoulders and hairy body are correct . . . the only thing wrong is the tooth![67] (Fig. 89)

●PILTDOWN MAN

Another reconstruction, Piltdown man, was likewise claimed as a crucial and significant find proving man's evolution. But Piltdown was later exposed as a reconstruction based upon an ape's jaw and human skull fragments that had been fraudulently doctored to give a "genuine"appearance. Piltdown man was exposed early in the 1900's as a fraud by Waterston, Boule, Miller, Ramstrom and others, yet continued as a central and classic proof for evolution in textbooks for almost 40 years thereafter.[68] (Fig.90)

●SOUTHWEST COLORADO MAN

Southwest Colorado Man was believed to be a link between man and primate until the single tooth used as its basis was found to belong to an extinct Eocene horse. Truly, as Harry Rimmer, an early critic of evolution wrote, "'Give us a tooth!' seems to be the cry of the experts; and they will supply all the rest from imagination and plaster of paris."[69]

●NEANDERTHAL MAN

The first Neanderthal skeleton was found in Europe at about the turn of the century. Since that time other skeletons have been found to verify that Neanderthal actually did exist. Although Neanderthal is posed often as an intermediary link, his brain capacity is larger than man's by more than 13%, he has been found in rock formations in which modern type man has also been found, and the stooped appearance of the reconstructed Neanderthals appearing in various texts is due not to the fact that these men were anatomically stooped, but rather because the original 1908 skeleton that was used for the reconstruction was diseased with the

---

67. *"THE EARLIEST MAN TRACED BY A TOOTH: AN ASTOUNDING DISCOVERY OF HUMAN REMAINS IN PLIOCENE STRATA," IN THE ILLUSTRATED LONDON NEWS, JUNE 24,1922, PP. 942,943.*
68. *SCIENCE NEWS LETTER,79 (1961):119; W. STRAUS: "THE GREAT PILTDOWN HOAX," IN SCIENCE,119 (1954):265-269.*
69. *H. RIMMER: THE THEORY OF EVOLUTION AND THE FACTS OF SCIENCE, (GRAND RAPIDS: EERDMANS, 1935), P. 123.*

Fig. **90** - Neanderthal & Piltdown
The Neanderthal reconstruction(top), giving a brutish appearance,
is based on a diseased specimen. Neanderthal was fully human.
Piltdown man(bottom), EOANTHROPUS DAWSONI, was fraudulently re-
constructed from ape and human parts. (A. M. Natural History)

crippling effects of osteo-arthritis. Other Neanderthal skeletons give every appearance of being fully erect, fully human.[70] The skeletal features of both Cro-Magnon and Neanderthal are essentially indistinguishable from those of modern man. Ceram reported in his writings a grave that was opened in 1856 in Dusseldorf and which, according to geological evidences, was of "remotest prehistory." The skeleton found therein was declared by Professor Mayr as a Cossack killed in 1814; Wagner of Gottingen maintained it was an old Hollander; Pruner Bay of Paris, that of an old Celt; Virchow, the famous pathologist, said it was an old man with gout. The skeleton was that of a Neanderthal![71] (Fig. 90)

●CRO-MAGNON MAN

Cro-Magnon man, although frequently cited as a link, was fully human. He had developed a sophisticated art and had a cranial capacity larger than that of many modern men. Anthropologists agree that the cave paintings and sculptured artifacts of Cro-Magnon in Europe prove he was in no way primitive, rather, he demonstrated great mastery and sophistication.

●HEIDELBERG MAN

Heidelberg man was reconstructed from a jawbone (mandible) found in Germany in 1907. But the difficulty with this "link" lies with the fact that the jaw structure of natives of New Caledonia is like the Heidelberg jaw--New Caledonians are fully human.[72](Fig. 91)

●KNM --ER 1470

Richard Leakey has recently found a skull in Africa, designated KNM--ER 1470, which is considered to be a true human form. The significance of this is that the 1470 skull is dated by evolutionary means as being a million or more years older than supposed links like Australopithecus, Pithecanthropus and Homo habilis.[73] In addition, Louis Leakey found fossils of Australopithecus, *Homo habilis* and *Homo erectus* in the same geological layer, below which

70. W. L. STRAUS AND A. J. CAVE: "PATHOLOGY AND POSTURE NEANDERTHAL," IN QUARTERLY REVIEW OF BIOLOGY, 132(1957):348-363; T. DOBZHANSKY:"CHANGING MAN," IN SCIENCE, 155(1967):410: C. BRACE & A. MONTAGU: MAN'S EVOLUTION (N.Y.:MACMILLAN,1965),P.130;TIME,MAY 17,1971 and 1973,PP.75,76; F. IVANHOE IN NATURE, AUGUST 8,1970.
71. C. W. CERAM: GODS, GRAVES AND SCHOLARS (N.Y.: KNOPF,1956), P. 22.
72. SCIENCE, 68(1928):124.
73. R. LEAKEY: NATIONAL GEOGRAPHIC, 143(1973):819.

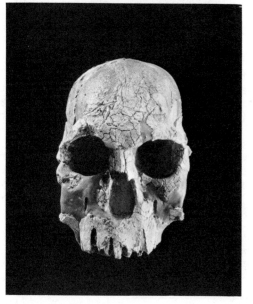

Fig. **91**- Heidelberg   Man   (top)
*Heidelberg man(Mauer man) is a reconstruction based upon a jaw
that is almost identical to the jaws of modern inhabitants of
New Caledonia. (Courtesy of American Museum of Natural History)*

Fig.**92**- KNM - ER   1470   (bottom)
*This reconstructed skull belongs, it is believed, to the human
genus. The fragments have been dated at "2.8 million years,"thus
predating human precursors. (Courtesy R. Leakey)*

he found a circular stone structure erected by true men![74] How could these fossils be precursors to modern men if modern men existed before them? (Other cases of modern type men predating precursors are discussed in Chapter 20) (Fig. 92) Contradictory evolutionary conclusions are not infrequent. Another case in point concerns the evidence that Australopithecus was a knuckle-walking ape, not an erect "man-ape." Contrasting evidence from skull casts show Australopithecus, *Homo habilis*, and skull 1470 to all be human in neurological development.[75]

This list of reconstructions is necessarily incomplete. However, it is apparent that the transitional stages in human evolution, the fabricated links in unverified "prehistory," are merely models, reconstructions of the imaginings of the reconstructor.[76] On the other hand, as far back as human civilization can be dated--history --man seems to be totally man. For example, mummified skeletons dating to 3400BC look identical to modern human forms.[77](Fig. 93) The parts used in reconstructions are either fraudulent, of questionable origin, far too scanty or are predated by modern true men types. No discovery as yet has given unequivocal evidence of man's "prehistorical" existence or his ancestral ties with primates.

•ARCHAEOPTERYX

A fossil skeleton that is held to be a link between birds and reptiles is Archaeopteryx. There are many characteristics of this feathered creature which supposedly argue for its half-bird, half-reptile classification. However, each of the features of Archaeopteryx is either found in true total birds, or not found in reptiles. For example:[78]
1. CLAWS--Claws are sometimes found in adult gallinaceous birds (domestic poultry), the ostrich(unfused metacarpals), the rhea, and the Hoactzin of S. America has claws when young and eight free carpal(wrist) bones making it--a true bird--more primitive than Archaeopteryx.
2. NECK RIBS--Found in recent birds.
3. SEPARATION OF THE PRE-ORBITAL GAP FROM THE PRE-ORBITAL HOLE--Found in the modern parrot.
4. LACK OF BONE PNEUMONICITY--Recent birds also have this characteristic and some reptiles(Pterosaurs) had pneumatic bones.

74. A. KELSO: *PHYSICAL ANTHROPOLOGY* (N.Y.: LIPPINCOTT,1970), PP. 221-223; M. LEAKEY: *OLDUVAI GORGE--VOL.III* (CAMBRIDGE: CAMBRIDGE U., 1971), PP. 24, 272; R. LEAKEY: "FURTHER EVIDENCE OF LOWER PLEISTOCENE HOMINIDS FROM E. RUDOLF, N. KENYA," IN *NATURE*, 231 (1971):241.
75. R. HOLLOWAY: IN *SCI. AMERICAN*, 231(JULY, 1974): 106-115.
76. I. LISSNER: *MAN, GOD AND MAGIC*(N.Y.: PUTNAM, 1961),PP.303-305.
77. P. GRAY: IN *MEDICAL RADIOGRAPHY & PHOTOGRAPHY*, 43(1967):34.
78. G. PINNA: *THE DAWN OF LIFE*(N.Y.: WORLD, 1972), P.2; H. NILSSON, (REF. 12) P. 1192; F. COUSINS, (REF. 79) PP. 89-99.

5. SCLEROTIC RING IN EYE--Found in birds and absent in many reptiles.
6. ABSENCE OF THE VERTEBRAL PROJECTION, THE PROCESSUS UNCINCOHIS-- Found absent also in the true birds, Aepyornix and Diaphorapteryx, of the "Pleistocene" and "Halocene" geological periods.
7. TAIL FEATHER ARRANGEMENT--Found in modern swans and hens; the extinct Pterodactyl reptiles had tails like modern birds.
8. ABSENCE OF TEETH--Many modern reptiles, like the turtle, have no teeth.
9. WINGS--Many modern true birds have wings but don't fly as did Archaeopteryx yet they are not held to be reptilian or mammalian, e.g., the kiwi, takahe, weka, kakapo, emu, logger-head duck, cassowary, rhea, tinamou, penguin, ostrich and the extinct moa.

How can Archaeopteryx be seriously posed as a bird-reptile link if the features that are to prove this are either possessed by true birds or absent in the reptiles? Penguins have wing-fins, why are they not advanced as a transitional stage to the fish? Bats and flying squirrels fly, why are they not mammal-bird transitions? No, Archaeopteryx is not a bird-reptile, he is a true bird. He has simply become a fossil patsy for wishful thinking as portrayed in the following quote from Heilmann's, *Origin of Birds* (1926):

> "The pressure of the air, acting like a stimulus, produces chiefly longish scales developing along the posterior edge of the forearm and the side edges of the flattened tail. By the friction of air, the outer edges of the scales become frayed, the frayings gradually changing into still longer horny processes, which in course of time become more and more feather-like, until the perfect feather is produced." (Fig. 94)

● HORSE

A classic proof for evolution, displayed prominently in museums and evolutionary texts, is fossil horses. The evolutionary tree begins with the tiny many-toed Eohippus and ends with the modern day horses. But what is not brought to our attention, for obvious reasons, is:

1. The sequence from small many-toed ancestors to large one-toed species is nowhere found in the fossil record. Every imaginable contradiction to the presumed order is found.
2. The Eohippus is almost identical to the African Hyrax. Both are the size of rabbits, have four front toes and three rear toes and live in brush.
3. Two modern type horses, *Equus nevadensis* and *Equus occidentalis*, have been found in the same geological strata as Eohippus. Thus we have modern day type horses grazing side by side with their precursors.
4. There are no gradations from one link to another. All suggested links appear suddenly in the fossil record.

5. Some present-day Shire horses are known to have more than one toe per foot but are still considered fully horses.[79] Thus, Westall of Durham University, for one, concluded that the "evolution" of Eohippus to Equus was all wrong.[80] (Fig. 94)

•SEYMOURIA

The gap between reptiles and amphibians is filled by the fossil called Seymouria. But the so-called stem-reptile, Seymouria, that is supposed to be a precursor to reptiles is dated by evolutionary methods as existing 20 million years after reptiles had already appeared.[81] (Fig. 95)

•LANTHANOTUS

The fossil *Lanthanotus borneansis* is believed to be a link between snakes and lizards. But recently, in Sarawak, Malaysia, one was found alive.[82] If Lanthanotus evolved into lizards from a half-snake, half-lizard condition, why didn't the fellows in Malaysia do the same? (Fig. 95)

A link can only be considered a true link if the transitional stages leading to it and from it are known (which are not), and the mechanism for transition is known (which is not). The creationist predicts, based upon the unlikelihood of DNA undergoing spontaneous improvements, that any proposed evidence suggesting transformations is either incorrectly understood or downright fraudulent. The creationist is intent upon making links crumble under the cutting weight of close scrutiny. He says: "Really, the 'missing links' are not missing. How could what was never there be missing?"
The fossil record is not sparse and incomplete as some would defensively argue. George wrote:
> "There is no need to apologize any longer for the poverty of the fossil record. In some ways it has become almost unmanageably rich, and discovery is outpacing integration.[83]

79. R.B.GOLDSCHMIDT:"EVOLUTION AS VIEWED BY ONE GENETICIST," IN AMERICAN SCIENTIST,40(1952):97; H.RIMMER, (REF.69); D.DEWAR: THE TRANSFORMIST ILLUSION(TENNESSEE:DEHOFF,1957),PP. 87-97; F.W. COUSINS:"THE ALLEGED EVOLUTION OF THE HORSE," IN SYMPOSIUM ON CREATION III,ED. D.W.PATTEN(GRAND RAPIDS:BAKER,1971),PP. 69-85.
80. "LITTLE EOHIPPUS NOT DIRECT ANCESTOR OF HORSE," IN SCIENCE NEWS LETTER,60(AUGUST 25,1951):118.
81. G. A. KERKUT, (REF. 53) P. 136.
82. C.SHUTTLEWORTH:MALAYAN SAFARI(LONDON:PHOENIX,1965), P. 48.
83. T.N.GEORGE:"FOSSILS IN EVOLUTIONARY PERSPECTIVE," IN SCIENCE PROGRESS, 48(1960):1.

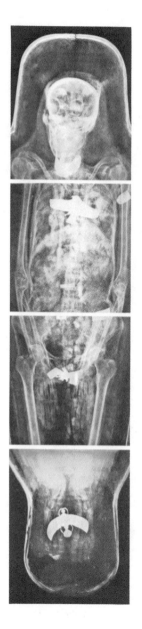
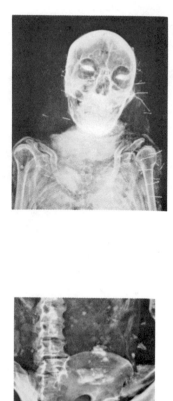

Fig. **93**- Mummies
These radiographs of ancient Egyptian mummies show skeletal features identical to those of modern men. The pelvis in the lower right corner is from a naturally dessicated body dating to 3400 BC. (Courtesy of P. Gray and Eastman Kodak)

Fig. **94**- Archaeopteryx and Horse Variety
Top photos are of Archaeopteryx, fossil and reconstruction. (A. Museum of Nat. History) Bottom photo is of "Gumba," an 18 inch tall American Miniature Yearling Stallion. Horses today vary from this size, and even smaller in Argentina, to the seven foot high, 3200 pound Clydesdales. Yet they are all considered fully horses. Similarly, modern-day antelopes vary from the 12 inch Suni to the six foot, 2000 pound Eland. Are these examples of evolution, or variety within a creationistic "kind?" (Joel Bridges)

Fig. **95** - Lanthanotus & Seymouria
*LANTHANOTUS BORNEANSIS in Sarawak, Malaysia(top). (Courtesy C.
Shuttleworth) Seymouria skeleton(bottom). (A. M. Nat. History)*

So the creationist is left with the faith that transitional forms will never surface--an extrapolation from DNA deductions and present evolutionary inadequacies; and the evolutionist has faith any current inadequacies will fade upon further research--an extrapolation from evidence of fossil and extant variations.

The Eye

Waddington wrote:
". . . we know of no other way than random mutation by which new hereditary variation comes into being . . ."[84]

How could something as intricate as the human eye ever arise by chance rearrangements (mutations) of the DNA code? This organ has long troubled evolutionists and served creationists bent on humiliating evolutionists by its complexity.

To form the eye, a constellation of beneficial mutations would have to occur. These mutations would not involve simple rearrangements of a few bases in DNA, but would first of all have to form sufficient DNA to work with, then mutations of this DNA would have to be integrated with other segments of DNA controlling the nervous, vascular, skeletal, muscular, and endocrine systems.

Two bony orbits must be "mutated" to house the globe of the eye. The bone must have appropriate holes (foramina) to allow the appropriate "mutated" blood vessels and nerves to feed the eye. The various layers of the globe, the fibrous capsule, the sclera and chorioid must be formed, along with the inner light sensitive retina layer. The retina, containing the special rod and cone neurons, bipolar neurons, and ganglion neurons, must be appropriately hooked up to the optic nerve which in turn must be appropriately hooked with the "mutated" sight center in the brain, which in turn must be appropriately hooked with the grey matter, brain stem and spinal cord for conscious awareness and lifesaving reflexes.

Random rearrangements in DNA must also form the lens, vitreous humor, aqueous humor, iris, ciliary body, canal of Schlemm, suspensory ligament, cornea, the lacrimal glands and ducts draining to the nose, the rectus and oblique muscles for eye movement, the eyelids, lashes and eyebrows. (Fig.96)

All of these newly mutated structures must be perfectly integrated and balanced with all other systems and functioning near perfect before the vision we depend upon would result. Deficiencies in any category would make vision not possible and make the whole mutated endeavor a useless waste.

Each of the gross features of the eye would be under the control of many genes (*Drosophila*--fruit fly--eye color is under the control of some 15 genes). Each gene consists of thousands

---

84. *C. WADDINGTON:THE NATURE OF LIFE(N.Y.:ATHENEUM,1962), P. 98.*

of nucleotides. The spontaneous mutation of sufficient DNA to code just the lens of the eye would be roughly equivalent to the formation of a chapter in a book from an explosion of letters. If we were to calculate the probability of the spontaneous formation or mutation of DNA sufficient to code an entire eye, the result would make our previous calculations concerning the improbability of the spontaneous formation of proteins appear pathetically puny by comparison.

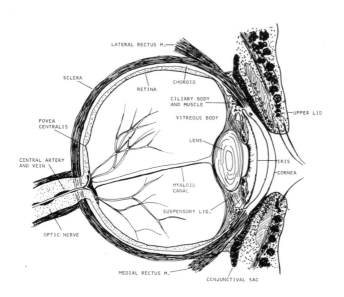

Fig. **96** - Eye   Anatomy
*Anything less than the complexity of a fully formed eye is useless. Could the eye have developed piecemeal through eons of time and escape the effects of natural selection? Could it develop **because** of natural selection?*

But many people believe the human eye has resulted from a long line of accumulated beneficial mutations preserved through the action of natural selection. A simple to complex gradation of eyes is said to have started with something akin to the simple pigment spots in protozoans and then accumulated complexity through the invertebrate-amphibian-reptile stages and finally culminated in the human eye. This idea is held to be eminently reasonable, in fact downright persuasive--until the mechanism for the transformations is examined, or until the evolution of the eye is examined in light of probabilities.

It seems unreasonable to believe DNA could undergo random changes and increase its information content. We say this because of what we have learned about the principles of information theory, i.e., random rearrangements in codes result in their ultimate destruction. But what is the probability of forming an eye through mutations and selection?

Let's assume that 1,000 mutations would be necessary to form an eye. (Millions more than this would in reality be necessary. Huxley estimates a million steps to produce a horse and considers this an underestimate.[85]) For the moment, let's forget the highly deleterious effects of mutations and assume mutations on the order of 50% beneficial. So if we are to get a chain of 1,000 beneficial mutations, then the probability of getting the eye would be like throwing heads with a coin 1,000 times in succession: $1/2^{1000} = 1/10^{300}$. So the chance of forming the eye would be one in ten followed by 299 zeros. In other words, it would not occur. (Borel says of a probability of $1/10^{200}$ that: "One can say with certainty that a phenomenon to which such a probability can be assigned has never been observed and will never be observed by any human in the entire universe."[86])

But evolutionists argue in terms of vast populations and oodles of time. Okay, let's begin with one million organisms per square foot of land all attempting to evolve an eye. We'll give them ten billion years, 50% beneficial mutations--with the other 50% being culled out by natural selection--plenty of DNA substrate to work with and mutations occurring at the rate of one per second. The probability that any of these organisms would form an eye would be: $1/10^{266}$! (Fig. 97)

A WHAT IS THE PROBABILITY OF FORMING AN EYE IF 1,000 BENEFICIAL MUTATIONS IN SUCCESSION WOULD BE NECESSARY AND MUTATIONS WERE 50% BENEFICIAL?

●THE PROBABILITY OF ONE BENEFICIAL MUTATION IS 1/2; THE PROBABILITY OF 1,000 BENEFICIAL MUTATIONS IS: 1/2 X 1/2 . . . FOR 1,000 TIMES = $1/2^{1000}$ = ... $1/10^{300}$

Fig. **97** - Eye Probability

B WHAT IS THE PROBABILITY THAT ONE OUT OF 1,000,000 ORGANISMS PER SQUARE FOOT OF LAND SURFACE(10^{14} FT.^{2}) WILL FORM AN EYE IF MUTATIONS OCCURRED AT THE RATE OF ONE PER SECOND FOR TEN BILLION YEARS, AND HARMFUL MUTATIONS WERE CULLED BY NATURAL SELECTION?

1 ONE ORGANISM WOULD REQUIRE 1,000 SECONDS TO ACHIEVE 1,000 MUTATIONS.

2 IN 10^{17} SECONDS(10^7 SECONDS IN ONE YEAR X 10^{10} YEARS), 10^{14} (10^{17} TOTAL SECONDS $\div$ 10^3 SECONDS FOR 1,000 MUTATIONS) ATTEMPTS BY ONE ORGANISM COULD BE MADE.

3 IF 10^{20} ORGANISMS(10^6 ORGANISMS PER FOOT X 10^{14} FT.^{2}) ARE MAKING ATTEMPTS, IN TEN BILLION YEARS THERE WOULD BE A TOTAL OF 10^{20} ORGANISMS X ATTEMPTS(10^{14}) = 10^{34} ATTEMPTS; $10^{34}/10^{300}$ = ATTEMPTS/POSSIBILITIES = ...$1/10^{266}$

---

85. J. HUXLEY: *EVOLUTION IN ACTION* (N.Y.: NEW AMERICAN LIBRARY, 1953), P. 41.
86. E. BOREL: *ELEMENTS OF THE THEORY OF PROBABILITY* (NEW JERSEY: PRENTICE-HALL, 1965), P. 59.

Even with these ridiculously lenient concessions, the eye still would not form.

It seems practically inconceivable to imagine the eye developing piecemeal through eons of time, when anything less than a fully formed functioning eye is useless and would be selected against. On the other hand, to believe that the eye appeared instantly through a symphony of mutations is ludicrous.

Actually, since our entire genetic makeup (our genotype) was once nothing but a diffuse brew of DNA letters (nucleotides) randomly dispersed in the primeval oceans, and our present DNA is supposedly the product of random arrangements and rearrangements of those letters, then we must be all mutation. Every gene controlling every structural and functional character of our bodies would be composed entirely of mutations. Scheinfeld wrote in this regard:

> "Nonetheless it is through the rare instances of favorable mutations, of innumerable kinds and in countless numbers, occurring successively over very extended periods, that the whole process of evolution may now be explained."[87]

If this be true--that our genetic makeup (genotype) is entirely mutations--then it is downright shocking that we even exist. Not only do the laws of information science argue against the possibility of mutations improving or even creating genes, but practical experience has forced the agreement among geneticists that all mutations (estimated more than 99.9%) are harmful. If our present genotype is dependent upon a long line of "beneficial" mutations, numbering in the millions, then we could have no genotype. If we have no genotype then we don't exist. But we do!

Mutations are rare and harmful. Mutations usually are recessive or semi-dominant (if they are compatible with life) which means that they usually will not show unless there is inbreeding. Further, no new organs form as a result of mutations nor have any new kinds of organisms been produced.

The creationist concludes, therefore, that fixity is the rule. Evolutionists see these problems as transient, stumbling blocks that will be removed upon further research. The creationist continues to point to biological discontinuities between kinds; the evolutionist points to the continuities within kinds. Each feels he has the upper hand.

Super Cow

If mutations were able to do what the evolutionist says, then with the artificial means available for increasing the rate of mutations, and imposing various selective forces, new kinds of

---

87. *A. SCHEINFELD: <u>THE NEW YOU AND HEREDITY</u> (N.Y.: LIPPINCOTT, 1950), P. 476.*

310

life and new organs might be formed. Surely this would be a most active scientific pursuit.

Personally, I have wanted a set of wings since boyhood. Most people wouldn't mind a new mutated pair. Also think of the changes that could be made in animals and plants to greatly benefit man. The following changes would be nicely in order for the domestic cow: mutate a couple of new udders for increased milk yield, mutate its legs to that akin to a horse's so it could be used for pleasure riding and racing; mutate its hair to wool so it could be sheared; mutate its reproductive system so that the fertilized eggs of any breed of animal could be artifically introduced into the cow's uterus and incubated there until birth (just think, no more difficult pregnancies or labor for women); mutate the regenerative ability of the tissues of the cow so that filet mignons could be stripped from it and the cow would then simply regrow the lost muscle; mutate its brain and change its IQ and vocal centers so that it could solve difficult problems and convey the answers to us in our language; and finally, mutate its digestive and urinary systems such that it could readily utilize any form of garbage as food and eliminate gold bricks and refined petroleum. Surely this would be "super cow!" The possibilities are endless. The creationist asks why these genetic feats are not being done by the intense efforts of men if they indeed have happened with such ease by spontaneous evolution.

Creating a "super cow" and wings for man is pure fantasy at this point in time. The science of eugenics (human genetic engineering) has its hands full just trying to rid man of harmful mutations. To create new organs is not within its present scope.

Simpson is of the opinion:

"The problems of tailoring a gene and inserting it in human sperm or egg, making it hereditary, are so many and so little understood at present that reasonable prediction would place that in a future very remote indeed. Moreover, the human (or any other viable and natural) gene system is so intricately balanced that insertion of a foreign element, however well specified in itself, would probably have disastrous effects."[88]

Plant and animal geneticists have found their capabilities limited to such activities as increasing milk yield from cows, or sugar from sugar beets to a maximum beyond which no further improvement is accomplished. Scientists, or nature, as far as we have direct evidence, only modify organisms and organs already in existence to a degree.

Some will say that we have deemphasized the most important

88. G. G. SIMPSON: BIOLOGY AND MAN (N.Y.: HARCOURT, BRACE, WORLD, JOVANOVICH, 1969), P. 129; IN HIS BOOK: TEMPO AND MODE OF EVOLUTION (N.Y.: COLUMBIA U., 1944), PP. 54,55, SIMPSON MADE SIMILAR PROBABILITY CALCULATIONS TO OURS AND ALSO SHOWED THE "INFINITESIMAL CHANCES" FOR SUCCESSIVE AND SUCCESSFUL MUTATIONS.

aspect of the evolutionary mechanism, natural selection. Mutations plus natural selection (neo-Darwinism) is believed to be the blend producing evolution. We've touched on natural selection in this chapter, let's look closer at Darwin's mechanism.

18 {NEO-DARWINISM

Natural selection is a process by which the environment selects the most fit organisms for survival. Natural selection is believed to occur analogously to a farmer selecting breeding lines. If the farmer desires to increase his egg production, he will select for breeding purposes those chickens laying the largest and most eggs. The progeny from these chickens will then be examined to select those producing the best, and these in turn will be used to breed subsequent chickens. In this way, with time, careful selection and surveillance, the farmer can increase his egg production.

Likewise, a changing environment is believed to select for survival those organisms most suited to live, and cull those not properly adapted. If members of each of the different varieties of dogs were suddenly forced into an arctic type environment, only those fit would survive. Thus the long legged, heavy coated breeds like the German Shepard, St. Bernard, Briard, Newfoundland, Norwegian Elkhound and Husky would probably survive. But hardly would the Pekingese, Dachshund, Hairless Chihuahua, Pug or Manchester Terrier be able to withstand the cold or be able to maneuver in heavy snows to find game.

Natural selection as a means for evolutionary change was formulated and popularized by Erasmus Darwin (Charles Darwin's grandfather), Malthus, Spencer and most notably, Charles Darwin himself. Today, natural selection is thought to be a key mechanism for the evolution of life. The modern theory of evolution is termed neo-Darwinism. Neo-Darwinism is a combination of mutations and natural selection. Mutations are believed to provide the "sports," the variants, from which nature can select. As a baseball scout looks for athletes showing unique and superior abilities, so nature looks for mutants that are unique and superior. Neither mutations nor natural selection alone could account for evolution according to modern neo-Darwinists.

The following quotations will attest to the acceptance of neo-

Darwinism by evolutionists:

A. W. Haupt states in a botany textbook:

"New forms arise spontaneously by mutations; natural selection then determines whether or not they will survive. If better suited to the environment than existing forms, they tend to be preserved; if not they are eliminated."[1]

The zoology textbook, *General Zoology*, by Villee, Walker and Smith comments:

"Early in the present century there was a heated discussion as to whether evolution was the result of natural selection or of mutation. As more was learned about heredity, it became clear that natural selection can operate only when there is something to be selected, that is, when mutations present alternate ways of coping with the environment. The evolution of new species, then involves both mutation and natural selection."[2]

The famed geneticist, Theodosius Dobzhansky, asserted:

"Therefore, the mutation process alone, not corrected and guided by natural selection, would result in degeneration and extinction rather than improved adaptiveness."[3]

Neo-Darwinian Examples

Neo-Darwinian examples abound in the literature. The peppered moth (*Biston betularis*) of Great Britain is a popular case. In the past there were many light colored moths that blended with the lichen growing on trees. Through the years, as industry spewed more and more pollution on cities, the lichen were killed and consequently the protective camouflage for the light colored moths was lost. As a result, the dark (melanic) form of the peppered moth (assumed to be a mutant) became predominant in the cities because the birds that enjoy these tasty morsels could not see them against the dark bark on trees. Prior to industrialization, the dark form was so rare it could hardly be found even in museum collections. Conversely, the light colored moth became predominant in the rural areas where pollution had not taken its toll in lichen. The change from the light to the dark moths in the cities is noted as a striking example of neo-Darwinism.

Then there are the numerous cases of bacterial resistance to antibiotics. *Escherichia coli*, the common inhabitant of the intestinal tract, has developed populations resistant to the effects of the antibiotic streptomycin. Although most *E. Coli* is susceptible

1. *A. W. HAUPT: AN INTRODUCTION TO BOTANY (N.Y.: MCGRAW-HILL, 1956), P. 258.*

2. *C. A. VILLEE, W. F. WALKER AND F. E. SMITH: GENERAL ZOOLOGY (PHILADELPHIA: SAUNDERS, 1963), P. 669.*

3. *T. DOBZHANSKY: "ON METHODS OF EVOLUTIONARY BIOLOGY AND ANTHROPOLOGY," IN AMERICAN SCIENTIST, 45(1957): 385.*

to the antibiotic, certain variants (assumed to be mutants) may be resistant. Therefore, although the drug may kill the majority of the bacteria, those resistant forms soon flourish in defiance of the antibiotic. The common use of antibiotics has "created" many strains that are resistant to routinely used antibiotics such as streptomycin and penicillin. This has produced a very real problem in medicine. Bacterial resistance is the reason for Staph. infections sweeping through hospitals and the underlying cause why many infections become deep seated, chronic and disseminating when they should normally clear readily.

Another example of neo-Darwinian evidence is the Golden Whistler bird (*Pachycephala pectoralis*). Varieties of this bird are found geographically separated on the Solomon Islands. There are the Nissan, Vella Lavella, Rendova, San Cristobal, Malaita and Bougainville subspecies. All of these differ in the amount of green and yellow colored plumage. Each island contains a characteristically colored Golden Whistler. It is believed that the separation of these birds geographically, ages ago, isolated genetic pools and mutant forms causing each island population to vary from one another. In this case, selection is said to have resulted from geographical distribution.

A final example I'll mention is sickle-cell anemia. You might recall how in North America the sickle-cell mutation is selected against because of its harmful effects. In Africa the condition is selected for and is quite widespread because it confers resistance to malaria. As beauty is in the eye of the beholder, mutations are only of benefit in the "eye" of natural selection.

Variation or Transmutation ?

The above examples strongly testify that organisms can vary, mutate, adapt to and be selected by the environment. The variation in bird plumage color, the selective breeding of chickens to increase egg yield and the fact that the moths most camouflaged will be the most likely to survive, are observed facts. But the evolutionist finds much more utility in mutations and natural selection than just to explain variety and change within existing types. He extrapolates from these observations and concludes that mutation-selection accounts for the ascent of all organisms from the ancestral amoeba. Now he has stepped on the creationist's toes. The creationist contends that no such amoeba to man extrapolation is possible from the empirical evidence available.

The operation of natural selection, adaptability and mutations clearly forces the conclusion that environment can effect changes. These observations are perfectly in line with the predictions of the micro-evolutionary model. However, do the observations go far enough to give direct testimony for transformations from one type into another?

The effect of environment on organisms resulting in their variations is not really predicted by the creationistic model, but it is not inconsistent with it either. When we think of evolution and creation in the larger sense--amoeba to man versus fixity of basic types--the conclusion that variations within existing types occur, does not speak directly for either position.

Does the evidence support the theory that neo-Darwinism produces changes beyond the limit of kinds, or does the evidence demonstrate fixity?

The biologist and evolutionist, Ernest Mayr, concludes:

". . . all the available evidence indicates that the origin of the higher categories is a process which is nothing but an extrapolation of speciation. All the processes and phenomena of macro-evolution and of the origin of the higher categories can be traced back to intraspecific variation, even though the first steps of such processes are usually very minute."[4]

The speciation Mayr here speaks of is the formation of new varieties from an original pure stock. An example would be the speciation of the Golden Whistler on the Solomon Islands referred to above.

Mathews, in the introduction to a 1971 edition of the *Origin of Species*, wrote concerning "evolution in action" examples such as the case of the melanic moths:

"The experiments beautifully demonstrate natural selection--or survival of the fittest in action, but they do not show evolution in progress, for however the populations may alter in their content of light, intermediate and dark forms, all the moths remain from beginning to end *Biston betularia*."[5]

Evolutionists in general recognize that their extrapolation from mini-changes to macrochanges bridges a gap that has not been filled by concrete data. Addressing himself to the gap between the actual data and evolutionary extrapolations, Julian Huxley states:

"'That is all very well,' you may say. 'It seems to be true that natural selection can turn moths black in industrial areas, can keep protective coloration up to a mark, can produce resistant strains of bacteria and insect pests. But what about elaborate improvements? Can it turn a reptile's leg into a bird's wing, or turn a monkey into a man? How can a blind and automatic sifting process like selection, operating on a blind and undirected process like mutation, produce organs like the eye or the brain, with the almost incredible complexity and delicacy of adjustment? How can chance produce elaborate design? In a word, are you not asking us to

---

4. E. MAYR: *SYSTEMATICS AND THE ORIGIN OF SPECIES* (N.Y.: DOVER, 1964), P. 120.
5. L. MATTHEWS: *"INTRODUCTION," IN THE ORIGIN OF SPECIES* (LONDON: J. M. DENT, 1971.

believe too much? The answer is no . . ."
   He then goes on to show how that the probability of a horse
arising through mutations is at least one thousand to the millionth
power.
   But the evolution of a horse with the aid of natural selection,
"is not too much to believe, once one has grasped the way the process operates!"[6] he says.
   The creationist retorts: "By this Huxley must mean: once one
learns how to extrapolate properly, expand upon the facts. Mr.
Huxley reasons, argues, persuades and extrapolates to transmutations. But no observable evidence is used by him to show this
'truth.' Melanism in moths and resistance in bacteria, even according to Huxley are different than 'reptile's leg into a bird's
wing, or monkey into a man.' Surely if evidences were available
to demonstrate the actual ability of natural selection to produce
new kinds, the evidences would be advanced instead of mere reasonings."

Applied Genetics

   The real observable evidences used to show the workings of
neo-Darwinism are merely examples of variation within certain bounds.
For example, from 1800 to 1878 the sugar content of beets was increased from 6% to 17%. Further breeding and selection from 1878
to 1924 did not increase the sugar content above 17%. The beet
had reached the limit of its genetic capacities.[7]
   This phenomenon observed in beets is not unique. Rather, it
portrays an all-pervading principle in genetics. Whether one
follows the genetic development of beets, corn, beans, peas, fruit,
milk, wool, beef, eggs, speed in horses or weight gain in pigs, improvement is limited and always confined to modification of existing traits within recognizable kinds of organisms. (For another
example, there has been "no substantial change in 7,000 years in
the fundamental botanical characteristics of the corn plant.")[8]
Even though Darwin and others have used the examples of man induced
changes in plants and animals as proof for evolution, never has
there been the formation of new characteristics resulting in the
transformation of one kind into a viable new kind.
   Addressing himself to the history of sugar beets, Tinkle, a
geneticist, explained:
           ". . . lest these examples seem strange to you (as they
           did to me at first) imagine that you have a bushel bas-

---

6. J. HUXLEY: *EVOLUTION IN ACTION* (N.Y.: NEW AMERICAN LIBRARY,
1953), PP. 40-42.
7. D. F. JONES: *GENETICS IN PLANT AND ANIMAL IMPROVEMENT* (N.Y.:
WILEY, 1924), P. 414.
8. P. C. MANGELSDORF, R. S. MACNEISH, W. C. GALINAT: "DOMESTICA-
TION OF CORN," IN *SCIENCE*, 143(1964):538.

ket filled with pairs of marbles of various sizes. In
sorting out the different sizes it may take you some
time to find the biggest ones, but once you have found
them, it is quite evident that the search is completed.
It is just as futile to expect a gene to develop a more
advanced characteristic as to expect a marble to grow
bigger."[9]

The genetic evidence shows that much of the variety we see
about us is simply a sorting of variants. In some cases genes
that are repressed, but still there, are "turned on" under the influence of various environmental influences. The variants thus
produced are not showing "new" traits but merely disrobing genetic
garments to reveal traits that have always been there.

Actual, practical, predictable and workable breeding, relies
upon gene stability. It is on this basis that the whole of the
modern practical science of heredity is based and works. Noting
the role of genetic fixity in the control of hereditable disease,
Riser, a veterinary scientist, wrote:

". . . Hip dysplasia is a polygenetic disease. Since
'like begets like' it is shown that breeding only dogs
with normal hips is an effective way to reduce the prevalence of canine hip dysplasia."[10]

The Hardy-Weinberg law in genetics, summed up by the formula,
$p + 2pq + q^2$, states that genetic frequencies in a freely inter-
breeding population do not change significantly from generation
to generation. In other words, if populations interbreed freely,
the frequencies of characteristics--eye color, blood types, etc.--
remain the same . . . genetically fixed. Although it is argued
that this law is true only in the absence of mutation, selection
and genetic drift, its implication is fixity.

In perusing several texts on evolution of a popular as well
as technical nature, I have found that every illustration depicting neo-Darwinism with actual organisms (as opposed to speculated
and extrapolated intermediates) simply represents variation within
an obvious kind: fruit fly evolution begins with fruit flies and
ends with fruit flies, finch evolution begins with finches and
ends with finches (the famed 13 species of Galapagos finches
Darwin studied in 1845 are the same 13 species today), mouse evolution begins with mice and ends with mice, dog evolution begins with
dogs and ends with dogs, bacteria evolution begins with bacteria
and ends with bacteria. Does the virtual absence of pictures representing the change of one organism to another reflect in turn a
very real lack of any such evidence? Surely, if examples of change
from one kind into another were available, evolution books would
contain the pictures.

---

9. *W. J. TINKLE*: <u>HEREDITY</u> *(GRAND RAPIDS: ZONDERVAN, 1970), P. 57.*
10. *W. H. RISER*: *"CANINE HIP DYSPLASIA: CAUSE AND CONTROL," IN*
<u>JOURNAL OF THE AMERICAN VETERINARY MEDICAL ASSOCIATION</u>*, 165*
(1974): 361.

When one sits back and looks at the forest and forgets the trees momentarily, he cannot help but be struck by the current and historic constancy of the basic types of plants and animals. Kellenberger wrote:

"Living things are enormously diverse in form, but form is remarkably constant within any given line of descent: pigs remain pigs and oak trees remain oak trees generation after generation."[11]

There are about 200 varieties of the dog, but they are all identifiable as dogs. Likewise, there are about 600 varieties of the fruitfly, 300 varieties of the pocket gopher, 250 species of the clam, Anadonta, are the same, 70 varieties of bluegrass, 1,500 varieties of the Hawthorn plant, several hundred varieties of sweet peas, 60 varieties of man and 50 varieties of violets. If variation is limitless, one cannot help but wonder why all of life is not a profusion of homogeneity making it impossible to clearly identify and delineate basic types.

On the other hand, speciation and variation is taken by evolutionists as disproof of creationistic fixity. However, the modern informed creationist does not (as we elaborated in Chapter 4) say that fixity is a fixity of "species." This idea--that creationistic fixity is fixity of species--originated with the eighteenth century botanist Linnaeus, who was a creationist. His dictum was: *"Species tot sunti, quot formae ab initio creatae sunt,"* which says, "There are as many species as forms were created in the beginning." Creationists today maintain that the Linnaean interpretation of creation was wrong and should not be taken as the last word, any more than Darwin's belief in inheritance of acquired characteristics, Lamarckism, should.

The sum total of man's efforts in breeding both plants and animals declares fixity of basic types. Sure, hybrids are formed, but they are sterile (mule) or limited in fertility (cattalo) to a few generations. Mutations are known to create infertility but never create fertility between intersterile kinds. Natural hybridization is uncommon if not absent, for animals in the wild state show a natural exclusiveness. Man has never been crossed with any other organism.

The rule of nature seems to be not the ascent of sports, but the descent to mongrels--reversion to type. Farmers can get pure lines of chickens, pigs, cows, and maintain them with proper surveilance. If the animals are allowed to intermingle, the pure lines of sleek tall slender beauties soon degenerate to boring, medium-sized, brown mutts--reversion to type. (Fig. 98)

Evolutionists, of course, don't see it that way. The fact that organisms can vary, adapt, change fertility and be molded by the environment makes evolution very reasonable, they feel.

---

11. E. KELLENBERGER: "THE GENETIC CONTROL OF THE SHAPE OF A VIRUS," IN *SCIENTIFIC AMERICAN*, 215(DEC., 1966):32.

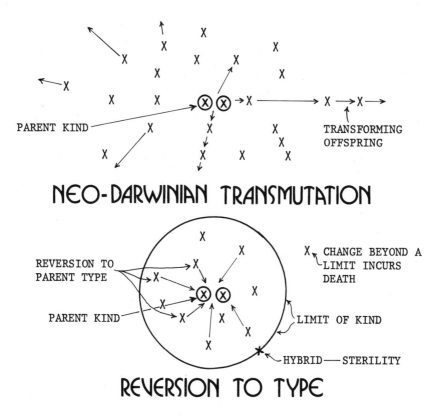

NEO-DARWINIAN TRANSMUTATION

REVERSION TO TYPE

Fig. **98**- Reversion to Type

Neo-Darwinism advocates limitless change and pressure towards the formation of new kinds--pressure away from the parent kind. Evidence from genetics and actual breedings testifies to fixity of basic kinds and pressure toward reversion to the parent type. Changes beyond certain limits renders the bearer sterile or dead.

Neo-Darwinism: A Negative Force?

Natural selection in itself does not produce anything new. Nature selects only what is already there. If one cuts down an entire field of corn except for one stalk, is the remaining stalk a new kind? Does the elimination of unfit organisms make the remaining fit organism a new kind? Natural selection is a weeding out of organisms, it is a destructive process. Further, what does nature have to select from? It is said mutations produce the new improved variants. Yet mutations are not known to increase the viability of organisms in natural environments. On the contrary, mutations, for all intents and purposes, are detrimental. Then, if natural selection cannot produce anything new, but only destroys organisms not fit (negative force), and mutations cannot produce new organisms, but only less fit ones (negative force), would not natural selection and mutations summated exert a negative force?

Environmental stress that is sufficient to require drastic changes of the sort believed to occur in evolution, could very well destroy existing organisms. If the environment stresses a population, that population may adapt to a degree, but if the environmental stress is enough, say to require development of wings from legs or eyes from pigment spots, then the entire population would surely perish.

It stands to reason that if organisms in a given environment are there and surviving because they are fit, a drastic change in that environment (enough of a change to, say, necessitate the creation of a new organ) would destroy those heretofore protected. Thus, certain areas in Antarctica are completely sterile, no bacteria have adapted to the rigors of that environment. There are countless examples of animals that have become extinct in the past (the dinosaurs for example) and many animals in the last couple of centuries that have become extinct or are nearing extinction. Certainly, if the biological organism has the limitless capacity to change, how is any extinction explained? Biological mechanisms are highly tuned and refined machines with some innate ability to adapt to varying stresses. However, just as a machine can only withstand so much abuse, so can living organisms.

Nowhere is this more obvious and clear than in medical practice. The body is programmed with an intricate set of control mechanisms for maintaining homeostasis (normality). Chemical receptors detect slight alterations in blood carbon dioxide, oxygen, electrolyte and sugar levels. Hormones and the autonomic nervous system control and make adjustments in blood pressure, cardiac output and respirations. If stress in the form of excess heat or cold, bacteria, protozoons or nematodes exceeds certain limits, the body's homeostatic mechanisms fail and death ensues. Survival depends upon <u>existing</u> structural and functional mechanisms. Although resistance to stress can vary from individual to individual, these differences are slight. A practitioner can usually predict (prognose) the outcome of certain diseases based upon evaluating to what degree the body is deviating from normal. The closer to normal, the more chance for survival, the farther from normal, the more chance for death.

Every segment of the biological world is "tuned" to a set of normals. Organisms have an ecological niche in which they are able to survive. Populations of organisms within a certain ecological niche can be stressed by the environment and change to a degree. For example, bacterial colonies grown on different mediums in culture plates will vary depending upon the medium, temperature and oxygen level. Never have organisms shown the ability to vary, mutate and be selected beyond a degree. If bacteria are put in a petri dish with no nutrient medium, they will eventually die, not develop the ability to digest glass; if a population of fish is removed from their ecological niche and thrown in the middle of a desert, they die, they don't mutate lungs and feet; if a population of land dwelling mammals are thrown in the middle of the Atlantic, they eventually die, they don't grow gills, flippers and revised kidneys allowing the consumption of salt water.

Evolutionists might say: "Such examples aren't fair. That isn't what we are saying. We say that changes occured over long periods of time and with gradually developing organs."

The creationist counters: "We have at our disposal the ideal test material for the assertion that time and vast populations yield new kinds. That material is the world of small, the prolific, and also the fossil record.

"We have irradiated millions of fruit flies and we can observe the reproduction of billions upon billions of bacteria and plankton, yet no changes are observed of the order needed for evolution. We have available to us the fossil record with untold millions of animals catastrophically preserved therein, (one quarter billion insects alone) and many of these, although supposedly many millions of years old, look essentially like their modern relatives extant today. Can time and vast populations complete that which has no evidence of a beginning?

"Why the present ecological scare? Why the concern over pollution? Does not the danger from damaging the environment tell us something? Namely, that if the environment is altered beyond a certain degree, survival is threatened. When it comes down to plain old practical belief, we find all people, including you evolutionists who believe you owe your existence to environmental stresses like pollution, fearing the ecological crises. Why are you not telling us ecological crises will result in biological improvement?"

Survival of the Unfit

To further illustrate the creationistic argument against neo-Darwinism, let's journey into our remote past. We'll consider us at the time when we had no arms. Since, according to neo-Darwinists, we all came originally from an amoeba-like ancestor which had no arms, and since we have arms today, we must have developed them. Anyway, back to our armless ancestor. We find him at the stage where he is to begin growing arms. What would make him need arms? Well, it could have been any number of things. Perhaps he was unable to escape from predators well and having arms would help him climb trees. Or maybe he was unable to implement his evolving ingenuity to create weapons and build fires without arms and hands. Or perhaps his wife was tired of being cuddled with only a hairy body and legs. In any case, he needed arms--having them was crucial to his survival.

This creates an interesting dilemma. If our ancestor needed arms, and having them was crucial to his survival, how would he be able to survive without them? He would need them immediately, not several million evolutionary years in the future. Yet, the neo-Darwinists tell us the evolution of organs took eons of time.

In order for natural selection to work, the environment must stress a population such that only some are able to survive-- only those with the new organ. So only those members of this ancient colony of our ancestors that had mutated newly formed arms would be able to survive. But wait, the evolutionist says evolution took time and, furthermore, it would be too incredible to believe the sudden mutation of an arm with its muscles, tendons, bone, cartilage, nerves, skin, arteries, veins, lymphatics and connective tissue. Then, evidently someone in the population would have first developed a slight nub in the area of the shoulder. He would pass this on to his children, and those of his progeny with a slightly larger nub would be selected and pass the larger nub on to their children. On and on this would go, and through the generations we could start to see the beginning of arms.

Those who were developing this arm, though, were experiencing some difficulties. It seems that the emerging arm nubs were absolutely no good to them. In fact, this arm precursor was getting them tangled in the brush when they tried to run from predators. Aside from that, not yet having good muscle and nerve control (that was to come in a couple of more million years), the arms would flip and flop when our ancestor would run, slap him in the face and eyes, temporarily blind him, and cause him to run into trees, trip, and be easily caught by his enemies. The women of the tribe also found the men with the largest partially formed arms quite unattractive and freakish looking; the men found the same to be true of the women that were developing the arm nubs. If this were the case, nature would have selected those without the useless developing arms as the most fit. Those that were developing the arm precursors would be killed off by natural selection.

If those of our ancestors who were not developing the arms were the ones to survive, what about the original environmental stress that was forcing arm evolution? Wouldn't natural selection kill those without arms? It follows from this that if those ancestors of ours who did not develop arms were exterminated, and those who began growing them were also culled, we had no ancestors. If we had no ancestors, then you and I do not exist--you are not reading this, and I am not writing it!

The same line of reasoning can be applied to the evolution of any organ in any organism. Organs not fully formed are of no benefit and would be selected against. Natural selection becomes the enemy of inventiveness. Furthermore, if organs develop slowly over eons of time, how does the organism know to keep adding to the developing organ until it's developed so that the organism can survive in an anticipated new environment millions of years yet in the future? Also, if the environment is forcing a change requiring a new organ and that organ does not mutate suddenly, completely and fully functioning, then the organism will die from the environmental stress.

Our Choice

Actually, almost all cases that are used to show the effect of neo-Darwinism cannot be directly proven to be a product of that mechanism. For example, the suitability of different beaks of birds to different forms of food usually cannot be directly shown to have resulted from mutations and natural selection. The creationist could as well argue that the reason beaks are shaped as they are is because they were created that way to enable birds to eat certain food. So, there is the choice· the food has dictated the beak, or the beak has dictated the food. The choice, in most cases, is simply a choice. No one has seen the beaks evolve, nor has anyone seen them be created.

We, the jurors, are faced with a choice between two extrapolations. The creationist asks us to extrapolate from present evidence of fixity and from like evidence in the fossil record, to the conclusion that life kinds have been fixed back to a creation. He pleads that empirical evidence from genetics and paleontology and the negative effects of the mechanism of neo-Darwinism make his extrapolation most valid.

The evolutionist is also asking us to extrapolate. Is it not true that belief that natural selection and mutations can result in new and different life forms is based solely on faith? Is not such belief credible only through the proper extrapolations--"grasping the way the process operates," according to Huxley? Belief in neo-Darwinism as a means to transmutation is based upon thoughts, ideas, reasonings, not hard core demonstrable facts. The direct evidence that natural selection has, does, or will result in complex new organ systems and organisms has plainly not surfaced. However, there is much evidence of variation. The evolutionist asks us to look at this for justification for an extrapolation to the large changes necessary for evolution in the amoeba-to-man sense.

The choice is ours.

19 { NEO-DARWINIAN PREDICTIONS

If neo-Darwinism is a valid scientific conclusion, then we should be able to make predictions based upon it. If the predictions are verified by observations, then neo-Darwinism is given real credibility. If the predictions are contradicted by the data, then neo-Darwinism should be discarded in favor of a more adequate explanation of the data.

The following is a listing of predictions based upon neo-Darwinism along with creationistic rebuttals and counter-interpretations.

-1-

● Prediction: Sub-populations with newly selected mutated characteristics should be more fit than the parent population.

Expert witness: C. H. Waddington, an evolutionist, states: "If by selection we concentrate the genes acting in a certain direction, and produce a sub-population which differs from the original one by greater development of some character we are interested in (such as higher milk yield or production of eggs), we almost invariably find that the sub-population has simultaneously become less fit and would be eliminated by natural selection."[1]
Expert witness: The population geneticist, H. T. Band, concluded from her work with fruit flies that those organisms showing a mutation and breeding true for it do not evidence increased viability.[2]

---

1. *C. H. WADDINGTON: "THE RESISTANCE TO EVOLUTIONARY CHANGE," IN NATURE, 175 (1955):51.*
2. *H. T. BAND: "GENETIC STRUCTURE OF POPULATIONS," IN EVOLUTION, 18 (1964):384-404.*

Creationist: "The very substance of evolution is the generation of new, more viable populations. Cited here are two experts who contend altered offspring populations are less viable than the parent stock. On the other hand, the creationist would predict that the further a population would vary from the original created kind, the less viable it would become. Sub-populations that are produced as a result of mutagenic changes in DNA should be less viable, for random changes in a complex integrated system should vitiate that system, not improve it."

-2-

● Prediction: Harmful mutations should be rigorously eliminated from populations.

Expert witness: The geneticist, Band, concluded that the evidence does not testify that harmful mutants retained in the recessive heterozygous condition are eliminated from populations-- the organisms with such mutations don't decrease viability.[3]

Creationist: "Natural selection is said to act by eliminating detrimental mutants, leaving for survival the more fit mutants. If harmful mutations are not rigorously eliminated from populations, even if they are in the recessive heterozygous condition, then harmful mutants would eventually accumulate in populations to the extent that future populations would be jeopardized. Here, an evolutionist and geneticist indicates that natural selection does not serve to rigidly select against harmful mutants. Natural selection must not only be able to cull those organisms with gross defects but must also be able to select against subtle changes in order to account for all of the various refinements we see in the biological world. In other words, natural selection must not only be able to select against an animal born without any eyes, but also select against organisms with 1% less retinal photoreceptors than others, or a slightly less functional lens, or cornea, or tear glands, or globe size or eyelids. If natural selection cannot eliminate subtle deficiencies, then the formation and bringing to perfection of organs such as the eye remain unaccounted for. Further, if harmful mutations accumulate in populations, then the net result of changes over time would be degeneration not improvement."

The creationist predicts that the accumulation of mutations would result in a net degenerative effect. He contends that gross abnormalities can be eliminated by the environment, but the environment could never force the evolution of the subtle refinements necessary to bring new organ systems and new kinds of organisms into existence.

-3-

● Prediction: There should be observed in nature a universal

---

3. H. T. BAND, (REF. 2) PP. 384-404.

aggressive struggle for survival of sufficient intensity to force transmutation.

Expert witness: *Scientific American*, (July, 1973) in reviewing the book, *Geographical Ecology*, says:
> "In the diversity of natural environments the species blend is rich. Competition for resource use must go before aggressive competition: surely there is no point to fighting unless some commonly useful resource is to be gained. For this main reason aggressive behavior . . . is far from universal in the animal kingdom."

Observation: All human societies usually condemn the same basic wrongs. Societies condemn murder, incest and lack of respect for private property.[4] Man's emphasis on moral conscience and higher laws of justice is what resulted in the conviction of the Nazi war criminals at Nuremberg. Moral regulations are counter to the amoral nature of evolution and tend to provide a climate of peace and respect for others rather than wanton aggression and abuse so necessary for natural selection.

> Could······amoral natural selection select moral human societies that penalize those who act amorally ?

Creationist: "The creationist argues that there has been a struggle for survival in nature subsequent to a perfect creation. Although nature is replete with competition, the evidence does not suggest that the struggle for existence is of sufficient intensity or exacting enough to account for the origin of all the various life forms. The existence of moral man, in fact, negates his origin from an amoral process."

-4-

● Prediction: Ancestral forms that were selected against to give rise to modern improved organisms should no longer exist.

Observations: The complex societal arrangements seen among bees and wasps are said to be evolutionary adaptations from less fit solitary ancestors. Yet we find bees and wasps that live solitary lives surviving just fine today.

Sexual reproduction is held to be the evolutionary improve-

---

4. A. MONTAGU: *ANTHROPOLOGY AND HUMAN NATURE* (BOSTON, P. SARGENT, 1957), PP. 58, 63, 64.

ment of asexual reproduction. Asexual reproduction is, in quantity, more abundant today than sexual reproduction. This is evidenced by asexual bacteria and other microorganisms making up 75% of all life on this planet.

The complexity and specialization seen today in modern human societies is thought to be the result of the survival of the fittest. If this be true, why do many primitive peoples in S. America, Australia, Africa and the Arctic survive and live contemporaneously with the "evolved" societies?

The intricately constructed and specialized nests of such birds as the megapode of Australia, the weaver bird and the tailor bird, are thought to be recent evolutionary adaptations from primitive simple nests. Generally speaking, however, the birds that make the least elaborate nests are the most abundant.

Fish with bones are thought to have developed from less fit fish with cartilaginous skeletons, yet cartilaginous fish (sharks) and bony fish exist side by side in present day oceans.

The botanist, Radcliffe Smith, makes the following observations of plants and "Hutchinson's Rules" for determining "primitiveness" and "advancement":

1. It is more "primitive" for a flower to have a number of separate carpels than to have a few united ones, however, on this basis the "primitive" Buttercup flourishes more in numbers than the "advanced" Love-in-a-mist.

2. Separate stamens are believed to be more "primitive" than united ones, however, on this basis the lime family in the tropics is found to be as, or more successful in numbers than the more "advanced" mallow family.

3. Trees and shrubs are suggested by Hutchinson to be more "primitive" than herbs, however, trees and shrubs take over the earth from herbs as vegetation progresses from grassland to scrubland to woodland.[5]

Deer are said to have developed antlers because they needed them for the defense of harems. Burton, in *The Illustrated London News*, February 25, 1961, noted that often an antlerless stag is a leader stag over other stags and will have the largest female harem. Thus the "more fit" antlered deer, and the "less fit" antlerless deer live side by side with the "less fit" dominating the "more fit."

Creationist: "If sexual reproduction developed because asexual reproduction was less fit, and highly cultured societies developed because primitive societies were less fit, and the ability to build elaborate nests developed because simple nests were less fit, and bony fish developed because cartilaginous fish were less fit, and more advanced vegetation developed to replace primitive vegetation, and antlered deer developed because antlerless

5. A. R. SMITH: *BOTANY AND EVOLUTION*, PAMPHLET #206 (GREAT BRITAIN: E. P. M., 1975).

deer were less fit, why do all the "less fit" organisms live side by side with their evolved modern ancestors, sometimes even dominating their "more fit" counterparts? The concurrent existence of ancestral forms with evolved forms is a contradiction to survival of the fittest. On the other hand, if life forms were created, there would be no reason why all living things, from the simple to the complex, could not coexist throughout time."

-5-

● Prediction: Organisms should not develop behavior that results in suicide for themselves or their progeny.

Observations: Some species of beetles and ants in the process of growing cultures of fungus will break open their own eggs to serve as fertilizer for the fungus.[6]

The ant, *Formica sanguinea*, captures and nurtures the insect parasite Lomechusa even to the exclusion of taking care of their own ant young. The Lomechusa parasite then kills off the Formica ant colony that has raised it.

Carpenter ants defend the Atemeles beetle larvae in preference to their own young. The Atemeles beetle then proceeds to feed on the larvae of the ants.

When an Anergates queen ant is found near a Tetramoria ant nest she is taken into the Tetramoria nest by Tetramoria workers and meticulously cared for. The Tetramoria ants then kill their own queen and care for the young born to the Anergates queen. By killing their queen, the Tetramoria have committed suicide for their colony.

Some ants tolerate caterpillars that in turn help spin silk for the nest of the ants, but the caterpillars also eat the ant larvae.

Opossums feign death when in danger, yet surely a predator would rather consume such a nonresisting passive meal, than a teeth baring, claw scratching one. The death feigning behavior of the opossum is suicidal. However, to the contrary, the opossum flourishes.

Birds of the cuckoo family practice what is known as social parasitism. The female cuckoo will lay eggs in the nest of various host birds such as Hedge sparrows, Meadow pits and Sedge warblers. The cuckoo young will hatch in about 12 days and then proceed to mount the eggs or newly hatched chicks of the foster parent on its back and push them over the edge. The foster parent then devotes all her time to the cuckoo. The young cuckoo may grow to three times the size of the foster parent thus forcing the foster mother to perch on the back of the young cuckoo to feed its gaping mouth. By tolerating and even rearing the cuckoo, the host

---

6. *SOME OF THE FOLLOWING INTERESTING BIOLOGICAL RELATIONSHIPS ARE TAKEN FROM EVAN SHUTE'S MOST EXCELLENT BOOK, FLAWS IN THE THEORY OF EVOLUTION (NEW JERSEY: CRAIG PRESS, 1961).*

birds are perpetuating a nemesis to their own kind. (Fig.99)

Fig.**99** - Cuckoo   Parasitism
*A young European Cuckoo is being fed by its foster parent, a
warbler. (Courtesy American Museum of Natural History)*

When renegade African lions attack herds of domestic goats,
the goats will often simply stand by and watch the slaughter of
their companions, apparently waiting for their own turn to be de-
voured. Lions usually only kill what they need to eat, but in
this case they have a field day, even killing entire herds.

Creationist: "It is difficult to understand how a process
(natural selection) that is supposed to result in the emergence of
organisms that are more fit for survival could generate organisms
that as a part of their behavior perform suicidal actions. Would
it be reasonable to believe that the most fit to survive are those
that commit suicide? The existence of insects that destroy their
own eggs to fertilize fungus, and insects that harbor species of
parasites that kill the insects' young, and animals such as the
opossum and goat that make themselves easily preyed upon, proves
that natural selection is not very selective. If nature tolerates
such suicidal misfits, how could it ever select the refinements
necessary for the formation of the human eye or brain?"

-6-

● Prediction: Organisms would not be expected to develop organs, behavior or characteristics for the sole benefit of another.

Observation: Humans provide a striking example of creatures who, with no hope of selfish benefit, often aid others. The true Christian ethic is one of selfless love. Modern societies have many philanthropic organizations designed to aid other starving or ravaged "less fit" humans, as well as animals. Man goes to great lengths to preserve human mutant freaks in institutions, through humane and antivivesection agencies, prevent the extermination or abuse of animals, and not interfere with the right of fellow humans to reproduce regardless of possible genetic consequences. Man, it is true, may seem to be basically selfish, but his goal, the horizon of progress he attempts to reach, is one based upon selflessness and loving concern for others. Could a selfish process like survival of the fittest produce a product striving for selflessness?

The plant, *Duvana dependens*, provides a special gall just the right size and shape and at the right time to house the moth *Cecidosis eremita*. The plant derives no known benefit from this relationship.

In some species of angler fish only the female catches food. She then voluntarily hooks up to the male through specially structured organs to unselfishly feed him intravenously.

The Amazon ant is helpless in feeding itself and rearing its young. If a slave ant does not selflessly aid the Amazon ant, the Amazon ant will die.

Leaf binding ants use their larvae to sew together leaves by holding the larvae in their jaws as the larvae exudes silk. The larvae's silk spinning ability seems to be for the sole benefit of the adult's nest building process.

The milkweed produces glycosides which are of no use to it, but protect the monarch butterfly feeding upon the plant.

Some ants herd and pasture certain caterpillars and aphids that secrete a milk for the ants to consume. The ants simply stroke their herded aphids properly and the aphids will either protrude special glands to be sucked, or simply extrude the milk. The milk organs on the caterpillars and aphids apparently serve only the ants.

Many plants and animals have coloration and architecture apparently perfected beyond any possible utility served. Deep sea crustacea, fish, sea cucumbers and sea anemones live in the black depths of the sea but are marvelously colored and structured. The sphinx moths are beautifully colored yet are active only at night when color could do them no good. Is such beauty only for the appreciation of man? Color may have utility, such as the absorption of heat in butterflies, but that function could be easily accomplished without intricate designs, symmetry and shadings. (It is commonly argued that coloration in butterflies serves for sexual attraction. However, it has been shown that female butterflies are not in the least influenced by male coloration. Then it seems that male butterfly coloration is in excess of functional need.) Color is important in flowers, but the beautiful designs

and hues of colors are not--actually are in excess of possible
utility. The cone shell has a beautiful pattern that is only visible if the shell is scraped. Leaves, diatoms and mollusks all
show ornate symmetry and architectural beauty which serves no function in reproductive attraction.

An obvious and striking example of selflessness which is common to all organisms is reproduction. Of what value is it to male
and female organisms to produce progeny? Of what value is it for
them to nurture and protect even to the death--their progeny? The
parents derive no benefit from this action, only the progeny gain.

Sagan wrote in this regard:

> "The animals are exceptionally motivated to reproduce
> themselves, even though there is no obvious material ben-
> efit which thereby accrues to them."[7]

Actually, the production of offspring brings pressure to bear
on the parents in terms of maternal demands and food-space competition. Does it follow from this that the very essence of life,
reproduction, refutes neo-Darwinism? (Fig. 100)

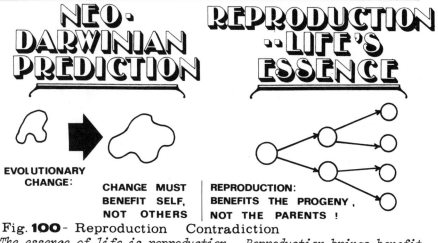

NEO-DARWINIAN PREDICTION

REPRODUCTION --LIFE'S ESSENCE

EVOLUTIONARY CHANGE:

| CHANGE MUST BENEFIT SELF, NOT OTHERS | REPRODUCTION: BENEFITS THE PROGENY, NOT THE PARENTS ! |

Fig. **100** - Reproduction   Contradiction
*The essence of life is reproduction. Reproduction brings benefit
to the progeny and competition to the parents. Neo-Darwinism predicts that characteristics could only develop if they greatly
benefit the evolving organism. Yet the essence of life, reproduction, benefits others, not self. Therefore, the creationist says,
neo-Darwinism is not true or life is not true--an easy choice.*

Creationist: "Natural selection is a selfish and competitive
process. Never would one expect the process to generate characteristics in one organism that could serve only another organism. A
created integrated biological world does not contradict benevolent

---

7. I. S. SHKLOVSKII C. SAGAN: *INTELLIGENT LIFE IN THE UNIVERSE*
(NEW YORK: DELL, 1966), P. 185.

relationships in nature."

-7-

● Prediction: Mechanisms that are proposed to explain the origin of various characteristics and traits should be consistently applicable. Ad hoc situations should not be common, rather the common evolutionary plan should.

Observations: Natural selection is said to have evolved females with the maternal instinct, other arrangements, being less fit, were to have been selected against, nevertheless:
The stickleback fish male attracts the female to a nest he has built. She deposits eggs and leaves; he fertilizes and remains to guard them. The male seahorse has a pouch into which the female deposits her eggs. He fertilizes and carries the eggs in this pouch until they are hatched. The male midwife toad twines the eggs laid by the female around his legs. He then dips them in water periodically to keep them moist and moves into the water just before they are ready to hatch. The male Tilapia fish hatches eggs in its mouth and allows the hatched young to use his mouth as a refuge. The banded pipefish male fertilizes, carries and nurses the young on its belly.
It is argued that feathers evolved for the purpose of enabling flight, yet bats fly and have no feathers, and some birds such as the ostrich and penguin have feathers and don't fly.
Why are insects and birds in identical environments colored differently?
The giraffe is said to have developed a long neck because this would make him the most fit, yet sheep have a short neck and live side by side with the giraffe. Thus each of these two animals are "more fit" than the other. One because he has a short neck, and the other because he has a long neck.
Sheep are to have evolved horns because this insured their survival, yet many breeds of sheep, such as the Shropshire, have no horns and live contemporaneously with horned sheep.
The horse has uncrowned teeth and a bushy tail to make it "fit for survival," yet the cow has crowned teeth and a tail with a tuft on the end. The cow grazes in the same field with the horse--evidently it, too, is perfectly fit.
The monkey is said to have developed a tail to better enable it to climb trees, yet the gibbon, manx cat and bear climb trees and have no tails; and the domestic cat has a tail, climbs well, but doesn't use the tail for that purpose.
The pinna of the ear is argued to have developed to make those needing more acute hearing abilities more fit, yet birds have highly sensitive hearing and have no ear pinna.
The protective melanic coloration of moths is used as a prime example of natural selection. It is said that the moths have the protective coloration to enable them to survive in darkened urban industrial areas. Why then do some moth species only endow the female with protective coloration, leaving the male with the nat-

ural colors?

The queen ant produces worker ants which are sterile and thus unable to pass on improvements to offspring--nor receive them from his ancestors.

The female glowworm phosphoresces to warn birds of its unpalatability. This ability is said to have arisen through natural selection, yet the male glowworm does not have this ability and survives well.

Some maintain that plants evolved the ability to produce berries to aid seed dissemination through their consumption and elimination by animals. Why then are some berries poisonous?

Cats of all varieties have in common a complex behavioral reaction to the active chemical ingredient in catnip, nepetalactone. But the catnip plant is indigenous only to the Old World. Why do cats from both the Old and New World have this catnip behavior? Did New World cats evolve catnip behavior in the absence of the influence of the catnip plant?

If asked why members of the cat family descend trees tail first an evolutionist will answer with "survival of the fittest." Why does the leopard survive well as the only member of the cat family that descends trees head first?

Why do female duke of burgundy butterflies walk on six legs while the males walk on four?

Creationist: "For almost every explanation of how natural selection forced the evolution of a particular organism or characteristic there can be found in nature a contradiction to that explanation. Rather than natural selection proving to be an all-embracing explanation of the origin of the biological world, it in reality explains only a few situations without contradiction. Where natural selection is contradicted, terms like "oddity" or "quirk of nature" are applied and ad hoc explanations are advanced. If creation be true, there should be no pervading mechanistic explanation for the origin of living forms. Nature would not be a continuum of some materialistic process, but rather the work of a creator artist. The biological world should be filled with "oddities" from an evolutionary viewpoint."

-8-

● Prediction: The interrelationships between organisms should be explainable through a step-wise sequence from the point at which the members of the relationship were independent of one another.

Observations: The following interrelationships creationists believe defy explanation through step-wise gradations:

Mites of the genus Antennophorus attach themselves to ants, steal food from the ant's mouth, reach out and steal food from passing ants and stroke the ant to make it regurgitate.

A spider lives within the pitcher plant of Malaya and eats the food caught by the plant. At the bottom of the pitcher is a pool of digestive enzymes which dissolve insects caught by the plant. The spider residing therein is able to immerse itself in this digestive soup when endangered with no harm to itself. Wouldn't the ancestors to these spiders themselves have been digested by the enzymes in the pitcher plant until such time that the special protective organs would have been fully developed? If so, we must reason, the ancestors of these Malaya spiders did not survive, and so neither do the spiders today. But they do!

Many parasites have the ability to prevent the coagulation of blood obtained from their host, some have no means of locomotion and have only insignificant nervous and digestive systems. Life in the absence of their specific host is impossible for them.

The rabbit is essentially the only species able to ingest the death cup toadstool (Amanita) containing the poisonous substance phallin with no apparent harm to itself. How could it have evolved this ability step-wise?

Insects would quickly overrun the world if birds did not keep them in check. How then could insects have existed millions of years, evolutionarily speaking, prior to the birds?

Some parasites require two or more hosts. For example, the dog heart worm, *Dirofilaria immitis*, resides in the heart chambers and great vessels of the dog and there produces larval forms (microfilaria) that are shed into the dogs blood stream. These larvae are unable to mature unless they enter a mosquito. When a mosquito feeds on the dog it sucks the larvae of the heart worm in with its blood meal. Within the mosquito the larvae mature. When the mosquito bites another dog, the matured forms enter the host along with the injected secretions from the mouth parts of the mosquito. The injected larvae then migrate through the tissues of the dog into the blood stream, travel to the heart and there grow to twelve or fourteen inches in length eventually killing their canine host. Here, as in numerous parasitic relationships, the host and means of sustenance of the parasite is killed; and the parasite depends upon the simultaneous existence of intermediate and final hosts that are widely separated in the evolutionary time-scale--here, the mosquito coming "millions" of years before the dog, and the parasite originating "millions" of years before either. (Fig. 101)

Some parasites exude a paralyzing substance that is offered to ants. The ants love it, eat it, are paralyzed and subsequently consumed by the parasite.

Certain wasps hunt caterpillars to serve as food for larval wasps. The wasp hunts in hot weather and if it killed the caterpillars they would soon putrefy when brought back to the wasp nest thus endangering the wasp young. The wasp has the ability to sting the caterpillar so that it is paralyzed yet still alive. In some cases the wasp demonstrates a tremendous understanding of caterpillar anatomy by stinging several specific ganglia in the various segments of the caterpillar yet not killing it. The caterpillar is still able to eat but unable to escape the larvae in the nest of the wasp which eat the caterpillar avoiding vital or-

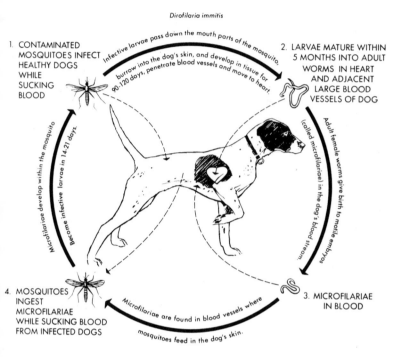

Dirofilaria immitis

1. CONTAMINATED MOSQUITOES INFECT HEALTHY DOGS WHILE SUCKING BLOOD

Infective larvae pass down the mouth parts of the mosquito, burrow into the dog's skin, and develop in tissue for 90-120 days, penetrate blood vessels and move to heart.

2. LARVAE MATURE WITHIN 5 MONTHS INTO ADULT WORMS IN HEART AND ADJACENT LARGE BLOOD VESSELS OF DOG

Adult female worms give birth to motile embryos (called microfilariae) in the dog's blood stream.

Microfilariae develop within the mosquito

Become infective larvae in 14-21 days.

4. MOSQUITOES INGEST MICROFILARIAE WHILE SUCKING BLOOD FROM INFECTED DOGS

Microfilariae are found in blood vessels where mosquitoes feed in the dog's skin.

3. MICROFILARIAE IN BLOOD

Fig. **101** - Heartworm   Cycle

Parasitic relationships present many enigmas to neo-Darwinism. The above diagram illustrates the life cycle of the dog heart- worm.   The parasitic worm kills its host and thus its means of sustenance and depends upon three widely separated organisms in evolutionary time, the dog, mosquito and heartworm.   This re- lationship seems to defy coherent evolutionary explanation.

gans so that the caterpillar remains alive as long as possible, in
some cases as long as nine months. (Fig.102)

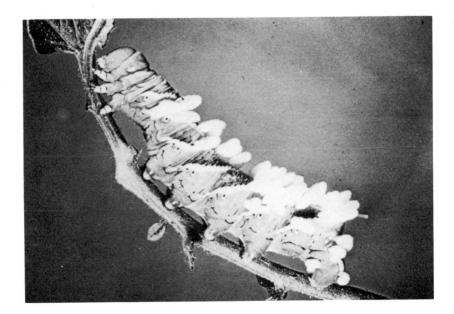

Fig. **102** - Wasp Parasitism

*Cocoons of the Braconid wasp have been laid on a host caterpillar.
(Courtesy of Wolfe Worldwide Films)*

In some cases the wasp is limited in its knowledge of anatomy
and only able to paralyze certain species of insects. When wasps
attack the preying mantis, they "know" to paralyze the treacherous
mantis arms first.

The Microstoma, a fluke-like worm, has stinging cells similar
to those found on hydroids. The Microstoma does not produce these
stinging cells itself, but rather gets them from eating polyps. The
stinging cells of the polyp discharge easily when touched, but the
Microstoma is able to eat the polyp without bursting the stinging
organs. The digestive tract of the Microstoma is structured so
that the stinging cells are swept via channels to the surface of
the Microstoma where they serve as a protective device. The Microstoma evidently does not eat the polyps for food, as it only
consumes enough to furnish itself with enough stinging cells, then,
even if hungry, it will no longer eat polyps.

Termites depend upon the infusoria within their digestive
tract to enable them to digest cellulose. Man depends upon certain
lowly bacteria within his digestive tract for the manufacturing of
Vitamin K, so necessary in blood clotting. Herbivorous animals,

like the cow and horse, have specially constructed digestive tracts to allow the digestion of food stuffs by microorganisms. How could termites, man and ruminants have survived without the coexistence of the lowly microorganisms?

The clownfish lives within the tentacles of the sea anemone. The anemone's tentacles paralyze other fish and thus the clownfish receives protection. The clownfish, in turn, feeds both itself and the sea anemone. The question becomes, as with the spider in the Malayan pitcher plant, how did the clownfish's ancestors survive the attempts to reside amongst the tentacles of the deadly sea anemone?

Lichen are a combination of algae and fungus. Both are absolutely dependent upon each other for survival but widely separated in evolutionary time.

Pollen masses picked up by insects from certain flowers will sometimes change position on the insect's body so as to be in the appropriate position for fertilization of the next flower on which the insect lands.

The yucca plant in the southwestern United States is dependent upon the pronuba moth for reproduction. At the appropriate time the pronuba moth emerges from its cocoon, flies to yucca flowers and gathers pollen in specially constructed mouth parts. The moth then pierces the ovary of a yucca flower with its ovipositer and deposits its moth eggs therein. The moth then climbs to the opening of the female part of the flower and ejects the pollen carried in its mouth. The moth thus fertilizes the flower and uses the flower as a nest for her eggs. The eggs of the moth hatch and the larvae feed on the yucca seeds but leave just enough so that the plant can reproduce itself. The yucca plant is unable to reproduce in any other way because of the structure of its reproductive organs; and the moth only reproduces in the presence of the yucca flower.

The Pseudomyrma ant lives in acacia trees and feeds on special fruits on the leaves of the plant. These fruits are not reproductive bodies and apparently serve no other function for the plant than to attract the Pseudomyrma which in turn benefits the plant by running off predators that would defoliate the tree in a matter of days.

Creationist: "Many relationships in nature are hard to envision coming about through piecemeal gradations. Some relationships such as the yucca-pronuba moth relationship involve organisms of widely separated ancestries. The complexity and specificity of these relationships speaks for fiat creation.

"We must agree with Dobzhansky, who, although an evolutionist, spoke to the complexity of human organs:

'For it seems that each of these systems is balanced so delicately that it can function only as such--intermediate systems combining the features of the two would be absurdly incoherent and unfit to survive.'"[8]

-9-

● Prediction: Since complex interrelationships between organisms are believed to be an improvement upon solitary living, ancient fossil records should show the absence of complex interrelationships.

Observation: Parasitic, commensal and symbiotic relationships among organisms are as old as the records. Fossilized plants and animals show complexity of form and evidences of fully functioning interrelationships from the beginning.

Creationist: "This speaks for creation, not evolution."

-10-

● Prediction: Organs and instincts should be envisioned as being able to come into existence through a series of meaningful gradations.

Observation: How could spiders develop the web spinning organs and the instinct to build webs. The spinneret organs of the spider have hundreds of apertures through which silk and glue are extruded. The spider also needs special oil secreting glands on its feet so it does not get stuck in its own web. Spiders are known to spin webs as large as nineteen feet in circumference and the silk can be as thin as a single molecule and surpassed in tensile strength only by fused quartz.
Some spiders (bolos spider) lasso their prey by swinging a ball of glue attached to a strand of silk around in the air, sometimes for fifteen minutes, throwing it at passing insects. Other spiders build a postage stamp size net and catch their prey by throwing the net over their victims. The *Dolometes fimbriatus* spider sews leaves together with silk making a raft. He then rides the raft in the water in search of insects.
The Evolution Protest Movement of Britain, confident that the web spinning organs of the spider cannot be explained through gradual transitions, has offered a $500 reward to anyone that can explain the evolution of the spider through gradual stages.[9]
The carnivorous plants, like the venus fly trap and the pitcher plant, show intricate design. These plants have the ability to not only attract but also capture and digest animal victims. Concerning the piecemeal evolution of the carnivorous plants, F. E. Lloyd in the introduction to *The Carnivorous Plants*, conceded that

---

8. T. DOBZHANSKY: "BIOLOGICAL ADAPTATION," IN SCIENTIFIC MONTHLY, 55 (1942):399.
9. CREATION OR EVOLUTION (GREAT BRITAIN: EVOLUTION PROTEST MOVEMENT), PAMPHLET NUMBER 89.

the evolution of the specialized organs of capture defy explanation. (Fig. 103)

Fig. **103** - Venus   Fly   Trap
A Venus Fly trap is nearly closed on its victim. (Wolfe Films)

How did human mothers develop mammary glands in a convenient location to nurse their young (on the chest as opposed to the back of the legs or neck), simultaneously evolving the alveolar and duct system of the glands, the appropriate hormonal control to stimulate milk production post-partum and milk ejection upon sucking stimulus. Furthermore, how did babies simultaneously develop the sucking instinct and lips that enable suction?

How did humans develop the involuntary ability to chew food, avoiding the tongue? Can you imagine having to think your tongue into the correct places in your mouth to manipulate food and avoid biting it prior to this involuntary ability? Surely, if this ability was developed gradually, macerated tongues would have been a definite problem while the transitional stages were evolving between voluntary tongue manipulations and involuntary control.

The enzymes and acids in the human stomach are sufficiently strong to digest an animal stomach when ingested. How did the stomach develop slowly the ability to digest stomachs, while not digesting itself? Furthermore, how did the digestive tract develop the ability to neutralize gastric acids entering the small intestine from the stomach, so the small intestine, which is not protected from these stomach juices, would not be digested?

The human body has the ability to control the acidity of blood with great precision. Through the blood's buffer systems, respirations and kidney excretion, pH (hydrogen ion concentration-acidity) is maintained between 7.35 and 7.45. The highest level of hydrogen ions is only 1/100,000,000 of a gram more than the lowest level!

Fish are said to have evolved into land creatures, yet the fish eye is absolutely useless outside of the medium of water.

How could the sexes develop coincidingly complementary sexual organs and instincts?

The human eye has the ability to see light coming through an aperture of only 3 microns (3/25,000 inch) and discern 10,000,000 different shades of colors (a designed machine can only discern about 40% as many colors). The intricacy of the human eye defies evolutionary description, by using one's evolutionary imagination or by attempting to find evidence for transitional stages in the fossil record.

The human brain weighs about three pounds, contains ten billion neurons with approximately 25,000 synapses (connections) per neuron. Each neuron is made up of 10,000,000,000 macro-molecules. The human mind can store almost limitless amounts of information, (a potential millions of times greater than the 10^{15} bits of information gathered in a lifetime--I. Asimov), compare facts, weigh information against memory, judgement and conscience and formulate a decision in a fraction of a second. The nervous system has numerous life saving reflexes, automatic controls of vital functions such as blood pressure and heart beat, connections with the endocrine system, and tremendous sensory abilities such as the ability of sensory nerve endings in the finger to detect a vibration of 0.02 microns (.08/100,000 inch). Creationists feel that to assert the gradual spontaneous development of the nervous system (setting aside the awful evolutionary enigma of a brain in excess of that which will ever be used) is to betray an ignorance of the tremendous complexity of that system.

The human heart beats faithfully about 100,000 times daily. Without our having to think about it the heart ejects the vital liquid of life at the rate of 10 tons per day and 80,000,000 gallons in a life time. The blood flows into a capillary network so extensive that the combined capillaries of four persons if placed end to end could reach all the way to the moon. Any part of our body not supplied with blood of the right composition and under the correct pressure is doomed. How could the cardiovascular system be less than perfect and produce fit human precursors? How could the complexities of that system arise spontaneously?

The bat, *Nictophilus geoffroyi*, can "see" fruit flies 100 feet away by echo location and catch as many as five in one second. The bat is able to hear frequencies of sound of 150,000 cycles/sec., whereas man can only hear 15,000 cycles/sec. The bat emits sounds of 70,000 cycles/sec. at a rate of 10 impulses/sec. at rest, and up to 100 impulses/sec. when in flight and approaching prey. He also has special muscles in his ears that close the ear to the bats own emitted sounds but opens them to receive the echo. How could such abilities and anatomical features develop piecemeal?

Whales have the ability to detect objects miles away through sonar, and determine if they are neutral, friend or foe.

It is presumed that the reptilian jaw hinge bones gave rise to the bones of the middle ear of mammals. A question: How did reptiles eat while the bones of their jaws were migrating through their skull to form the bones of the ear?

The strength in the hands of the human infant is commonly suggested as being a carry over from the time our ape-like ancestors had to hold onto the hair of their mother when being transported. In a popular book on childbirth the comments are made: "Put your finger in his palm; immediately his fingers will grasp yours firmly. Nobody taught him to do this. It is a very good skill to have, particularly if you evolved originally from a species that had to hang on to things in order not to fall off! It's purely biological."[10] How did the young survive as our ancestors were losing hair to become hairless humans?

The heads of certain Colobopsis ants look like cork and are used to plug the entryway to the ants nest.

Rows of spines forming comb-like structures on skin parasites, such as the dog flea, prevent the flea from easily being scratched off. Breeding cycles of some fleas depend upon host hormones.

The water beetle,*Stenus bipunctatus* , escapes from its enemies by ejecting a detergent substance from a special gland. The detergent releases surface energy propelling the beetle forward very rapidly and the insect chasing the beetle is doomed to sink in the water treated with the detergent because the surface tension is destroyed by the detergent.

The male spider, *Hypomena bituberculata*, has two knobs on its head which the female (prospective mate) bites into when he comes-a-courting. Her intent is to kill him, but instead she is rendered harmless by being caught in these structures. This allows him to mate with her and escape with his life.

Many organisms have developed structures, colors and mannerisms intended to mimic something else to provide protection. Lycaenidae butterflies have antennae-like structures on the hind portion of their wings along with an eye spot. The butterflies wave the structures as if they were antennae. When a bird attacks, it bites at the rear (apparent front) of the butterfly, and the butterfly wings away in the opposite direction. The common walking stick worm has joints that look like plant nodes. The caterpillar of the lobster moth of Britain will assume a terrifying position when attacked, and if this does not turn its enemy away, it will expose wounds to give the idea that it has already been

---

10. E. WRIGHT: *THE NEW CHILDBIRTH* (NEW YORK: HART PUBLISHING, 1966),P. 79.

parasitized. The Malayan hooded locustid is known to open a cleft exposing entrails in an apparent wound when attacked. The singhalese grasshopper will expose ominous eyespots to an attacking mynah bird. Animals such as the ptarmigan, arctic fox, chameleons, iguanas, flounders and reef fish change color to fit the environmental background. The leaf butterfly, Kallima, is boldly colored until it lights on a leaf at which time it blends with the leaf background apparently disappearing. Flata plant bugs will cluster together on stems to look just like flowers: the green bugs will look like buds and the pink bugs will arrange themselves to look like the flower. There is a spider in Java that lies on its back on leaves to look just like bird droppings. The green hairstick butterfly lands and situates its wings in the sun so as to cast a minimal shadow. The hawkmouth looks like bark only if it settles on trees head up, whereas the geometrid tissue moth resembles bark only if it arranges itself horizontally. Ants have six legs, and spiders have eight legs; so when a spider mimics an ant it uses its front two legs to appear as antennae. The clearwing moth resembles wasps and will even fly during the day like wasps whereas moths are normally night fliers. Many insects will pretend to sting when attacked, and certain snakes as well as the wryneck bird will oscillate and hiss to mimic dreaded snakes. The Amazon leaf fish floats downstream like a leaf toward its prey. The pod of the plant species, Scorpiurus, resembles a centipede. When birds pick it up and fly away with it the pod distributes its seeds.

Near eastern lizards will put a stick sideways in their mouth to prevent being swallowed by snakes. Creationists ask: "Did lizards develop this ability by selection; a selection of lizards who happened to routinely carry sticks in their mouths?"

The instinctive abilities of many other animals are amazing and likewise defy evolutionary description. Some insects will lay their eggs on only certain species of plants and are able to identify the plant even before its characteristic flowers have emerged. Ants cultivate species of fungi that are no longer found in nature apart from the ant colony. The ants prepare compost for the fungus and cause the fungus to produce bud structures which the ants consume. The purple emperor caterpillar rests on the midline of the leaf it is eating, then moves to the stem when it pupates apparently "knowing" that leaves drop in the fall. When birds and bees travel they have the ability to orient to the sun to find directions and also have the ability to compensate for the time of day. Bees dance to tell the source of a new food find and can even communicate, via the dance, how attractive the flower is. Bees fan the hive to cool and dehydrate the nectar, spread water on the combs to cool them in the summer and will aggregate to heat the combs in the winter. The bee could have made its honey cells out of many different geometric structures but instead it uses the hexagon which provides the ultimate volume in proportion to the amount of wall built and provides the greatest circumference to allow room to work. The abilities of the bee, which are at best still poorly understood, reside in a brain that is smaller than a pinhead.

The migrating abilities of animals are truly amazing. Fur seals, bats, whales, turtles, birds, salmon and eels are known to travel thousands of miles. The monarch butterfly migrates: different generations make   different parts of the journey. The barn swallow migrates a distance of 9,000 miles from N. Canada to Argentina, and the arctic tern will migrate 14,000 miles. How could such navigational abilities along with the instinctive urge to migrate develop by chance? (Fig. 104)

Fig. **104**-Tern Vs DC-9
The arctic tern(top) can migrate some 14,000 miles. For man to accomplish similar navigation, sophisticated instrumentation such as seen in this DC-9 is needed(bottom). (Wolfe Worldwide Films)

What makes birds of the same kind produce the same kinds of· nests? The megapode bird of Australia builds a nest of sand and leaves in which it buries its eggs. The temperature outside the nest can vary from 20° to 100°F, yet the megapode checks the temperature of her nest and maintains the heat therein at about 92° by adjusting the amount of cover and decaying compost. The indian tailor bird makes its nest by punching holes in leaves and weaving them together with spiders' silk and cotton.

How do animals of the same kind recognize each other and only mate within their own sphere?

The horse bott (Gastrophilus), cow warble (Hypoderma) and sheep bott (Oestris ovis) lay eggs on their hosts. Somehow the larvae of these flies know how to make the appropriate migrations through their hosts. The presence of these flies has been known to panic herds of horses, sheep and cows even though the fly merely lays the eggs on the hair of these animals. The herd seems to instinctively know that several weeks or months henceforth, these miniscule eggs will hatch into larvae producing sinus (sheep), digestive (horse) and cutaneous (cow) diseases.

The water bug, Argyroneta, weaves a diving bell of silk and after submerging in the water attaches the bell to roots. She then surfaces gathering bubbles of air to take below into the diving bell. The bell becomes filled with air and there she lays her eggs and rears her young replenishing the air periodically so they will not suffocate.

Creationist: "The development of organs demands the simultaneous appearance and perfection of the parts, otherwise the organisms would be selected against because of useless appendages. The organs, instincts and abilities of every member of the biological community cry out for creationistic interpretations. Design, perfection, purpose and beauty demand a designer. It seems that no matter what we examine in 'nature,' close scrutiny always reveals the stamp: made by a creator!

"The evolutionist, on the other hand, for example, confronts us with logic like this to explain the origin of biological characters: 'It now seemed as though the hawk had sharp eyes because it was the sharp eyed hawks that survived . . .' We must agree with Professor Pantin when he went on to say: 'There is a very great deal of truth in that . . .'[11] For what has he said? Namely this, hawks have sharp eyes because they have sharp eyes. Profound! The doctrine of the survival of the fittest as an explanation for origins is nothing but a tautology, a redundancy."

-11-

● Prediction: Life should consist of a few elite highly fit organisms if natural selection is true.

Observations: Living organisms are highly diverse with many variations and characteristics all fitting the same environment. For example, the cow uses its tongue to grasp food while the cat uses it to lap liquid. The snake uses the tongue as a sensing organ and the dog uses his to cool. Man uses his tongue for speech, the toad for attack and the anteater for entrapment.

Creationist: "If natural selection is such a powerful force as to bring life into existence and produce organs, surely it would refine living forms so that so much diversity would not exist."

---

11. *C. F. A. PANTIN: "THE ORIGIN OF SPECIES," IN A SHORT HISTORY OF SCIENCE (N.Y.: DOUBLEDAY, 1951), P. 101.*

-12-

● Prediction: Beneficial organs should be maintained in a population. If man is the acme of evolution, he should have carried with him the most beneficial characteristics.

Observations: The opposing toe of our ape-like ancestors would certainly be a nice asset. One would be able to pick things up without bending over, as well as use the feet for third and fourth hands.

A female chimpanzee has been known to pull 1,260 lbs. with one arm, whereas a man of the same size could only pull about 1/6th as much. Certainly such strength would be an asset to man.

An owl can see 100 times better than man at night. The golden eagle can see a rabbit at two miles.

Lowly trees and turtles are known to outlive man.

Many lowly animals have fantastic smelling abilities. Some butterflies can smell a female from several miles away. The male silkworm moth can smell the scent of a female emitting 0.0001 mg of chemical from a distance of seven miles. Dogs have been known to track by scent up to 800 miles.

The cheetah can run at speeds to 70 mph. and the sailfish can swim at speeds to 70 mph. The protozoan, *Monas Stigmatica*, can move at a rate of 40 times its own length in one second; man can't even cover seven times his length in one second.

Fish can withstand several thousand pounds of pressure at depths to 35,000 ft.; and the alpine chough bird can withstand an altitude of 27,000 ft. above sea level.

A flea can jump 130 times its own height and thus overcome a force of 200 g's. Man has only been able to withstand about 82 g's.

The crotalid snake has an infra red organ in its head that can detect temperature changes of 1/100th of a degree.

The eye of the trilobite (an organism supposedly extinct for some 300 million years) is said to have "possessed the most sophisticated eye lenses ever produced by nature." Levi Setti feels that the trilobite's eye lenses implied knowledge of "Fermat's principle, Abbe's sine law, Snell's law of refraction and the optics of birefringent crystal." Concluding, Setti states: "It didn't happen by accident. It proves that evolution can produce this kind of thing . . . the lenses look like they were designed by a physicist."[12]

A snail can pull 60 to 200 times its weight and lift 10 times its weight. In order to match this, man would have to pull four to thirteen tons and lift 1,500 pounds!

Can any man match the industriousness of the bee which flies the equivalent of twice around the world to make just one pound of honey?

---

12. *L. J. SHAWVER: "TRILOBITE EYES: AN IMPRESSIVE FEAT OF EARLY EVOLUTION," IN SCIENCE NEWS, 105 (FEB. 2, 1974): 72,73.*

The hero shrew of Uganda, Africa, measuring only six inches long, can support a 160 pound man on its back. No human could survive under a comparably proportionate weight.

Toads can fast one year, lungfish four years, ticks eighteen years and nematodes up to 39 years. This ability would be obviously advantageous for men in starving nations.

Creationist: "Why did the human not retain such obviously beneficial characteristics in his evolution? Why do lowly creatures outdo us in so many areas of ability? Why did we 'leave behind' beneficial characteristics in our evolutionary ascent?"

-13-

● Prediction: Neo-Darwinism should result in irreversible evolution. Organs and characteristics lost in the course of evolution should not reappear--Louis Dollo's Law of evolution.[13]

Observations: Most evolutionists now agree that the course of evolution has changed. For example, reptiles and mammals are said to have arisen from an aquatic environment and then returned (whales, sea snakes, etc.). Some birds (ostrich, etc.) started on land, took to flight then returned to land.

Organs are known to reappear by reverse mutations. Eye color in fruit flies will occasionally revert to a previous color. Modern-day shire horses are known to occasionally have three toes, a condition supposedly lost millions of years ago. And guinea pigs that normally have three toes on their rear feet, will occasionally experience a reverse mutation resulting in four toes on the rear feet, again a condition supposedly lost millions of years ago.

Creationist: "Reverses in mutations would stunt evolutionary progress: two steps forward, one step back; one step forward, two steps back, etc."

Adding It Up

Understanding the complexities of the biological world is by no means a simple feat. The goal of science should be to comprehend biology in terms of the simplest and most comprehensive generalization explaining the origin of and the changes in life. Many think that neo-Darwinism is just such a generalization. Many feel they can easily explain away the creationistic objections raised above. Some evolutionists will assert, as would Huxley, that one must "properly understand" the process in order to "see" how these objections are not valid. The deficiencies in neo-Darwinism, some will say, are dismissed with a sweep of the

---

13. H. BLUM: _TIME'S ARROW AND EVOLUTION_ (PRINCETON: PRINCETON U., 1968), PP. 173,175.

hand by properly understanding "mimicry," "convergence," "geographical speciation," "differential population growth," "selective pressure," "sexual selection," "selective value," "genetic
drift," "environmental context" and "gene frequencies." And, of
course, many feel the difficulties will vanish given a million
billion quintuplatillion umptaplatillion, multuplatillion impossi-
bidillion fantasticatrillion years. We must decide whether the
predictions listed above are valid neo-Darwinian predictions and
whether they are consistent with or contradicted by the evidence.

In like manner we must ask ourselves whether the creationistic
prediction, that life will not transmutate in the amoeba to man sense,
is bolstered or thwarted by the evidence. Rather than explaining
all of the variety we see about us through some natural mechanism,
the creationist invokes design. In other words, he would say the
reason things are as they are is the same reason the oceans are
so near their shores--they were made that way.

20 { GEOLOGIC EVIDENCE

The record of the rocks is probably one of the most popular evidences used to demonstrate evolution. And doesn't the record show life to have great antiquity? Doesn't it in fact show a gradation of life over time from simple to complex? Yes it does--at least as we see that record presented in geology texts. The geologic timetable spreads life over about 2 billion years and depicts the least complex and smallest organisms as the oldest, and the most complex organisms as the youngest. The charts on historical geology are supposedly a representation of the historical record of life as it has been retained for our examination in the form of fossils. The geologic timetable is in chart form what we should find if we dug into the ground and examined the fossils of each successive strata. (Fig.105)
Is that the case? Can we dig into the ground and find the invariable progressive succession of life from the complex to the small? Further, upon what basis are the ages of the fossils determined?

A Cozy Circle

Surprising as it may seem, the only real evidence for the geological succession of life, as represented by the timetable, is found in the mind of the geologist and on the paper upon which the chart is drawn. Nowhere in the earth is the complete succession of fossils found as they are portrayed in the chart.
For example, if you want to find Pre-Cambrian or Paleozoic strata you must go to the Grand Canyon. If you want to find Mesozoic you must travel to eastern Arizona. To find Tertiary, you must then travel to New Mexico. In order to find the entire succession, from Cenozoic to Archeozoic, one would have to turn

ERA	PERIOD	EPOCH	RECORDS OF DISTINCTIVE LIFE	MILLIONS OF YEARS AGO
cenozoic ▼	QUATERNARY	RECENT		
		PLEISTOCENE-	-EARLY MAN-----------------2+	
		PLIOCENE----	-LARGE CARNIVORES----------10	
	TERTIARY	MIOCENE------	-WHALES,APES,GRAZERS--------27	
		OLIGOCENE---	-LARGE BROWSING ANIMALS-----38	
		EOCENE------	-RISE OF FLOWERING PLANTS---55	
		PALEOCENE---	-FIRST PLACENTAL MAMMALS----70	
mesozoic ▼	CRETACEOUS---------------		-DINOSAURS EXTINCT MODERN FLORAS-------------130	
	JURASSIC-----------------		-DINOSAURS ZENITH PRIMITIVE BIRDS FIRST SMALL MAMMALS--------180	
	TRIASSIC----------------		-APPEARANCE OF DINOSAURS----225	
paleozoic ▼	PERMIAN-----------------		-CONIFERS ABUNDANT REPTILES DEVELOPED--------260	
	CARBONIFEROUS: -PENNSYLVANIAN-----------		-FIRST REPTILES COAL FORESTS--------------300	
	-MISSISSIPPIAN----------		-SHARKS ABUNDANT-----------340	
	DEVONIAN----------------		-RISE OF AMPHIBIANS FISHES ABUNDANT-----------405	
	SILURIAN----------------		-EARLIEST LAND PLANTS AND ANIMALS---------------435	
	ORDOVICIAN--------------		-FIRST PRIMITIVE FISHES-----480	
	CAMBRIAN----------------		-ALL SUBKINGDOMS OF INVERTEBRATE ANIMALS TRILOBITES BRACHIOPODS---------------570	
PROTEROZOIC ARCHEOZOIC	PRECAMBRIAN---------------		NO INDISPUTABLE FOSSILS-----570 TO 1,500+	

Fig. **105**- Geologic Time Table

shovels all over the world flitting from one place to another in order to see the "proper" sequential geologic column.[1]
The authors, Von Engeln and Caster, state concerning the geological column:
"If a pile were to be made by using the greatest thickness of sedimentary beds of each geological age,

1. A. CLARK: *FOSSILS, FLOOD, AND FIRE* (ESCONDIDO: OUTDOOR PICTURES, 1968), P. 55.

it would be at least 100 miles high. . . . It is of
course, impossible to have even a considerable fraction of this at any one place . . ."[2]
The writers, Brown, Monnett and Stovall, state similarly:
"Whatever his method of approach, the geologist must
take cognizance of the following facts . . . There is
no place on the earth where a complete record of the
rocks is present . . . To reconstruct the history of
the earth, scattered bits of information from thousands of locations all over the world must be pieced
together. The results will be at best only a very
incomplete record. If the complete story of the earth
is compared to an encyclopedia of thirty volumes, then
we can seldom hope to find even one complete volume
in a given area. Sometimes only a few chapters, perhaps only a paragraph or two, will be the total geological contribution of a region; indeed, we are often
reduced to studying scattered bits of information more
nearly comparable to a few words or letters."[3]
If the complete sequence of fossils is not found in the
rocks as it is portrayed on the geologist's paper, upon what
basis do geologists make the time scale? I might illustrate
their method this way.

A geologist digs in the rocks and finds a clam fossil.
When he arrives home he asks his neighbor, an authority on
evolution, "When do you believe this clam fossil would have
evolved?" His neighbor says: "Well, the clam fossil is less
complex than the crab fossil you found last week, and more complex than the trilobite fossil you found last month. Since we
know evolution progressed from simple to complex, the proper
place for the clam fossil is in between the crab and the trilobite."

The geologist makes the appropriate entry on a chart he is
devising to show the history of life on earth. As the months
go by, and our geologist brings back to his home fossil specimens found all over the world, he is able to complete his chart
with the aid of his evolutionary friend.

The evolutionary neighbor in turn finds much utility in the
chart his geology friend has devised: When someone needs proof
that evolution occurred, just point them to the chart; the
record of fossils and their arrangement from simple to complex
surely is proof that evolution has occurred!

So the chart of the geological column rests on the a priori
assumption: "since life is here, life evolved." The assumption

2. *O. VON ENGELN AND K. CASTER*: <u>GEOLOGY</u> (N.Y.: MCGRAW-HILL,
1952), PP. 417,418.
3. *H. BROWN, V. MONNETT, J. STOVALL*: <u>INTRODUCTION TO GEOLOGY</u>
(BOSTON:GINN, 1958) P. 11.

of evolution is used to arrange the sequence of fossils, then
the resultant sequence is advanced as proof of evolution.

The following quotations will further demonstrate this
circular reasoning used by evolutionary geologists:

The geologist, Carl Dunbar:

"We now know, of course, that different kinds of
animals and plants have succeeded one another in time
because life has continually evolved; and inasmuch as
organic evolution is world-wide in its operation, only
rocks formed during the same age could bear identical
faunas . . . Although the comparative study of living
animals and plants may give very convincing circumstantial evidence, fossils provide the only historical
documentary evidence that life has evolved from
simpler to more and more complex forms."[4]

Sir Archibald Giekie stated:

"We may even demonstrate that strata have turned completely upside down if we can show that fossils in
what are the uppermost layers ought properly to lie
underneath those in the beds below them."[5]

O. Schindewolf contends:

"The only chronometric scale applicable in geologic
history for the stratigraphic classification of rocks
and for dating geologic events exactly is furnished
by the fossils. Owing to the irreversibility of
evolution, they offer an unambiguous time scale for
relative age determinations and for world-wide corre-
lations of rocks."[6]

Errol White of the British Museum of Natural History wrote
in the forward to the book, *The Dawn of Life*:

"The book brings home very clearly one of the chief
practical uses of fossils: that of correlating rocks
of the same age." (How is it determined that the
rocks are of the same age? Let's read on.) "In other
words, because the succession of the faunas and floras
has been established, (i.e., since evolution is true)
the finding of fossils in widely separated regions can
help the geologist to determine the relative ages of
the rock formations the world over. . . . This last
system is based on the concept that each epoch of
Earth's history has had characteristic animal and
vegetable types, which are not comparable with those

---

4. C. DUNBAR: _HISTORICAL GEOLOGY_ (N.Y.: JOHN WILEY, 1961),
PP. 9,47.
5. A. GIEKIE: _TEXTBOOK OF GEOLOGY_ (LONDON:MACMILLAN, 1903),
P. 387.
6. O. H. SCHINDEWOLF: "COMMENTS ON SOME STRATIGRAPHIC TERMS,"
IN _AMERICAN JOURNAL OF SCIENCE_, 255(1957):394.

in any other earlier or later epoch, and on the basis
of a study of fossils it is thus possible both to
arrive at the position that they occupied in geological time, and to ascribe an age to the rock that contains them . . . Paleontological discoveries are in
fact among the most important proofs of evolution
itself and have made it possible to establish and
confirm the relationships between the great animal
groups."[7] (paranthetical words added)

And finally, we'll quote Professor Pantin:
"Now geologists are very interested in species--you
recognize particular kinds of rocks by the particular
species of fossils you find in them."[8]

Dating   Strata

Since the arrangement of fossils is arbitrary, i.e., based
upon the a priori assumption of evolution, then the geological
column can not be used to demonstrate evolution or vast age.
How are ages assigned to the strata? We must first realize that
even if there were an evolutionary succession, the succession
could only show relative positions of fossils in the stream of
time. That clams are placed above trilobites speaks nothing to
the amount of time between them or to ages in an absolute sense.

Very simply, fossil dates are determined by two methods:
(1) Since the earth is assumed to be billions of years old, and
life is assumed to have evolved over many millions of years
(the proportion of fossil bearing strata to total strata), then
one can approximate ages by spreading the fossils over the total
time assumed for their evolution; (2) Radioactive datings and
age estimates based upon strata thicknesses are then used to
substantiate the order and assign more specific ages to the
fossils in the geological column.

Professor Walter Elasser of the University of Maryland
observes:
"As is well known, the order of the geological strata
is fixed entirely by means of fossils; thus the geological method presumes the existence in these periods
of living beings of gradually increasing complexity.
By means of radioactive dating methods it is possible
to ascertain definite lengths for the periods of

---

7. G. PINNA: *THE DAWN OF LIFE* (N.Y.: WORLD, 1972), FORWARD
AND PP. 10-12.
8. C. F. A. PANTIN: "THE ORIGIN OF SPECIES," IN *A SHORT HISTORY
OF SCIENCE* (N.Y.: DOUBLEDAY, 1951), P. 97.

geological history . . . "9

Adolph Knopf brings to our attention that of all the radioactive dates that have been determined on rocks and their associated fossils, only three are used to date the geological column. He says:

"An urgent task for geology is to determine, in years, the length of the eras, periods, and 'ages' (time spans of the stages) and, eventually of the zones. Not a single one of them--eras, periods, and ages, let alone zones--has yet been reliably determined. This statement is possibly surprising in view of the fact that almost any modern writer can produce a geologic timetable that gives precise datings and lengths of eras and systems and even of some of the smaller subdivisions . . . All other absolute ages have been derived from the three radioactive tie points by interpolation based on thickness of strata or by 'reasoned guesses' . . . "10

Regarding estimating time on the basis of strata thickness, Twenhofel says such analyses "are hardly worth the paper they are written on . . . "11

Let's back up and walk through the reasoning used to arrive at the geological timetable. First, it is assumed that since life is here, life evolved. Then, if life evolved and all natural events are proceeding today essentially as they have throughout history (uniformity), then the deeper the strata in the earth, the older its age. It follows also that the older the strata, the more primitive (simple) assemblage of organisms it should portray.

Assuming these 'truths', fossils are gathered from around the world (no complete succession being found in any one place) and assembled in a progressive order from simple to complex on a chart. Time is then alloted to the various divisions of the geologic chart on the assumption that the earth is billions of years old--it must be, of course, because evolution would take that long to occur. The fossils are spread in a reasonable (evolutionary) order throughout the assumed antiquity of life's existence, then substantiation and more exact dates are determined on the basis of measuring strata thicknesses and radioactive elements.

Strata thicknesses are dated upon the assumption that strata were laid down in the past at the same rate as today: about one foot every five thousand years. Radiodatings (based upon a set of assumptions that likewise assume uniformity) that fit the

9. W. M. ELASSER: "ORIGIN, COMPOSITION AND AGE OF THE EARTH," IN ENCYCLOPEDIA BRITANNICA, 7(1973):850.
10. A. KNOPF: "MEASURING GEOLOGIC TIME," IN SCIENTIFIC MONTHLY, 85(1957):227.
11. A. KNOPF, (REF. 10) P. 227.

preconceived order of the geologic column are accepted as accurate and advanced as corroborative proof of the order in the column. Those radiodates not fitting the "correct" order of the strata are rejected. (The time allotments to the geological column were assigned before radiodating techniques.) If any contradictions to the preconceived order of the column are found, i.e., radioactive datings showing a "wrong" age, or fossils out of "correct" sequence, these contradictions are explained away. For example, if the radioactive dates do not coincide with the order, this "anomaly" is accounted for by simply arguing that the radiodate was in error; if fossils are found out of sequence, this is explained on the basis of geological faulting, folding, thrusting and intense erosion whether or not there is evidence for such. (Fig. 106)

Spieker wrote:

> "And what essentially is this actual time-scale? On what criteria does it rest? When all is winnowed out and the grain reclaimed from the chaff, it is certain that the grain in the product is mainly the paleontological record and highly likely that the physical evidence is the chaff."[12]

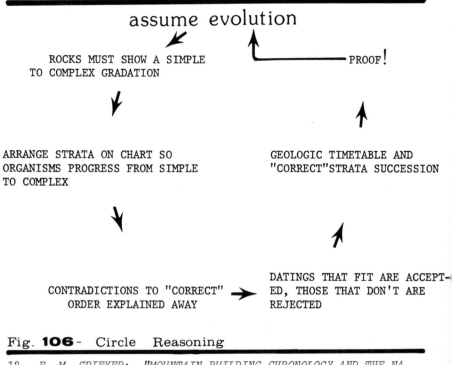

assume evolution

ROCKS MUST SHOW A SIMPLE TO COMPLEX GRADATION

PROOF!

ARRANGE STRATA ON CHART SO ORGANISMS PROGRESS FROM SIMPLE TO COMPLEX

GEOLOGIC TIMETABLE AND "CORRECT" STRATA SUCCESSION

CONTRADICTIONS TO "CORRECT" ORDER EXPLAINED AWAY

DATINGS THAT FIT ARE ACCEPTED, THOSE THAT DON'T ARE REJECTED

Fig. **106** - Circle Reasoning

12. E. M. SPIEKER: "MOUNTAIN BUILDING CHRONOLOGY AND THE NATURE OF THE GEOLOGIC TIME-SCALE," IN BULLETIN OF THE AMERICAN ASSOCIATION OF PETROLEUM GEOLOGISTS, 40(1956):1806.

Fossilization

The creationist believes that if the geological and fossil data are examined without evolutionary bias, a totally different picture of earth history can be concluded. He sees the fossil and geological records as proof of catastrophe and rapidity, not uniformity and eons. He reasons as follows:

Consider for a moment the fact that the earth is surrounded by thousands of square miles of sedimentary strata. Sedimentary strata, by definition, speaks to water deposition. It is within these strata that the vast majority of fossils are found. What causes fossilization? Practically every known mechanism for fossilization demands sudden catastrophic burial.

Even Darwin recognized, as expressed in the conclusion to his second edition of the *The Origin of Species*, that fossilization required unique rapid processes, not slow uniformitarian ones:

> "The accumulation of each great fossiliferous formation will be recognized as having depended on an unusual concurrence of favorable circumstances . . . "

Giovanni Pinna, the Deputy Director of the Museum of Natural History in Milan, although a firm believer in uniformitarianism, wrote:

> "In fact, when an organism dies, the substances that compose its soft parts undergo more or less rapid decay, due to such factors as attack by bacteria and erosion by water (particularly the sea) . . . If an an organism is to be preserved, it must be protected from destructive agents as quickly as possible . . . And the sooner that this consolidation occurs, the more likely it is that the organism will be preserved . . . there are also certain layers, such as those formed from extremely fine-grained calcareous rocks, which have consolidated so rapidly as to permit the preservation of the most delicate structures of many organisms."[13]

In further testimony, consider this. Not many years ago there were millions of bison roaming the North American Continent. Today there are but a handful. What happened to the thousands killed by the infamous Buffalo Bill and his cohorts? Where are their fossils? There are none because the carcasses of the bison met the inevitable eventuality of all other dying things in the absence of sudden burial by catastrophe. They were scavangerized,

---

13. *G. PINNA: THE DAWN OF LIFE (N.Y.: WORLD, 1972), PP. 1, 2.*

they rotted, decayed and slowly were dissipated by the elements.
There is no preservation by dust slowly blowing over a carcass
or by a few leaves falling upon it.

The authors of the book, *The Birds*, would have us believe
that fossils can be produced by animals simply falling in the
mud, even preserving parts which normally decompose in a matter
of hours. Notice this explanation for the preservation of the
archeopteryx fossils which, as you may recall, contain even
feather detail:

> "We can easily imagine the predicament which led to the
> fossilization of the three individuals so long ago.
> They were probably forced into reluctant flight by some
> pursuing reptilian predator, only to flop down on the
> water and mud from which they could not rise."[14]

In the earth's crust we find the record of billions of animals and plants preserved. The fossil record is not "incomplete,"
as the evolutionist might argue (incomplete because it does not
contain the links he needs), but is quantitatively huge and
qualitatively rampant with about as many species as are alive
today.[15]

The vast oil and coal reserves in the earth, even in the polar regions, are almost impossible to explain without invoking the
catastrophic burial of billions of plants and animals. There
are literally trillions of tons of coal in the earth with some
seams extending to 100 feet thick. Many indications are given
that these deposits of coal (fossil plants) were swept into
position, layered and produced by water catastrophe, not by the
slow accumulation of organic material in fresh water swamps:
fossil trees are found extending through several layers of coal,
some trees are upside down; seams are sometimes split with marine sediments in between; large boulders are found in some coal
beds; fossils of exclusively marine Spirobis tubeworms are found
in coal; many coal beds have no fossil-type soil under them; no
modern peat bogs grade into coal seams. On this basis, the argument that coal was formed by periodic cycles of in-place organic
buildup, as Hollingsworth wrote, "has an element of unreality."[16]

About 1/7 of the earth's surface, from Siberia into Alaska,
is a frozen muck containing the remains of millions of mammoths.
Some were frozen so rapidly that their flesh is still edible
today.[17] There are many places around the world containing

14. R. PETERSON: *THE BIRDS* (N.Y.: TIME 1963), P. 10.
15. *THE FOSSIL RECORD*, EDS. W. B. HARLAND AND OTHERS (LONDON:
GEOLOGICAL SOCIETY, 1967).
16. S. NEVINS: "STRATIGRAPHIC EVIDENCE OF THE FLOOD," IN *SYM-
POSIUM ON CREATION III*, ED. D. W. PATTEN (GRAND RAPIDS: BAKER,
1971), PP. 44-46; S. HOLLINGSWORTH: "THE CLIMATE FACTOR IN THE
GEOLOGICAL RECORD," IN *JOURNAL OF THE GEOLOGICAL SOCIETY OF
LONDON*, 118(1962):13.
17. HENRY HOWARTH: THE *MAMMOTH AND THE FLOOD* (LONDON: LOW,

virtual log jams of fossil dinosaur bones. The Dinosaur National Monument in Utah contains over 300 different kinds of dinosaurs. In Wyoming, two Anatosaurus fossils are preserved so well as to show the wrinkled and bruised hide over their bodies.[18] Besides the huge fossil beds of plants (coal) there are the hippopotamus graveyards in Sicily, the remains of 6,000 vertebrates in Geiseltal Germany, the masses of amphibians in the Permian beds of Texas, millions of fossil closed clams in a three foot thick stratum in Texas, (however, clams do not live packed together like this, and unless buried before death, the shells will separate and not remain closed), the horrible shoals of billions of fish fossilized in contorted states of agony spread over 10,000 square miles with as many as 1,000 fish in one square yard in the Old Red Sandstone of England, and the Miocene herring fossil bed of California, and there are innumerable other fossil graveyards with carcasses of every conceivable kind strewn, mangled and twisted together.[19] There are millions of fossil trilobites rolled into defensive balls and, although marine, are found 7,000 feet high on mountains. In the Karoo formation of South Africa alone there are about 800 billion fossils of amphibians and reptiles covering an area 200,000 miles square.[20] And, most amazing is the fact that it is estimated that one percent or less of the fossil species that have been preserved have as yet been described.[21]

Even evidence as easily lost as ripple marks (even at great depths in the sea), rain drops, fish odor, worm trails, animal tracks, sponge detail, droppings, insect wing detail, feathers and chemicals are preserved in the fossil record. Sharks have been found flattened to 1/4 inch in thickness with the tail still upright suggesting sudden catastrophic burial.[22] (Figs. 107-109)

Could the vast beds of sedimentary strata (covering about 3/4 of the earths surface and reaching to as much as 40,000 feet in depth) with their entombed biological remains result from the yawning slow--one foot per five thousand years--processes we see

SEARLE AND RISINGTON, 1887); I. TOLMACHOFF: *THE CARCASSES OF THE MAMMOTH AND RHINOCEROS FOUND IN THE FROZEN GROUND OF SIBERIA*, ARTICLE I, VOL. 23 (PHILADELPHIA: AMERICAN PHIL. SOC., 1929).
18. G. PINNA: *THE DAWN OF LIFE* (N.Y.: WORLD, 1972), P. 5.
19. H. MILLER: *THE OLD RED SANDSTONE* (BOSTON, 1865); H. S. LADD: *SCIENCE*, 129(1959):72; S. NEVINS, (REF. 16) PP. 36, 37.
20. I. VELIKOVSKY: *EARTH IN UPHEAVAL* (N.Y.: DELL, 1955), PP. 13-71; N. NEWELL: *JOURNAL OF PALEONTOLOGY*, 33(1959):495; G. NICHOLAS: *SCIENTIFIC MONTHLY*, 76(1953):301.
21. T. GEORGE: "FOSSILS IN EVOLUTIONARY PERSPECTIVE," IN *SCIENCE PROGRESS*, 48(1960):4.
22. B. NELSON: *THE DELUGE STORY IN STONE* (MINNEAPOLIS: BETHANY, 1968), PP. 44, 101-105; W. H. TWENHOFEL: *TREATISE ON SEDIMENTATION* (N.Y.: DOVER, 1961), PP. 644, 675; E. H. COLBERT: *DINOSAURS* (N.Y.: DUTTON, 1961), P. 183.

Fig. **107** - Fossil Graveyards

•*This north wall of the Dinosaur National Monument in Utah is virtually solid with fossil dinosaur bones. From 1909 to 1924, 300 skeletons were removed from the site. (Ambassador College Photo)*

•*The Agate Springs, Nebraska fossil bed(bottom) contained an estimated 9,000 fossil animals in one hill. Rhinoceroses, camels, pigs and others appear here. (Courtesy Denver Museum Natural History)*

Fig. **108** - Fossil   Gluttons

•*The Eocene varves of fossil lake in Wyoming, yielded this find(top) of a perch swallowing a herring.   It is estimated that a foot of rock here would require 2,000 years to form.   Some, however, feel that burial must have been rapid to preserve the "action" and details of the specimens. (Courtesy of Princeton Museum Nat. Hist.)*
•*These fossil fish(bottom) are on display at the Hall of Paleontology at Kansas State College.   The smaller six-foot ingested fish, Gillicus, shows no signs of digestion by the larger fourteen-foot fish, Portheus. Was burial rapid, or slow? (Courtesy Mary Frey)*

Fig. **109** - Evidence for Catastrophy

•*Fossil shark squashed to one-quarter inch thick with tail still upright(top left).* •*Intricate detail of a fossil dragonfly wing is preserved perfectly(top right).* •*Ephemeral ripple marks fossilized in the Red Deer River in Alberta(bottom). (A. M. Nat. History)*

occurring today. Where is one example of fossilization occurring on a scale today, equivalent to the magnitude seen in the plethora of fossil graveyards around the world? Conditions might fortuitously happen today that might result in the fossilization of a few animals (a cliff dropping in the water and burying a few fish, clams, insects, etc.), but never have we observed any cataclysm on a scale like that which would have been necessary in the past to account for the thousands of square miles of solid heaps of fossils.

Creationists insist: "Fossilization is unnatural, abnormal, catastrophic, quick, unique, exceptional, cataclysmic. When we see fossilization world-wide, when we note that water is the agency that has presented the conditions for fossilization, then we must conclude that there was a world-wide water cataclysm in the past. The geological column is not a record of the coming of life, it is a record of its going, its departure, its demise."

The scientific community is not naive to this evidence. Some simply shelve it or ignore it in order to maintain faith in uniformitarianism. Others have taken note and are now seriously questioning the doctrine that the "present is the key to the past:"

Heylmun:
> "There are many other reasons why we should not blindly accept the doctrine of uniformitarianism . . . ";

Gretener:
> "Accepting the principle of the rare event as a valid concept makes it even more desirable to retire the term 'uniformitarianism.'";

Gould:
> "Substantive uniformitarianism as a descriptive theory has not withstood the test of new data and can no longer be maintained in any strict manner.";

Krynine:
> "Conventional uniformitarianism, or 'gradualism,' i.e., the doctrine of unchanging change, is verily contradicted by all post-Cambrian sedimentary data and the geotectonic histories of which these sediments are the record.";

Valentine:
> "It seems unfortunate that uniformitarianism, a doctrine which has so important a place in the history of geology, should continue to be misrepresented in introductory texts and courses by 'the present is the key to the past,' a maxim without much credit."[23]

---

23. *E. HEYLMUN: "SHOULD WE TEACH UNIFORMITARIANISM?" IN JOURNAL OF GEOLOGICAL EDUCATION, 19(1971):36; P. GRETENER: "SIGNIFICANCE OF THE RARE EVENT IN GEOLOGY," IN BULLETIN OF THE AMERICAN ASSOCIATION OF PETROLEUM GEOLOGISTS, 51(1967):2205; S. GOULD: "IS UNIFORMITARIANISM USEFUL," IN JOURNAL OF GEOLOGICAL*

Lastly, we must mention Immanuel Velikovsky and his growing following who attempt documentation of the cataclysmic history of our planet and rejection of uniformitarianism, though not opting for a creationistic interpretation.[24]

Pre-Cambrian Void

We are also faced with the clear evidence that about two-thirds of the earth's geological record, the "Pre-Cambrian period," does not contain any significant quantities of indisputable fossils (some contend it contains absolutely none).

The following quotations will testify to this void in the record. Axelrod, of the University of California, confessed:

"One of the major unsolved problems of geology and evolution is the occurrence of diversified, multicellular marine invertebrates in lower Cambrian rocks on all the continents and their absence in rocks of greater age . . . These sediments apparently were suitable for the preservation of fossils, because they are often identical with overlying rocks which are fossiliferous, yet no fossils are found in them."[25]

T. George wrote:

"There is, however, one gigantic gap in the record that is of a different kind--the gap of Pre-Cambrian times. Despite intensified search by many hundreds of geologists, the rocks older than the oldest fossiliferous Cambrian sediments remain almost as barren of fossils as when they were first studied 150 years ago. Some of them are displayed in thicknesses of many thousands of feet, they may be as unaltered and as undeformed as many fossiliferous rocks of later ages, they provide clear indications of having accumulated in environments, lacustrine and marine, apparently wholly favorable to both plant and animal life, and they sometimes underlie Cambrian in a unitary suite of strata little affected by changing geography. Yet they have yielded few fossils that are recognizable as plants, and none that are certainly animals.

EDUCATION, 15(1967):150; P. KRYNINE: "UNIFORMITARIANISM IS A DANGEROUS DOCTRINE," IN *PALEONTOLOGY, 30(1956):1004; J. VALENTINE:* "THE PRESENT IS THE KEY TO THE PRESENT," IN *JOURNAL OF GEOLOGICAL EDUCATION, 14(1966):59,60; CITED IN SCIENTIFIC CREATIONISM, ED. H. MORRIS (SAN DIEGO: CREATION-LIFE PUBLISHERS, 1974), PP. 92-94.*
24. *I. VELIKOVSKY: EARTH IN UPHEAVAL (N.Y.: DELL, 1955); PENSEE, A JOURNAL, P.O. BOX 414, PORTLAND, OREGON.*
25. *D. I. AXELROD: "EARLY CAMBRIAN MARINE FAUNA," IN SCIENCE, 128(1958):7.*

"On the other hand, the earliest Cambrian rocks, formed about 500 million years ago, are relatively richly fossiliferous and contain a fauna already highly diversified . . . Moreover, the major phyla when they first appear display an evolutionary differentiation that implies a complex phyletic history in Pre-Cambrian times . . . Granted an evolutionary origin of the main groups of animals, and not an act of special creation, the absence of any record whatsoever of a single member of any of the phyla in the Pre-Cambrian rocks remains as inexplicable on orthodox grounds as it was to Darwin ('To the question why we do not find rich fossiliferous deposits . . . prior to the Cambrian system, I can give no satisfactory answer')."[26]

Harland and Rudwick wrote in *Scientific American* about the sudden proliferation of fossils at the Cambrian:

" . . . they were complex organisms that clearly belonged to the various distinct phyla, or major groups of animals, now classified as metazoan. In fact, they are now known to include representatives of nearly every major phylum that possessed skeletal structure capable of fossilization.

" . . . yet before the Lower Cambrian there is scarcely a trace of them. The appearance of the Lower Cambrian fauna . . . can reasonably be called a 'sudden' event.

"One can no longer dismiss this event by assuming that all Pre-Cambrian rocks have been too greatly altered by time to allow the fossils ancestral to the Cambrian metazoans to be preserved . . . even if all the Pre-Cambrian ancestors of the Cambrian metazoans were similarly softbodied and therefore rarely preserved, far more abundant traces of their activities should have been found in the Pre-Cambrian strata than has proved to be the case. Neither can the general failure to find Pre-Cambrian animal fossils be charged to any lack of looking."[27]

Kay and Colbert query:

"Why should such complex organic forms be in rocks about six hundred million years old and be absent or unrecognized in the records of the preceeding two billion years? . . . If there has been evolution of life, the absence of the requisite fossils in the rocks older than the Cambrian is puzzling."[28]

26. T. N. GEORGE: "FOSSILS IN EVOLUTIONARY PERSPECTIVE," IN *SCIENCE PROGRESS*, 48(1960):4,5.
27. W. B. HARLAND AND M. RUDWICK: "THE GREAT INFRA-CAMBRIAN ICE-AGE," IN *SCIENTIFIC AMERICAN*, 211(1964):34-36.
28. G. M. KAY AND E. H. COLBERT: *STRATIGRAPHY AND LIFE HISTORY*

364

Simpson of Harvard laments about the Pre-Cambrian void that
it is "not only the most puzzling feature of the whole fossil
record but almost its greatest apparent inadequacy."[29] (Fig. 110)

Fig. **110** - Cambrian Diorama
A diorama of life as it may have appeared immediately after "Pre-Cambrian" times. (Courtesy of the American Museum of Natural Hist.)

After the Pre-Cambrian void we see a vast fossil record in
the sedimentary rocks (water deposited) showing huge arrays of
life. Finally, today, and for the past few thousand years, no
fossilization to speak of is taking place.

So the record of the rocks argues: there was a time in the
past when uniformitarian conditions were not opportune for fossilization (Pre-Cambrian); then there was a time when hordes of

(N.Y.: WILEY, 1965), PP. 102, 103.
*29. G. G. SIMPSON: "THE HISTORY OF LIFE," IN <u>EVOLUTION AFTER
DARWIN - THE EVOLUTION OF LIFE</u>, VOL. 1, ED. SOL TAX (CHICAGO:
UNIVERSITY OF CHICAGO, 1960), P. 144 .*

animals and huge blankets of plants were catastrophically buried
by sediment (the fossil record); then there has been the time
since, when uniformitarian conditions again are not ripe for
fossilization. What are we saying? Just this: the creationist
insists that the geological column and timetable that is spread
over almost two billion years and used to support the thesis that
life has evolved, is actually a record of the demise of animals
through the agency of a world-wide aqueous cataclysm, i.e., a
record of life's departure, not its coming. (Fig. 111)

Evolution Model		Creation-Flood Model	
P R E S E N T thousands	P R E S E N T	NO SIGNIFICANT FOSSILIZATION OR SEDIMENTATION	thousands
G E O L O G I C T I M E T A B L E b i l l i o n s	F L O O D	AQUEOUS BURIAL OF BILLIONS OF LIVING FORMS--FOSSILS VAST EROSION AND SEDIMENTA-TION	months
P R E C A M B R I A N b i l l i o n s	P R E F L O O D	CRYSTALLINE BASEMENT ROCKS: PREFLOOD ROCKS MINUS THOSE REMOVED BY THE FLOOD	thousands

Fig.**111**- Revised Geologic Timetable
*The classical geologic column and timetable spreads the record of
the fossils over millions of years. The creationist looks at the
same data and concludes the "geologic timetable" is a record of one
large devastating flood that accomplished the majority of its work
in a few months--a record of life's departure, not its arrival.*

Flood Evidence

The creationist feels that there is not one piece of substantiated evidence that argues against the idea that geological
history could be understood on the basis of a creation and subsequent world-wide flood that have occurred within the last few
thousand years. What does he offer to speak directly for this
interpretation? The following is a partial list of evidence
the creationist proffers to support his contention:

366

A PRE-CAMBRIAN VOID
The Pre-Cambrian void provides no record for the evolutionary history of the vast array of animals that suddenly appears in
the Cambrian. The Pre-Cambrian—Cambrian demarcation portrays
pre-flood basement (minus that worked up by the flood) and post-
flood sediment respectively.

B FOSSILIZATION
The very existence of billions of fossils, oil beds and
coal seams found world-wide and preserved through aqueous agency
speaks to watery cataclysm. (It has even been calculated that
the total amount of coal within the earth--4.49 x 10^{12} metric
tons of carbon--could have been produced by the sudden world-
wide amassing of an earth full of pre-flood tropical vegetation--
3.24 x 10^{12} metric tons of carbon.)[30]

C EPHEMERAL MARKINGS
Preservation of transitory markings like ripple marks,
tracks and rain drops testify to sudden complete burial.

D POLYSTRATE TREES
Spanning through several strata are found trees preserved
as well at their tops as at their bottoms. The fossil trees
bridge an evolutionary time span (as determined by dating the
strata through which the trees span) that would preclude their
"in place" growth and fossilization. This, of course, shows that
the sediments and the trees were moved into place and deposited
at the same approximate time; and also throws the evolutionary
contention that the strata were laid down over hundreds of thousand of years into serious question.[31] (Figs. 112,113)

E EVOLUTIONARY CONTRADICTIONS
Every conceivable contradiction to the proposed order of
the geological column is found in the field. Price has stated:
> "Any kind of fossiliferous beds whatever, 'young' or
> 'old' may be found occurring conformably on any other
> fossiliferous beds, 'older' or 'younger'."[32]

If 'younger' fossils are found on top of 'older' fossils,
then the evolutionist argues that this was due to faulting,

30. DETAILS ARE OUTLINED IN H. WIANT, JR.: "A QUANTITATIVE COM-
PARISON OF THE CARBON IN THE BIOMASS AND COAL BEDS OF THE WORLD,"
IN CREATION RESEARCH SOCIETY QUARTERLY, 11(1974):142.
31. A. GIEKIE, (REF. 5) PP. 654, 655; C. DUNBAR: GEOLOGY
(N.Y.: WILEY, 1960), P. 227.
32. G. M. PRICE, QUOTED IN B. NELSON: DELUGE STORY . . . ,
(REF. 22) P. 146.

Fig.**112** - Nova Scotia Polystrate Trees
*The fossil tree impression pictured here(top) spans over twelve
feet through sedimentary strata. The impression was exposed by a
tidal cut into this Carboniferous strata in Joggins, Nova Scotia.
It is difficult to imagine this tree being buried by means other
than catastrophy. Slow deposition of rock(uniformity) would not
allow a tree to be fossilized before it would rot and fall. A
short distance from the tree impression in the top photo is found
this fossil tree(bottom) spanning several feet through sedimentary
strata posing similar problems for an evolution-uniformity interpretation. (Courtesy R. Cranson)*

Fig. **113** - Polystrate Trees

*This fossil tree penetrates a visible distance of ten feet through
volcanic sandstone of the Clarno formation in Oregon. Potassium-
Argon dating of the nearby John Day formation suggests that 1,000
feet of rock was deposited over a period of about seven million
years or, in other words, at the rate of the thickness of this page
annually! However, catastrophic burial must have formed the rock
and caused the fossilization, otherwise the tree would have rotted
and collapsed. (Details in S. E. Nevins: CREATION RESEARCH SOCIETY
QUARTERLY, 10(1974):191-207.) This Lepidodendrid tree trunk(bottom)
found in Tennessee, has its base on the Pewee coal seam and extends
twenty feet through sedimentary rock. (Courtesy Steve Minkin)*

thrusting and folding, i.e., the 'correct' order was there in the beginning, however, one land mass broke from another, lifted itself on top of the adjacent mass and slid on top of it; the top of the sliding mass was then eroded away leaving the 'appearance' that younger fossils came before older fossils.

The following examples are suggested to be overthrusts:[33]

1. LEWIS OVERTHRUST: In Montana, "Pre-Cambrian" rocks lie on top of "Cretaceous" rocks that are supposed to be 500 million years younger. This contradiction is explained by a thrust in which a piece of land 350 miles wide and six miles thick(about 10,000 square miles in area) picked itself up and slid 40 miles on top of the "Cretaceous" strata.
2. FRANKLIN OVERTHRUST: In Texas, rocks 450 million years old lie on top of rocks 130 million years old.
3. MYTHEN PEAK: The Mythen Peak in the Alps has rocks 200 million years old on top of rocks 60 million years old. The thrust is believed to have pushed all the way from Africa to Switzerland.
4. GLARUS OVERTHRUST: In Switzerland, rocks 180 million years old lie on top of rocks 60 million years old. Rock a mile in thickness is believed to have been moved 21 miles.
5. HEART MOUNTAIN THRUST: In Wyoming, about 2,000 square miles of rock supposedly 300 million years old rests on top of rock 60 million years old.
6. MATTERHORN: The Matterhorn in the Alps has supposedly been thrust from 60 miles away resulting in "younger" rocks on top of "older" rocks.(Fig. 114)

Spieker wrote:

"...lying on the crystalline basement are found from place to place not merely Cambrian, but rocks of all ages."[34]

Creationists feel that these frequent contradictions to evolutionary succession in the rocks are testimony against uniformity and evidence for catastrophe. Are overthrusts simply a ploy to explain away contradictions? Creationists think so. They draw our attention to the physical difficulties in moving large masses of rock many miles over other rocks(the Lewis Overthrust would have weighed 800,000,000,000,000 tons) and the lack of evidence at the rock interfaces that any thrusting has occurred at all.[35]

---

33. *C. ROSS AND R. REZAK: THE ROCKS AND FOSSILS OF GLACIER NATIONAL PARK(U.S. GEOLOGICAL SURVEY PROFESSIONAL PAPER 294-K, 1959), PP. 422, 424; W. PIERCE: BULLETIN OF THE AMERICAN ASSOCIATION OF PETROLEUM GEOLOGISTS, 41(1957):592-598,625; D. GISH: CREATION RESEARCH SOCIETY QUARTERLY, 12(1975):34-36; J. WHITCOMB AND H. MORRIS: THE GENESIS FLOOD(PHILADELPHIA: PRESBYTERIAN,1961), PP. 180-211.*
34. *E. SPIEKER: "MOUNTAIN BUILDING CHRONOLOGY AND NATURE OF GEOLOGIC TIME-SCALE," IN BULLETIN OF THE AMERICAN ASSOCIATION OF PETROLEUM GEOLOGISTS, 40(1956):1805.*
35. *SEE LAST TWO REFERENCES IN FOOTNOTE #33.*

The following fossil finds and archeological evidence further contradict the notion of universal evolutionary succession:

1. POLLEN IN PRE-CAMBRIAN: Pollen from Angiosperm and Gymnosperm trees has been found in "Pre-Cambrian" rocks. This would place, according to evolutionary ideas, the reproductive pollen hundreds of millions of years prior to the existence of the mother trees. Some spores are stained with red oxide from the surrounding rocks, thus proving they are not from present-day contamination. The evolutionists, Leclerq and Axelrod, have found spores and fragments of woody plants representing dozens of genera(Axelrod found 60 genera) in "Cambrian" rocks.[36] Woody plants supposedly did not arrive on the evolutionary scene until over 200 million years after the "Cambrian!" (Fig. 115)

2. ARTHROPODS IN PRE-CAMBRIAN: Arthropod fossils have been found by a U.S.G.S. team in "proterozoic--younger Pre-Cambrian" rocks age-dated at 1.2 billion years. This discovery from the Sierra Ancha area of northern Arizona, in 1972, and age-dated by the University of Arizona, puts the Arthropods hundreds of millions of years before they were supposed to have evolved. (Fig. 116)

3. THE NAMPA IMAGE: A baked clay figurine was obtained from a well being bored in 1889 at Nampa, Idaho. In attempting to obtain artesian water, the figurine was pumped up from rocks over 300 feet deep under a "Tertiary" lava sheet. This would date the artifact--and its human maker--at about 12 million years old according to the evolutionary geologic timescale. Most evolutionists, however, feel that man has evolved from a primate precursor in only about the last three million years.[37] (Fig. 117)

4. GOLD CHAIN IN COAL: In 1889, Mrs. S. W. Culp broke a chunk of coal and found embedded therein a ten inch, eight-carat gold chain. This would place the human maker of the chain far beyond that which even the most liberal evolutionist would imagine for the antiquity of man.[38]

---

36. R. STAINFORTH: IN NATURE, 210(1966):292; MICROPALEONTOLOGY, 10(1964):518; C. BURDICK: IN C.R.S.QUARTERLY, 3(1966):38; S. LECLERQ: IN EVOLUTION, 10(1956):109; D. AXELROD: IN EVOLUTION, 13 (1959):264.
37. PROCEEDINGS OF THE BOSTON SOC. NAT. HIST., 24(1890):424; I. VELIKOVSKY: EARTH IN UPHEAVAL (N.Y.: DELL, 1955), P. 90; F. WRIGHT: IN AMERICAN GEOLOGIST, 23(1899):267; A. BIRD: BOISE THE PEACE VALLEY, (IDAHO: CAXTON, 1934), PP. 17-26; B. DEFENBACH: IN SUNDIAL, 1(JUNE, 1935), P. 5.
38. MORRISONVILLE, ILLINOIS TIMES, JUNE 11, 1891.

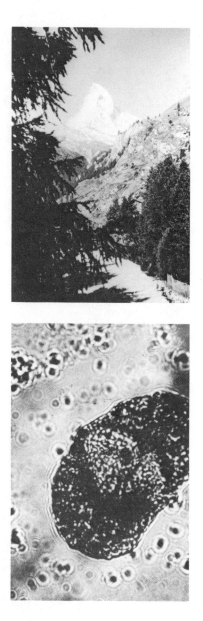

Fig.**114** – Matterhorn
The Matterhorn is believed to have been thrust from some 60 miles away, to rest now on younger rocks. (Wolfe Worldwide Films)

Fig.**115** – Pre - Cambrian Pollen
A fossil Conifer Gymnosperm spore or pollen found in the Grand Canyon Hakati Shale, "Proterozoic." (Courtesy C. Burdick)

Fig. **116** – Pre-Cambrian Arthropods
"Proterozoic" fossils tentatively identified as Arthropods, from Sierra Ancha area of Arizona. (Courtesy C. Burdick)

Fig. **117** – Nampa Image
The Nampa figurine retrieved from rocks estimated at 12 million years old. (Courtesy Idaho Historical Society, Davis Museum)

5. IRON POT IN COAL: Professor W. Rusch has reported an iron pot encased in coal dated, by evolutionary standards, at 300 million years old.[39]

6. CONTEMPORANEOUS HUMAN AND DINOSAUR PRINTS: Human footprints, both normal size and giant size, sometimes side by side with dinosaur prints, have been found in Mexico, New Mexico, Arizona, Texas, Missouri, Kentucky, Illinois and in other U.S. locations. The tracks were probably first preserved by being dried and hardened, then, they were probably covered by pulses of sediment leaving a cleavage seam at that level. Some believe that the prints are frauds because dinosaurs were supposed to be extinct at least 70 million years before man arrived. However, the following counterarguments suggest otherwise: (a) The tracks are widely distributed; (b) The impressions are usually only exposed by flood erosion or bulldozers; (c) Two paleontologists are on record as having pronounced them genuine--Dr. Camp of the University of California and Dr. G. Westcott of Ypsilanti, Michigan; (d) Strings of from 15 to 23 right-left tracks have been uncovered; (e) Upon sawing through the tracks, the rock particles found underneath the impressions are more compressed than the particles surrounding the prints; (f) The associated dinosaur fossil tracks are accepted as valid; (g) Some prints have ridges of mud pushed up around them.[40] (Figs. 118-121)

7. CALAVERA AND CASTENODOLO SKULLS: The human Calaveras skull from the U.S.(1886), and the Castenodolo skull from Italy(1860) predate, according to the geologic column, humans by millions of years. These fossils were found in "Pliocene" strata.[41]

8. SKULL IN COAL: In the coal collection of the Mining Academy of Freiberg, Germany, "is a puzzling human skull

39. W. RUSCH: "HUMAN FOOTPRINTS IN ROCKS," IN *CREATION RESEARCH SOCIETY QUARTERLY*, 7(1970):201.
40. A. G. INGALLS: "THE CARBONIFEROUS MYSTERY," IN *SCIENTIFIC AMERICAN*, 162(1940):14; C. L. BURDICK: "CHANGING CONCEPTS CONCERNING EVOLUTION," IN *THE NATURALIST*, 16(1957):38-41; R. T. BIRD: "THUNDER IN HIS FOOTSTEPS," IN *NATURAL HISTORY*, MAY, 1939, P. 255; W. SMITH: *MAN'S ORIGIN, MAN'S DESTINY* (WHEATON: HAROLD SHAW, 1968), FIGS. 6-21.
41. *HOW THEY CHOOSE OUR ANCESTORS* (GREAT BRITAIN: EVOLUTION PROTEST MOVEMENT); A. KEITH: *THE ANTIQUITY OF MAN* (PHILADELPHIA: LIPPENCOTT, 1928), P. 119; D. DEWAR: *THE TRANSFORMIST ILLUSION* (TENN.: DEHOFF, 1957), PP. 117, 118; W. HOWELL: *MANKIND SO FAR* (1946), P. 103.

374

Fig.**118** - Paluxy River   Tracks
•*Fossil dinosaur trackway along the Paluxy River in Glen Rose, Texas(top). (Courtesy A. M. Natural History) •Shod fossil footprint in a line of 23 along the Paluxy River bed(bottom right). •Allosaurus and Tyrannosaurus tracks along Paluxy(bottom left). (Burdick.*

Fig. **119**- Human and Dinosaur Tracks
•*Trail of human fossil tracks along Paluxy River(top).* •*Bottom photograph shows Brontosaurus track with human print at the end of the stick, top center. (Reprinted by permission from MAN'S ORIGIN, MAN'S DESTINY, by A. Smith; published Bethany Fellowship, Inc., Minneapolis, Minnesota 55438; Copyright 1968 by A. Smith.) Such evidence has prompted the saying: "Evolution may be fun, but dinosaurs bite!"*

Fig. **120** - Giant Human Prints
•*Quarried dinosaur and giant human fossil prints from the Paluxy River(top). (Courtesy C. Burdick)* •*Bottom photograph shows two giant human prints chiseled out of the Paluxy River bed. (Courtesy R. Cranson)*

Fig. **121**- Paluxy Excavation
•*Bulldozers at work along the Paluxy River have uncovered trails of crossing human and dinosaur tracks(top).* •*The bottom photograph is a close up of an 18 inch man track only 17 inches from a three-toed dinosaur imprint. (Courtesy Films for Christ)*

composed of brown-coal and magniferous and phosphatic li-
monite, but its source is unknown."[42]

9. TRILOBITES IN FOSSIL SANDAL IMPRESSION: William Meister
unearthed a fossil shod footprint in the "Wheeler Mid-Cambrian"
strata at Antelope Springs, Utah in June of 1968. The track
split in half with the top portion being the mud that had
sifted in to fill the depression the foot had made. Portions
of trilobites are found embedded in both heel and toe. Seven
other tracks were also found in the same area precluding this
being a "geological quirk." The contemporaneousness of man
and trilobite would effectively collapse about 500 million
years of the geological column.[43] (Fig. 122)

10. SCULPTURES OF EXTINCT BIRDS: Jose Diaz-Bolio, a Mexican
archeologist discovered an ancient Mayan relief sculpture of
a bird he feels resembles the Archaeopteryx or Archaeornis.
This discovery, from Totonacapan, in Veracruz, Mexico, would
create a discrepency of about 130 million years between when
the Archaeopteryx became extinct and man first appeared. If
evolution be true, "the twain(Mayan and serpent-bird) never
should have met."[44]

11. FIVE-TOED LLAMA ETCHINGS: Five-toed llamas, according
to evolutionary formulations, were extinct some 30 or more
million years ago. However, in the early nineteen hundreds
an archeologist digging in Bolivia found pottery with five-
toed llama etchings on it. Skeletons of five-toed llamas
were also found in association with the Tiahuanacan culture.[45]

12. DINOSAUR PICTOGRAPHS: Pictographs of a dinosaur, ibex,
elephant and other beasties have been found on the walls of
the Havasupai Canyon by S. Hubbard, Honorary Curator of Arch-
eology of the Oakland Museum, and others, in the late 1800's.
Does this speak for the contemporaneity of man and dinosaur?[46]
(Fig. 123)

13. MASTODON PETROGLYPHS: Several petroglyphs of mastodons
have been found on the sandstone cliffs of the Colorado River

42. *O. STUTZER: GEOLOGY OF COAL(CHICAGO: U. OF CHICAGO, 1940),
P. 271.*
43. *M. COOK: IN WHY NOT CREATION (GRAND RAPIDS: BAKER, 1970), PP.
185-193.*
44. *"SERPENT BIRD OF THE MAYANS," IN SCIENCE DIGEST, 64(NOV., 1968).*
45. *E. COLBERT: EVOLUTION OF THE VERTEBRATES (N.Y.: WILEY, 1955),
P. 386; P. HONORE: IN QUEST OF THE WHITE GOD (N.Y.: PUTNAM, 1964),
PP. 164,165.*
46. *E. SCOYEN: IN ARIZONA HIGHWAYS, 27(JULY, 1951): 36-39.*

Fig. **122**- Squashed   Trilobites
This shoe impression, showing heels, has trilobites squashed in the toe and heel. Actually, there is only one imprint that has split in half like a book. The arrow points to the trilobite in the heel. (Courtesy C. Burdick)

Fig.**123**- Dinosaur   Pictograph
If this pictograph is actually a representation of a dinosaur,
about 70 million years of the geologic column is collapsed.

gorge, within ten river-miles of Moab Valley in Utah. Some suggest, however, that man has only been in America 3000 years, and mastodons went extinct about 12 thousand years ago.[47] (Fig. 124)

14. 100 MILLION YEAR OLD HUMANS: F. A. Barnes reported the recent find of two human skeletons in "100 million year old" Utah rock. The strata in which the fossils were found were classified as "Lower Dakota," or "Upper Morrison." J. Marwitt, an anthropologist at the University of Utah,declared that the bones were obviously human and found in situ, i.e., they were not washed into position. Fifteen or more feet of rock above the bones was bulldozed off and was reported as continuous and unbroken with about six feet being solid rock. The skeletons were articulated(bones were together at the joints) and stained green by the copper salts from the surrounding rocks. In turn, the surrounding rocks were stained by the organics from the bodies. By its position in the rocks, the discovery places man about 97 million years before any of his speculated evolutionary precursors![48] (Fig. 125)

15. FURTHER CONTRADICTIONS: Erich von Fange has made an extensive listing of contradictions to classical evolutionary successions:
(a) Fossil human footprints in S. America, Indiana, Missouri, Texas, New York, Nevada, Kentucky and Nicaragua;
(b) Fossil leather sole imprint, size 13 with a double line of sewed stitches, found in "Triassic" rock estimated to be 225 million years old;
(c) Fossil sole imprint with visible sewed thread in coal estimated at 15 million years old;
(d) Flint carvings on extinct saurian(reptilian) bones estimated to be 180 million years old;
(e) Artifacts found down to 300 feet under the earth;
(f) Human skull at a depth of 130 feet under 5 separate layers of lava;
(g) Paved tile in Colorado "Miocene" rock estimated to be 27 million years old.[49]

In summary, there can be little doubt that the record in the rocks does not consistently present a gradation of simple to complex. Evolutionists attempt to explain the anomalies or simply

47. A. LOOK: *1000 MILLION YEARS ON THE COLORADO PLATEAU* (DENVER: GOLDEN BELL, 1947), PP. 279,280.
48. F. A. BARNES: "THE CASE OF THE BONES IN STONE," IN *DESERT*, 38(FEB., 1975):36.
49. E. VON FANGE: "TIME UPSIDE DOWN," IN *CREATION RESEARCH SOCIETY QUARTERLY*, 11(1974):19-; ALSO SEE DISSENT IN 12(1975):121-, ISSUE.

Fig. **124** - Mastodon Petroglyph
Petroglyph of extinct mastodon. (F. Barnes, Moab, Utah)

Fig. **125** - Bones in 100 Million Year Old Rock
This is one of two skeletons found in rock that is age-dated at 100 million years old. Note articulations. (F. Barnes, Moab, Utah)

ignore them. Creationists seize upon the"anomolies" as evidence against evolution and for a creation-flood interpretation. They conclude that the very nature of the sedimentary strata and the mechanism for fossilization, plus the randomization of fossil order, speak to sudden catastrophic burial. This would mean, judging from the finds mentioned above, that prior to the flood man did indeed live contemporaneously with trilobites and dinosaurs, that the plants and animals that led to the formation of the coal and oil beds likewise were contemporaneous with man, and that the whole of the fossil record is simply a book with pages of sedimentary strata depicting preflood life.

F FLOOD FOSSIL SORTING
In some places in the world, fossils are found in sedimentary rocks which show a gradation from simple to complex. This, as we have mentioned, is held to prove evolutionary progression through time. However, this general progression would also be expected if the fossils were produced from the action of a flood. The dense spherical marine creatures would be the first to be layered out due to the sorting effect of hydrodynamic selectivity, i.e., the more dense and spherical creatures(simpler) will sediment out more rapidly than the less dense more irregular creatures(complex). Furthermore, it would be reasonable that after the smaller marine creatures were overwhelmed from sediments and associated toxicities, that more and more complex organisms(less dense, less spherical) would layer out on top of one another. Then, as the waters would continue to rise, the slow moving shore creatures would be trapped(amphibians), then slow moving reptiles, and finally the flood waters would overwhelm the fleeing land creatures(birds, mammals, man, etc.) The final effect in the sediment would be a general progression of organisms from simple to complex, although contradictions to this order would be expected due to the randomization from flood action. (Fig. 126)

G FLOOD TRADITIONS
Flood traditions have been carried by essentially every culture on earth. A survey of 120 tribes in North, South and Central America, revealed that all of them without exception had flood traditions.[50] A post-flood population would be expected to carry with it ideas of such a world-wide cataclysm as it dispersed around the world. With time the accounts would be expected to change and be incorporated into newly emerging mythologies. The basic theme, nevertheless, would be expected to remain the same: universal flood, some sort of ark of safety, few survive. Most of the traditions compare to the Bible's account in describing

50. *INTERNATIONAL STANDARD BIBLE ENCYCLOPEDIA*, VOL. II, P. 822.

384

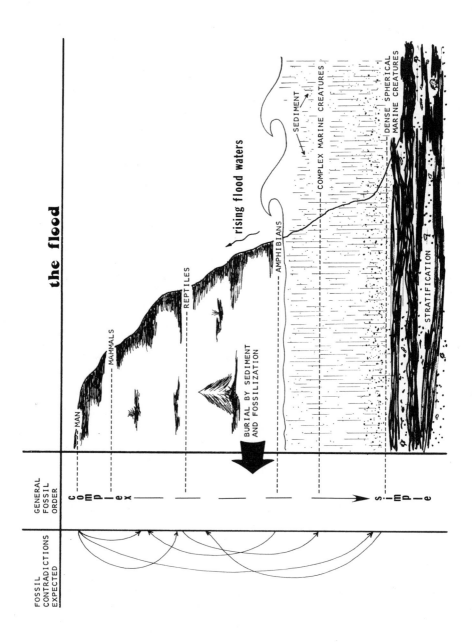

Fig. 126 – Flood Fossil Order
A flood would create, in general, a fossil order from simple to complex due to hydrodynamic selectivity, ecological zonation, and attempts to flee to higher elevations. A flood might also explain the frequent contradictions to this general order.

an earth-wide flood where only a few were saved via an ark.[51](Fig. 127) The notion of an earth-wide flood and an ark of safety is not at all incredible to creationists. If the evidence points to a world-wide flood, and life was preserved through it--obviously, since life is here today--there must have been a means of preservation. Elephants and rhinoceroses either treaded water or were on board an ark! The ark was not, according to the Bible anyway, a quaint little boat with a streamlined bow and stern so often pictorialized(actually "cartoonized") with Noah standing at the helm and a giraffe's head sticking smilingly from a window. Rather the ark would have been a gigantic rectangular three-storied chest designed simply to float, not pull skiers. The ark would have contained 1.5 million cubic feet of space(the equivalent of about 522 railroad boxcars); calculations show that the vessel would have been practically impossible to capsize; and only representatives of the basic "kinds" needed to have been taken aboard-- not all varieties or "species." Plants could have survived by being carried on the ark, by floating rafts of vegetation, and by simply sprouting after the waters subsided--1000 year old Manchurian Lotus seeds have germinated and grown. Calculations have also shown that the ark only needed to have been one-half full in order to carry representatives of all kinds that could not have survived in the waters outside the ark![52]

H **EARLY BELIEVERS**
The foundations of modern stratigraphy, sedimentology and geomorphology were laid in the 17th and 18th centuries by men like Steno, Grandius and Woodward. These men and other careful and informed scientists of that day interpretated the sedimentary and fossilized records in the rocks in terms of the great world-wide flood of Noah.[53] Creationists draw our attention to the fact that modern evolutionary uniformitarianism was formulated by "novices" like Smith, a surveyor, Chambers, a journalist, Hutton, an agriculturalist, Buckland, a theologian, and Lyell, a lawyer.

51. B. NELSON, (REF. 22) PP. 165-190; W. KELLER: *THE BIBLE AS HISTORY* (N.Y.: W. MORROW, 1956), PP. 25-35.
52. BIBLICAL DIMENSIONS IN CUBITS: *GENESIS 6:14-16;* DETAILS ON ARK SIZE, STABILITY, DIMENSIONS, ANIMAL CAPACITY, ETC., FOUND IN: B. NELSON, (REF. 22) PP. 153-; J. WHITCOMB AND H. MORRIS: *THE GENESIS FLOOD*(PHILADELPHIA: PRESBYTERIAN, 1970), PP. 7-14; 63-88; H. MORRIS: "THE ARK OF NOAH," IN *C.R.S.QUARTERLY*, 8(1971):142; A. REHWINKEL: *THE FLOOD* (ST. LOUIS: CONCORDIA, 1951), PP. 57-77.
53. J. WOODWARD: *AN ESSAY TOWARD A NATURAL THEORY OF THE EARTH* (1695); N. STENO: *A TREATISE ON A SOLID BODY ENCLOSED BY NATURAL PROCESS WITHIN A SOLID*(1669); J. GRANDIUS: *ABOUT THE TRUTH OF THE UNIVERSAL DELUGE. . .*(1676); AN EXCELLENT SUMMARY OF EARLY FLOOD THINKING IS IN: B. NELSON, (REF. 22) PP. 7-68.

	MAN TRANSGRESSES	DIVINE DESTRUCTION	FAVORED FAMILY	ARK PROVIDED	WATER DESTRUCTION	HUMAN SEED SAVED	ANIMAL SEED SAVED	UNIVERSAL DESTRUCTION	LANDING ON MOUNTAIN	BIRDS SENT OUT	SURVIVORS WORSHIP	DIVINE FAVOR ON SAVED
ASSYRIO-BABYLONIA (A)	X	X	X	X	X	X	X	X	X	X	X	X
ASSYRIO-BABYLONIA (B)		X	X	X	X	X	X	X	X	X	X	X
PERSIA (A)			X	X	X	X	X	X		X		
PERSIA (B)	X	X			X			X				
SYRIA	X			X	X	X	X	X				
ASIA MINOR			X	X	X			X		X		
GREECE		X	X	X	X	X		X	X		X	
EGYPT	X	X			X	X		X			X	X
ITALY	X	X	X	X	X	X		X	X		X	
LITHUANIA	X	X		X	X	X						
WALES				X	X	X	X					
SCANDINAVIA (A)				X	X							
SCANDINAVIA (B)				X	X	X						
LAPLAND				X	X	X		X				
RUSSIA		X		X	X	X	X	X				X
CHINA				X	X	X				X		
INDIA (A)		X	X	X	X	X			X			
INDIA (B)	X	X	X	X	X	X						
ALASKA			X	X	X	X	X					
ESQUIMAUX(CANADA)				X	X	X						
THLINKUT (A)	X			X	X	X						
THLINKUT (B)				X	X	X						
CREE				X	X	X	X	X		X		
CHEROKEE(U.S.)			X	X	X	X		X				
MANDAN				X	X	X		X			X	
LENNI LENAPE	X			X	X	X		X				
TAKOE	X				X	X						
PAPAGOS(MEXICO)			X	X	X	X				X		
PIMAS			X	X	X	X						
TOLTECS				X	X	X		X				
AZTECS			X		X	X		X				
MICHOACAN					X	X				X		
NICARAGUA				X	X	X		X				
PERU			X	X	X	X		X				
BRAZIL				X	X	X		X				
LEWARD ISLANDS	X	X	X	X	X	X		X				
FIJI ISLANDS (A)				X	X	X						
FIJI ISLANDS (B)	X			X	X	X		X				
ANDAMAN ISLAND	X			X	X	X		X		X		
HAWAII	X			X	X	X		X			X	X
SUMATRA				X	X	X			X			

Fig. **127** - Flood Legend Features

The above chart depicts principle ideas from flood traditions of some cultures around the world that hold non-Biblical accounts. The "X's" represent either partial or full representation of Biblical features. (Modified from B. Nelson, (Ref. 22) p. 169)

❚ RADIOCARBON DEATH - DATES
   If there were a world flood in the past, then the destruction
of life at that time should eclipse and be markedly contrasted
with the destruction of life previous to and after that event.
Also, as we discussed above, the conditions for fossilization and
thus the vast majority of fossils should coincide with the time of
the flood. The C-14 dating method has been shown to be reasonably accurate within the time span of human history and thus might
aid us in determining if such evidence does exist for the flood.
In other words, if the flood is responsible for the majority of
fossilization, then a vast quantity of fossils should date to the
time of the flood. R. Whitelaw, of Virginia Polytechnic Institute,
graphed 25,000 radiocarbon dates published through 1970.[54] The
samples were of men, animals and vegetation taken above and below
sea level. After correcting the published dates for the disparity
between C-14 production and disintegration discussed in Chapter
10, the resulting graph proves to peak with the greatest number
of deaths occurring about 4000 years ago. (Fig. 128)

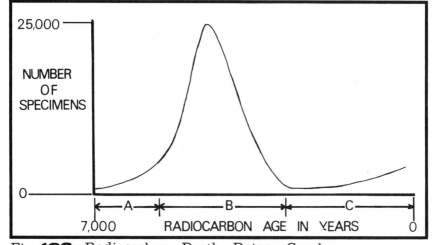

Fig. **128**- Radiocarbon Death Dates Graph
*This graph schematically portrays Whitelaw's 25,000 C-14 correct-
ed datings. The peak in the graph(B) represents the huge destruction of life at the time of the flood. Section(A) would represent
the slow increase in dateable remains as life slowly increased in
numbers after creation. Section(C) of the graph would represent
the slow increase in dateable remains as life grew from the small
post-flood nucleus. The 7,000 year creation date is based upon
comparing C-14 production and disintegration. (See Chapter 10)*

---

*54. R. WHITELAW: "TIME, LIFE AND HISTORY IN THE LIGHT OF 15,000
RADIOCARBON DATES," IN C.R.S.QUARTERLY, 7(1970):56.*

J. **FLOOD - CANOPY   IMPLICATIONS**
If there were a world-wide flood in the past, something had
to have caused it. Rain along with geotectonic disturbances that
would flatten the earth surface could have served the purpose.
If it rained to the degree necessary to cause world-wide flooding,
then prior to the rain there must have been an excessive amount
of atmospheric water. There must have been a water canopy of sorts.
A vast pre-flood water canopy would imply several things. Many of
which are verified somewhat by scientific findings:
(1) GREENHOUSE EFFECT-- A water canopy surrounding the earth would
be expected to produce an earth-wide greenhouse effect. The atmospheric water would have captured the long-wave radiation(heat)
from the sun between the canopy and the earth. The result would
be similar to that produced by greenhouses, i.e., the earth would
have been heated. Similarly, it is believed the dense clouds of
Venus heat that planet's surface and smooth out temperature differences. So, it is most interesting that we have pole to pole evidence that the earth was once subtropical. Heylum wrote:
> ". . . there is little evidence that climatic belts existed
> in the earlier history of the earth. . .This anomalous sit-
> uation is difficult to explain. . . It is obvious, therefore,
> that climatic conditions in the past were significantly
> different from those in evidence today."[55]

Under the ice caps are found palm leaves, fruit trees and tropical
marine crustaceans. Vast forests of luxuriant subtropical plant
life are also buried under the polar caps.[56] And, on the other
extreme, the great deserts of the world show evidence of once being
humid and subtropically rich areas. Thus, there is evidence for
a uniform tropical-like environment in the past which could be
explained by a pre-flood water canopy. (See Fig. 129)
(2) OZONE AND LONGEVITY-- The water canopy would absorb long-wave
radiation, and then, by preventing its reflection back into space,
trap these long-waves between the canopy and the earth.[57] This
would indirectly result in an increase in the ozone above the
canopy since ozone is normally destroyed by long-wave radiation
being reflected by the earth unimpeded into the atmospheric ozone
layer. On the other hand, there would be a decrease in the level
of ozone near the earth's surface since the ozone destroying long-
wave radiation would be more intense in this area beneath the water
canopy. (Fig. 129) The net effect of the water canopy on ozone
would therefore be high ozone concentrations outside of the canopy,

---

55. E. HEYLUM: "SHOULD WE TEACH UNIFORMITARIANISM?" IN JOURNAL OF
GEOLOGICAL EDUCATION, 19(1971):36.
56. D. E. HOOKER: THOSE ASTOUNDING ICE AGES (N.Y.: EXPOSITION,
1948), P. 44.
57. DETAILS IN: D. PATTEN: "THE PRE-FLOOD GREENHOUSE EFFECT," IN
SYMPOSIUM ON CREATION II(GRAND RAPIDS: BAKER, 1970), PP. 11-41.

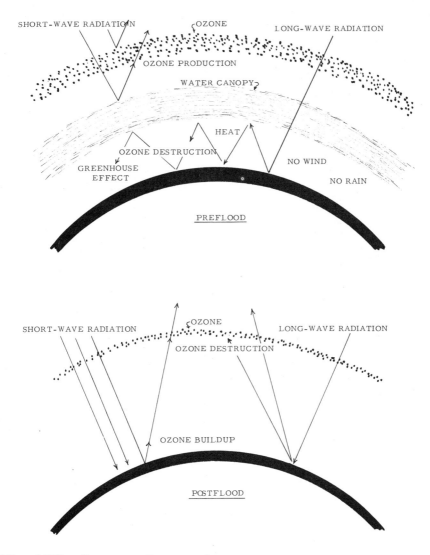

Fig.**129**- Canopy Implications
*These two drawings depict hypothetical atmospheric conditions before
and after the flood. In pre-flood times the water canopy would be
expected to: (1) shield the earth from short-wave radiation; (2)
trap long-wave radiation near the earth; (3)thicken the ozone canopy
due to the entrapment of ozone-destroying long-wave radiation under
the canopy; (4) level temperatures--greenhouse effect; (5) high
longevity due to decreased mutations. With the loss of the canopy
after the flood we would expect(bottom): (1) ozone buildup on earth;
(2) increased short-wave radiation on earth; (3) temperature diff-
erentials yielding winds, rain, freezing and baking; (4) a drop in
longevity due to increased ozone, radiation and mutations.*

and low concentrations beneath the canopy near the earth. ("High" and "low" would be in comparison to present levels.) Ozone, it has recently been learned, has a deleterious effect upon organisms. It increases susceptibility to degenerative diseases and decreases life span in much the same way as do x-rays.[58] Therefore, since the water canopy would have resulted in a low concentration of ozone near the earth's surface, we would expect less biological degeneration and longer life spans for pre-flood organisms, including man. In this regard there is evidence that men of the past did live much longer than we do today. Skulls have been found in Europe and other places around the world with teeth that are worn almost to the gumline. This, of course, is not proof that the great wear was the result of long life for a coarse diet could do the same, but may in fact be evidence we should at least consider in support for the greater longevity of men of the past. The Bible, although viewed with a skeptical eye by many, does record that man prior to the flood lived to great ages, but men soon after the flood lived only to the present day average of about 70 years.[59] (Fig. 130)

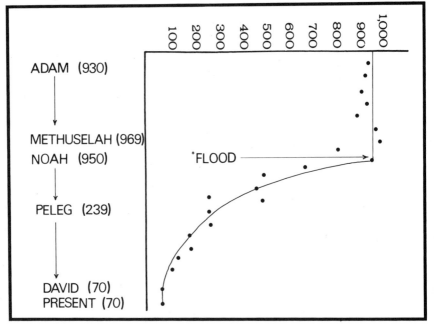

Fig. **130** - The Flood and Longevity
This chart depicts pre-flood and post-flood ages of men as they are recorded in the Bible.

58. R. FETTNER: IN *NATURE*, 194(1962):793.
59. COMPARE THE AGES LISTED IN GENESIS CHAPTER 5 TO GENESIS CHAPTER 11; ALSO SEE PSALM 90:2.

(3) RADIATION, SIZE AND LONGEVITY-- The pre-flood water canopy
plus the resultant greater ozone canopy would also have greatly
increased the shielding of the earth and its inhabitants from
short-wave radiations--the cosmic rays, the ultraviolet light
and other harmful rays issuing from space. (This would, of course,
significantly affect the cosmic ray dependent production of C-14.
Thus the C-14 dating method would be invalid prior to the time of
the flood.) You may recall it mentioned in a previous chapter
that the present ozone canopy prevents contemporary life from being destroyed by harmful short-wave radiation. Short-wave radiation is dangerous because it causes the degradation of biochemicals. It also increases the rate of mutations which in turn has
been shown to increase the rate of aging.[60] Therefore, if these
harmful rays were shielded from the earth in pre-flood times by
the water canopy and greater ozone canopy, we would expect greater health, life span and perhaps size of pre-flood creatures.
Could it be that this is the explanation for so many fossilized
creatures being so large as compared to present-day organisms:
insects with two-foot wing spans, birds with 30 foot wing spans,
giant mammals and 50 ton reptiles?
(4) VOLCANISM-- If there were crustal movements and contortions
in addition to the rain, we would expect, associated with the flood,
seismic fissures, volcanism, earthquakes, tidal waves, etc. Such
geological activity could account for the flood being universal:
Pre-flood ocean basins would lift spilling their water over the
land masses that would be concomitantly dropping(tectonic and
diastrophic geologic activity). The reverse of this could occur
after the flood, perhaps accounting for why deep sea marine creatures and even whales are found fossilized on top of the highest
of mountains. Also, vast volcanic action would produce huge lava
flows accounting for present day formations like the Indian Deccan
Plateau containing volcanic rock two miles deep, and the American
Columbian Plateau stretching over 200,000 square miles and aver-
aging 3,000 feet deep. The volcanic ash spewing from these volcanoes into the upper reaches of the atmospheric pre-flood canopy
could have provided the source for the nuclei of dust which
would be necessary for the condensation of the water vapor into
rain drops.
(5) MAMMOTHS AND THE CANOPY-- We have previously mentioned the
frozen mammoths found entombed in the arctic. These mammoths, the
most notable being the Beresovka mammoth of Siberia, give every
evidence of being suddenly buried in mucky water and quickly frozen. (Some estimate temperatures must have been far below-100° F)
The flesh of the Beresovka mammoth was edible, the stomach contained about 30 pounds of food consisting of subtropical vegetation

---

60. *H. J. CURTIS: "BIOLOGICAL MECHANISMS UNDERLYING THE AGING
PROCESS," IN SCIENCE, 141(1963):686; L. E. ORGEL: "AGING OF MAMMA-
LIAN CELLS," IN NATURE, 243(1973):441; R. HOLLYDAY: "ALTERING EN-
ZYMES IN AGING FIBROBLASTS," IN NATURE, 238(1972):26.*

still in an undigested state, and the mouth was filled with partially masticated food. The eyes and red blood cells were extremely well preserved, and the separation of water in the cells--
which proceeds rapidly after death--was only partial. All of this
speaks to the sudden and maintained freezing of the carcass.
Might the explanation for the sudden freezing of mammoths lie with
the drop of the insulating pre-flood canopy(or perhaps ice as some
suggest) plunging the polar regions suddenly into arctic temperatures?61

Conclusion

Evolutionists see the record in the rocks speaking to the
vast antiquity of life and gradual evolutionary progression through
time. Evolutionists begin with the assumption that evolution is
true, and from there they gather data and assemble charts to fit
this preconception. Facts counter to the geologic column are considered in error, explained through geologic mechanisms like faulting or thrusting, whether or not there is supporting physical
evidence, or simply shelved as quirks of nature.

The evolutionary interpretation of the rocks and fossils is
vogue today and needs little if any documentation. Even young
school children "know," for example, that dinosaurs were extinct
millions of years before man appeared. In this chapter I have
tried to bring to light some data that is not popularly known--
quirks, if you will, oddities that creationists, at least, view
as contradicting evolutionary interpretations.

With the information taught to us in school, and the evidence
pointed out here at our disposal for consideration, do the rocks
point to a gradual evolution of life through eons of time, or does
the record speak to catastrophe and, by implication, creation?

---

61. H. HOWARTH: <u>THE MAMMOTH AND THE FLOOD</u>(1887); D. PATTEN, (REF.
57) P. 21.

21 { ARGUMENTS FROM SIMILARITY

Carl Sagan wrote:
"The inner workings of terrestrial organisms--from microbes to men--are so similar in their biochemical details as to make it highly likely that all organisms on the Earth have evolved from a single instance of the origin of life."[1]

Much of the case for amoeba to man evolution is built upon arguments from similarity. Evolutionists argue that if similarity can be shown between organisms through comparative anatomy, embryology, vestigial organs, cytology, blood chemistry, protein and DNA biochemistry...then evolutionary relationship can be proven. For example, as Sagan noted above, biochemical similarity among all creatures is taken to prove evolutionary relationship in a general biological sense. Additionally, man-primate similarities, amphibian-reptile similarities and amphibian-fish similarities prove relationships in a more specific sense.

Similarity, it is agreed, can show relationship. Note the similarities among closely related families of people or animals. Similarity, however, can also mean common design as can be noted by the similar features of different buildings designed by one architect. Obviously, creationists will opt for this latter interpretation.

Contradictions

If the law of similarity can be used to show evolutionary re-

---

1. *I. S. SHKLOVSKII & C. SAGAN: INTELLIGENT LIFE IN THE UNIVERSE (N.Y.: DELL, 1966), P. 183.*

lationships, then dissimilarities can be used to show a lack of relationship and, any similarity must show relationship. I will list some examples of how the argument from similarity, if consistently applied, leads to evolutionary contradictions:

1. The octopus eye, pig heart, pekingese dog's face, milk of the ass and the pronator quadratus muscle of the Japanese salamander are all very similar to analogous human structures. Do these similarities show evolutionary relationships?
2. The weight of brain in proportion to body weight is greater in the dwarf monkey of South America, the marmoset, than in man. Since this proportion is used to show relationship between primates and man, is the marmoset, therefore, more evolved than man?
3. The plague (*Pasteurella pestis*) afflicts only man and rodent. Does this similarity show close relationship?
4. Plant nettle stings contain acetylcholine, 5-hydroxytryptamine and histamine. These chemicals are also found in man.[2] Are man and plant closely related?
5. The root nodules of leguminous plants and the crustacean, Daphnia, contain hemoglobin, the blood pigment found in man.[3] Are these organisms closely related to man?
6. If certain specific gravity tests are run on the blood of various animals, the frog and snake are found to be more similar to man than the monkey is to man.
7. Mothers with certain types (ABO and Rh systems) of blood can bear children with blood which contains antibodies against the mother's type. Thus, if the blood of the mother and child are mixed, agglutination occurs. Their blood is incompatible. Since the blood of mother and child are dissimilar, does this prove the mother is not related to the child?
8. If the concentration of red blood cells in animals is compared (millions per cu. mm. of blood), man is more similar to frogs, fish and birds than to sheep.
9. Since bones are often used to show relationships, bone chemistry should likewise be helpful in this regard. If the calcium/phosphorus ratio is plotted against bone carbonate, man proves to be close to the turtle and elephant, the monkey close to the goose, and the dog close to the horse but distant from the cat.[4]
10. Dragonfly larvae can be sent into a trance by stroking their abdomens. Does this prove their relationship to the African cobra?
11. Some efforts have been made to show chromosome content and DNA

2. G. A. *KERKUT*: *THE IMPLICATIONS OF EVOLUTION* (LONDON: PERGAMON, 1960), PP. 8,9.
3. G. KERKUT: (REF. 2);KEIL, D. AND WANG, Y.: "HAEMOGLOBIN IN THE ROOT NODULES OF LEGUMINOUS PLANTS," IN *NATURE*, 155(1945):223.
4. E.D.PELLIGRINO AND R.M.BILTZ(1968), CITED IN *EVOLUTION IN THE GLARE OF NEW KNOWLEDGE* (GREAT BRITAIN: EVOLUTION PROTEST MOVEMENT PAMPHLET, #186, 1971).

similarities. How do the following facts fit into the evolutionary simple to complex scheme:
a) Human cells contain 7 picograms of DNA/cell, whereas the frog contains more, and the African lungfish contains 100 picograms of DNA/cell!
b) Human cells contain 46 chromosomes, ferns 72, donkeys 62, crayfish 200, paramecium several hundred, and the protozoan, Aulacantha, 1600! Shouldn't we expect DNA content and chromosome content to increase as we move up the evolutionary ladder?[5]

12. The tetrapyrole chemical ring is found in plant chlorophyll, in hemoglobin and other animal respiratory pigments, sporadically as a coloring pigment in molluscan shells, and also in the feathers of some bird species. How does tetrapyrole similarity speak for relationship?[6]

13. Another modern biochemical proof of evolution is derived by comparing amino acid sequences of various organisms.[7] This proof might be suggestive of evolutionary relationships if it applied consistently. For example, Cytochrome C is a coenzyme found in most organisms. If we compare its amino acid sequences among organisms we find many similarities. However, what about the similarities in Cytochrome C that show man closer than the snapping turtle to the rattlesnake, or man closer than the rattlesnake to the bullfrog, or man closer than bread mold to the sunflower![8]

Evolutionists look at general trends and conclude evolutionary relationships. Creationists focus on contradictions and inconsistencies and conclude the law of similarity is fraudulent. (Fig. 131)

Man - Animal   Gap

There is much to-do made over the similarities between man and other animals, especially the primates. Little is normally said about the dissimilarities. But the contrasts, the differences between man and animal, man and primate, are quite remarkable:
1. Only man can benefit from transmitted and accumulated knowledge

5. *A. MONTAGU: HUMAN HEREDITY (N.Y.: NEW AMERICAN LIBRARY, 1963), P. 29; T. DOBZHANSKY: GENETICS AND THE EVOLUTION PROCESS (N.Y.: COLUMBIA U. 1970), P. 17.*
6. *H. BLUM: TIME'S ARROW AND EVOLUTION (PRINCETON: PRINCETON U. 1968), PP. 175,176.*
7. *R. V. ECK AND M. O. DAYHOFF: ATLAS OF PROTEIN SEQUENCE AND STRUCTURE (MARYLAND: THE NATIONAL BIOMEDICAL RESEARCH FOUNDATION, 1966).*
8. *E. O. WILSON AND OTHERS: LIFE ON EARTH (CONNECTICUT: SINAUR, 1973), P. 803.*

and wisdom. Only man makes history.
2. Only man is religious.
3. Only man has an innate sense of morality, of right and wrong, good and bad. Only he suffers the agony of a violated conscience. Animals must have "morality" trained into them, man must have it trained out of him.

CRITERION	SIMILAR	DISSIMILAR
EYE ANATOMY	MAN–OCTUPUS	
HEART ANATOMY	MAN–PIG	
PRONATOR QUADRATUS	MAN–JAPANESE SALAMANDER	
PLAGUE	MAN–RODENT	
ACETYLCHOLINE-HISTAMINE	MAN–PLANT	
BLOOD SPECIFIC GRAVITY	MAN–FROG	MAN–MONKEY
RED BLOOD CELL CONCENTRATION	MAN–FISH	MAN–SHEEP
HEMOGLOBIN	MAN–ROOT NODULES	
ABO AND RH BLOOD FACTORS		MOTHER–CHILD
CALCIUM-PHOSPHORUS-CARBONATE	MAN–TURTLE	DOG–CAT
CYTOCHROME C	MAN–SUNFLOWER	MOLD–SUNFLOWER
	MAN–BULLFROG	RATTLESNAKE–FROG

Fig. **131**-Similarity Contradictions
There are many similarities that can be used to support proposed evolutionary relationships. However, the argument from similarity cannot be consistently applied since some similarities and dissimilarities contradict evolutionary relationships.

4. Only man produces art and adornment for aesthetic non-utilitarian purposes.
5. Only man has a language of sentences allowing conversation and conveyance of abstract thoughts. Only he writes, invents and composes.
6. Men sing, apes don't. Only man can musically harmonize with others.
7. Only man has mind in the sense of having insight, foresight, self-awareness, pride, reason, will, abstract and conceptual thought, judgement and the ability to be educated and not just trained.
8. Man needs government. He is not instinctively self-sufficient.
9. Only man can make and use fire, and make and use tools.
10. Only man blushes.
11. Only man conceptualizes eternity.

12. Only man surrounds death with ceremony and funerals.
13. Only man has power and dominion over all other animals. Thus, man rides the elephant and not vice versa. Man trains, rules and studies the animals. Never is the converse true.
14. Only man sets and pursues willed goals and purposes.
15. Man is unique physically. He is biochemically unique, skeletally unique, muscularly unique, posturally unique (only he has an upright heel-toe walk), endocrinologically unique, neurologically unique and, in short, totally unique when compared carefully with any other creature.

The creationist reasons that if man-primate similarities prove a close relationship between the two, the dissimilarities noted above prove the opposite--man and primate are not related.

Vestigial Organs

Professor Packard wrote: "To those who believe in special creation the presence of vestigial organs has proved a stumbling block--an insuperable obstacle."[9]

Vestigial organs are rudimentary organs supposedly retained from evolutionary ancestors. For example, the human appendix is believed to be a rudiment of a cecum such as the herbivorous horse has. The similarity between the appendix and cecum argues for man's ancestral ties with herbivorous animals.

Not too long ago man was imputed to have 180 vestiges. Organs like the appendix, tonsils, thymus, pineal gland and thyroid gland were on the list.

Today, all former vestigal organs are known to have some function during the life of the individual. If the organ has any function at any time it cannot be called rudimentary or vestigial. For example, it would be incorrect to term the gonads vestigial just because they are more or less dormant until puberty.

As man's knowledge increased, the list of vestigial organs decreased. So what really was "vestigial?" Was it not man's rudimentary knowledge of the intricacies of the body?

Nevertheless, vestigial organs are still cited in modern texts as proof of evolution. For example, some argue that because we have so many problems with the appendix, and it can usually be removed without harm to the individual, that it therefore is vestigial. But we know the organ is part of the reticulo-endothelial system of the body and, like the tonsils, fights infection. Just because appendicitis is common, how can we conclude that the organ is vestigial? We have far more respiratory infections than appendix problems, yet the respiratory system is hardly considered vestigial. Nor does the fact that the appendix can be removed

---

9. *PACKARD, QUOTED IN EVAN SHUTE: FLAWS IN THE THEORY OF EVOLUTION (NEW JERSEY: CRAIG, 1961), P. 49.*

with apparently no harm speak to the organ's vestigial nature. We
can manage without an arm, without one kidney, without one eye,
are these structures likewise vestigial?

Another example often cited is the coccygeal vertebrae in the
human. These vertebrae are located at the end of our spine similar to the tail vertebrae in animals. Are the coccygeal vertebrae
vestigial? Hardly, these vertebrae serve as an important attachment site for the levator ani and coccygeus muscles that form the
pelvic floor. These muscles have many functions, among which is
the ability to support the pelvic organs. Without these muscles
(and their sites of attachment) pelvic organs would prolapse, i.e.,
drop out.

There is a very basic fallacy in the argument from vestigial
organs. An organ is supposedly vestigial because we "don't need"
the organ anymore. The development or loss of organs based upon
need, use or disuse was an idea advanced by Lamarck and soundly
dislodged by modern genetics.[10] Organs can only appear or disap-
pear if there is a genetic alteration in the chromosomes, or DNA,
so that the characteristic (or loss of) can be transmitted to the
offspring. Use or disuse has absolutely no effect on offspring.

One has to be very discerning when listening to evolutionary
argumentation because scientists still use the argument of inheritance of acquired characteristics--"use," "disuse," "need," "lack
of need."[11] But one can undergo intensive muscular exercises and
build himself into a brute of a fellow, or one can put his arm in
a sling till it withers and atrophies to skin and bone, and the
tails of mice can be cut off for generation after generation.
Will these acquired characteristics affect offspring? No, certainly not. To affect the offspring, you must alter the DNA in the sex
cells of the gonads. Even if DNA is altered, how could the sex
cells "know" which organs to lose or develop based upon need?

The Lamarckian mechanism, by which it is argued that vestigial
organs arise, is fallacious. Additionally, there are no evidences
of the transitional stages between functioning organs and useless
organs. Really, useless appendages would prove degeneration, not
evolution. Evolution is the rise of new, different and functioning organs, not the wasting away of organs. The creationist asks:
"Where are the nascent organs? Vestigial organs show degeneration,
devolution, not evolution."

One final point to consider in this regard. If man does have
180 vestigial organs, organs that were once functioning, then in
the past he would have had more organs than he now has. In the

10. FOR DOCUMENTATION SEE ANY MODERN BIOLOGY TEXT DISCUSSION OF
LAMARCKISM OR INHERITANCE OF ACQUIRED CHARACTERISTICS; ALSO SEE OUR
PREVIOUS DISCUSSION OF LAMARCKISM IN CHAPTER 17.
11. DARWIN WAS HEAVILY INFLUENCED BY THE ERRONEOUS VIEWS OF LAMARCK.
--A. MUNTZING: "DARWIN'S VIEW ON VARIATION UNDER DOMESTICATION IN
THE LIGHT OF PRESENT-DAY KNOWLEDGE," IN PROCEEDINGS OF THE AMERICAN
PHILOSOPHICAL SOCIETY, 103(1959):191; OTHER REFERENCES IN CHAPTER 17.

past, he would have been developing the organs that he presently has plus he would have had the 180 functional vestigial organs. So the farther we go back in time, the more complex the organism! Rather an interesting evolutionary twist.

Embryology

The argument from embryology is based primarily upon the ideas of Haeckel (1866). He advanced the law of recapitulation or, as it is also termed, the biogenetic law. In erudite descriptive form this law means "ontogeny recapitulates phylogeny." Or, in other words, an individual will summarize his evolutionary history by passing through similar evolutionary stages during his embryological development.

So it has been popularly believed that man has a gill stage, a hair stage, tail stage, protozoan stage, worm stage, etc. Embryo similarities is an evidence all are exposed to even in elementary biology courses.

Surprising as it may seem, however, this evidence has been rejected by practically all competent biologists.

Sir Arthur Keith wrote in 1932:

"It was expected that the embryo would recapitulate the features of its ancestors from the lowest to the highest forms in the animal kingdom. Now that the appearances of the embryo at all stages are known, the general feeling is one of disappointment; the human embryo at no stage is anthropoid in its appearance."[12]

The famous embryologist, Gavin de Beer, said:

"Until recently the theory of recapitulation still had its ardent supporters . . . It is characteristic of a slogan (ontogeny recapitulates phylogeny) that it tends to be accepted uncritically and die hard."[13]

Elsewhere, deBeer and his coauthor, Swinton, state of the biogenetic law:

". . . . a theory that in spite of its exposure, its effects continue to linger in the nooks and crannies of zoology."[14]

G. H. Waddington wrote:

"The type of analogical thinking which leads to theories that development is based on the recapitulation of ancestral stages or the like no longer seems at all convincing or even very interesting to biolo-

12. A. KEITH: *THE HUMAN BODY (1932)*, P. 94.
13. G. DEBEER: *EMBRYOS AND ANCESTORS (NEW YORK: OXFORD U. 1954)*, P. 6.
14. G. DEBEER AND W. E. SWINTON: *STUDIES IN FOSSIL VERTEBRATES*, ED. T. S. WASTALL (LONDON: ATHLONE, 1958).

gists."[15]

G. Moment, in his zoology text, stated in regard to recapitulation:

"In this form the theory runs into so many difficulties it clearly cannot be true."[16]

In the book, *Animal Form and Function*, W. Breneman concludes:

"This law has been so seriously questioned and is so obviously inapplicable in many instances that as a law it now is of historical interest only."[17]

The authors of *Concepts of Zoology* conclude:

". . . we no longer believe we can simply read in the embryonic development of a species its exact evolutionary history."[18]

Bock wrote of Haeckel's recapitulation theory that it has ". . . been demonstrated to be wrong by numerous subsequent scholars."[19]

And Oppenheimer said that Haeckel was a "fanatic" who should have never been considered a "professional embryologist." She also felt that Haeckel's "law" was "damaging to science" and "delayed rather than accelerated the course of embryological progress."[20]

In spite of this testimony, recapitulation continues to be used as proof of evolution in both popular and technical writings. To this day I find students quickly alluding to "the stage where man had gills" as a prominent proof of evolution.

Superficially it may appear that the human embryo resembles other creatures. But since man develops from one cell how could he help but at the beginning stage look like a protozoan; since he must develop endocrine glands (thymus, parathyroids), eustachian tubes, blood vessels to the head, jaws and neck parts, how could he help but have a stage when he would have folds and furrows in the neck region (gills?) to serve as the substructures for this development? How could he help but look like a worm when he had no arms and legs?

Sound science, however, operates above superficiality. At no time does man actually have gills, at no time is he a protozoan and at no time is he a worm.

If we use the argument from embryology then let's use it con-

---

15. G. H. WADDINGTON: *PRINCIPLES OF EMBRYOLOGY* (LONDON: GEORGE ALLEN AND UNWIN, 1956), P. 10.

16. G. B. MOMENT: *GENERAL ZOOLOGY* (BOSTON: HOUGHTON MIFFLIN, 1967), P. 243.

17. W. R. BRENEMAN: *ANIMAL FORM AND FUNCTION* (BOSTON: GINN, 1959), P. 521.

18. H. FRINGS AND M. FRINGS: *CONCEPTS OF ZOOLOGY* (TORONTO: COLLIER MACMILLAN CANADA LTD., 1970), P. 267.

19. W. J. BOCK: "EVOLUTION BY ORDERLY LAW," IN *SCIENCE*, 164 (1969):684

20. J. OPPENHEIMER: *ESSAYS IN THE HISTORY OF EMBRYOLOGY AND BIOLOGY* (MASS.: M.I.T., 1967), PP. 148-.

sistently. Why does the "law" not apply at all to the embryology of plants? If the horse has come from a four-toed ancestor, where is his four-toed embryological stage? If the whale has come from a four-legged land animal, where is its four-legged embryological stage? Birds supposedly sprung from reptiles but at no time in bird embryology are there socketed teeth. If every stage in embryology represents an ancestor, then we humans must have had an ancestor with an umbilical cord and placenta attached. Insects pass through a pupal stage and, therefore, one of its ancestors must have been a dormant pupa. Maggots will more or less dissolve themselves when developing into a fly. Therefore, one of the fly's ancestors was a dissolved maggot. Chickens have an embryological stage where a huge yolk-sac is attached to their abdomen, therefore, a chicken ancestor would likewise have had a yolk-sac attached that was larger even than the chicken itself.

The contradictions and exceptions that must be made to the "biogenetic law" are more numerous than the consistencies. Professor Leach says:

"The undeniable tendency of a complex animal to pass through some developmental stages reminiscent of the adult conditions of a selected and graduated series of lower forms has long been described as 'The Biogenetic Law.' But as a 'Law' inscribed by nature it is perhaps more full of 'loopholes' and 'bypasses' than any law thus far inscribed by man."[21]

The embryological development of every kind of plant and animal is unique--if one bothers to look through the scales covering the eyes of prejudice. At any stage the biochemical and genetic uniqueness (DNA sequence) of every organism can be differentiated from that of any other kind.

The drawings by Haeckel that were designed to show the similarities between embryos of different animals were spuriously altered to fit his preconceived ideas. Thompson says:

"When the convergences of embryos was not entirely satisfactory, Haeckel altered the illustrations of them to fit his theory. The alterations were slight but significant. (e.g., human head on an ape embryo) . . .The biogenetic law as a proof of evolution is valueless."[22]

Creationists are up in arms about the evolutionists' use of recapitulation: "The 'biogenetic law' continues to be foisted upon the populace. And Haeckel's pictures will constitute proof even though his drawings were exposed as frauds by A. Brass in 1907. In spite of its disproof it will continue to be termed a 'law' because it proves the preconceived 'law' of evolution. While at the same time, the law of biogenesis (life cannot come from nonlife),

21. J. W. LEACH: _FUNCTIONAL ANATOMY--MAMMALIAN AND COMPARATIVE_ (N.Y.: MCGRAW HILL, 1961), P. 44.
22. W. R. THOMPSON: "INTRODUCTION," IN _THE ORIGIN OF SPECIES_ BY C. DARWIN (N.Y.: E. P. DUTTON, 1956).

a law scientifically established and verified,will only be given the status of a 'principle.'

"The only real evolutionary contribution of Haeckel was the slogan 'ontogeny recapitulates phylogeny.' Evolutionists seem to enjoy throwing words like these around as if concoctions of words alone prove their case. But learn this slogan. Use it. You'd be surprised how much respect you can gain by uttering it forth!

"No, it is not the creationist who is anti-intellectual. It is the materialist that uses as 'proofs' information that is offensive to a thinking person. Danson argues in *New Scientist*:

'. . . despite the hostility of the witness provided by the fossil record, despite the innumerable difficulties . . . evolution survives . . . Can there be any other area of science, for instance, in which a concept as intellectually barren as embryonic recapitulation could be used as evidence for a theory?'[23]

"The 'proof' from embryology as well as from similarity and vestigial organs simply consists of sloppy superficial so-called science and gaping unjustified extrapolations. These 'proofs' rely upon only that data that fits the preconceived materialistic dogma, and the rejection, alteration or ad hoc explanation of the data not consistent. If the case for evolution stands on these 'proofs,' there is no case.

"Evolutionists will continue to exclude the alternative explanation of origins, a creator, at the beginning then wonder why they do not find him at the end."

With this we end our survey of the evidence as it relates to the two propositions. With our succeeding and final chapter we will be invited to use the information we have become acquainted with to render a decision. Which of the two propositions, in light of the evidence, within the context of our prescribed methodology, comes out on top?

R. DANSON: NEW SCIENTIST, 49(1971):35.

22 {RENDERING A DECISION

Fredrich Nietzsche once wrote:

> "No one can draw more out of things, books included,
> than he already knows. A man has no ears for that to
> which experience has given him no access."

How true this is. Man is a captive of his own biases, a slave to
selfish prejudices. So much of what we see depends upon what we're
looking for. However, contrary to this pessimism, men have and do
rise above their own leanings. The combination to the lock that
imprisons us is: turn toward the desire for truth; turn away from
egotism; turn toward the willingness to act upon truth regardless
of what it is; turn away from the goal of simply saving face; turn
toward the eagerness to expose personal views to open dissection
and criticism; turn away from hiding cherished opinions from outside attack; turn toward letting the facts, reality, force the
conclusions; turn away from forcing conclusions on the facts.

We should all be interested in letting the creation-evolution
controversy do more than entertain us. The information we have
considered should, in conjunction with other facts we have at our
disposal, be used to reach a conclusion. It is true that it's
never too late to learn, let's not be among those who learn it too
late.

In this final chapter we will summarize arguments, dismiss
the complaint that "truth" on origins cannot be reached, and review some methodological guidelines to allow us to make a decision.

Extrapolations

Blum wrote:

> "All speculation regarding the origin of life is, of

course, essentially an extrapolation."[1]
No one observed the origin of life, therefore, one can only extrapolate backwards from present observations to a conclusion on how
life did originate. Likewise, no one has observed life from its
beginning to testify whether it has evolved or remained fixed. We
can only extrapolate to a conclusion from what we see today.

Similarly, no one has observed earth history throughout its
time, so one can only extrapolate from present data and observations to determine whether the earth has experienced uniformity
or catastrophe.

Both creationists and evolutionists extrapolate. For example,
here are some of the evolutionary extrapolations:

The fact that science has been able to remove the cloak of
mystery from many of life's processes through naturalistic explanations is taken as testimony that science will be able to explain
the origin of life through naturalistic mechanisms; Since tremendous strides have been made in science and technology since the
time of Darwin, then it follows that the evolutionary proposition
is a fruitful scientific idea; If amino acids arise in experimental
spark-discharge tubes, then they can form spontaneously in a primeval ocean; If amino acids can form in spark-discharge tubes,
then giant protein molecules, specifically sequenced, stereospecific and having tertiary structure can form by chance; If the
components of DNA can be experimentally synthesized, then huge
DNA molecules, stereospecific and specifically sequenced to carry
information exceeding that contained in millions of volumes of
encyclopedias can form by chance; Since proteins from living tissue
can be teased apart, randomly mixed, and then observed to orient
themselves in the orderly state they were in before being separated,
then spontaneously formed chemicals will automatically aggregate
and assume the symmetry and order characteristic of life;[2] Since
an event whose probability is 1/1,000 will change to 63/100 if
attempted 1,000 times, then likewise, no matter how improbable an
event is, its probability will increase to surety given sufficient
time and attempts; Since canyons are now being cut at a snail's
pace, erosion is only proceeding slowly and rocks are now only
being formed lazily, then this is the way earth history has always
proceeded; Since religion has always had to retreat whenever it
stuck its nose into science, it will be forced to retreat on the
issue of origins.

In his book, *The Origin of Life*, Keosian draws our attention
to the time in the past when life was made mystical because of the
belief that organic compounds could only be made through the cell.
He then states: ". . . now with abiotic synthesis life is no mystery!"[3] With this argument we are being led to believe that the

---

1. H. BLUM: _TIME'S ARROW AND EVOLUTION_ (PRINCETON, PRINCETON U.,
1968), P. 168.
2. M. CALVIN:"CHEMICAL EVOLUTION," IN _PROGRESS IN THEORETICAL
BIOLOGY_, 1 (1967):28,29.
3. J.KEOSIAN: _THE ORIGIN OF LIFE_ (N.Y.:REINHOLD,1968),PP. 15,16.

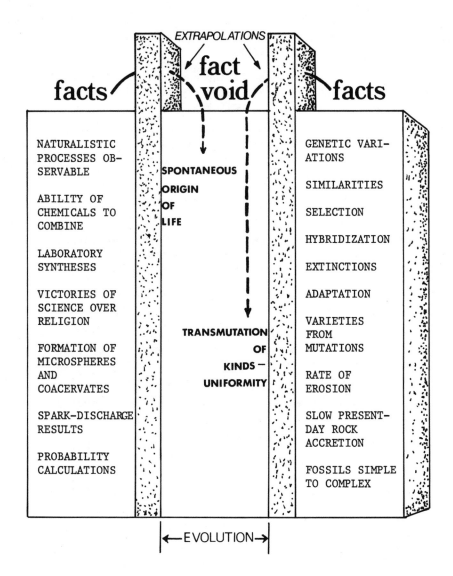

Fig. **132**-Evolutionary   Extrapolations
The tenets of evolution are (1) spontaneous origins; (2) trans-mutation of kinds and; (3) uniformity.   There is no direct evidence for the first two and, although there is direct evidence for uni-formity, there is no direct testimony it has always been true. Therefore, "proof" for evolution relies upon extrapolations from present knowns, to hypothetical unknowns.

ability of atoms to form organic molecules, like amino acids, proves their ability to spontaneously form life. There is, of course, much extrapolation necessary before one could conclude the spontaneous formation of life based upon what products have been obtained by abiotic syntheses.

In like manner, evolutionists extrapolate from the simple genetic variation we see occurring constantly in nature, to transmutations of kinds. The gap between what has been observed in genetics and what we are to believe occurred in the past is filled by reasonings, analogies and extrapolations. (Fig. 132)

On the other hand, creationists extrapolate in this way: Since man has been unable to synthesize life to this point in time, he will never do so; If intelligence is needed to form the components of life now, then intelligence would have been necessary in the beginning; Since DNA contains information, and information requires intelligence, DNA must have been created by intelligence; Since highly complex machines and structures require intelligence for their manufacturing, the complexity of the universe and life would likewise require intelligence for their formation; Since we have not yet found fossil transitional series between the various categories of life, no transitions exist; Since genetics has been unable to demonstrate the ability of organisms to vary limitlessly, organisms are bound to a law of fixity; Since fossilization today requires catastrophic burial, the vast fossil beds in the earth speak to an earth-wide catastrophe; Since practically every spontaneous thing we observe, in the absence of some kind of predesigned motor, runs down, decays, loses order, chemicals could never spontaneously wind themselves up into the order characteristic of life; Since mutations vitiate now, they always have vitiated, not invented improved, complexified. (Fig. 133)

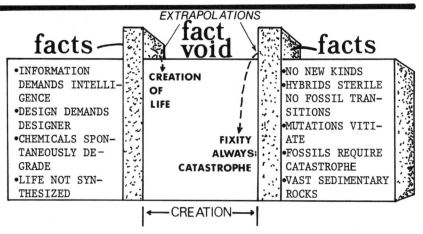

Fig .**133**-Creationistic   Extrapolations
Proof for creation is not direct. Rather, the "proof" depends upon extrapolations from present knowns to hypothetical unknowns.

Fig.134- Extrapolations from Variation
There is a remarkable degree of variety among dogs and cats. The evolutionist extrapolates to the conclusion that variety is limitless. The creationist extrapolates to the conclusion that variety is confined within the bounds of identifiable kinds, i.e., dogs stay dogs. cats stay cats. (Courtesy of Purina)

So it becomes obvious that any conclusion we reach on the controversy is an extrapolation. No one can brag of having reached an "absolute scientific truth" on the matter. Faith is involved. This need not discourage us. Actually almost all conclusions we reach in any field are extrapolations and require faith.

How do we know that if we throw a ball into the air, it will return to the ground? Are we not predicting, extrapolating from what we have had previous experience with, or from what we have been taught in school or told by others? How do we know that a stone tablet with writing on it unearthed from an archeological site is the product of human hands? Are we not extrapolating from what we know to be true now--that writing is only now being produced by humans? We make conclusions based upon extrapolations constantly, with ease and no compunction. Why distrust a conclusion on origins because it is an extrapolation?

This is not to say any extrapolation is valid. Extrapolations are legitimate only if the event they attempt to establish is practically possible. For example: Since it is possible for a man to jump six feet in the air, with time and training will he eventually be able to jump 20 feet, 50 feet, 100 feet or to the moon? If someone can lift five pounds, does this prove that one day he will be able to lift 1,000,000 pounds? If a coin is flipped and the 1/2 chance of obtaining heads is obtained twice in a row, does this prove he can flip heads a billion times in succession? If letters thrown haphazardly on the floor form the word "an," does this mean that a novel could be written by the same process?

So, an extrapolation can be valid and reasonable, or it can be nonsense, folly, gobledygook. When we extrapolate to a conclusion on origins, we must be sure our extrapolation is the best-- most in tune with the facts, the evidence, reality. The extrapolation that requires the least amount of extrapolation is the one we should opt for. In other words, if we flip heads with a coin once and predict that we can do it three times, this extrapolation is much more legitimate than the prediction that we can flip heads a billion times.

With this said, let's give the evolutionists and creationists each a chance to sum up their cases. We'll give each free license to throw their final punches. Let's first listen to the evolutionist.

Evolutionary Summation

"Why not accept evolution--which is an extension of naturalistic philosophy--when the present and the past have revealed continued naturalistic explanations for what is observed in the biological and physical worlds? True, experimental evidence may not be complete, but it has shown--contrary to creationists' hopes --that many of the components of life can be formed without inserting a supernatural creator. A list of chemical biases is growing that shows the chemicals of life are together as they are because they like it that way. Matter shows a predetermination toward forming life.

"Organisms are seen to vary freely and be influenced in their variations by the environment. Given time, and the proper environmental stresses, why couldn't life have evolved into the panorama of life we see today?

"Everywhere we look we see the operation of naturalism. Where is the hand of the creator in the orbiting of the planets, in the formation of a tornado, in the fury of a thunder storm, in the growth of a tomato, in the heat from the sun, in the etiology of diabetes, in the contagion of poliomyelitis, in the fall of darkness at the day's end, in the birth of a chicken from an egg or in the origin of life itself? Why the need to thrust the hand of a creator into what appears to be the natural outworking of natural processes?

"Just because I (evolutionist) cannot explain 'life' or 'consciousness' by studying the intracacies of the molecules that are organized in such a fashion as to result in 'life' or 'consciousness,' does not mean 'life' and 'consciousness' are not natural. Hydrogen and oxygen combine to form water which is 'wet.' The characteristics of hydrogen and oxygen do not help us to understand what 'wetness' is, but is 'wetness' not natural because it cannot be explained by reductionistic analysis? Does 'wetness,' because it cannot be explained by reductionism, point to a divine hand? If not, why should 'life' or 'consciousness' point to the divine?

"Evolution is unencumbered by the faith, emotionalism and bigotry of religion. Why is it that practically all modern scientists, philosophers and other men with high academic training opt for evolution? Evolution is so much a part of all scientific disciplines, that progress would stop if it were rejected. Blum expresses this sentiment:

> 'The concept is not unique to biology; the astonomer regards the universe in the same way, and the geologist, and others too, find evolution essential to the understanding of the broader aspects of their subjects.'[4]

"One final reason for rejecting creation: If a creator made everything, how do we account for disease, suffering, religious confusion and travail of men through the milleniums? Is not the creator responsible for these things? Are these not effects demanding a cause? Would he not be responsible for the gruesome parasitic relationships in nature, for the natural cataclysms that devastate populations, in short, would not these less pleasant characteristics of the 'creation' throw the existence of a creator into question?

"Evolution is unencumbered by the blind dogmas, rituals and mythologies of religion. Evolution, or naturalism, deals with what we can see, what we can test, not with a dimension to which

---

4. H. BLUM, (REF. 1) P. 3.

man has no access, the spiritual.

"All creationists try to do is poke holes in our arguments without offering any alternative except, 'God did it.' The creationistic reliance upon a supernatural being of unlimited resources allows them to escape from any difficulty. This reasoning makes anything and everything possible for them and impossible for us. Their solutions remind me of the answer to the puzzle: If a person is left in a room with no windows or doors, and there is a mirror on the wall and a table on the floor, how can he get out? The answer: Look in the mirror, see what he saw. Take the saw, cut the table in half. Two halves make a hole--crawl out through the hole!"

Creationistic Summation

"Rather than evolution being science, the exposé of, the objections to, the criticisms are science. Scientific facts, laws and principles must be dismissed or seriously altered and tampered with to maintain one's belief in evolution.

"The specific chemical precursors to the cell are known(remember, science means dealing with what is known, not unknown) to form naturally only through the cell itself. Therefore, the chemicals of life could not predate the cell. (Fig. 135) Life's chemicals

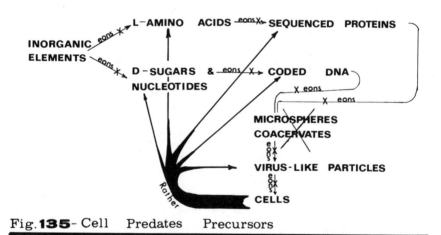

Fig. **135**- Cell Predates Precursors

could only arise after the cell. It follows from this that the real problem for evolutionists is explaining how a cell in all of its complexity could arise suddenly from simple inorganic atoms. However, even the most devout evolutionist, if not grossly naive, must concede that a cell could not arise suddenly and naturally from inorganic materials. The cell is far too complex, the probabilities too remote for such a 'natural supermiracle.' The sudden 'poof!' formation of a cell would demand a supernatural act by an agent with supernatural power and intelligence.

"In like manner, the physiological and anatomical integration in organisms, the ecological interdependence and the interdependence of the physical world with natural laws, speak to sudden "poof!" creation. Since no part of the universe is autonomous, but rather vitally dependent upon the simultaneous existence of other parts and laws, they all must have been formed relatively quickly and simultaneously.

"We are therefore forced to invoke 'poof!' creation. That a creator could have sufficient competence to perform such a feat is difficult to imagine. Nevertheless, since the speed of any synthesis or construction is dependent upon the expertise and effort applied, an omnipotent creator, by definition could hold the competence.

"Consideration of probabilities, molecular stereospecificity, the principles of information science as they apply to the formation and modification of DNA, the futility of biochemical bias, mutations and natural selection, evidences of design, the law of mass action, the hostility of the primitive environment and its effect upon chemical kinetics and concentrations, the law of biogenesis, the laws of thermodynamics, the transcendent un-reductionistic nature of life, the paleontological and geological evidence against uniformity and for a world flood, evidence for a recent creation, and much more, best fit creation.

"True, one is free to still believe in evolution but it appears he must simply give up math, physics, chemistry, thermodynamics, etc., to keep the faith. Time is no panacea either, for how can time change laws that clearly say no to evolution?

"Considering the evidences for creation, the questions loom over us: Why do people believe evolution? Why is it taught? Why are contrary positions and facts suppressed?

"The testimony for creation is so blatant, the failure to see it can only be due to a blindness of some sort or failure to be truly honest. The dishonesty is inexcusable. Blindness, if it is not by design, can be understood. Why? Simply because the facts in support of creation are suppressed in education at all levels. On the other hand, evolutionism is rampant. Many scientists and laymen who believe in evolution are honest, intelligent and sincere. They have merely been brainwashed by an evolutionary educational-social-political world system. They are, in effect, blinded by naturalistic philosophy. The same type of blindness, the same syndrome is common with racists, religionists and political activists. For most, not realizing the seriousness of origins, they become imprisoned, indoctrinated and, in turn, well intentioned missionaries naively spreading the same dogmas they have been subtly coerced to believe.

"But when you think about it, the evidence for creation is not really suppressed. It is all about us. The Earth, Universe and life are all design. Those who cannot see this are diseased with the contagion of spiritual blindness that comes from social and educational immersion and baptism in naturalistic philosophy.

"Life is here, it is reality, it is an effect. All real effects have a real cause, ergo, life must have a real cause. The character of life, its orderliness and complexity, points to a cause that is not only real, but highly intelligent. Any other proposed cause would be glaringly inept.

"There is much insight on the nature of the creator that can be learned simply by applying cause and effect relationships. Some examples are: The cause of time-space infinity must be infinite and eternal; The cause of perfect order must be orderly; The cause of life must be alive; The cause of aesthetic values must be aesthetic; The cause of morality must be moral; The cause of free will must be volitional; The cause of infinite energy must be omnipotent; The cause of love must have love; The cause of science must be scientific; The cause of communication skills must communicate. Thus, although limited as to details, there is much that reason alone can reveal to us about our creator. Since each of the effects we have listed is real, we must impute their cause to atoms (an absurdity since we would end up with living, moral, communicating, aesthetic atoms), or to a creator personage.

"Everyone concludes naturally and comfortably that highly or- dered and designed items (machines, houses, etc.) owe existence to a designer. It is unnatural to conclude otherwise. But evolu- tion asks us to break stride from what is natural to believe and then believe in that which is unnatural, unreasonable and . . . unbelievable.

- HOUSE(ORDERED EFFECT)······DEMANDS·······A COMPETENT CAUSE-- INTELLIGENCE

- COMPUTER SYSTEM(MORE········DEMANDS·······A COMPETENT CAUSE-- ORDERED EFFECT)   MORE INTELLIGENCE

- LIFE(A VASTLY ORDERED······DEMANDS·······A COMPETENT CAUSE-- EFFECT)   VAST INTELLIGENCE

- CHAOS AND DEGRADATION······DEMANDS·······A COMPETENT CAUSE-- (AN EFFECT WITH NO ORDER)   NATURAL, MINDLESS SPONTANEOUS PROCESSES

"We are told by some that all of reality--the universe, life, etc.--is without an initial cause. But, since the universe oper- ates by cause and effect relationships, how can it be argued from science--which is a study of that very universe--that the universe is without an initial cause? Or, if the evolutionist cites a cause, he cites either eternal matter or energy.   Then he has suggested a cause far less than the effect.

"The basis for this departure from what is natural and reason- able to believe is not fact, observation or experience but rather unreasonable extrapolations from abstract probabilities mathemat- ics and philosophy.

"There was a recent television program covering the intriguing questions raised by Stone Henge in Great Britain. The initial question concerning it was who or what had formed it. The ordered, patterned, designed, and meaningful arrangements of concentric rocks and holes, even allowing certain astronomical predictions, pointed unequivocally to an intelligent cause. Scientists were in agreement on this. There remain many questions still unresolved: How were the rocks moved into place? How did ancient men possess knowledge enabling them to construct an astronomical observatory? Why was it built? But the fact remains, scientists concur, mind was the cause of Stone Henge.

"This television commentary presented a situation paralleling the question of the origin of life. We see life and ask the question as to what formed it. We examine life, observe its functions, contemplate complexity that defies duplication by intelligent men, and what are we to conclude? Well, Stone Henge could have been formed by the erosion of a mountain, hurricanes and tidal waves moving stones into place, and meteorites forming the ring of holes. But never once was this possibility even mentioned by the television commentator. And surely, no scientist has seriously entertained the notion. With the question of the origin of life, hundreds of thousands of people are not only entertaining the notion that life is accounted for by blind mindless physical processes, but advocating it as fact, as the pure, scientific and only reasonable truth.

"In the 1973 edition of the *Encyclopedia Britannica*, in the section on 'Intelligent Life Beyond the Solar System,' is a photograph of the earth in the vicinity of Ontario, Canada from a Tiros weather satellite. Faintly visible is a crisscross pattern. The caption to the photograph reads: 'The crisscross pattern in white shows logging swaths, a sign of intelligent life on earth.'[5] This is taken as an example of how space explorers might be able to discern whether intelligence is on another planet. In other words, a few parallel lines indicate intelligence! If this be true, and the relative simplicity of Stone Henge demands an intelligent cause, then would it not be the height of absurdity to 'look down upon' life and conclude anything but that its cause is likewise intelligent? (Fig. 136)

"Calvin, in his book, *Chemical Evolution*, discusses at some length the possibility of life on other planets. Therein he discusses the hope of receiving signals from intelligent life elsewhere in the universe. The deciding factor as to whether signals originate with intelligence, or are emanating from an unintelligent source, is order in the signals in the form of a decipherable code.[6] So a sign of intelligence is order and codes! Is not DNA

---

5. *C. SAGAN: "EXTRATERRESTRIAL LIFE," IN* ENCYCLOPEDIA BRITANNICA, *13 (1973):1086.*

6. *M. CALVIN:* CHEMICAL EVOLUTION *(N.Y.: OXFORD U., 1969), PP. 243-248, AND APPENDIX.*

414

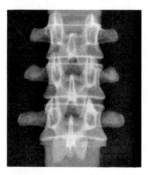

Fig. **136** - Signs of Intelligence
The top photograph is from a Tiros weather satellite, of a region in Ontario. The parallel lines in the upper left hand corner(logging swaths) are a sign of intelligent life on earth. Scientists look for similar signs on other planets to indicate intelligent life. The bottom photograph is a radiograph of three human lumbar vertebrae. Do the parallel lines and order seen here suggest an intelligent creator? (Top photo. Courtesy NASA)

a code? Is not life the pinnacle of orderliness? Must we not attribute the existence of life and its encoded molecules to an intelligent source as well? Calvin unintentionally implies that we should do that, but spends hundreds of pages in the same book trying to prove life has an unintelligent source!

"By applying everyday practical experience and common sense, the evolutionist's proposition is reduced to absurdity. That not only science, but almost the entire world has embraced the evolutionary notion as the explanation for the origin of life is the most baffling and gross intellectual inconsistency ever adopted by the human race. It is truly incredible how much intelligence has been used to prove a lot of nonsense.

"For those familiar with the very real mechanistic and probabilistic difficulties in evolution there is nothing for them but to accept creation or invoke infinite improbabilities. I (creationist) once talked with a graduate student who was a devout evolutionist. I acquainted him with some of the more difficult objections to the evolutionary proposition but he continued to maintain that time and probability were the key. I then looked around the room and drew his attention to an electric typewriter.

"I said to him: 'Suppose that you visited me this evening and, having never seen a typewriter, asked me what was the strange machine on the desk. I turned the machine on, inserted some paper and demonstrated how it worked by spinning out a quick Pulitzer Prize winner. In amazement you looked on. Dying of curiosity you asked, "Where did you get such a thing?" Oh, I would say, well a long long long time ago my great-great-great-great-grandfather took pieces of chrome, iron, silicon, cloth and other materials and put them all in a large vat and sealed it. He then heated it, cooled it and shook it. Each succeeding son had his try at subjecting the vat to various other physical abuses. The vat was irradiated, bombarded with electrical discharges, heated, cooled, vacumized, pressurized, and what have you. Last week, I could stand it no longer, I took a torch, opened the vat, and lo and behold--an electric typewriter, cord and all! Would you believe such a story?'

"He said, smiling, 'No!'

"'How then can you believe that life, which dwarfs the typewriter in complexity to an exceeding degree, could get here by like random processes?'

"'Well,' he said, 'given enough time and the infinitudes of space I believe a typewriter could spontaneously arise.'

"'Do you believe then that somewhere in space there is such a typewriter floating around?'

"'Yep,' he said boldly, gaining confidence.

"Of course, I then had nothing left but to ask him if he thought it were in English.

"Questioning others along a similar line reveals that floating in space are not only typewriters, but television sets, couches, chairs, radios, automobiles (442's with four on the floor, of course), mixmasters and toasters. No wonder there is such great danger in space travel!

"Wald, in discussing the possibility of viable biochemicals arising spontaneously, wrote:

'What we ask is to synthesize organic molecules without such a machine. I believe this to be the most stubborn problem that confronts us--the weakest link at present in our argument. I do not think it by any means disastrous, but it calls for phenomena and forces some of which are as yet only partly understood and some probably still to be discovered.'[7]

The professor does not explain away the 'stubborn problem' through science, facts, data, etc. . . . instead he finds it necessary to invoke unknown and 'partly understood' forces of nature.

"Invoking the unknown is an evolutionary ploy. The problems in the evolutionary position are very real, natural and scientific. The supposed basis for materialistic philosophy is nature, the known, the scientific. How can what is unknown about nature-- 'unknown and partly understood forces'--be submitted as proof for evolution when it is what is known from nature that is heralded as the definitive testimony to the factualness of the proposition? If it is proper to invoke unknown forces to prove a position, then any position can be so 'proven,' e.g., man coming from cheese.

"Has not the evolutionist also contradicted himself by invoking the unknown as proof for his case, while at the same time berating creationists because they deal with the supernatural, the 'unknown?'

"Now let's turn our attention to another scientist, Robert Tocquet. Speaking of the chemicals of life, he states:

'The inclusion of nucleins, glucosides, lipides, etc., besides the many varieties of protein, which are all substances distributed in the precise order appropriate to the performance of vital functions and to psychic expression, calls for so complex a coordination of physico-chemical factors, that, to put it simply, reason is offended by the assumption of such an accumulation of "natural miracles!"'[8]

"Life is a miracle, as even the evolutionist is able to see. Not only the origin of life speaks to the miraculous, but so does everyday observable growth and reproduction. Man is vividly incapable of duplicating, or even clearly explaining, the structure and physiology of a simple blade of grass.

"What is a miracle? Is it not a departure from the natural? So a miracle cannot be a 'natural miracle' (a natural unnaturalism), as Tocquet argues. 'Natural' and 'miracle' are opposites . . . antithetical. Life being a miracle means that it is <u>un</u>natural. Then life is <u>un</u>naturalism which is the same as <u>un</u>materialism which

---

7. G. WALD: "THE ORIGIN OF LIFE," IN <u>THE PHYSICS AND CHEMISTRY OF LIFE</u> (N.Y.: SIMON AND SCHUSTER, 1955), P. 9.

8. R. TOCQUET: <u>LIFE ON THE PLANETS</u>(N.Y.: GROVE,1962), P. 33.

is the same as <u>un</u>evolutionism! What does all this add up to? Evolution is <u>un</u>done.

"Regarding the transformation of kinds, the burden is upon the evolutionist to show that transformations have or do happen. This he has not done. The fossil record and the whole of genetics testifies to fixity of basic types. The evolutionist must imagine links for which there is not evidence of existence, the creationist rests his case on what is evident--fixity.

"Perhaps religionists have been wrong in the past, this does not force the conclusion that everything a creationist says will be in error. Evolutionists are guilty of perpetrating outright frauds to attempt proof of their position. What about Nebraska man, Piltdown man, Heidelberg man and all of the reconstructions that are taken as proof that man has an ape-like ancestry? These "precursors" even have true humans coming before them according to their own geological time-scale.

"What about the junk that was dredged up from the ocean's bottom, given the name *Bathybius haeckelii*, described as moving, responding to stimuli, assimilating food, and considered the 'mother of protoplasm?' This amorphous material was thought to be the evolutionary mother of life itself, but had to be abandoned when chemical analysis showed it to be a precipitate of calcium sulphate deposited when alcohol was added to ocean water. Not even a trace of organic material was found.[9] Thus, *Bathybius haeckelii*, like all evolutionary links, came to an inglorious end.

"So, are evolutionary guesses immune from being pushed aside with the advancement of scientific knowledge?

"Evolution may be more popular, may be more widely taught than creation, but if 50 million people say a foolish thing, it is still a foolish thing. Popularity means nothing relative to truth. As for the notion that scientific progress would stalemate if creation were accepted, we must ask then how science ever developed in the first place.

"Modern science was primarily developed within Christendom at a time when creationism was taken seriously and literally. Most of the fathers of the various scientific disciplines were creationists. Some examples are: Cuvier, d'Archiac, d'Orbigny, Barrande, Pictet, Murchison, Agassiz, Forbes and Sedgwick--fathers of comparative anatomy and paleontology (fossil study); John Ray--founder of systematic botany; Davy--chemist and discoverer of potassium and sodium; Boyle--one of the founders of modern chemistry; Joule--physicist and discoverer of the first law of thermodynamics; Kelvin--physicist and discoverer of the second law of thermodynamics and telegraphic instruments; Galileo--father of mechanics and experimental physics; Kepler--father of modern dynamical astronomy; Faraday--physicist and discoverer of electrolysis, the power generator and electromagnetic fields; Maxwell--physicist and developer

---

9. *C. P. IDYLL: <u>ABYSS--THE DEEP SEA AND THE CREATURES THAT LIVE IN IT</u> (N.Y.: CROWELL, 1971), P. 236.*

of the unifying concept of the electromagnetic theory of light; Samuel Morse--inventor of the telegraph; Newton--physicist, mathematician and originator of the binomial theorem, differential calculus and the reflecting telescope as well as discoverer of the nature of white light, colors and the gravitational forces on the moon; Pasteur--chemist, microbiologist and discoverer of the microbial nature of disease, vaccines, stereochemistry and pasteurization; and, of course, the recent scientists Einstein and Von Braun have espoused belief in a creator.

"So the majority of modern scientific advancement is based upon discoveries and scientific methods originated by creationists.

"As for the allegation that science could not advance without evolution, at least two highly respected scientists disagree. Bounoure, Director of Research at the National Center of Scientific Research in France, stated:

> 'Evolutionism is a fairy tale for grown-ups. This theory has helped nothing in the progress of science. It is useless.' 10

Heribert Nilsson has similar sentiments:

> '. . . the evolution theory can by no means be regarded as an innocuous natural philosophy, but that it is a serious obstruction to biological research. It obstructs --as has been repeatedly shown--the attainment of consistent results, even from uniform experimental material. For everything must ultimately be forced to fit this theory. An exact biology cannot, therefore, be built up.' 11

"Which scientifically established truth supposedly owing its existence to evolutionary philosophy could not as well have been elucidated within the framework of creationism?

"It is true that creation implies religion, but so does evolution. Evolution can be thought of as sort of a magical religion.

"Magic is simply an effect without a cause, or at least a competent cause. 'Chance,' 'time' and 'nature' are the gods enshrined at evolutionary temples. Yet these gods cannot explain the origin of life. These gods are impotent. Thus, evolution is left without competent cause and is, therefore, only a magical explanation for the existence of life. And, like other cultures practicing magic, evolution has its witch doctors. But their dance is not performed in the glimmer of bonfires, rather, it is performed in the various temples found on campuses around the world, in subsidized research institutions and in the light cast by spark discharge tubes. The incantations and ravings can be heard by simply listening to the radio, watching the television, or reading a child's biology text.

"Is it not fairy tales that spin wild yarns of physical trans-

---

10. *LE MONDE ET LA VIE* (OCTOBER, 1963).
11. *H. NILSSON: SYNTHETISCHE ARTBILDUNG* (LUND,SWEDEN:GLEERUP,1954)P.

formations--mice into horses, gingerbread into men, children into spiders? Of course, it is not the fairy's word or a witch's spell that causes evolutionary transformation, it is the intellectually acceptable power of the star dust of the time-chance-nature diety.

"Those who doubt, who lack faith in the rites of the evolutionary high priests are fitting only for exorcism: the exorcism of the spirit of an open mind, and the possession by the spiritual dogma: 'Since life is here, life evolved.'

"Evolutionists attribute to time, chance and nature the capacities that creationists attribute to God. Time, chance, and nature is the holy pagan trinity of the evolutionist. But this trinity has not left the materialist with a revelation as to how the creation was accomplished. When examined closely, this three-headed god provides the power for degeneration and decay rather than complexification and synthesis. Rather a traitorous religion this evolutionary trinitarianism.

"Evolution requires plenty of faith: a faith in L-proteins that defy chance formation; a faith in the formation of DNA codes which if generated spontaneously would spell only pandemonium; a faith in a primitive environment that in reality would fiendishly devour any chemical precursors to life; a faith in experiments that prove nothing but the need for intelligence in the beginning; a faith in a primitive ocean that would not thicken but would only hopelessly dilute chemicals; a faith in natural laws including the laws of thermodynamics and biogenesis that actually deny the possibility for the spontaneous generation of life; a faith in future scientific revelations that when realized always seem to present more dilemmas to the evolutionist; faith in probabilities that treasonously tell two stories--one denying evolution, the other confirming the creator; faith in transformations that remain fixed; faith in mutations and natural selection that add to a double negative for evolution; faith in fossils that embarrassingly show fixity through time, regular absence of transitional forms and striking testimony to a world-wide water deluge; a faith in time which proves to only promote degradation in the absence of mind; and faith in reductionism that ends up reducing the materialist's arguments to zero and forcing the need to invoke a supernatural creator.

"The evolutionary religion is consistently inconsistent. Scientists rely upon the rational order of the universe to make accomplishments, yet the evolutionist tells us the rational universe had an irrational beginning from nothing. Due to a lack of understanding about mechanisms and structure, science cannot even create a simple twig. Yet the evolutionary religion speaks with bold dogmatism about the origin of life. Ontogeny (observed, testable, calculable, individual life history) is not understood, but the evolutionist boasts of his knowledge of phylogeny (unobserved, untested, unknown evolutionary ancestral history). The evolutionist insists that only evolutionists can competently criticize evolution; however, non-scientists are free to write and expound pro-evolutionism.

"Although it claims to, the evolutionary religion offers no real hope or salvation for man. Sagan argues that biological existence and hope lies with the birth and death of stars like our sun. The births of stars, by their mutagenic rays, 'generate the planetary nurseries of life, and the hope for intelligent beings is that 'they may at least derive some comfort from the thought that the death of their star, the event that will cause their own extinction, will, nevertheless, provide the means for continued biological advance of the starfolk on a million other worlds.'[12]

"Somehow the evolutionist expects us to take hope and derive comfort from the knowledge that if our star dies and we are all annihilated, the energy derived from the explosion of our bodies will help generate and mutate some other starfolk! Some religion, some hope!

"Problems that exist in the world do not cancel the existence of a creator any more than a murder in a house proves that the house was not built by an architect.

"In considering present world conditions, one might ask why, if man did spring from monkey, didn't he spring far enough, or, put another way, if man descended from the monkey, when is he going to quit descending?

"But the evolutionary religion is not without its optimistic prophets. However, as the author Philip Hughes stated:
'A philosophical fancy, which is admittedly unsupported by any demonstrative evidence, can scarcely be accepted as offering substantial encouragement to believe that mankind is steadily advancing towards the goal of a good state.'[13]

"So why is evolution believed? Some believe because their scientific training and work is so highly specialized that they cannot through overview see the contradictory issues . . . it's the ole 'can't see the forest for the trees' problem. Scientists in each narrowed corner simply assume that other scientists in other narrowed corners have the proofs all worked out. Few have ever seen in perspective the real issues. Few scientists have knowledge of, or have come to grips with problems like the circle reasoning in the geological column, the contradictions between evolution and biogenesis, or the second law of thermodynamics, or information science, the implications of the mechanism of fossilization, or the fossil contradictions. In fact, when renowned scientists are faced with these problems they are usually dumbfounded and whirl in the disbelief that such information has not been circulated.

"There is one final point. The evidence provides a final reason for rejecting so-called theistic evolution. This compromising position, first inaugurated by Aristotle, suffers from the logical

12. C.SAGAN: *THE COSMIC CONNECTION* (N.Y.: DELL, 1973), P. 262.
13. P.E.HUGHES: *CHRISTIANITY AND THE PROBLEM OF ORIGINS* (PHILADELPHIA: PRESBYTERIAN AND REFORMED, 1973), P. 12.

fallacy of 'misuse of contradictory alternatives,' the belief in antithetical positions, or, this is kind of like believing that if you set white and black balls side by side they become grey. Now, we have found that there is no scientific evidence for evolution. Thus, theistic evolution finds no basis in logic or in science. If evolution has occurred, be it materialistic or theistic, where is the evidence? Surely a vast all-pervading uniform evolutionary process operating through eons of time would have left some signs. But there seem to be none. On the other hand, there is much to force us to the conclusions that history has been ununiform, being marked by at least one great world catastrophe, that basic kinds of life are fixed and that there was a sudden miraculous and com- plete creation. There is no need to dub evolution with the finger of the creator. Evolution is wrong. To associate a crea- tor with it would throw him into suspect. "

Predictive Value

A characteristic of truth is its ability to make predictions which realize fulfillment, or consistency, with actual facts. If we make as many predictions as we can from each model and set these against pertinent evidence from the real world, we should be able to tell which position is most consistent with the data. The more correct position would find itself less often in the position of having to "explain" and "tailor" the facts to make them consistent with the model. The proposition best predicting the evidence could be judged the more useful scientific tool. The proposition having to continually rework or omit the facts becomes a cumbersome scien- tific appendage that always gets in the way. (Fig. 137)

Making the Tally

We agreed in the beginning, in the chapter on Methodology, that there were only two possible explanations for the origin of life. If we reject evolution, we are left with creation; if we reject creation, we are left with evolution. To decide which position is more likely true, we simply decide which proposition is most consistent with the facts as we know them. Just as we did in the Gnoof-Xert controversy, we look at the tally after we have made the listing, and formulate our conclusion.

It will be proper to cite deficiencies in the evolutionary proposition as testimony for the truthfulness of creation, and vice versa. Is not the ascertaining of truth often dependent upon seeing weaknesses in a position, and as a consequence, forc- ing a reevaluation of former conclusions? Price puts it this way in describing scientific investigation:

". . . it appears to me that you can very seldom conduct

Fig. **137**- Predictions   VS   Evidence

pREdicTiONs: dATA:

cr·ETERNAL OMNIPOTENT CREATOR ev·ETERNAL MATTER	►	UNIVERSE BEGAN; MATTER DEGRADES; LIFE HIGHLY ORDERED
c NATURAL LAWS AND CHARACTER OF MATTER UNCHANGING e MATTER AND LAWS EVOLVE	►	LAWS CONSTANT; MATTER CONSTANT; NO NEW LAWS
c TREND TOWARD DEGRADATION e TREND TOWARD ORDER	►	SECOND LAW OF THERMODYNAMICS
c CREATION OF LIFE THE ONLY POSSIBILITY e SPONTANEOUS GENERATION PROBABLE	►	BIOCHEMICAL IMPROBABILITIES
c LIFE UNIQUE e LIFE-MATTER CONTINUUM	►	LIFE-MATTER GAP; BIOCHEMICALS FORMED NATURALLY FROM NONLIFE
c NO CURRENT CREATION e CONTINUAL CREATION	►	FIRST LAW OF THERMODYNAMICS
c LIFE ETERNAL e LIFE BEGAN	►	LAW OF BIOGENESIS
c BASIC CATEGORIES OF LIFE UNRELATED e ALL LIFE RELATED	►	LAW OF BIOGENESIS; REVERSION TO TYPE; FOSSIL GAPS; HETEROGENEITY; SIMILARITIES
c WORLD CATASTROPHE e UNIFORMITY	►	FOSSILS; SEDIMENTARY STRATA; FROZEN MUCK; PRESENT UNIFORMITY
c ORGANS ALWAYS COMPLETE e GRADUAL EVOLUTION OF ORGANS	►	ORGANS ALWAYS FULLY DEVELOPED; NATURAL SELECTION CULLS
c MUTATIONS HARMFUL e MUTATIONS CAN IMPROVE	►	MUTATIONS VITIATE; LAWS OF INFORMATION SCIENCE
c LANGUAGE, ART AND CIVILI- ZATION SUDDEN e CIVILIZATION GRADUAL	►	ARCHEOLOGY AND ANTHROPOLOGY SHOW CIVILIZATION SUDDEN
c MAN UNIQUE e MAN AN ANIMAL	►	MAN-ANIMAL SIMILARITIES, ALSO GAP: ART, LANGUAGE, RELIGION
c DESIGN MANIFEST e NATURALISM	►	LIFE COMPLEX AND HIGHLY ORDERED; NATURAL SYNTHESES

experiments that prove anything. All you can do is arrange an experiment (in our case an evaluation of the data) that will disprove one of the possible points of view."[14]

Is not the real error the persisting in a proposition to the point of twisting data to conformity so that the proposition remains inviolate? Have we not shown the error in a position if the alleged evidences supposedly showing it true are found to be fallacious? If we see that the tally seems to be going in the wrong direction for us, why not take the trouble to notice we may be facing the wrong direction?

One additional point to remember before making a decision. If the data does not support our belief, yet we cling to our preconceptions, what does our belief become? Would it not be a blind, credulous and, depending upon the vigor with which we defended it, fanatical religious faith? If we accept the proposition most consistent with the data would this not be the honest, rational, scientific approach? (Fig. 138)

Truth   on   Origins

Some, however, will still balk at making a decision. They argue: "Isn't it egotistical for man to feel he can know truth? Who is to say we have all the facts? How do we know that 'truth' is not merely an illusion, a passing fancy, a will-o'-the-wisp like old scientific 'truths' such as the flat earth, a geocentric universe, the corpuscular nature of light, phlogistan and ether? Why, who is to say what future science will reveal? In any investigation, do we not simply show the sufficiency of an explanation? Sufficiency does not mean necessity."

The answers to these questions lie with the asking of others. Most who have read these pages have previously passed many grades in school. Many have even accomplished several years of college work. But to pass grades at any level requires our submission to evidence and acquiescence to "truths." We have believed and submitted to truths revealed to us from language, mathematics, physics, chemistry, history, economics, biology, sociology, etc. And this we have done willingly, with confidence and often with much less investigation and thought than was required to digest the evidence outlined in this book. The very fact that we pass grades testifies to our acceptance of basic truths. Why then can we not make a decision on origins?

If our efforts were directed toward, for example, proving that the force of the wind depends upon invisible atoms, would you hesitate to accept this thesis if all of our current knowledge supported it? How about if we similarly attempted to prove the

---

14.   *N.W.PIRIE IN THE ORIGINS OF PREBIOLOGICAL SYSTEMS AND THEIR MOLECULAR MATRICES, ED. S.W.FOX (N.Y.: ACADEMIC, 1965), P. 56.*

CREATION - EVOLUTION   EVIDENCE

1. BIOCHEMICAL STEREOSPECIFICITY
2. PROTEIN AND DNA PROBABILITIES
3. DNA AND INFORMATION SCIENCE
4. EFFECT OF MUTATIONS
5. GENETIC AND FOSSIL FIXITY
6. LACK OF TRANSITIONS
7. REVERSION TO TYPE
8. BIOCHEMICAL BIAS
9. COMPLEX ORGANS AND RELATIONSHIPS
10. SELFISH NATURAL SELECTION VS SELFLESS REPRODUCTION
11. MASS ACTION VS AQUEOUS SYNTHESIS
12. SECOND LAW OF THERMODYNAMICS
13. NEED FOR INTELLIGENT MANEUVERINGS IN EXPERIMENTS
14. REDUCTIONISM
15. LAW OF BIOGENESIS
16. EFFECT OF TIME
17. LIFE VERIFIED TO ONLY ABOUT 3000 BC
18. FOSSILS LOOK LIKE MODERN FORMS
19. PRE-CAMBRIAN VOID
20. FIRST LAW OF THERMODYNAMICS
21. EFFECT CANNOT BE GREATER THAN CAUSE
22. PRESENT-DAY UNIFORMITY
23. FOSSIL GRAVEYARDS SUGGESTING CATASTROPHE
ETC. . . . .

CREATION: EVOLUTION:

CREATION:	EVOLUTION:
1.	1.
2.	2.
3.	3.
4.	4.
5.	5.
6.	6.
etc.	etc.

Fig. **138** The Tally

If we wish to make a decision on the controversy, we simply list the evidence under the proposition it best fits. The reader may wish to extend the list. Nevertheless, in the end we should accept the proposition most consistent with the data and reject the proposition contradicted by the data.

existence of the invisible force of gravity? If the data supported its existence, if effects pointed to this force as the cause, would you not make a commitment? Would you not believe? In the same vein, if we set about the task of proving that metal is mostly composed of space,the space between and within atoms (if 200 million pounds of concrete were condensed, the resultant mass could fit in a pencil eraser), and the evidence bore this out, even though we have no direct observational basis and the notion is counter to human sensation--all metal feels solid--would we not accept it as true? We must all answer yes to these questions for we have all accepted these truths in our schooling.

It must necessarily follow, even though the cause of creation is a cause unseen, for there are no direct observations of who or what created, that we must be unhypocritical and not apply a double standard to the resolving of origins. We have no ego objection to accepting a round earth, nor do we refuse to accept this truth because of what "science may reveal in the future." No more, no less is expected on the issue of origins.

True, we cannot be totally dogmatic and argue that all of the ideas we presently hold are fixed and immutable. But this does not stop us from believing that the earth is round or that order is the opposite of disorder or that two plus two is four. We believe basic truths because they consistently ring true with reality. No facsimile of normal human life, let alone scientific progress, would be possible without such submission.

Rene Descartes said: ". . . when it is not in our power to determine what is true, we ought to follow what is most probable . . ." If one or the other of the propositions on origins proves totally consistent with reality, why not accept it? To refuse to can only be an emotional reaction, not a scientific one, for all of science demands submission to that which is most certain. To argue an erroneous position, or neutrality, after examining the evidences and then to flaunt either of these views as honest and open-minded smells of intellectual halitosis.

Hesitancy to decide on the issue of origins can be only a reaction, emotionally, against the implications of believing either creation or evolution. After putting two and two together, we may wish we had kept them apart. This common reaction proves the thesis we made in the opening chapters of this book, i.e., origins is not a bland, isolated academic matter. It has profound effects upon each of us personally.

This tells us something. The importance of the controversy compels us to make an informed decision, a decision that is as correct as we can make it. Ignorance is only an opiate that lulls an inquiring mind to sleep. However, it seems that often the least popular item on the menu is food for thought, especially if it gives us tastes we are not accustomed to.

We should remember that although truth may hurt, it is the lie that scars us. Reworking our conclusions on the matter of origins may be traumatic for us. Submitting to the truth may be difficult. We may be left with the feeling that just when we think we have all the answers, some jerk changes the questions. Nonetheless, realizing the far-reaching influence our position on origins has on our lives, we are compelled to follow through with an honest and open-minded decision.

ᴄAPPENDIX

Most of the references cited throughout this book have been either neutral or sympathetic to the evolutionary position. Any who wish to pursue evolutionary argumentation can consult the bibliography. It is extremely difficult to gain access to scientific literature critical of evolution or published material that is pro-creationism. For this reason I make the following list for those who wish to pursue the scientific aspects of creationism. Some of these references discuss both creation and evolution but opt for creation, others are simply critical of certain aspects of evolution without advocating creation as an option:

Acts and Facts 2716 Madison Ave., San Diego, California: Institute for Creation Research)--Periodical.

Barnes, Thomas G.: Origin and Destiny of the Earth's Magnetic Field (San Diego: Institute for Creation Research,1973).

Barzun, Jacques: Darwin, Marx, Wagner (New York: Doubleday, 1958).

Bernhard, R.: "Thinking the Unthinkable--Are Evolutionists Wrong," in Scientific Research, 4 (9-1-69):28.

Bible-Science Newsletter (Box 1016, Caldwell, Idaho: Bible-Science Association)--Periodical.

Blick, E. F.: "The Second Law of Thermodynamics and Living Organisms," Paper presented at Entropy in Life session of the American Society for Engineering Education 82nd Annual Conference, Rensselaer Polytechnic Institute

(Troy, New York, June 18, 1974).

Bliss, R.: "Can Science Teachers Change Their Attitudes Toward the Teaching of Origins in the Classroom?" in Wisconsin Society of Science Teachers Newsletter, 13 (Jan., 1972):4.

Blum, Harold F.: Time's Arrow and Evolution (Princeton: Princeton University Press, 1962).

Bonner, J.T.: "Review of Kerkut's Book," in American Scientist, 49 (1969):240.

Clark, Harold W.: Fossils, Flood and Fire (Escondido, Calif.: Outdoor Pictures, 1968).

Clark, Robert E.D.: Darwin: Before and After (Chicago: Moody Press, 1967); The Universe: Plan or Accident (Grand Rapids: Zondervan, 1972).

Cook, Melvin A.: Prehistory and Earth Models (London: Max Parrish Co., 1966).

Coppedge, James: Evolution: Possible or Impossible? (Grand Rapids: Zondervan, 1973).

Cousins, Frank W.: Fossil Man (Hants, England: Evolution Protest Movement, 1966).

Creation Research Society Quarterly (2717 Cranbrook Rd., Ann Arbor, Mich.: Creation Research Society)--Periodical.

The Creationist (P.O.Box 173, Malverne, N.Y.: Christian Evidence League)--Periodical.

Daly, Reginald: Earth's Most Challenging Mysteries (Nutley, N.J.: Craig Press, 1972.

Davidheiser, Bolton: Evolution and Christian Faith (Nutley, N.J.: Presbyterian and Reformed Publ. Co., 1969).

Dewar, Douglas: The Transformist Illusion (Murfreesboro, Tenn.: DeHoff Publ., 1965).

Dewit, Duyvenne J.J.: A New Critique of the Transformist Principle in Evolutionary Biology (Kampen, Neth.; Kok, 1965).

Doorway Papers (P. O. Box 291, Brockville, Ontario Canada: A. C. Custance)--Periodical.

England, D.: A Christian View of Origins (Grand Rapids: Baker, 1972).

Enoch, H.: Evolution or Creation (Madras: Union of Evangelical
    Students of India, 1966).

E.P.M. Pamphlets (110 Havant Rd., Stoke, Hayling Island, Hants,
    PO11 011: Evolution Protest Movement)--Periodical.

Ethridge: "Evolution Still Unproven," in The Miami Herald (Nov.
    17, 1972).

Fairbairn, J.W.: Nature, 241 (1973):225.

Frair, Wayne & Davis, Wm. P.: The Case for Creation (Chicago:
    Moody Press, 1972).

Gish, Duane T.: Evolution: The Fossils Say No! (San Diego: Insti-
    tute for Creation Research, 1973).

Gish, Duane T.: Speculations and Experiments on the Origin of
    Life (San Diego: Institute for Creation Research, 1972).

Goldschmidt, R. B.: "Evolution, As Viewed by One Geneticist,"
    American Scientist 40 (1952): 97.

Gray, J.: "The Mechanical View of Life," in Nature, 132 (1933):
    661-664.

Hall, M. and S.: The Truth: God or Evolution (Nutley: Craig,
    1974).

Haller, John S.: Outcasts from Evolution (Urbana: University of
    Illinois, 1971).

Hayword, A.T.J.: Nature, 240 (1972):557.

Hull, D.: "Thermodynamics and Kinetics of Spontaneous Generation,"
    in Nature, 186 (1960):694.

Kerkut, G.A.: Implications of Evolution (London: Pergamon Press,
    1960).

Klotz, John W.: Genes, Genesis and Evolution (St. Louis: Concordia,
    1970).

Lammerts, W.E., ed.: Scientific Studies in Special Creation (Phil-
    adelphia: Presbyterian and Reformed Co., 1971).

Lammerts, W.E., ed.: Why Not Creation? (Philadelphia: Presbyterian
    and Reformed Co., 1970).

Lewis, D.S.: Christian Reflections (Grand Rapids: Eerdmans,
    1967).

Macbeth, Norman: Darwin Retired (Boston: Gambit, Inc., 1971); "The Question: Darwinism Revisited," in Yale Review, June, 1967, pp. 662-.

Marsh, Frank L.: Life, Man and Time (Escondido, Calif.: Outdoor Pictures, 1967); Evolution, Creation and Science (Washington: Review and Herald, 1967).

Martin, C.P.: "A Non-Geneticist Looks at Evolution," in American Scientist, 41 (1953): 103.

Matthews, L. Harrison: "Introduction" to Origin of Species (London: J. M. Dent and Sons, Ltd., 1971).

Monsma, ed.: The Evidence of God in an Expanding Universe (N.Y.: Putnam, 1958).

Moore, John N. and Slusher, Harold S., eds.: Biology: A Search for Order in Complexity (Grand Rapids: Zondervan, 1974).

Moore, J. N.: "Evolution and the Scientific Method," in The American Biology Teacher, 35 (1973):23.

Moorhead, P. S. and Kaplan, M.M. eds.: Mathematical Challenges to the Neo-Darwinian Interpretation of Evolution (Philadelphia: Wistar Institute Press, 1967).

Mora, P. T.: "The Folly of Probability," in The Origins of Prebiological Systems and Their Molecular Matrices, ed. S. W. Fox (New York: Academic Press, 1965) p. 41.

Mora, P. T. : "Urge and Molecular Biology," in Nature, 199 (1963):217.

Morris, Henry M. and Whitcomb, John C.: The Genesis Flood (Philadelphia: Presbyterian and Reformed Co., 1961).

Morris, Henry M.: The Twilight of Evolution (Grand Rapids: Baker Book House, 1964).

Morris, Henry M., Boardman, Wm. W., and Koontz, Robert F.: Science and Creation (San Diego: Creation-Science Research Center, 1971).

Morris, Henry M., and Others; A Symposium on Creation (Grand Rapids: Baker Book House, 1968).

Nelson, B.: After Its Kind (1967); The Deluge Story in Stone (1968) (Minneapolis: Bethany).

Nilsson, H.: Synthetische Artbildung (Lund Sweden: Gleerup,1954).

Origins (Loma Linda, California 92354: Geoscience Research Institute, Loma Linda University)--Periodical.

Pattee, H.: "The Recognition of Description and Function in Chemical Reaction Newworks," in Chemical Evolution and the Origin
of Life, ed. R. Buver and C. Ponnamperuma (N.Y.: American
Elsevier Pub. Co., Inc., 1971), p. 43.

Patten, D.W., ed.: Symposium on Creation II (1970); III (1971);
IV (1972) (Grand Rapids: Baker).

Patterson, R. J.: "Life Is Not a Chemical Accident," in Science
Digest, 76 (1974) 10.

Polanyi, M.: "Life Transcending Physics and Chemistry," in
Chemical and Engineering News, 45 (August 21, 1967):54-66.

Rimmer, H.: The Theory of Evolution and the Facts of Science
(Grand Rapids: Eerdmans, 1935).

Salisbury, Frank B.: "Doubt About the Modern Synthetic Theory of
Evolution," in American Biology Teacher (September, 1971),
p. 338.

Shute, Evan: Flaws in the Theory of Evolution (Philadelphia:
Presbyterian and Reformed, 1966).

Siegler, H. R.: Evolution or Degeneration--Which? (Milwaukee:
Northwestern Publishing House, 1972).

Simpson, G. G.: "The Non Prevalence of Humanoids," in Science,
143 (1964):769.

Slusher, Harold S.: Critique of Radiometric Dating (San Diego:
Institute for Creation Research, 1973).

Thompson, W. R.: "Introduction" to C. Darwin's, The Origin of
Species (New York: E. P. Dutton and Co., Inc., 1956);
Science and Common Sense (N.Y.: Magi. 1965).

Velikovsky: Earth in Upheaval (New York: Dell Pub. Co., Inc.,
1955).

Wigner,E.P.: "The Probability of a Self Reproducing Unit," in
The Logic of Personal Knowledge (London: Routledge and Kegan
Paul, 1961), p. 231.

Zirkle, Conway: Evolution, Marxian Biology, and the Social Scene
(Philadelphia: University of Pennsylvania Press, 1959).

Bibliography

Abell, G.: EXPLORATION OF THE UNIVERSE (N.Y.: Holt, 1969).

Abelson, P.: ANNALS OF THE NEW YORK ACADEMY OF SCIENCE, 69(1957); PROCEEDINGS OF THE NATIONAL ACADEMY OF SCIENCE, 55(1966).

Abercrombie, M., and others: A DICTIONARY OF BIOLOGY (Baltimore: Penguin, 1961).

Ackerknecht, E.: ENCYCLOPEDIA BRITANNICA, 23(1973).

Adler, I.: HOW LIFE BEGAN (N.Y.: New American Library, 1957).

Agranoff, B.: SCIENTIFIC AMERICAN, 216(1967).

Anderson, J.: JOURNAL OF PHYSICAL RESEARCH, 76(1972).

Anderson, J., and Spangler, G.: PENSEE, 4(Fall, 1974).

Andrews, R.: MEET YOUR ANCESTORS (N.Y.: Viking, 1956).

Angrist, S.: SCIENTIFIC AMERICAN, 218(1968).

Antevs, E.: JOURNAL OF GEOLOGY, 65(1957).

Anthony, C., and Kolthoff, N.: TEXTBOOK OF ANATOMY AND PHYSIOLOGY (St. Louis: Mosby, 1971).

Arnold, C.: AN INTRODUCTION TO PALEOBOTANY (N.Y.: McGraw-Hill, 1947).

Asimov, I.: LIFE AND ENERGY (N.Y.: Doubleday, 1962); SCIENCE DIGEST, 45(1959); 69(1971).

Axelrod, D.: EVOLUTION, 13(1959); SCIENCE, 128(1958).

Ayala, F.: PHILOSOPHY OF SCIENCE, 37(1970).

Bada, J.,and others: PROC. OF THE NATIONAL ACADEMY OF SCIENCE, 71 (1974).

Bainbridge, R.: PHYSICAL REVIEW, 90(1953).

Baker, E.: AN INTRODUCTION TO ACAROLOGY (N.Y.: MacMillan, 1952).

Band, H.: EVOLUTION, 18(1964).

Barnes, F.: DESERT, 38(Feb., 1975).

Barnes, T.: ACTS AND FACTS, 3(July-August, 1974); ORIGIN AND DES-TINY OF THE EARTH'S MAGNETIC FIELD (San Diego: Institute for Creation Research, 1973).

Barnett, L.: THE UNIVERSE AND DR. EINSTEIN (N.Y.: New American Library, 1957).

Barzun, J.: DARWIN, MARX AND WAGNER--CRITIQUE OF HERITAGE (N.Y.: Doubleday, 1958).

Bernal, J.: MARX AND SCIENCE (N.Y.: International, 1952).

Berrill, N.: YOU AND THE UNIVERSE (N.Y.: Dodd, Mead, 1958).

Bewkes, E., and others: EXPERIENCE REASON AND FAITH(N.Y.: Harper, 1940).

BIBLE-SCIENCE NEWSLETTER, 13(1975).

Bird, A.: BOISE, THE PEACE VALLEY (Idaho: Caxton, 1934).

Bird, R.: NATURAL HISTORY, (May, 1939).

Blick, E.: AMERICAN SOCIETY OF ENGINEERING EDUCATION PAPER, (June 18, 1974).

Blum, H.: TIME'S ARROW AND EVOLUTION (N.Y.: Harper, 1962; Princeton: P. U. Press, 1968).

Bock, W.: SCIENCE, 164 (1969).
Bogert, C.: SCIENTIFIC MONTHLY, 76 (1953).
Bolin, B.: THE ATMOSPHERE AND THE SEA IN MOTION (N.Y.: Rockefeller Institute, 1959).
Borel, E.: ELEMENTS OF THE THEORY OF PROBABILITY (New Jersey: Prentice-Hall, 1965).
Brace, C. and Montagu, A.: MAN'S EVOLUTION (N.Y.: MacMillan,1965).
Bremermann, H.: PROGRESS IN THEORETICAL BIOLOGY, 1 (1967).
Breneman, W.: ANIMAL FORM AND FUNCTION (Boston: Ginn, 1959).
Brinkman, R.: JOURNAL OF GEOPHYSICAL RESEARCH, 74 (1969).
Brown, H. and Others: INTRODUCTION TO GEOLOGY (Boston:Ginn,1958).
Brues, C.: SCIENTIFIC AMERICAN, 185 (1951).
Burdick, C.: CREATION RESEARCH SOCIETY QUARTERLY, 3 (1966); THE NATURALIST, 16 (1957).
Burton, M. and R., edd.: THE INTERNATIONAL WILDLIFE ENCYCLOPEDIA, (N.Y., Marshall Cavendish, 1969).
Butler, J.: THE LIFE PROCESS (London: George Allen and Unwin,1970).
Buver, R. and Ponnamperuma, C., edd.: CHEMICAL EVOLUTION AND THE ORIGIN OF LIFE (N.Y.: American Elselvier, 1971).
Callender, H. and Mathews, D.: ENCYCLOPEDIA BRITANNICA, 11 (1973).
Calvin, M.: CHEMICAL EVOLUTION (N.Y.: Oxford U., 1969); PROGRESS IN THEORETICAL BIOLOGY, 1 (1967).
Cannon, H.: THE EVOLUTION OF LIVING THINGS(Manchester: Manchester U., 1958).
Caullery, M.: GENETICS AND HEREDITY, (N.Y.: Walker, 1964).
Ceram, C.: GODS, GRAVES AND SCHOLARS (N.Y.: Knopf, 1956).
Chaney, R.: AMERICAN SCIENTIST, 36 (1948).
Clark, A., ed.: THE NEW EVOLUTION: ZOO GENESIS, (Baltimore: Williams and Wilkins, 1930).
Clark, H.: FOSSILS, FLOOD, AND FIRE (Escondido: Outdoor Pictures, 1968).
Clark, R.: DARWIN: BEFORE AND AFTER (London: Paternoster, 1948).
Clementson, S.: CREATION RESEARCH SOCIETY QUARTERLY, 7 (1970).
Colbert, E.: DINOSAURS (N.Y.: E. P. Dutton, 1961); EVOLUTION OF THE VERTEBRATES (N.Y.: Wiley, 1955).
Cook, J. and Wisner, W.: THE NIGHTMARE WORLD OF THE SHARK, (N.Y.: Dodd, 1968).
Cook, M.: NATURE, 179 (1957); PREHISTORY AND EARTH MODELS (London: Max Parish, 1960).
Coppedge, J.: CREATION RESEARCH SOCIETY QUARTERLY, 8 (1971); EVOLUTION: POSSIBLE OR IMPOSSIBLE (Grand Rapids: Zondervan 1973).
Core, E.: GENERAL BIOLOGY (N.Y.: John Wiley & Sons, 1961).
Creation or Evolution (Great Britain: E.P.M.) Pamphlet #89.
Crow, J.: BULLETIN OF THE ATOMIC SCIENTISTS, 14 (1958).
Curtis, H.: SCIENCE, 141 (1963).
Custance, A.: THE EARTH BEFORE MAN (Ottawa: Doorway Papers).
Danson, R.: NEW SCIENTIST, 49 (1971).
Darwin, C.: BULLETIN OF THE ATOMIC SCIENTISTS, 114 (1958).
Davidson, C.: PROCEEDINGS OF THE NATIONAL ACADEMY OF SCIENCE, 53 (1956).
Davis, P. and Solomon, E.: THE WORLD OF BIOLOGY (N.Y.: McGraw-Hill,

1974.)

DeBeer, G.: EMBRYOS AND ANCESTORS (N.Y.: Oxford U., 1954).

deGrazier, A., ed.: THE VELIKOVSKY AFFAIR (N.Y.: University Books, 1966).

Delevoryas, T.: MORPHOLOGY AND THE EVOLUTION OF FOSSIL PLANTS,(N.Y.: Holt 1962).

Descartes, Rene: DISCOURSE ON METHOD AND MEDITATION (N.Y.: Bobbs Merrill, 1960).

Dewar, D.: THE TRANSFORMIST ILLUSION, (Tennessee: Dehoff, 1957).

Dickey, P. and Others: SCIENCE, 160 (1968).

DID MAN GET HERE BY EVOLUTION OR CREATION (N.Y.: WTBTS, 1967).

Dixon, M. and Webb, E.: ENZYMES (N.Y.: Academic, 1964).

Dobzhansky, T.: AMERICAN SCIENTIST, 45 (1957); EVOLUTION, GENETICS AND MAN (N.Y.: John Wiley and Sons, 1955); GENETICS AND THE EVOLUTION PROCESS (N.Y.: Columbia U., 1970); GENETICS AND THE ORIGIN OF SPECIES (N.Y.: Columbia U., 1951); MANKIND EVOLVING (N. Haven: Yale U. Press, 1962); SCIENCE, 155 (1967); SCIENTIFIC MONTHLY, 55 (1942).

Dodson, E.: A TEXTBOOK OF EVOLUTION (Philadelphia: W. B. Saunders 1952).

Dort, W.: ANTARCTIC JOURNAL OF THE U.S., 6 (1971).

Drane, J.: MAIN CURRENTS IN MODERN THOUGHT, 29 (1972).

Dubos, R.: AMERICAN SCIENTIST, 53 (1965).

Dunbar, C.: GEOLOGY (N.Y.: Wiley, 1960); HISTORICAL GEOLOGY (N.Y: Wiley, 1961).

Dunn, L. and Dobzhansky, T.: HEREDITY, RACE AND SOCIETY (N.Y.: New American Library, 1952).

Eck, R. and Dayhoff, M.: ATLAS OF PROTEIN SEQUENCE AND STRUCTURE (Maryland: National Biomedical Research Foundation, 1966).

Eddington, A.: THE NATURE OF THE PHYSICAL WORLD (N.Y.: MacMillan, 1930).

Ehrensrard, G.: LIFE: ORIGIN AND DEVELOPMENT (Chicago: U. of Chicago, 1962).

Eisenberg, L.: IMPACT OF SCIENCE ON SOCIETY, 23 (1973).

Elasser, W.: ENCYCLOPEDIA BRITANNICA, 7 (1973).

ENCYCLOPEDIA BRITANNICA FILM #2140.

Epstein, J.: PROCEEDINGS OF THE NATIONAL ACADEMY OF SCIENCE, 170 (1973).

EVOLUTION IN THE GLARE OF KNOWLEDGE (Great Britain: Evolution Protest Movement, 1971), Pamphlet #186.

EVOLUTION VERSUS THE NEW WORLD (N.Y.: WTBTS, 1950).

Faul, H.: NUCLEAR GEOLOGY (N.Y.: Wiley, 1954).

Fettner: NATURE, 194 (1962).

Fisher, A.: POPULAR SCIENCE, 202 (1973).

FORT WAYNE NEWS SENTINEL (July 11, 1950), editorial page.

Fowler, W.: SCIENTIFIC MONTHLY, 84 (1957).

Fox, S.: AMERICAN BIOLOGY TEACHER, 36 (1974); INTERNATIONAL MOSCOW SEMINAR (August 2, 1974), P. 13; NATURE, 205 (1965); THE ORIGINS OF PREBIOLOGICAL SYSTEMS AND THEIR MOLECULAR MATRICES (N.Y.: Academic Press, 1965).

Fox, S. and Others: ARCHIVES OF BIOCHEMISTRY AND BIOPHYSICS, 102

(1963).

Fox, S. and Harada, K.: JOURNAL OF THE AMERICAN CHEMICAL SOCIETY, 82 (1960).

Fried, J.: THE MYSTERY OF HEREDITY (N.Y.: John Day, 1971).

Frings, H. and M.: CONCEPTS OF ZOOLOGY (Toronto: Collier MacMillan 1970).

Fromm, E.: BEYOND THE CHAINS OF ILLUSION--MY ENCOUNTER WITH MARX AND FREUD (N.Y.: Simon and Schuster, 1962).

Funkhouser and Others: BULLETIN VOLCANOLOGIQUE, 29 (1966).

Funkhouser, J. and Naughton, J.: JOURNAL OF GEOPHYSICAL RESEARCH, 73 (1968).

Gardner, E.: PRINCIPLES OF GENETICS, (N.Y.: John Wiley and Sons, 1964).

Gardner, M., ed.: GREAT ESSAYS IN SCIENCE (N.Y., Pocket Books, 1957).

Garrels, R. and MacKenzie, F.: EVOLUTION OF THE SEDIMENTARY ROCKS (N.Y.: W. W. Norton, 1971).

Garrido, J.: CREATION RESEARCH SOCIETY QUARTERLY, 10 (1973).

Gentry, R.: AMERICAN JOURNAL OF PHYSICS, 33 (1965); MEDICAL OPINION AND REVIEW, 3 (1967).

GEOCHRONICLE, 2 (1966).

George, T.: SCIENCE PROGRESS, 48 (1960).

Giekie, A.: TEXTBOOK OF GEOLOGY (London: MacMillan, 1903).

Gish, D.: CREATION RESEARCH SOCIETY QUARTERLY, 12 (1975); SPECULATIONS AND EXPERIMENTS RELATED TO THEORIES ON THE ORIGIN OF LIFE, (San Diego: ICR Publishing, 1972).

Goldschmidt, R.: AMERICAN SCIENTIST, 40 (1952).

Gould, S.: JOURNAL OF GEOLOGICAL EDUCATION, 15 (1967).

Grandius, J.: ABOUT THE TRUTH OF THE UNIVERSAL DELUGE AND THE REMAINS THAT ARE FOUND AT GREAT DISTANCE FROM THE SEA (1676).

Gray, J.: NATURE, 132 (1933).

Greene, E.: PRINCIPLES OF PHYSICS (New Jersey: Prentice-Hall, 1962).

Gretener, P.: BULLETIN OF THE AMERICAN ASSOCIATION OF PETROLEUM GEOLOGISTS, 51 (1967).

Guthrie, W.: A HISTORY OF GREEK PHILOSOPHY (Cambridge University Press, 1962).

Haines, R.: QUARTERLY REVIEW OF BIOLOGY, 33 (1958).

Hall, M. and S.: THE TRUTH: GOD OR EVOLUTION (New Jersey: Craig, 1974).

Haller, J., Jr.: OUTCASTS FROM EVOLUTION: SCIENTIFIC ATTITUDES OF RACIAL INFERIORITY (Urbana: U. of Illinois, 1971).

Hanawalt, P. and Haynes, H.: SCIENTIFIC AMERICAN, 216 (February, 1967).

Harada, K.: NATURE, 200 (1963).

Harland, W. and Others, ed.: THE FOSSIL RECORD (London: Geological Society, 1967).

Harland, W. and Rudwick, M.: SCIENTIFIC AMERICAN, 211 (1964).

Hart, R. and Setlow, R.: PROCEEDINGS OF THE NATIONAL ACADEMY OF SCIENCE, 71 (1974).

Haupt, A.: AN INTRODUCTION TO BOTANY (N.Y.: McGraw-Hill, 1956).

Hendrix, C.: THE CAVE BOOK (Mass.: Earth Science, 1950).

Heylmun, E.: JOURNAL OF GEOLOGICAL EDUCATION, 19 (1971).
Heymann, D. and Others: SCIENCE, 167 (1970).
Hochhuth, R.: THE DEPUTY (N.Y.: Grove Press, 1964).
Hofstadler, R.: SOCIAL DARWINISM IN AMERICAN THOUGHT (N.Y.: George Braziller, 1959).
Hokin, M. and L.: SCIENTIFIC AMERICAN, 213 (1965).
Hollingsworth, S.; JOURNAL OF THE GEOLOGICAL SOCIETY OF LONDON, 118 (1962).
Holloway, R.: SCIENTIFIC AMERICAN, 231 (July, 1974).
Hollyday, R.: NATURE, 238 (1972).
Holter, H.: SCIENTIFIC AMERICAN, 205 (1961).
Honore, P.: IN QUEST OF THE WHITE GOD (N.Y.: Putnam, 1964).
Hooker, D.: THOSE ASTOUNDING ICE AGES (N.Y.: Exposition,1948).
HOW THEY CHOOSE OUR ANCESTORS (Great Britain: E.P.M.).
Howarth, H.: THE MAMMOTH AND THE FLOOD (London: Low, 1887).
Howell, W.: MANKIND SO FAR (1946).
Hoyle, F.: THE NATURE OF THE UNIVERSE (N.Y.: Harper, 1960).
Hughes, P.: CHRISTIANITY AND THE PROBLEM OF ORIGINS (Philadelphia: Presbyterian and Reformed, 1973).
Hull, D.: NATURE, 186 (1960).
Hunt, E. and Karlin, J., edd.: SOCIETY TODAY AND TOMORROW (N.Y.: MacMillan, 1961).
Huxley, J.: EVOLUTION IN ACTION (N.Y.: New American Library, 1953).
Idyll, C.: ABYSS--THE DEEP SEA AND THE CREATURES THAT LIVE IN IT (N.Y.: Crowell, 1971).
Ingalls, A.: SCIENTIFIC AMERICAN, 162 (1940).
THE ILLUSTRATED LONDON NEWS, (June 24, 1922).
Ivanhoe, F.: NATURE (August 8, 1970).
Jastrow, R.: NATURAL HISTORY, 83(1974).
Jepsen, G.: SCIENCE, 154 (1966).
Jepsen, G. and Others, edd.: GENETICS, PALEONTOLOGY AND EVOLUTION (New Jersey: Princeton U., 1949).
Johlige, H.: PHYSICAL REVIEW C--NUCLEAR PHYSICS, 2 (1970).
Joly, J.: NATURE, 109 (1922); PHILOSOPHICAL TRANSACTIONS OF THE ROYAL SOCIETY OF LONDON--A, 217 (1917).
JONES, D.: GENETICS IN PLANT AND ANIMAL IMPROVEMENT (N.Y.: Wiley, 1924).
JOURNAL OF GEOPHYSICAL RESEARCH, 74 (1968).
Jueneman, F.: INDUSTRIAL RESEARCH, 14 (1972).
Kay, G. and Colbert, E.: STRATIGRAPHY AND LIFE HISTORY (N.Y.: Wiley, 1965).
Keeton, W.: BIOLOGICAL SCIENCE (N.Y.: Norton, 1972).
Keil, D. and Wang, Y.: NATURE, 155 (1945).
Keith, A.: THE ANTIQUITY OF MAN (Philadelphia: Lippencott, 1928); EVOLUTION AND ETHICS (N.Y.: G. P. Putnam's Sons, 1949); THE HUMAN BODY (1932).
Kellenberger, E.: SCIENTIFIC AMERICAN, 215 (Dec., 1966).
Keller, W.: THE BIBLE AS HISTORY (N.Y.: W. Morrow, 1956).
Kelso, A.: PHYSICAL ANTHROPOLOGY (N.Y.: Lippencott, 1970).
Kelvin, Lord: MATHEMATICAL AND PHYSICAL PAPERS (Cambridge: Cambridge U., 1882); POPULAR LECTURES AND ADDRESSES (London:MacMillan,1889).

Kenyon, D. and Steinman, G.: BIOCHEMICAL PREDESTINATION (N.Y.:
   McGraw-Hill, 1969).
Keosian, J.: THE ORIGIN OF LIFE (N.Y.: Reinhold, 1968).
Kerkut, G.: IMPLICATIONS OF EVOLUTION (N.Y.: Pergamon, 1960).
Kieth, M. and Anderson, G.: SCIENCE, 141 (1963).
Klein, M.: SCIENCE, 157 (1967).
Knopf, A.: SCIENTIFIC MONTHLY, 85 (1957).
Koch, L.: SCIENTIFIC MONTHLY, 85 (1957).
Kovarik, A.: BULLETIN #80 OF THE NATIONAL RESEARCH COUNCIL, June,
   1931.
Krinov, E.: PRINCIPLES OF METEORITICS (N.Y.: Pergamon, 1960).
Krynine, P.: PALEONTOLOGY, 30 (1956).
Ladd, H.: SCIENCE, 129 (1959).
Lammerts, W., ed.: SCIENTIFIC STUDIES IN SPECIAL CREATION (Grand
   Rapids: Baker, 1971); WHY NOT CREATION (Grand Rapids: Baker,
   1970).
Laughlin, A.: JOURNAL OF GEOPHYSICAL RESEARCH, 74 (1969).
Leach, J.: FUNCTIONAL ANATOMY--MAMMALIAN AND COMPARATIVE (N.Y.:
   McGraw-Hill, 1961).
Leakey, M.: OLDUVAI GORGE--VOL.III, (Cambridge: Cambridge U.,1971).
Leakey, R.: NATIONAL GEOGRAPHIC, 143 (1973); NATURE, 231 (1971).
Leclerg, S.: EVOLUTION, 10 (1956).
LE MONDE ET LA VIE,(October, 1963).
Levy, O.: THE COMPLETE WORKS OF NIETZSCHE, (1930).
Lewis, G. and Randall, M.: THERMODYNAMICS (N.Y.: McGraw-Hill,1961).
Lewis, C.: CHRISTIAN REFLECTIONS (Grand Rapids: Eerdmans, 1967).
Libby, W.: AMERICAN SCIENTIST, 44 (1956); RADIOACTIVE DATING
   (Chicago: University of Chicago, 1952).
LIFE, (April 3, 1939).
Lingenfelter, R.: REVIEWS OF GEOPHYSICS, 1 (1963).
Lindsay, R.: AMERICAN SCIENTIST, 56 (1968).
Lindsey, W.: PRINCIPLES OF ORGANIC EVOLUTION (St. Louis: C.V.
   Mosby, 1952).
Lissner, I.: MAN GOD AND MAGIC (N.Y.: Putnam, 1961).
Litynski, Z.: SCIENCE DIGEST, 51 (1961).
Loebsack, T.: OUR ATMOSPHERE (N.Y.: New American Library, 1961).
Loetscher, L., ed: TWENTIETH CENTURY ENCYCLOPEDIA OF RELIGIOUS
   KNOWLEDGE (Grand Rapids: Baker, 1955).
Look, A.: 1,000 MILLION YEARS ON THE COLORADO PLATEAU (Denver:
   Golden Bell, 1947).
LUNAR SCIENCE IV (1973).
Luoff, A., ed: BIOCHEMISTRY AND PHYSIOLOGY OF PROTOZOA (N.Y.:
   Academic Press, 1951).
Lyttleton, R.: THE MODERN UNIVERSE (N.Y.: Harper, 1956); MYSTERIES
   OF THE SOLAR SYSTEM (Oxford: Clarendon, 1968).
Macbeth, N.: DARWIN RETIRED (Boston: Gambit, 1972); YALE REVIEW,
   June, 1967.
Macleod, A. and Cobley, L., edd.: EVOLUTION IN CONTEMPORARY
   BOTANICAL THOUGHT (Chicago: Quadruple, 1961).
Mangelsdorf, P. and Others: SCIENCE, 143 (1964).
Margenau, H. and Murphy, G.: THE MATHEMATICS OF CHEMISTRY AND PHYSICS

(N.Y.: Von Nostrand, 1943).
Marsh, F.: EVOLUTION CREATION AND SCIENCE (Wash.: Review & Herald, 1947).
Marshall, A., ed.: BIOLOGY AND COMPARATIVE PHYSIOLOGY OF BIRDS, (N.Y.: Academic, 1960).
Marsland, D.: PRINCIPLES OF BIOLOGY (N.Y.: Holt, Rinehart and Winston, 1957).
Martin, C.: AMERICAN SCIENTIST, 41 (1953).
Mason, B.: METEORITES (N.Y.: Wiley, 1962); PRINCIPLES OF GEOCHEMISTRY (N.Y.: Wiley, 1952).
Matthews, L.: THE ORIGIN OF SPECIES (London: J. M. Dent and Sons, 1971).
Mayr, E.: POPULATIONS, SPECIES AND EVOLUTION (Mass: Harvard U., 1970); SYSTEMATICS AND THE ORIGIN OF SPECIES (N.Y.: Columbia University Press, 1942; Dover, 1964).
McWhirter, N. and R.: GUINESS BOOK OF WORLD RECORDS (N.Y.: Sterling, 1973).
Mickey, A.: INTERNATIONAL HARVESTER (1945).
MICROPALEONTOLOGY, 10 (1964).
Middlehurst, B. and Kuiper, G., edd.: THE MOON, METEORITES AND COMETS (Chicago: U. of Chicago, 1963).
Miller, H.: THE OLD RED SANDSTONE (Boston, 1865).
Miller, S.: JOURNAL OF THE AMERICAN CHEMICAL SOCIETY, 77 (1955); SCIENCE, 130 (1959).
Moment, G.: GENERAL ZOOLOGY (Boston: Houghton Mifflin, 1967).
Montagu, A.: ANTHROPOLOGY AND HUMAN NATURE (Boston: Sargent, 1957); HUMAN HEREDITY (N.Y.: New American Library, 1963).
Moon, P. and Spencer, D.: JOURNAL OF THE OPTICAL SOCIETY OF AMERICA, 43 (1953).
Moorhead, P. and Kaplan, M.: MATHEMATICAL CHALLENGES TO THE NEO-DARWINIAN INTERPRETATION OF EVOLUTION (Philadelphia: Wistar Inst., 1967).
Mora, P.: NATURE, 199 (1963).
Mormon, J.: A HISTORY OF FISHES (N.Y.: Hill and Wang, 1963).
Morowitz, H.: MAIN CURRENTS IN MODERN THOUGHT, 28 (1972); PROGRESS IN THEORETICAL BIOLOGY, 1 (1967).
Morris, H.: CREATION RESEARCH SOCIETY QUARTERLY, 8 (1971); SCIENTIFIC CREATIONISM (San Diego: Creation-Life Publishers, 1974).
Morrison, R. and Boyd, R.: ORGANIC CHEMISTRY (Boston: Allyn and Bacon, Inc., 1963).
MORRISONVILLE ILLINOIS TIMES (June 11, 1891).
Motulsky, A.: SCIENCE, 185 (1974).
Muller, H.: BULLETIN OF THE ATOMIC SCIENTISTS, 11 (1955).
Muntzing, A.: PROCEEDINGS OF THE AMERICAN PHILOSOPHICAL SOCIETY, 103 (1959).
Nelson, B.: AFTER ITS KIND (Minneapolis: Bethany, 1967); THE DELUGE STORY IN STONE (Minneapolis: Bethany, 1968).
THE NEW ORLEANS TIMES--PICAYUNE (May 7, 1964).
Newell, N.: JOURNAL OF PALEONTOLOGY, 33 (1959); PROCEEDINGS OF THE AMERICAN PHILOSOPHICAL SOCIETY, 103 (1959).
Newman, J., ed.: WHAT IS MAN (N.Y.: Simon and Schuster, 1955).

Nicholas, G.: SCIENTIFIC MONTHLY, 76 (1953).

Nilsson, H.: SYNTHETISCHE ARTBILDUNG (Lund: Gleerup, 1954).

Noble, C. and Naughton, J.: SCIENCE, 162 (1968).

Norman, J.: A HISTORY OF FISHES (N.Y.: Hill and Wang, 1963).

Ommanney, F.: THE FISHES (N.Y.: Time, 1964).

Oparin, A.: LIFE, ITS NATURE, ORIGIN AND DEVELOPMENT (Edinburgh: Oliver and Boyd, 1961; N.Y.: Academic Press, 1964).

Oppenheimer, J.: ESSAYS IN THE HISTORY OF EMBRYOLOGY AND BIOLOGY (Mass: M.I.T. Press, 1967).

Orgel, L.: NATURE, 243 (1973); THE ORIGINS OF LIFE: MOLECULES AND NATURAL SELECTION (N.Y.: Wiley, 1973).

Pantin, C.: A SHORT HISTORY OF SCIENCE (N.Y.: Doubleday, 1951).

Pasachoff, J. and Fowler, W.: SCIENTIFIC AMERICAN, 230 (May, 1974).

Patten, D., ed.: SYMPOSIUM ON CREATION II (1970), III (1971), (Grand Rapids: Baker).

Pauling, L.: COLLEGE CHEMISTRY (San Francisco: W. H. Freeman, 1964).

Peterson, R.: THE BIRDS (N.Y.: Time Inc., 1963).

Petterson, H.: SCIENTIFIC AMERICAN, 202 (1960).

Pierce, W.: BULLETIN OF THE AMERICAN ASSOCIATION OF PETROLEUM GEOLOGISTS, 41 (1957).

Pinna, G.: THE DAWN OF LIFE (N.Y.: World Publishing, 1972).

Pirie, N.: ANNALS OF THE NEW YORK ACADEMY OF SCIENCE, 66 (1957).

Polanyi, M.: CHEMICAL AND ENGINEERING NEWS, 45 (1967).

Pope, C.: THE GREAT SNAKES (N.Y.: Knopf, 1961).

Poynting, J.: NATURE, 71 (1905).

PROCEEDINGS OF THE THIRD LUNAR SCIENCE CONFERENCE, 2 (1972).

PROCEEDINGS OF THE BOSTON SOCIETY OF NATURAL HISTORY, 24 (1890).

Quastler, H.: THE EMERGENCE OF BIOLOGICAL ORGANIZATION (New Haven: Yale U., 1964).

Raven, C.: A SHORT HISTORY OF SCIENCE (N.Y.: Doubleday, 1951).

RECENT OPINIONS OF BIOLOGISTS ON EVOLUTION (Great Britain: E.P.M., 1948).

Reed, C.: SCIENCE, 130 (1959).

Rehwinkel, A.: THE FLOOD (St. Louis: Concordia, 1951).

Rickover, H.: SATURDAY EVENING POST, 236 (March 30, 1963).

Riley, J. and Skirrow, G.: CHEMICAL OCEANOGRAPHY (N.Y.: Academic Press, 1965).

Rimmer, H.: THE THEORY OF EVOLUTION AND THE FACTS OF SCIENCE (Grand Rapids: Eerdmans, 1935).

Riser, W.: JOURNAL OF THE AMERICAN VETERINARY MEDICAL ASSOCIATION, 165, (1974).

Robertson, H.: RELATIVITY AND COSMOLOGY (Philadelphia: Saunders, 1968).

Robson, G.: ENCYCLOPEDIA BRITANNICA, 15 (1957).

Rohlfing, D. and Oparin, A., edd.: MOLECULAR EVOLUTION: PREBIOLOGICAL AND BIOLOGICAL (N.Y.: Plenum, 1972).

Ross, C. and Rezak, R.: THE ROCKS AND FOSSILS OF GLACIER NATIONAL PARK (U.S. Geological Survey paper 294-K, 1959).

Rubey, W.: BULLETIN OF THE GEOLOGICAL SOCIETY OF AMERICA, 62 (1951); SCIENCE, 112 (1950).

Rusch, W.: CREATION RESEARCH SOCIETY QUARTERLY, 7 (1970).

Sagan, C.: THE COSMIC CONNECTION (N.Y.: Dell, 1973); ENCYCLOPEDIA
  BRITANNICA, 13 (1973).
Salisbury, F.: AMERICAN BIOLOGY TEACHER (Sept., 1971).
Samec, R.: CREATION RESEARCH SOCIETY QUARTERLY, 12 (June, 1975).
Savage, J.: EVOLUTION (N.Y.: Holt, 1965).
Scheinfield, A.: THE NEW YOU AND HEREDITY (N.Y.: Lippincott, 1950).
Schindewolf, O.: AMERICAN JOURNAL OF SCIENCE, 255 (1957).
Schultz, J. and Cleaves, A.: GEOLOGY IN ENGINEERING (N.Y.: Wiley,
  1955).
SCIENCE, 68 (1928).
SCIENCE, 116 (1952).
SCIENCE, 181 (1973).
SCIENCE DIGEST, 49 (1961).
SCIENCE DIGEST, 64 (1968).
SCIENCE NEWS (Dec. 1, 1973).
SCIENCE NEWS LETTER, 60 (Aug. 25, 1951).
SCIENCE NEWS LETTER, 79 (1961).
SCIENTIFIC MONTHLY, 78 (1954).
Scoyen, E.: ARIZONA HIGHWAYS, 27 (July, 1951).
Shapely, H.: VIEW FROM A DISTANT STAR (N.Y.: Basic Books, 1963).
Shawver, L.: SCIENCE NEWS, 105 (Feb. 2, 1974).
Shklovskii, I. and Sagan, C.: INTELLIGENT LIFE IN THE UNIVERSE
  (N.Y.: Dell, 1966).
A SHORT HISTORY OF SCIENCE—A SYMPOSIUM (N.Y.: Doubleday, 1951).
Shroeder and Others: THE PEPTIDES (N.Y.: Academic Press, 1965).
Shultz, J. and Cleaves, A.: GEOLOGY IN ENGINEERING (N.Y.: Wiley,
  1955).
Shute, E.: FLAWS IN THE THEORY OF EVOLUTION (New Jersey: Craig
  Press, 1961).
Shuttleworth, C.: MALAYAN SAFARI (London: Phoenix House, 1965).
Sillen, L.: SCIENCE, 156 (1967).
Simpson, G.: BIOLOGY AND MAN (N.Y.: Harcourt, Brace...,1969);
  LIFE OF THE PAST (New Haven: Yale U. Press, 1953); THE MAJOR
  FEATURES OF EVOLUTION, (N.Y.: Columbia U. Press, 1953); THE MEAN-
  ING OF EVOLUTION (New Haven: Yale U. Press, 1967); SCIENCE, 131
  (1960); SCIENCE, 143 (1964); TEMPO AND MODE OF EVOLUTION (N.Y.:
  Columbia U., 1944).
Sinnott, E.: TWO ROADS TO TRUTH (N.Y.: Viking, 1953).
Smith, A.: BOTANY AND EVOLUTION (Great Britain: E.P.M., 1975),
  Pamphlet #206.
Smith, A. and Bellware, F.: SCIENCE, 152 (1966).
Smith, H.: FROM FISH TO PHILOSOPHER (N.Y.: Little Brown, 1953).
Smith, W.: MAN'S ORIGIN, MAN'S DESTINY (Wheaton: Harold Shaw,
  1968).
Snell, F., ed.: PROGRESS IN THEORETICAL BIOLOGY, 1 (1967).
Spieker, E.: BULLETIN OF THE AMERICAN ASSOCIATION OF PETROLEUM
  GEOLOGISTS, 40 (1956).
Srb, A., ed.: GENES, ENZYMES AND POPULATIONS (N.Y.: Plenum Press,
  1973).
Stainforth, R.: MICROPALEONTOLOGY, 10 (1964); NATURE, 210 (1966).
Steno, N.: A TREATISE ON A SOLID BODY ENCLOSED BY NATURAL PROCESS

WITHIN A SOLID (1669).
Stevenson, P.: CREATION RESEARCH SOCIETY QUARTERLY, 12 (June, 1975).
Stokes, W.: ESSENTIALS OF EARTH HISTORY (New Jersey: Prentice Hall, 1960).
Storer, T.: GENERAL ZOOLOGY (N.Y.: McGraw Hill, 1957).
Straus, W.: SCIENCE, 119 (1954).
Straus, W. and Cave, A.: QUARTERLY REVIEW OF BIOLOGY, 132 (1957).
Studier, M. and Others: SCIENCE, 149 (1965).
Stutzer, O.: GEOLOGY OF COAL (Chicago: U. of Chicago, 1940).
Suess, H.: JOURNAL OF GEOPHYSICAL RESEARCH, 70 (1965).
Sutherland, M.: NATIONAL GEOGRAPHIC, 104 (Oct., 1953).
Sverdrup, H. and Others: THE OCEANS (N.Y.: Prentice-Hall, 1942).
Talbott, S.: PENSEE, 2 (1972).
Tax, S., ed.: EVOLUTION AFTER DARWIN (Chicago: U. of Chicago,1960).
Taylor, J.: LAWNS (Ontario Dept. of Agriculture Publication #448).
Thimann, K., ed.: THE PHYSIOLOGY OF FOREST TREES (N.Y.: Ronald, 1958).
Thompson, W.: THE ORIGIN OF SPECIES (N.Y.: E.P.Dutton, 1956).
TIME MAGAZINE (Nov. 11, 1946).
TIME MAGAZINE, 87 (Feb. 25, 1966).
TIME MAGAZINE (May 17, 1971 and 1973).
Tinkle, W.: HEREDITY (Grand Rapids: Zondervon, 1970).
Tocquet, R.: LIFE ON THE PLANETS (N.Y.: Grove Press, 1962).
Tolmachoff, I.: THE CARCASSES OF THE MAMMOTH AND RHINOCEROS FOUND IN THE FROZEN GROUND OF SIBERIA (Philadelphia: American Philosophical Society, 1929).
Trop, M. and Shaki, A.: CREATION RESEARCH SOCIETY QUARTERLY, 11 (1974).
Twenhofel, W.: TREATISE ON SEDIMENTATION (N.Y.: Dover, 1961).
Urey, H.: PROCEEDINGS OF THE NATIONAL ACADEMY OF SCIENCE,38(1952).
Valentyne, J.: JOURNAL OF GEOLOGICAL EDUCATION, 14 (1966).
Velikovsky, I.: EARTH IN UPHEAVAL (N.Y.: Dell, 1955).
Villee, C. and Others: GENERAL ZOOLOGY (Philadelphia: Saunders, 1963).
Von Engelen, O. and Caster, K.: GEOLOGY (N.Y.: McGraw-Hill, 1952).
Von Fange, E.: CREATION RESEARCH SOCIETY QUARTERLY, 11 (1974).
Waddington, C.: NATURE, 175 (1955); THE NATURE OF LIFE (N.Y.: Antheneum, 1962).
Waddington, G.: PRINCIPLES OF EMBRYOLOGY (London: George Allen, 1956).
Wald, G.: ANNALS OF THE NEW YORK ACADEMY OF SCIENCE, 66 (1957); FRONTIERS OF MODERN BIOLOGY (Boston: Houghton Mifflin, 1962); PHYSICS AND CHEMISTRY OF LIFE (N.Y.: Simon and Schuster, 1955).
Wastall, T., ed.: STUDIES IN FOSSIL VERTEBRATES (London: Athlone, 1958).
Watson, D.: NATURE, 123 (1929).
Weaver, K.: NATIONAL GEOGRAPHIC, 145 (1974).
Weaver, W.: SCIENTIFIC MONTHLY, 78 (1954).
Weidel, W.: VIRUSES (Ann Arbor: U. of Mich., 1959).
Weisz, P.: THE SCIENCE OF BIOLOGY (N.Y.: McGraw-Hill, 1959).
Whitcomb, J. and Morris, H.: THE GENESIS FLOOD (Philadelphia:

Presbyterian and Reformed, 1970).
White, A. and Others: PRINCIPLES OF BIOCHEMISTRY (N.Y.: McGraw-Hill, 1964).
Whitelaw, R.: CREATION RESEARCH SOCIETY QUARTERLY, 7 (1970).
WHY I BELIEVE IN CREATION (Great Britain: E.P.M., 1968).
Wiant, H.: CREATION RESEARCH SOCIETY QUARTERLY, 11 (1974).
Wigner, E.: THE LOGIC OF PERSONAL KNOWLEDGE (London: Routledge, 1961).
Wilson, E. and Others: LIFE ON EARTH (Connecticut: Sinaur, 1973).
Woodward, J.: AN ESSAY TOWARD A NATURAL THEORY OF THE EARTH (1695).
Wright, E.: THE NEW CHILDBIRTH (N.Y.: Hart, 1966).
Wright, F.: AMERICAN GEOLOGIST, 23 (1899).
Young, L.: EVOLUTION OF MAN (New Jersey: Oxford U., 1970).
Zucherman, S.: FUNCTIONAL ACTIVITIES OF MAN, MONKEYS AND APES (1933).

Index